# New Directions in
# Educational Leadership

# New Directions in Educational Leadership

Edited and
Introduced by

## Paul Harling

The Falmer Press
(A member of the Taylor & Francis Group)
London and Philadelphia

UK      The Falmer Press, Falmer House, Barcombe, Lewes, East Sussex, BN8 5DL

USA      The Falmer Press, Taylor & Francis Inc., 242 Cherry Street, Philadelphia, PA 19106-1906

First published in 1984

**Library of Congress Cataloging in Publication Data**

Main entry under title:

New directions in educational leadership.

    Includes bibliographies and indexes.
    1. Education and state—Great Britain—Addresses, essays, lectures. 2. School management and organization —Great Britain—Addresses, essays, lectures. 3. Leadership—Addresses, essays, lectures. I. Harling, Paul.
LC93.G7N47   1984   379.41   84-13494
ISBN 0-905273-60-5
ISBN 0-905273-59-1 (pbk.)

Jacket design by Leonard Williams

Typeset in 10½/12 Plantin
by Imago Publishing Ltd., Thame, Oxon.

*Printed in Great Britain by Taylor & Francis (Printers) Ltd, Basingstoke*

*To Penny, Caroline and Justin*

# Contents

# Contents

## General Editor's Preface

The educational system calls for leadership at many levels: national and local, political and professional, in primary, secondary and tertiary education. This collection of papers deals with leadership at all these levels and with more besides. Twelve of the papers were specially commissioned for this volume from people with close experience of the system and its leadership needs, and the rest have all been completely revised.

It is clear from even a cursory glance at the contributions to this volume that theory and practice in educational leadership are inexorably linked. It is equally clear that the role of theory is to illuminate practice to cast light into its darker corners and to expand our sensitivities to relevant issues, our way of envisioning how educational leadership may be improved. It has been the aim in this volume to do just this, and Paul Harling's own experience in educational leadership has been crucial. He has brought an astute awareness to issues in educational leadership and produced not only a timely reader but one which should prove an excellent introduction to the field for all students.

*Philip H. Taylor*
Birmingham
December 1983

# Foreword

Leadership consists of efforts to shape the behaviour of groups of people, or individuals, within an organization or system in such a way that benefits will ensue and the purposes of the organization or system will be fulfilled. It consists of interpersonal influence exercised within the broad boundaries of the system towards the attainment of specified goals. It is exercised through formal and informal channels of communication and involves persuasion and influence to link and reconcile the often disparate goals of the participants within the system. It is multi-directional, involving reflection, compromise and modification on the part of all involved. It is dynamic, concerned fundamentally with change in the system rather than mere maintenance.

The main thrust of the argument conducted within the papers included in this collection is that the last twelve or fifteen years have seen significant changes in educationalists' understanding and application of the concepts of leadership, and because of these changes (1) the relationships between the participants have changed; and (2) policy and practice have changed.

The papers have been specially commissioned, or in some cases reprinted from previously published sources, with this thesis in mind. Each of them examines leadership and/or influence with special reference to one or more aspects, sectors, roles or interests within the educational system in England and Wales. The authorship of the papers is of the highest quality and each possesses total credibility with fellow educationalists.

Within these pages readers will find description, reflection and analysis of recent changes in styles of educational leadership which have effectively defined the future of our educational system. Most are written by active participants in the educational process, or in the case of one or two papers, they have been produced after careful and systematic observation of the real world in which we work. Each paper examines, within its particular topic, the role of the specified sector, group or individual in 'leading' the various branches of education in

1 establishing and revising aims and objectives;
2 facilitating and improving teaching, learning and the curriculum;
3 improving the structure and organization of education;
4 providing facilities and a climate for personal and professional growth;
5 ensuring the provision of sufficient human and material resources.

The book is intended for students of education, management and social administration at all levels. It has been designed as a source book for teachers and others interested in the educational process and will find a place in the reading lists of certificate, diploma and degree courses. It is a book of questions, not answers, and is expected to provoke comment and meaningful discussion about many of the ideas, concepts and practices of educational management. However, most of the papers contain a large number of recent additional references in the subject for those readers motivated to search for answers to their own, more specific, questions.

Clearly with so many authors, topics and sources readers will, after selective reading, find their own road to educational salvation but perhaps a quotation from Lao Tze, included within Joan Dean's paper, will help to set the scene.

> A leader is best
> When people barely know he exists,
> Not so good when people obey him and acclaim him,
> Worst when they despise him,
> Fail to honour people
> They fail to honour you
> But of a good leader who talks little,
> When his work is done, his aim fulfilled,
> They will say, 'We did it ourselves.'

(Lao Tze, *The Way Of Life*)

*Paul Harling*
Chorley
December 1983

*1*
*Introduction:*
*The Organizational*
*Framework for*
*Educational Leadership*

# The Organizational Framework for Educational Leadership

*Paul Harling*
*All Saints' CE School, Chorley*

## The Educational Organization

The educational system in England and Wales can be regarded as a 'complex social organization' (Katz, 1964).[1] It is 'complex' because it includes many different persons who interact in their performance of many different functions. It is 'social' because 'the participants are interdependent and their actions are socially promulgated and enforced' (Katz, 1964).[2] This emphasis on people and their influence on other people is echoed by Kelly who writes that 'the most important thing to know about organizations is that they do not exist — except in people's minds' (Kelly, 1974),[3] and by Etzioni who refers to organizations as 'social units that pursue specific goals which they are structured to serve' (Etzioni, 1964).[4] At risk of being pedantic it is therefore clear that the educational system as a whole is 'an organization' and that it possesses constituent 'organizations' at various levels. All the participants are thus part of the same organization — although at times the behaviour of some sectors would seem to suggest otherwise.

The distinctive characteristic of an organization is therefore that it has been formally established for the explicit purpose of achieving certain goals. Every organization has a formally instituted pattern of authority and an official body of rules and procedures which are intended to aid the achievement of those goals. However, alongside this formal aspect of the organization are networks of informal relationships and unofficial norms which arise from the interaction of individuals and groups working within the formal structure. Every 'leader' has to be aware of both these aspects since it is their interaction which determines the level and nature of his autonomy and therefore his ability to lead other participants and influence the system as a whole. The importance of considering such theoretical viewpoints is emphasized by Sergiovanni and Starratt when they refer to the various theories of administration, management and leadership as 'alternative windows through which the educational practitioner can view [educational] problems and issues'.[5] They point out that the practitioner is the one qualified to 'build prescription from theory ... in view of the uniqueness and complexity of the circumstances he faces.'[6] This advice has been followed to the letter in the choice of authors and contributions to this book.


## The Bureaucratic Model

The most widely recognized framework for understanding formal administrative and supervisory structures is the bureaucratic model first articulated methodically by Max Weber. Contrary to the popular view of a bureaucracy being characterized by layers of inefficient functionaries Weber sees bureaucracy as a form of organization which strives continuously for maximum efficiency through rationally defined structures and processes. Indeed, he believes that 'the decisive reason for the advance of bureaucratic organization has always been its purely technical superiority over other forms of organization.'[7]

Abbott (1965),[8] among others, has outlined Weber's model of ideal bureaucracy, noting how its features are present to some degree in most organizations, including schools and educational systems and sub-systems. It is worth considering these briefly in turn to ascertain the extent of their presence and effect on educational leadership, decision-making and organization.

Firstly, organizational tasks are distributed among the various positions as official duties. This implies a division of labour and a degree of specialization enabling the organization to employ personnel on the basis of specific skills and experience. The DES is divided into branches, LEAs are divided into administrative districts and by type of educational institution. Similarly schools are divided into types, departments are established within schools and there is a clear distinction, except in the case of headteachers, between the administration function and the teaching function.

Secondly, in the classical Weberian model, the positions and offices are organized into a hierarchical authority structure, usually a pyramid. Thus the DES and Parliament have powers of control over LEAs who in turn 'lead' school governors who 'lead' headteachers who 'lead' classroom teachers.

Thirdly, there is a formally established system of rules and regulations governing official decisions and actions. The regulations ensure a degree of uniformity of operation and together with the authority structure make possible the coordination of the various activities. Such regulations provide a degree of continuity regardless of changes in personnel, thus promoting stability. In fact there is considerable standardization of textbooks, syllabi, examinations and the like to provide for orderly behaviour, and each LEA has a system of issuing bulletins and memoranda on matters of safety, health and the legal rights and obligations of teachers.

Fourthly, officials are expected to assume an impersonal orientation in their contact with 'clients' and other officials. Such detachment is designed to prevent the personal feelings of officials from distorting their rational judgement in carrying out their duties. In schools and LEAs authority has been generally established on the basis of rational considerations rather than charismatic qualities, participants are expected to apply rules with strict impartiality and thus, by operating in a spirit of 'formalistic impersonality' the typical school system and school has succeeded, to a large extent, in separating organizational rights and obligations from the private lives of individuals.

Fifthly, employment by the organization constitutes a career for participants based on expertise and qualifications. Officers and teachers are appointed by 'normal' competitive procedures and 'career advancements are according to seniority or to achievement or both' (Blau and Scott, 1962).[9] Such features are easily recognized as fundamental to the conditions of employment in the educational organization and encourage the development of 'fair' styles of leadership.

The Weberian model therefore projects an image of certain 'leaders' deliberately controlling the educational system or sub-system by adjusting the 'levers of authority' (Hanson, 1976–77).[10] A recurring theme of the papers in this book is whether in fact the bureaucratic model accurately reflects the structure, the mode of decision-making, and therefore the style of leadership in the schools and local authorities. To some degree the educational system is a unique type of organization and, as Parsons[11] and Gouldner,[12] among others, have stressed, Weber's approach fails to recognize the effects of the presence of personnel with 'professional' tendencies and orientations on the process of leadership and decision-making in education. The distinction appears to be one of differentiating between the existence of the educational system as an entity in its own right and the 'life' and 'action' which are brought in by the human participants. This distinction is highlighted in the model of administrative and supervisory behaviour which discusses schools in terms of social systems analysis and which was developed by Getzels and Guba.[13]

## The Social Systems Model

The constituent organizations of our educational system individually and collectively respond to stimuli from their social environment, and also affect the environment with their 'output'. Getzels and Guba suggest that the context and process of management, of which leadership is a part, can be examined from structural, functional and operational perspectives. Structurally, management and leadership consist of a series of superordinate-subordinate relationships within the system. Functionally, this hierarchy of relationships is the basis for allocating and integrating roles, personnel and facilities on behalf of the goals of the system. Operationally, the management process occurs totally through interpersonal relationships. The emphasis is therefore on people and on the resulting uniqueness of each organization as the participants bring into it needs, interests, expectations and attitudes.

The manager/leader must therefore be aware of, and work within, two dimensions. Firstly, he is concerned with the nomothetic dimension representing the ongoing structure of education which exists and persists regardless of the particular staff employed at a particular time. The structure is defined in terms of roles, such as Secretary of State, Chief Education Officer, Headteacher, or Teacher. The roles are defined in terms of the expectations, of the incumbent and others, which are associated with the roles and from which he as the 'leader' will develop his actions. This dimension conveys a model of our educational system as a relatively stable pattern of roles, within which incumbents conform to the expectations attached to them.

However, such a dimension takes no account of the differences between people, and hence is balanced by the idiographic or personal dimension. In this dimension the individual has personally determined goals which are expressed through unique personalities according to unique needs. The idiographic dimension thus represents the idiosyncratic aspect of an organization, which is a function of differences between people. The fundamental concern for a consideration of leadership is therefore whether the educational system uses people to accomplish organizational ends or whether people use the educational system to accomplish human ends.

This model therefore highlights the major dilemma facing someone who wishes to lead. Since the educational system is a human organization the task must be based on both the nomothetic and idiographic dimensions. Leaders are concerned not only with survival and maintenance of the school system, but also with the appropriateness of educational goals, the welfare and development of staff, and with the intellectual, social and emotional development of the 'clients' — the children and students who use and benefit from educational provisions. The dilemma is a recurrent theme of this book but it seems probable that with clear human concerns the system is required to serve its participants and clients, rather than the suggested bureaucratic way which requires individuals, to a large extent, to serve the system.

Consideration of the scope and intensity of the autonomy of leaders and decision-makers must depend partly on the nature of this 'organization versus individual' dilemma and whether indeed such a dilemma exists at all. Its persistence as a theme of management and leadership discussions therefore requires some consideration of authority systems in education, with particular emphasis on the authority and power of those participants who find themselves in the role of 'leader'.

## Authority Systems in Education

It has already been suggested that Weber's bureaucratic model of organizational structure and implied behaviour is fundamental. Similarly, Weber's formulation of authority types provides a background for discussion of any participant's organizational authority, power and leadership.

Weber distinguishes three kinds of authority on the basis of their acceptance as a common feature for a particular group within the educational system.[14] Given that 'power' refers to the ability to control the actions of others, 'legitimation' refers to social approval and 'authority' refers to legitimized power, Weber distinguishes three major types of authority and therefore sources of legitimation: legal/rational, charismatic/affective and tradition.[15]

Legal/rational legitimation rests on the acceptance of the supremacy of law and social norms, and compliance is the result of the application of impersonal principles and rules. It is this form of authority which provides a basis for the ideal bureaucratic organization and is particularly applicable to the situation of the secretary of state and parliament in relation to the educational system as a whole. In a similar way heads of maintained schools are bound by articles of government which set broad limits on their autonomy. Draft articles were set down in a central government White Paper[16] and virtually all LEAs obeyed the advice almost to the last comma.

Therefore any challenge to the authority of the headteacher to 'lead' his school, perhaps by the staff of the school or 'outsiders', may be countered by reference to the legal establishment of that authority. In addition, headteachers, for example, 'may draw legal legitimation from the many circulars, reports and recommendations which come to them from the local authority administration, the inspectorate, the Department of Education and Science, and from the various consultative committees of the Department' (King, 1973).[17] Some of these are demands, others advisory. King adds to this by pointing out that 'a rational belief in the value of an action can be an important source of legitimation for that action, without an accompanying legal or official codification.'[18] It is therefore a subtle but powerful tool of the leader in the educational system.

Charismatic or affective legitimation rests on a profession of faith in the correctness of a course of action, although that action may not be rationally justifiable to a majority of interested parties. A recent example is the use of corporal punishment which, although discredited by a significant body of expert psychological, sociological and legal advice, is still included as part of the disciplinary code of many schools and local authorities. The recent (Summer 1983) decision of the secretary of state to allow parental choice in the matter has created problems for LEAs with regard to their legal/rational authority to 'lead' the schools under their control and the leadership of the headteacher will in future have to be based on his charismatic/affective authority. He can decide upon any rules or codes of discipline for his school, with official (i.e. LEA and legal) support, but if his affective legitimation is faulty he will meet significant opposition from his employers, the parents, and possibly the children. To reinforce the previous emphasis on the educational system being a human organization, effective leadership requires the development of both charismatic/affective and legal/rational legitimation.

Traditional legitimation of the educational leaders' authority derives largely from historical beliefs about the role of leaders, and is sometimes based upon outdated practices. There are still some people who believe that leaders at all levels 'know best' what is good for the rest. With regard to central government the development of local authority associations and the increased and diverse influence of the unions and other pressure groups has shown that leadership is not the prerogative of the chosen few. Similarly schools which have encouraged the development of political — with a small p — parents' associations have found that traditional views, merely because they are based on tradition, are quickly challenged by people of equal or greater intelligence than the proponent of the views. This point is repeatedly stressed in the articles and papers of this book.

The developing professionalism (including relevant knowledge, skills and attitudes) of teachers and administrators at all levels has produced a fourth source of organizational authority based on professional norms and skills. It is a suitable tool for consideration of the 'organization versus individual' dilemma, mentioned earlier, which bedevils leaders in the educational system. It is particularly noticeable that in schools 'organizational norms and rules often conflict with educo-professional norms.'[19]

The work of Peabody[20] is of great value when, in summarizing the work of Weber, Simon, Bennis and Presthus,[21] he identifies four broad categories of authority: authority of legitimacy, authority of position (including the sanctions which may be part of a leadership decision), authority of competence (including professional skills and experience), and authority of person (including human relations skills). Peabody notes that teachers seemed to value authority of competence higher than authority of person, position or legitimacy, and that authority of position and person were next in importance. In other words, the professional orientation of subordinates is a potent force for a leader, and he needs to recognize and utilize the fact that professionalism exists if he wishes to have an effective base of authority on which to build his decision-making and leadership.

The indications would seem to be, therefore, that in general leaders in the educational system are finding that their bases of authority are changing. The popular view of the leader as one who possesses legal rights, with powers by virtue of his position to impose sanctions and rewards, is being upstaged by his need to display superior competence and possess those leadership qualities as an individual which encourage his views to be adopted. This view will be reinforced in the readings which follow this introduction.

## Power Bases in Schools

Given such changes and increasing limitations on previously accepted authority, it is of value to consider briefly some of the bases of power. Authority, as it has been considered in the previous section, is directed towards a broad basis for action rather than at a small group or individual. Power, on the other hand, is derived from authority and is directed towards winning compliance of subordinates on behalf of the superordinates in the organization.

French and Raven have identified five bases for the social power which person L can exert over person F.[22] Firstly, reward power, based on F's perception that L has the ability to reward him. It is a particular characteristic of benevolent but paternalistic environments. Rewards consist of scale posts in schools, the warm, light classrooms and so on.

Secondly, coercive power, based on F's perception that L has the ability to punish him and impose sanctions. Financial penalties imposed on recalcitrant LEAs are on example; the withholding of good confidential references by headteachers is another.

Thirdly, expert power, based on F's perception that L has some special knowledge or expertise, is similar to the competence authority base, and is the ability to command compliance on the basis of professional knowledge, information and skills. The fact that Chief Education Officers receive informal notification of 'developments' before official pronouncements is a case in point. Similarly the fact that a headteacher has first notice of, and easiest access to, significant developments in education during INSET and through the issue of circulars is of significance.

Fourthly, referent power, based on F's identification with L. If a headteacher can be obeyed because of his personality, then he has referent power. It is a point of interest here that headteachers have all been classroom teachers and thus have common roots. The same cannot always be said of the relationship between schools' personnel and the LEA.

Fifthly, legitimate power, based on F's perception that L has a legitimate right to prescribe behaviour for him, by virtue of the office he holds. This source of power is in constant use in the relationships between the LEAs and schools. It is also the basic point which is usually clarified by a head in his first encounter with a new teacher and is indeed probably the first base of power to be utilized with any new staff. It is also clearly stated in the articles of government issued to all new members of staff and so all teachers are at least implicitly aware of the head's legal responsibilities.

A study by Bachman *et al.* throws some light on the problems of power and school leadership.[23] They find that the most important reason for complying with the wishes of superordinates was a response to expert power and legitimate power. Referent and reward power were less important and coercive power the least likely reason for compliance. It would seem likely therefore that a headteacher (or indeed an LEA or agent of the central government) could well find great value in the days spent on the wide variety of available courses for teachers.

## The Informal Organization of the School

Much of the preceding discussion has concerned the formal structure of the educational system, although at all levels and stages the formality has had to be refined and/or qualified because of the informal influences which occur in any human organization. As Banks (1976) points out, there are 'networks of informal relations and unofficial norms which arise out of the social interaction of individuals and groups working together within the formal structure'.[24] Iannacconne has contributed perhaps the best-known work on informal organizations in educational systems and the bearing they have on power and constraints in educational leadership.[25] Fundamentally, the informal organization is related conceptually to the idiographic dimension of Getzels and Guba in its stress on the fact that interaction in organizations is between people, and not just between roles. As people, members of organizations seek others with whom they can associate. Iannacconne refers here to the individual's need for a 'primary group affiliation'[26] with people, in addition to his professional affiliation with the formal organization. Personal characteristics such as age, sex, marital status, career status and professional sub-sector involvement appear to affect which members are included in a primary informal group.

Owens writes, 'there is abundant evidence that informal organization is essential to the functioning and administration of an organization, and the primary groups of the informal organization have great powers.'[27] It is impossible to conceive of an educational organization which is so well structured and planned as to eliminate the human factor. But more importantly it is almost impossible to conceive of an educational organization which does not recognize the need of its personnel to develop primary group affiliations that will reward them with generally sought social and psychological satisfactions. For the headteacher of a school, or a district education officer, the power of the informal organization is of great practical concern because the leader's basic interest is in getting things done and it is the informal group which, to a large extent, can set the behavioural norm for the staff. Struggles to gain acceptance of the leader's leadership are not merely the conflict of official authority and an individual member of staff. In reality the individual may have the support of one or more primary groups in facing the authority and style of leadership of the superordinate. If attempts are made to use raw legal power to influence a subordinate, while disregarding the group power which may support the individual, the result may be a shift in the primary group's behavioural norm to a reduced level of cooperation. Iannacconne refers to this as the exercise of extra-legal power.

Of great significance to leadership of the school or sub-system in education is Iannacconne's observation of two situations. One is where the informal primary groups are linked through an individual who is a member of both. In this case he is referred to as an 'articulation'. If two individuals in different primary groups regularly interact, their link is called a 'bridge'. The leader's ability and willingness to recognize and nurture the individuals in these two categories can extend his influence more widely through the primary groups of the informal organization. Perhaps there is strength in the idea of an 'old boys' network' after all! By the same token, however, conflict with the members of a bridge or an articulation can marshall widespread opposition. The paper by David Reynolds and Steve Murgatroyd is a particularly interesting case in point, illustrating shifting allegiances within a particular school setting.

## Professional Tendencies in Education

It seems very likely, in view of the foregoing discussion, that a purely formal model of organizational structure, control and leadership in our educational system would not be useful for any more than a very simplistic analysis of the actual processes of decision-making. As Lortie points out with reference to the schools sector, 'the bureaucratic model, in emphasising the formal distribution of authority, does not prepare us for many of the events that actually occur in public schools. Teachers, for example, lay claim to and get, informally, certain types of authority despite lack of formal support for it either in law or in school system constitutions.'[28] Bidwell, in his classic analysis of the school as a formal organization, stresses that we have limited knowledge about the 'interplay of bureaucratization and professionalism in the schools'.[29] This is also true among schools, school governors and LEAs. Hanson adds that the interplay issue is quite significant in understanding questions of educational leadership and decision-making 'because teachers as professionals claim allegiance to a set of normative principles representative of the profession as well as to a specialised colleague group.'[30] On the other hand, local education authority officers, and to some extent head-teachers, 'must be loyal to the organization that employs them.' In this instance Lortie writes, 'the several strands of hierarchical control, collegial control and autonomy become tangled and complex.'[31] Clearly to refer to the school and educational system as a *complex* organization is no exaggeration.

We must therefore assume that any consideration of the educational system will need to take into account the existence of professionally oriented personnel. This is because professionally oriented organizations possess authority and power systems which are different from those in 'pure' bureaucracies. This type of organization tends to be characterized by the development and application of a more pluralistic power structure which is, relative to the bureaucratic power structure, more dispersed throughout the organization on the basis of ability and competence; more dynamic, in the sense that it moves from person to person depending on the job to be done; more interdependent, in that personnel are specialists who need to cooperate with other specialists to command overall authority in a particular situation; and more functional, in that it is constantly re-examined and refined to meet changing circumstances. Such a professionally oriented organization tends to use power bases which are related to the job to be done, rather than to the characteristics of particular individuals.

To function in such an organization the people involved need to be themselves professionally oriented. Lieberman lists the characteristics of a profession as, first, the provision of a unique, definite and essential social service; second, an emphasis on intellectual techniques in performing the services; third, a long period of specialized training; fourth, a broad range of autonomy for both the individual practitioner and for the occupational group as a whole; fifth, an acceptance by the practitioners of broad personal responsibility for judgements made and acts performed within the scope of professional autonomy; sixth, an emphasis upon the services to be rendered, rather than the economic gain to the practitioners; and seventh, a comprehensive self-governing organization of practitioners.[32]

Without going into these characteristics in depth it seems quite clear that the personnel of many sectors of our educational system do not fully match the criteria for definition as a profession. Perhaps the nearest manifestation is in higher education, especially universities, examined by Brian Fidler in this book. However, all sectors do suffer from a number of deficiencies with regard to strict definitions of 'professional' and it seems fair to assume that Etzioni's use of the term 'semi-professional'[33] is more apt. But it must also be noted that the orientation is there and seems to be increasing in all sectors of the system. Its effects have been clearly identified in most of the contributions to this book.

## Concluding Comments

Sergiovanni and Starratt suggest that there are three fundamental dilemmas for a leader in the educational system,[34] and each of them is echoed time and again during the discussions in this book. Firstly, there is the problem of reconciling for himself, and on behalf of the clients of the system, the increasing bureaucratization and professionalism which Corwin,[35] for example, sees as simultaneous but conflicting trends in schools and school systems and which require different modes of leadership.

Secondly, there is the ability-authority dilemma of choosing and reconciling the right to decide with the ability to decide. Thirdly, there is the autonomy-coordination dilemma. As teachers have become specialized relative to non-teachers in terms of training and performance, the teachers' demands for autonomy have increased while at the same time demands for accountability and justification have also increased. To complicate matters further, teachers, by increasing their degree of specialization, have become more dependent upon each other to achieve educational goals and the leadership problem becomes one of finding means of coordinating activities.

Bidwell places the whole issue of educational leadership in perspective when he writes 'the looseness of the system structure and the nature of the teaching task seem to press for a professional mode of school system organization, while demands for uniformity of product and the long time span over which cohorts of students are trained press for rationalisation of activities and thus a bureaucratic base of organization.'[36] Thus, as Hanson suggests, 'the instructional mission of the school becomes the organising principle of the teachers' professionalism, whereas the need for efficient resource allocation and rational planning procedures becomes the organising principle for the administrators.'[37] Thus there are apparently two very different sources of organizational leadership in the educational system, one rooted in the classical bureaucratic tradition of formal centralized authority, and the other rooted in the informal professionalism of the teacher.

With regard to the autonomy of teachers, Lortie argues that the source is physical and social separation of the teachers' work space.[38] Behind closed doors teachers are isolated from immediate supervision. Headteachers are similarly protected, but in a crisis the pattern is probably much more fragile than it appears, as the situation at William Tyndale School showed.

Katz adds further insight into the question when he points out that teachers and administrators are specialists in pursuit of their respective tasks and need protection from one another to allow for 'personal manoeuvres'.[39] Such diversity, he believes, is a valuable resource for schools and school systems, and properly coordinated plays a key role in promoting spontaneity and creativity. Significantly Gouldner has pointed out that organizations are structured to control, link and interrelate parts, but also to establish, separate and preserve areas of functional autonomy,[40] and Argyris suggests that the true essence of an organization is found in the pattern of semi-autonomous but interdependent parts rather than its formally stated goals and structure.[41]

It would seem, therefore, that when trying to understand issues of the nature and focus of school and educational system leadership and decision-making the purely formal models are inadequate but certainly not defunct. Since virtually all models of organizational structure, control, authority and leadership appear to be footnotes to Weber's work then the models which tend to stress centralized decision-making will be correct only to a point. Elements which are troublesome to the classical formal models continually arise. They are the raw material of the rest of this book. The authors are seeking answers to the vexed questions of who can and should lead whom, to what end, by what means and for what purpose. Only time will tell whether they have indeed recognized the New Directions in Educational Leadership.

## Notes

1 KATZ, F.E. (1964) 'The school as a complex social organization', *Harvard Educational Review*, 34, 3.
2 *Ibid.*, p. 428.
3 KELLY, J. (1974) *Organizational Behaviour*, New York, Irwin, p. 1.
4 ETZIONI, A, (1964) *Modern Organizations*, Englewood Cliffs, Prentice Hall, p. 4.
5 SERGIOVANNI, T.J. and STARRATT, R.J. (1971) *Emerging Patterns of Supervision: Human Perspectives*, New York, McGraw Hill, p. 31.
6 *Ibid.*, p. 31.
7 GERTH, H. and WRIGHT MILLS, C. (1947) *From Max Weber; Essays in Sociology*, London, Routledge and Kegan Paul, p. 214.
8 ABBOTT, M.G. and LOVELL, J.T. (Eds) (1965) *Change Perspectives in Educational Administration*. Auburn, Auburn University Press.
9 BLAU, P.M. and SCOTT, W.R. (1962) *Formal Organizations: A Comparative Approach*, San Francisco, Chandler, pp. 32–3.
10 HANSON, M. (1976–77) 'Beyond the bureaucratic model: A study of power and autonomy in educational decision making', *Interchange*, 7, 2, p. 28.
11 PARSONS, T., Introduction, in WEBER, M. (1947) *The Theory of Social and Economic Organization*, Trans. by HENDERSON, A.M. and PARSONS, T., Glencoe, Free Press, pp. 58–60.
12 GOULDNER, A. (1954) *Patterns of Industrial Democracy*, London, Routledge and Kegan Paul, pp. 22–4.
13 GETZELS, J.W. and GUBA, E.G. (1957) 'Social behaviour and the administrative process', *School Review*, 65, pp. 423–41.
14 HENDERSON and PARSONS (1947), *op. cit.*
15 GERTH and WRIGHT MILLS (1947), *op. cit*, p. 9.
16 *Principles of Government in Maintained Secondary Schools* (1944) London, HMSO.
17 KING, R. (1973) 'The head teacher and his authority', in FOWLER, G. *et al.* (Eds) *Decision Making in British Education*, Ch. 21, London, Heinemann p. 425.
18 *Ibid.*
19 SERGIOVANNI and STARRATT (1971), *op. cit.*, p. 39.
20 PEABODY, R.L. (1962) 'Perceptions of organizational authority: A comparative analysis', *Administrative Science Quarterly*, 6, 4.
21 WEBER, M. in HENDERSON and PARSONS (1947) *op. cit.*; URWICK, L. (1944) *The Elements of Administration*, London, Heinemann; SIMON, H.A. *et al.* (1950) *Public Administration*, New York, Macmillan; BENNIS, W.G. (1959) 'Leadership theory and administrative behaviour; the problem of authority', *Administrative Science Quarterly*, 4; PRESTHUS, R.V. (1960) 'Authority in organizations', *Public Administration Review*, 20.
22 FRENCH, J.R.P. and RAVEN, B. (1960) 'The bases of social power', in CARTWRIGHT, D. and ZANDER, A.F. (Eds) *Group Dynamics: Research and Theory*. Evanston Row and Peterson.
23 BACHMAN J.D. *et al.* (1968) 'Bases of supervisory power: A comparative study in five organizational settings', in TANNEBAUM (Ed.), *Control in Organizations*, New York, McGraw Hill, p. 236.
24 BANKS, O. (1976) *The Sociology Of Education*, 3rd ed., London, Batsford, p. 192.
25 IANNACCONNE, L. (1964) 'An approach to the informal organization of the school', in GRIFFITHS, J. (Ed.) *Behavioural Science and Educational Administration*, Chicago, University of Chicago Press.
26 *Ibid.*, p. 234.
27 OWENS, R.G. (1970) *Organizational Behaviour in Schools*, p. 50.
28 LORTIE, D.C. (1964) 'The teacher and team teaching; suggestions for long term

research', in SHAPLIN, J.T. and OLDS, H.F. (Eds) *Team Teaching*, New York, Harper and Row, p. 273.

29  BIDWELL, C. (1965) 'The school as a formal organization', in MARCH, J.G. *Handbook of Organizations*, Chicago, Rand McNally, p. 992.

30  HANSON (1976–77), *op. cit.*, p. 27.

31  LORTIE (1964), *op. cit.*, p. 1.

32  LIEBERMAN, M. (1956) *Education As a Profession*, Ch. 1, Englewood Cliffs, Prentice Hall.

33  ETZIONI (1964), *op. cit.*, p. 76.

34  SERGIOVANNI and STARRATT (1971), *op. cit.*, p. 61.

35  CORWIN, R.G. (1965) 'Professional persons in public organizations', *Educational Administration Quarterly*, 1, 3, p. 15.

36  BIDWELL (1965) *op. cit.*, pp. 976–7.

37  HANSON (1976–77), *op. cit.*, p. 30.

38  LORTIE (1964), *op. cit.*, p. 274.

39  KATZ (1964) *op. cit.*, p. 438.

40  GOULDNER, A. (1959) 'Organizational tensions', in MERTON, R.K. *et al.* (Eds) *Sociology Today*. New York, Basic Books.

41  ARGYRIS, C. (1959) 'Understanding human behaviour in organizations: One viewpoint', in HAIRE, M. (Ed.) *Modern Organizational Theory*, New York, Wiley, p. 125.

## 2
## *The Nature of*
## *Educational*
## *Leadership*

# *Introduction*

The literature concerning the nature of educational leadership is vast and many volumes could be compiled which merely list the available sources. What is required is an outline of some of the general issues and trends to be found in considerations of educational leadership in England and Wales. This has been supplied for the reader in this section of the book.

The first contribution is by Alan Paisey, one of the country's leading writers on educational management. The paper was specially commissioned for this book. In it he successfully outlines developments in the thinking and action concerning educational management since the Second World War. He discusses four conflicting movements of thought and experience concerning leadership within educational institutions at the present time:

the 'leadership has no appeal' movement;
the 'there should be a return to leadership' movement;
the 'leadership has never been absent' movement; and
the 'leadership should be shifted from individuals to groups' movement.

He points out the fact, often disregarded, that leadership is about routine organizational matters as well as major initiatives, and makes it clear that the structure of our educational system does not function automatically but requires a great deal of skill and application by all concerned.

This point is reiterated in the second paper, by Steve Murgatroyd and Harry Gray, who examine the nature of leadership required to produce an effective school, defined as one which responds to individual pupil and staff needs and to the changing face of the community in which it is placed. The dynamic, human aspect of leadership is therefore emphasized as the authors seek to define the characteristics of the leader who wishes to establish 'helping relationships' in school. In the article they attempt to list the particular skills associated with this kind of leadership, and consider the kinds of support leaders require to enable them to maintain leadership of a suitable quality.

# Trends in Educational Leadership Thought

*Alan Paisey*
*Bulmershe College of Higher Education*

The Second World War proved to be a dramatic watershed in education. The post-war world chose education as a major vehicle for social reconstruction and prosperity. This was a daunting task to give to it but especially so since a substantial growth of population took place at the same time. Consequently, there followed an unprecedented growth in the number, range and size of educational institutions. In the first instance, the approach to managing these institutions reflected pre-war practice overlaid with the experience of those who returned to education or who entered it for the first time from war service.

The many preoccupations of national communities everywhere allowed the re-establishment, expansion and development of educational institutions to proceed apace and unhindered. Progress was subject to the dynamics and internal controls of the constituent parts of the system itself but not to the explicit and direct surveillance of interests outside education. The prospect of independent assessments of what was value for money in education and notions of public accountability lay thirty years ahead.

However, educational institutions then, as now, in common with all institutions were required to operate within the values, expectations and practices of the community being served, as enshrined in its laws. The prevailing climate of opinion in the wake of the shock of war was fashioned by the conditions and perceived causes which gave rise to it. Notable among these was the prevalence in Europe of totalitarian government. This could be recognized by its uniformity, directive practices, hierarchical attitude and offices, and centralized institutions but, above all, by its immovable ruling élite, bulwarked by suitable theories, the exercise of leadership and the deification of the leader.

Leadership thus came to be associated with destruction and suffering in post-war society. It was an unpopular word. The new age wanted to emancipate the ordinary citizen, to enlarge the status and contribution of the very individuals whom leadership allegedly reduced to anonymity. At that time it would have been imprudent if not impossible to offer courses on leadership in education and there were far more pressing subjects for research. Today, in contrast, the climate is very different. Leadership as a subject for courses and research is in vogue. New expectations of leadership have been articulated.

> Over the past few years nearly every major educational report has stressed the importance of leadership roles in schools. . . . In general the evidence suggests that if those who lead have appropriate experience, personal qualities and appropriate skills, they will support and develop the work of colleagues (Surrey Inspectorate, 1982).

Leadership is a characteristic of schools as of any other kind of organization. This is an assertion based on a common sense notion of leadership as the conduct of an individual or group used to influence others in respect of their values, attitudes, knowledge, skills and behaviour. Leadership so broadly defined is present in every classroom or teaching group. The teacher clearly exercises leadership in this sense in relation to young people, though it may prove progressively more elusive for the teacher to do so over the whole age-range for compulsory schooling. The attributes of leadership in a classroom with 5-year-olds are different from those required in a classroom with 16-year-olds.

Similarly, one teacher may exercise leadership in relation to a colleague or a member of the non-teaching staff of the school, and it is not uncommon for a member of the non-teaching staff to exercise leadership in relation to members of the teaching staff. Generally, certain organizational members are expected to exercise leadership because of their formal positions in the school. This applies particularly to the head of school. The expectation is clear and direct in the case of the small school. In the case of the large school the expectation may be expressed more in terms of collective leadership or that of a senior management team with the head as its central figure.

The common sense definition of leadership used so far does not indicate anything about the direction of the influence exercised. The conduct of an individual or group which affects others can create values, attitudes, knowledge, skills and behaviour of all kinds. The concept of leadership, however, is certainly intended to convey the idea that the direction of these variables is in favour of a certain purpose and not antipathetic to it. Thus leadership is a unifying activity. It may be exercised effectively for the organization as a whole. This is centripetal leadership. On the other hand, it may be exercised in respect of a part or several parts of an organization leading to the formation of coalitions, perhaps fragmentation, and even schism. This is centrifugal leadership and represents a failure of the individual or group responsible for the organization as a whole to exercise leadership in relation to those members who themselves can exercise leadership in incompatible ways.

If it is a fact that leadership is currently a subject for courses for personnel in education and also a focus for educational research, it is not a fact that leadership is clear in concept and practice. The teaching profession does not uniformly appear to regard leadership as the *sine qua non* of professional expertise, institutional structure and general expectation.

The rest of this chapter, therefore, will be directed to two purposes: firstly, to consider the concept of leadership; secondly, to identify and discuss four conflicting movements of thought and experience concerning leadership within educational institutions today.

### The Concept of Leadership

Discussion about leadership is confused because the word is used ambiguously. Many different assumptions are made about it, but in practice it seems that four models are predominantly in use:

the congenital model
the situational model
the management model
the followership model

In the *congenital model*, leaders are born rather than fashioned by the environment. The strength of this model is that it allows the energies of society to focus on *finding* the necessary leaders rather than creating or training them. Credibility lies in the attributes conferred by the accident of birth rather than personal effort and record of performance. Leadership is an ascribed rather than an achieved quality. The weakness of this model is in the obvious fact that in the contemporary world leadership must be exercised in so many different fields, each based on its own special knowledge. Unless it is held that leadership is never dependent upon specifics in any occupation or activity but only on the common and general human factor (Knipe and Maclay, 1973), then clearly it is hard to assert that anyone can automatically be leader in any field because of innate, superlative qualities alone.

In contrast, *the situational model* stresses the relative nature of leadership. Circumstances create leaders in that opportunities for leadership arise from an expressed need or demand and the availability of an individual relatively able at that time to meet it. This model owes much for its development to the work of Bion (1961) whose studies of the behaviour of individuals in groups during the Second World War showed that leadership could be a transitory, revolving quality among group members, variously exercised to generate conflict, reconciliation, the creation of coalitions or sub-groups, and the discharge of production or work itself. The situational model, therefore, stresses that leadership is a ubiquitous quality. Given the appropriate circumstances, anybody can be a leader. The strength of the model can be stated in terms of its emphasis on the essential, potential value of every person. Energies in organizations should be focussed on erecting a structure which gives all members the chance to find maximum motivation and commitment through being in situations in which they can lead. The weakness of the model lies in its failure to take account of the undoubted differences between individuals, both at birth and at every other subsequent point of life. Furthermore, it overlooks the question of will and ambition. There are patently present in organizations some members who are unable or unwilling to let another lead by using extraneous devices to this end. The model presupposes a measure of objectivity and detachment which may not exist in practice. Individuals can be greedy for power to the point of lacking recognition of the leadership capacity of others in terms of this model.

The *management model* identifies leadership with the formal positions held by individuals in working organizations. Leadership in this model depends not so much on birth as in the congenital model, nor on relative circumstances as in the situational model, but on appointment (National Association of Secondary School Principals, 1982). Leadership is associated with hierarchical names and levels. It is bulwarked by the guarantees and instrumentalities placed in the hands of the individual by the appointing body and sanctioned by social rites and expectations. All bureaucratic organizations exhibit the management model, including education, public sector industries, the armed services, the civil service, the church, and the health and social security services. The strength of the model is that if leadership is by definition either in short supply (the congenital model), or expensive to create or unreliable in appearance (the situational model), it can provide at least a semblance of leadership. It makes the most of inadequacy and raises the possibility of achieving exceptional results with unexceptional resources in unpropitious circumstances (Paisey, 1981a). The weakness of the model is clearly that leadership in its quintessential sense might never be exercised. Organizations may simply be maintained or stagnate, starved of the leadership towards new fields and the adaptation needed. Furthermore, individuals other than the formal postholders evidently can and do exercise leadership to the discomfiture of the latter and to the point when the organization may be imperilled.

The fourth and final leadership model may be paradoxically called the *followership model*. Much attention is given to the qualities, qualifications and behavioural patterns of leaders. Too little attention is given to the reasons why individuals are prepared to be followers as an explanation of the incidence and nature of leadership. The interest lies in the fact that everyone, it seems, is willing to be a follower either on a permanent basis, or in certain circumstances. The point is that a leader does not always know that he or she is a leader. Even if there is recognition of it, the individual may not cherish the fact. Even where leadership is desired and actively sought, there is still no guarantee that it will be exercised. In other words, sovereignty lies with the follower. Followers provide the leader with a raison d'être. The reasons for followership can vary from the bizarre and irrational to the fully explicit and rational. Nevertheless, the leader cannot always know why he or she is a leader and, therefore, cannot always generate a following in order to satisfy a desire to lead. The strength of the model is that it provides insight into the conditions and events in organizations for the purpose of analyzing the micropolitics for managerial purposes. It has the merit of giving scope to the role of third parties. Leadership can be regarded as the product of triangulation. An individual perceives that a second is prone to acknowledge leadership in a third. This is obviously an important observation to be able to make accurately if the first individual happens to be the head of an institution. It enables him or her to make and modify the organizational structure to the best advantage of all. The weakness of the model is that organizations, because of their collective and public purpose, must require *constrained* behaviour as well as *facilitated* behaviour (Kynaston-Reeves, 1967). Thus, there is lack of consideration of why members of an organization *ought* to recognize and be willing to follow a leader, as catered for by the management model.

## Conflicting Movements of Thought and Experience

For the purposes of reviewing the conflicting movements of thought and experience concerning leadership in educational institutions, the following four movements are identified. Each of these is presented and discussed in turn:

'leadership has no appeal' movement;
'there should be a return to leadership' movement;
'leadership has never been absent' movement;
'leadership should be shifted from individuals to groups' movement.

### *'Leadership Has No Appeal' Movement*

There are those who are hostile or indifferent to the idea of leadership in schools. Its lack of appeal arises from three sources: the nature and purpose of the learning process, the professional mode of the teacher, and the preferences for an existential approach to organizational life. In educational institutions there are distinct estates or interest groups: the governing body representing the public interest; the teaching staff; the pupils or students; ancillary staff supplying all manner of support services; and administrative staff. Leadership is expressed and may be studied separately within each of these estates. Relations between them in terms of leadership may also be considered. Size of institution, however, is important in this regard. Small schools have had to share governing bodies with other schools. They may also have the services of only a part-time secretary to help with administration. In contrast, a large school will have large sub-organizations of each. Nevertheless, whatever the size of institution, day-by-day working conditions are dominated by the practices and requirements of the teaching-learning activity which is the productive aspect of the school as a workplace. Consequently, the ethics and values of teachers in relation to pupils or students and to each other characterize the institution as a whole. Specifically the growth and development of learners, whether children, young people or adults, is a path from dependence to independence. This applies to the various domains of the human personality — physical, emotional, intellectual, social, aesthetic and spiritual. Leadership is thought by some to be an irrelevant concept in this process. True, a teacher of young children cannot help but obtrude into their lives, if only on account of physical stature and knowledge. But this is not synonymous with the notion of leadership as a deliberate and sought-after imposition of values and direction of conduct by one person on another. The deferential or 'other-regarding' ethic has as its goal the production of freely cooperating individuals. The teacher's role is essentially recessive or instrumental. To some extent this makes for a dichotomy between teachers of younger children and teachers of older children.

Undoubtedly, however, the most critical field of application for the concept and practice of leadership is among the teaching staff. All discussion in schools of organizational unity, common purposes, cooperative action, conformity and uniformity presupposes the crucial part played by the teaching staff. Whether they are prepared to work together or whether they are not prepared to work together are the issues of primary importance. Leadership is often thought to make the difference between the two. Yet actual circumstances suggest that either leadership is not the requisite factor or, if it is so, then leadership is not sufficiently common.

It seems that leadership is a measure of the credibility gap between leader and led. The very natural and unavoidable differences between the teacher and young children provide the model for such leadership. There is a quantitative and qualitative differential which the child cannot ignore. Such a model, however, seldom applies among adults. No longer is even the head of an institution automatically superior in qualification, experience, wisdom, or any other variable, to other colleagues of the teaching staff. Educational opportunities, social values, employment, legislation and external scrutinies and controls have all combined to reduce the possibilities of an unambiguous ascendancy of one person in relation to colleagues.

In addition, in education there is a strong tradition of teacher autonomy. Some believe this to be more apparent than real. Others believe it to be more characteristic of education in Britain than anywhere else. It is, however, clearly a feature in teaching because of the nature of the job, even in more centralized and formally directive systems. In some countries it would be unthinkable within a school for a teacher to compromise his hard-earned qualifications and professional standing by having a leader.

French secondary schools, for example, do not have the elaborate middle management arrangements which typify those in Britain. Heads in countries like France and West Germany fulfil a more strictly administrative role than is expected in Britain. The autonomy of the teacher is nearly always defined in terms of freedom to decide something, such as what the teaching content should be, or it may be defined in terms of freedom to use something, such as materials or available money. Typically autonomy has been over *what* is done as well as over *how* it is done. Currently it is argued that autonomy should extend only to how it is done, leaving what is done to be decided by the community (Hornsby, 1983). It may also be defined, however, in terms of independence from, at worst, colleague domination and, at best, colleague leadership. The case is that numerous teachers acting independently but intelligently, and cooperating freely can guarantee the liberties and flexibilities needed to provide education with all its ambiguity for a heterogeneous school population.

The whole case of the 'leadership has no appeal movement' turns on those assumptions and principles associated with the existentialist point of view and way of life (Paisey, 1981a). This seeks to restore to the individual his freedom of thought and action, unshackled from the constraints of custom, obligation and leaders. He is not *obliged* to have such freedom but he has the right to choose it if he wishes. Fundamentally, this movement of thought vitiates the possibility of leadership of institutions or sub-parts of them. It is not the differential merits and qualities of an individual that may be acceptable or unacceptable. It is the very idea itself of leadership exercised by another or by oneself. Leadership has no necessary appeal in principle.

### 'There Should Be a Return to Leadership' Movement

The view has been common that teachers are people who in temperament and in practice are somehow removed from the real world (Stinnett, 1967). Certainly there are characteristic differences between schools as organizations and economic organizations generally (Paisey and Alan-Smith, 1983). These differences do not include, however, and, it is contended, never have included, the absence of leadership in educational institutions. Nevertheless, it is felt by many that the nature of teaching and the visible resilience of the school as a 'remarkably invulnerable' institution (Cuban, 1982) is evidence enough of the relative isolation of the school from external influences and its imperviousness to internal efforts to change, both of which require the mediation of leadership. Critics may charge educational institutions with complacency but advocates point to the essential needs of the job — a stable, orderly, predictable but stimulating organization and institutional climate (Paisey, 1981b).

Brameld (1965) felt it necessary to encourage a resurgence of leadership among teachers both inside and outside the school; the kind of leadership required was creative, audacious, directive, convergent, committed, confronting, involved and controlling. Evidently this was a stronger form of leadership than was seen to be in vogue. In the intervening period, however, the need for leadership has been based on two considerations. People have sometimes wondered if *anyone* was in charge or if *anyone* spoke with authority about education. Now there is a plea for a reformulation of the purposes of public education: leadership is at a premium (Tyack and Hansot, 1982). Certainly instructional leadership in terms of time spent in classroom observation and teacher supervision is *not* the central focus of headteachers (Morris *et al.*, 1982).

Diagnosis of the ills of educational institutions has led some to the conclusion that it has become too comfortable not to lead. *Transactional* behaviour predominates over *transformational* behaviour. Using the term 'management' to mean the former, Enochs (1981) has put the matter succinctly:

> Too many school administrators are more interested in managing than leading, and the reasons are apparent. Merely managing is less demanding and less risky. If you diffuse responsibility, you don't have to accept it; nor are you accountable for the consequences of taking on responsibility. Managing may be an artful way of preventing a job from exceeding the limits of its holder.

Studies of the actual use of working time provide evidence of this. It has been concluded from such studies that the head is no longer the leader of the school and no longer captain of his ship, but merely the pilot or helmsman steering through the shallows and between the rocks. There is a need to reduce the technical-organizational content of the head's work in favour of greater pedagogical leadership with teaching-learning-leadership conceptual tasks as the foremost activity (Hopes, 1982).

Thus, the inevitable duality of leadership in educational institutions noted by Hughes (1970) is subject to the need for continual review. The balance between the executive leadership and professional leadership must be adjusted from time to time. At this particular time the direction of change required seems to be in favour of the latter.

### *'Leadership Has Never Been Absent' Movement*

Leadership for many people precludes the involvement of organization members in the ways implied by the use of the word 'participation'. Leadership is seen as the antithesis of participation. Thus, low participation levels would be expected with the extensive exercise of leadership and vice versa.

The participation of members in educational organizations, however, may be reduced as well as increased according to the needs of the institution (Paisey, 1982). Recent trends in practice have been towards increased participation, aided by studies such as the Taylor Report and the legislative provisions of the Education Act of 1980. Schools generally are less characterized by the stern, and sometimes harsh, autocratic rule which used to be more prevalent. Yet relative to organizations at large they still are — and perhaps must be — subject to directive regimes, however disguised they may be, owing to the nature of their work.

If all schools are taken into account, it is arguable that a majority of heads and senior staff believe in strong leadership and find it necessary to use it. It may often be personalized and idiosyncratic. Many may have paid tribute to or toyed with newer ideas for exercising control and direction. Nevertheless, they remain conscious of their ultimate legal responsibilities and therefore assert their own leadership (Barrell, 1982; 1983).

One of the mainstays for those who take this view is the argument that if an individual has a prescribed responsibility he or she should not be for ever asking others what should be done. Consultation and deference can be pressed to the point of abdication of duty. Manifestly, the opinions and judgemental ability of persons are not equal. The opinion and judgement of anyone may be expressed as of right but should always be weighed against those of another who has consistently shown wisdom in his or her opinion and judgement.

Since heads of school and other senior staff have been appointed inter alia because their opinion and judgement have been considered better than those passed over, it makes most sense that they should continue to exercise those qualities as leadership (Enochs, 1981).

Those who call for a return to leadership, therefore, are basing their case on faulty observations and wrong assumptions. Germane to their case, however, is the extent to which local education authorities determine whether leadership in schools can be exercised, and may carelessly frustrate it (Esp, 1982).

Nevertheless, it can be admitted that leadership is not the prominent and inclusive phenomenon in schools that it once was. One view is that leadership is more of an optional quality found among many other attributes which are highly desirable in the head and senior members of the teaching staff. These may include problem-solving, organizational ability, powers of communication, sensitivity and tolerance of stress (National Association of Secondary School Principals, 1982). Thus, if leadership has indeed never left the schools, it may only remain as relative and selective conduct.

Clearly the definition of leadership is at stake. All powers and abilities of vital worth to an organization used to be swept up under the generic title of 'leadership'. Now it seems there is a trend towards a finer discrimination of concepts, assigning a limited connotation to the word 'leadership'.

Whether inclusive or selective definitions of leadership are used, those who say that leadership has never left the schools can point to new models which support their position (National Association of Secondary School Principals, 1982). Leadership is necessary and present but is exercised in ways not readily recognized. Notably leadership is called for in respect of living with and handling the *ambiguities* of school life, the *expertise* on which it relies, the *coalitions* which may bind the organization together and ensure the discharge of its work according to plan or may create division and the dislocation of work, the constraints of *time* which govern all, and the *information* which sustains the entire organization (March, 1974).

The leadership which exists today and which has never left the schools is assertive, achievement-oriented, directed towards an orderly, purposeful, and peaceful school climate, high expectations for staff and pupils, and well-designed instructional objectives and evaluation (Shoemaker and Fraser, 1981).

### *'Leadership Should Be Shifted from Individuals to Groups' Movement*

One of the most striking features of contemporary life in schools is the yawning gap between the needs and demands of organization and the capacity of any one individual to meet them. It is very much a matter of infinite possibilities and finite means. The judicious determination of objectives, from the point of view of both the number of objectives adopted and the stringency of any particular one of those objectives, is of crucial importance (Jackson, 1975). The exposure of schools to external publicity and pressures, added to the turbulent flow of internally generated variables, has led to new attitudes and practices for dealing with more complex situations effectively, and tempted schools to do too much.

If one person alone can no longer be expected to cope adequately as the leader of an educational institution, a small group of people is thought to be better able to do so. Thus the idea of the *management* team has grown as a serious attempt to maintain organizational viability.

The *teaching* team during the 1960s and 1970s was an antecedent based on the same principle. Schools in the middle age-range found themselves becoming very large. Maintaining an integrated and exciting curriculum required more than any one teacher could give. The teaching team was a response to complex and increasing demands. With contraction and the renewed emphasis on basic subject programmes this form of teaching organization is now probably less common.

So too with the management team. The large school, complex issues and difficult circumstances create the demand for it. Should the size of school fall and the scrutiny and controversy surrounding schooling become less acute, it might be expected that the management team will be less in evidence. It may still remain in more benign conditions, however, on a basis of preferences in principle.

At the moment, the management team in one form or another is common. It can take the form of an executive group which is led by the head of school. In a secondary school the team might consist of two or three deputy heads, the senior teacher, and the head of school, or it might also include the heads of faculty. In a primary, junior or middle school it might consist of the deputy head, scale post holders, such as curriculum coordinators and team leaders, and the head of school. In a small school of any kind it may simply consist of all the teaching staff with the head of school.

The management team might also be the name for the senior staff as a group, irrespective of functions other than those which each member discharges as assigned work appropriate to his or her rank. The management team might also consist of those whom the head of school habitually consults and uses to steer the school in the desired direction through their ability to obtain the necessary support of staff, pupils, parents and others.

The term 'management' might or might not be synonymous with leadership in the title 'management team'. However, it is undoubtedly the use of the title 'management team' meaning 'leadership team' which is of current significance. The deliberate composition of a group to provide widely-based and consummate collective leadership is probably the most important constitutional act in the life of the school. Typically, such teams consist of members who are there by right of rank, occasionally by reason of patronage. If original appointments have been faulty or if the passage of time has found the holder of a senior post wanting, this basis for composing the management team is automatically weak, placing a handicap on the idea of team leadership from the start.

If the purpose of the management team really is to supply effective leadership and an unmistakable impact, then its members might best be chosen according to the critical contribution each can make to it. Particular knowledge, skills and energy are important in this regard. Temperament or disposition, however, may be the key factor. In short, the many variables which enter into the concept of management style are involved (Paisey and Paisey, 1980).

Belbin (1983) has powerfully demonstrated in the case of industrial and commercial managers that the most effective management team is one composed of members who between them share a number of specific propensities or qualities. Eight of these have been identified during empirical investigation. In a management team of eight members, each should be in the team because he or she is able to offer one of the eight qualities. If a team of four people is required then it would be necessary for each of them to be able to contribute two qualities so that all eight are fully represented. The differential functions of the members which arise from these qualities in the team gives it its strength and effectiveness. The presence and balance of all eight qualities in the team is the variable of greatest significance when the team's work output and achievement are being considered.

Consequently, particular *people* are needed in preference to particular *ranks* which people may happen to hold. Membership determined on this basis might actually preclude some members of staff who carry senior rank. The corollary is also true. Membership might favour some individuals who carry lower or no formal rank in the school hierarchy but who eminently possess a quality which the team needs. Once the membership has been established it may also occur that the essential functions which each member contributes to make it a team may bear no correlation with the formal ranks held. The most dramatic example of this is when the head of school really does not function as the chairman.

## The Missing Factor

Most people work in formal organizations. Teachers spend their working lives in them. Wherever leadership is sought and discussed, the expectation usually is that it will emanate from those who hold formal positions of some seniority. As often as not, those expectations also are that leadership is by definition behaviour directed towards innovation and the characteristic handling of dramatic events (Corbett, 1982). The working life of most people in educational institutions today, however, in spite of the uncertainties and complexities which abound, consists essentially of steady application, a good deal of repetition, and attempts to make existing arrangements work well.

Leadership should be identified with the routine organizational day as well as with the events which call for significant initiatives. The organizational structure of an educational institution consists of the distribution of a particular set of jobs, authority and positions. The well-being, motivation, job satisfaction, and work output of members are greatly influenced by the structure. Unfortunately, more attention is given to designing the structure or considering what it ought to be than in making the existing structure work properly. Thus, in ordinary circumstances leadership may be seen as the possession and exercise of political will to make the existing structure work well. It is a mistake to think that structures work automatically.

In educational institutions there is a vast amount of self-restraint, good sense, objectivity and rationality, but these in themselves do not guarantee the effective and efficient operation of the structure to achieve the ends which the institution exists to serve. There is still the need for leadership to make the structure work as intended, to make the minor adjustments to it that are constantly and inevitably required, and to reiterate frequently the values of the organization (Weick, 1982), as well as to face and survive crises and the more turbulent events which unavoidably occur.

## References

BARRELL, G. (1982) 'Accountability in school management', *Education Today*, 32, 2, pp. 3–8.

BARRELL, G. (1983) 'Knowing the law', in PAISEY, A. (Ed.) *The Effective Teacher*, London, Ward Lock Educational, Ch. 2, pp. 19–37.

BELBIN, R.M. (1983) *Management Teams: Why They Succeed or Fail*, London, Heinemann.

BION, W.R. (1961) *Experiences in Groups*, London, Tavistock.

BRAMELD, T. (1965) *Education as Power*, New York, Holt, Rinehart and Winston.

CORBETT, H.D. (1982) 'Principals' contributions to maintaining change', *Phi Delta Kappan*, 64, 3, November, pp. 190–2.

CUBAN, L. (1982) 'Persistent instruction: The high school classroom, 1900–1980', *Phi Delta Kappan*, 64, 2, October, pp. 113–18.

ENOCHS, J.C. (1981) 'Up from management', *Phi Delta Kappan*, 63, 3, November, pp. 175–8.

ESP, D.G. (1982) *Training Approaches in Various European Countries: An Overview*, Strasbourg, Council of Europe.

HOPES, C. (1982) *Problems of Relating Selection Criteria and Training Needs: Research and Evaluation Attempts in the Federal Republic of Germany*, Strasbourg, Council of Europe.

HORNSBY, J. (1983) 'Perceiving the purpose of schooling', in PAISEY (1983), *op. cit.*, Ch. 1, pp. 10–18.

HUGHES, M. (Ed.) (1970) *Secondary School Administration: A Management Approach*, Oxford, Pergamon.

JACKSON, K. (1975) *The Art of Solving Problems*, London, Heinemann.

KNIPE, H. and MACLAY, G. (1973) *The Dominant Man*, London, Fontana.

KYNASTON-REEVES, T. (1967) 'Constrained and facilitated behaviour: A typology of behaviour in economic organizations', *British Journal of Industrial Relations*, 5, 2, July, pp. 145–61.

MANGAN, G. (1982) *The Biology of Human Conduct*, Oxford, Pergamon.

MARCH, J.G. (1974) 'Analytical skills and the university training of educational administrators', *The Journal of Educational Administration*, 12, 1, May, pp. 17–44.

MORRIS, V.C. *et al.* (1982) 'The urban principal: Middle manager in the educational bureaucracy', *Phi Delta Kappan*, 63, 10, June, pp. 689–92.

NATIONAL ASSOCIATION OF SECONDARY SCHOOL PRINCIPALS (1982) *The Effective Principal*, Reston, Va., NASSP.

PAISEY, A. (1981a) *Organization and Management in Schools*, London, Longman.

PAISEY, A. (1981b) *Small Organizations: The Management of Primary and Middle Schools*, Windsor, NFER-Nelson.

PAISEY, A. (1982) 'Participation in school organization', *Educational Management and Administration*, 10, 1, February, pp. 31–5.

PAISEY, A. (Ed.) (1983) *The Effective Teacher*, London, Ward Lock Educational.

PAISEY, A. and ALAN-SMITH, K. (1983) 'Educational management — is it something different?' *School Organization*, 2, 4, pp. 333–40.

PAISEY, A. and PAISEY, T. (1980) 'The question of style in educational management', *Educational Administration*, 9, 1, Autumn, pp. 95–106.

SHOEMAKER, J. and FRASER, H.W. (1981) 'What principals can do: Some implications from studies of effective schooling', *Phi Delta Kappan*, 63, 3, November, pp. 178–82.

STINNETT, T.M. (1967) 'Teacher professionalization: Challenge and promise', in HAVIGHURST, R.J. *et al.* (Eds) *Society and Education*, Boston, Allyn and Bacon, pp. 352–9.

SURREY INSPECTORATE (1982) *Management in Education*, County Hall, Kingston, Surrey County Council.

TYACK, D. and HANSOT, E. (1982) 'Hard times, hard choices: The case for coherence in public school leadership', *Phi Delta Kappan*, 63, 8, April, pp. 511–15.

WEICK, K.E. (1982) 'Administering education in loosely coupled schools', *Phi Delta Kappan*, 63, 10, June, pp. 673–6.

# Leadership and the Effective School[*]

*Steve Murgatroyd*
*Open University in Wales*
*and*
*H.L. Gray*
*Huddersfield Polytechnic*

The importance of leadership in the process of innovation and change within an educational organization is widely acknowledged (see Halpin, 1966; Gray, 1979). What is also acknowledged is that the dynamic features of leadership — style, quality of followership and types of negotiation, for example — are far more critical to effectiveness, innovation and change than the attributes of the leader. Possession of leadership attributes by a person does not ensure either followership or effectiveness. What matters is the quality of followership a leader can stimulate and sustain. In thinking about the effective school — a school which responds to individual pupil and staff needs and to the changing face of the community in which it is placed — the nature of its leadership is clearly a critical variable.

Leaders use different styles within organizations. Sadler (1970) highlights four leadership styles used in the film *Styles of Leadership* (1962). These are: (1) *the tells style* — the leader issues instructions in the expectation that they will be obeyed; (2) *the sells style* — the leader seeks to persuade others of the wisdom and benefit of the decisions she has made; (3) *the consults style* — the leader makes decisions only after the fullest possible consultation with her staff colleagues; (4) *the joins style* — the leader sees her task in terms of enabling the staff to examine a problem requiring action and to ensure that the staff, mindful of the constraints under which the organization functions, reach a decision about action acceptable to the majority of those present. According to Sadler's own research, 'most people are able to describe their own managers in terms of one of these four styles'. But such descriptions of style confuse the holding of a decision-making position within an organization (e.g., head, deputy head, year head) with

[*] This is an edited version of the article which appeared in *School Organization*, 2, 3, 1982, pp. 285–95.

being a leader. There is no necessary connection between leadership and the holding of management positions.

What is clear from these descriptions of the decision-making style of those with management responsibility in an organization is that different styles of management create very different kinds of organizations. Bates (1974), for example, suggests that different styles can lead to three different forms of organization. These are: (1) *hierarchical and formal organizations* with 'top-down' management — decisions are handed down like the ten commandments and enforced by middle management acting as accolites for the head; (2) *hierarchical informal organizations* in which different kinds of hierarchy exist for different kinds of purposes; and (3) *diffuse and informal organizations* in which participation by all staff (but not pupils) is maximized — this is sometimes referred to as 'bottom-up' management.

These descriptions of style and the resulting organizations are of value in that they help to make objective a very subjective process. For leadership is essentially a description of a particular form of relationship between people sharing common aims which they seek to achieve by different objectives. At the same time, the language of organizations often obscures the fact that discussions about 'management' and 'leadership' are discussions about the nature and quality of interpersonal relationships within an organization. This is why there is a systematic attempt to define leadership in terms of the position a person holds ('He is the head therefore he must be the leader!') rather than the dynamics of the group processes within a school. This is also why a failure to deal with certain problems (e.g., truancy, delinquency, academic weakness) is generally attributed to management rather than to the collective body of the staff. The language of management neglects the interpersonal qualities of organizations and readily permits scapegoating.

In this paper we seek to define the effective school in terms of the quality of interpersonal relationships which exist within it and to examine the role leadership plays in the development of such an institution. In addition, we describe an in-service training activity offered at Huddersfield Polytechnic designed to facilitate leadership in educational organizations. However, it needs to be made clear at the outset that the notion of an 'effective school' is grossly problematic. Reynolds *et al.* (1980) seek an operational definition in terms of the outputs of the school — attendance rates, reported rates for delinquency and academic achievement. Whilst focussing upon 'products' is a conventional way of viewing organizational effectiveness, in educational institutions such a focus is not adequate. There needs to be a process focus too. A school can be good at producing O and A-level performers, have a high level of attendance and low rates of delinquency and be an oppressive environment in which to work. An understanding of the 'effective school', if such an organization exists, will involve an appreciation of staff:staff relationships, staff:pupil relationships and school:other relationships. In addition, the degree of acceptance a person within the organization feels and the willingness to admit failure and embrace change all appear crucial to organizational effectiveness.

## The Place of the Person in the Effective School

In studies of effective helping relationships four qualities are regarded as essential. These are: (1) *empathy* — the ability to see another person's problem as if it were one's own without losing that 'as if' quality; (2) *warmth* — the vitality of sharing; (3) *genuineness* — the acceptance of another person's right to their attitudes, values, beliefs and assumptions and to be honest and accepting in transactions with others; and (4) *concreteness* — the ability to focus upon present issues rather than constantly looking back or to the future. Whilst different researchers use different terms for these qualities, these are both necessary and sufficient qualities for helping others (Rogers, 1957; Carkhuff, 1967; Lieberman *et al.*, 1973).

Schools set themselves up as helping institutions. Teachers and other school personnel speak of the school's role in 'helping students learn'. Networks are created within school to help the person make subject choices, to help them make career-relevant decisions, to help them cope with family disturbance or illness. Both the 'academic network' and the 'pastoral network' aim at helping pupils learn; helping them realize their potential; helping them cope. What is more, the helping role extends beyond helping pupils cope with present demands. The school also aims to help pupils prepare for future roles in the community. Helping is very much a currency-word in the language of the school.

Yet schools are rarely evaluated in terms of the necessary and sufficient conditions outlined above. What is more, these conditions are often regarded by teachers and managers in schools as potential disruptors, as recipes for revolution; as a beginning manifesto for pupil-power. One headmaster, in reviewing the research associated with these constructs, wrote 'whilst they may be of value in every other helping context they are not valid in the context of school: no pupil can learn whilst his teachers are trying to understand him from his point of view, trying to be warm and trying to be genuine. It's not in the nature of the school.' Another, following a similar review, wrote 'schools are not person-centred they are subject-centred', despite the voiced concern to educate the 'whole-person'.

There is a view amongst some who look at schools from the outside that they are primarily concerned with encouraging pupils to learn cognitive skills. The emphasis on academic achievement gives rise to schools not treating their pupils or their staff as whole-persons. Pupils are rewarded for imaginative compliance to the regime of the school rather than for being warm, genuine, empathic persons. Whatever the merits of this view, those who advance it view the position of the 'person' within the school as marginal to its purposes. One problem with this view of the school is that it assumes that the school is able to determine its own purposes and that it is desirable for personal development to be regarded as the key to these purposes. Schools serve many functions on behalf of constituencies not represented by those who occupy the schools' rooms. They act as regulators for the daytime behaviour of young people. They act as gatekeepers of knowledge on behalf of those who develop and sustain that knowledge. They are expected to promote employability even at times of high unemployment. Finally, they are expected to care for their pupils as would a careful parent. So many purposes and so many potential conflicts between them. Yet the point being made by these outsiders — people like Carl Rogers (1980), Reinhard Tausch (1978) and others (Aspy, 1972; White, 1974) — is that learning about a subject, like chemistry, French, poetry or maths, need not, and indeed cannot, be divorced from learning about one's self (Murgatroyd, 1976). The question that needs to be addressed, therefore, is the extent to which people in school are enabled to learn about themselves as well as the subjects they are studying. Another way of expressing this is to ask how much of what happens in the process of schooling is due to the people who participate in this process. There is considerable evidence that the achievement of pupils in a subject is a function of: (1) the quality of their interpersonal relationships with their teachers (Aspy, 1969; Dickenson *et al.*, 1970; Moon, 1966); (2) the quality of interpersonal relations with peers (Hargreaves, 1967); (3) the strength of their positive self-concept (Brookover *et al.*, 1967); and (4) the strength of their internal focus of control (Barr-Tell *et al.*, 1980) Whilst other features of the situation — resources, social support, level of intellectual ability — are also important, the features described above seem critical. What is interesting about these features is that they are intensely personal qualities: they are about people *not* about skills. What is more, these characteristics are best enabled by the use of the necessary and sufficient conditions mentioned above: empathy, warmth, genuineness and concreteness. Finally, they can be stimulated by leadership in the classroom.

## Classroom and Organizational Leadership

There would appear to be a strong relationship between the style of leadership and type of negotiation within the classroom and that which exists in the organization at large. The classroom acts as a mirror for the relationships which exist in the school organization. Classrooms are not islands, they are very much sections of a larger community. Whilst some teachers are able to run their classrooms as if they were islands within the school, the pupils arriving in these classes bring with them the ethos of the school and their experience of its regime. Teachers seeking to run their classes in ways radically different from the way the organization operates thus have a great deal to do. One teacher working in a school run very much as a 'top-down' institution with a 'tells' style of management ran a class along the lines of a teacher-initiated negotiation group only to be constantly interrupted by colleagues saying things like 'I came in to quell a riot, I didn't realise that this is what you call teaching!' When the same teacher tried to run a participative assembly he was advised by the deputy head to 'stick to the well established formula of two hymns, a prayer and a bollocking!' In subtle but significant ways these and related incidents brought strong pressure to bear on the teacher to conform to the normative classroom behaviour expected of teachers within the school.

Reynolds (1976) has argued that schools may be viewed as arenas of potential conflict. Reynolds suggests that for many pupils in a school the aims of the teachers and their own aims are not compatible. As Waller (1932, pp. 195–6) observed:

> The teacher represents the established social order in the school, and his interest is in maintaining that order, whereas pupils only have a negative interest in that feudal superstructure. . . . Pupils are the material in which teachers are supposed to produce results. Pupils are human beings striving to realize themselves in their own spontaneous manner, striving to produce their own results in their own way. Each of these hostile parties stand in the way of the other, in so far as the aim of either are realized, it is at the sacrifice of the other.

What is important to note, according to Reynolds, is that this underlying conflict rarely shows itself. He explains this in terms of the idea of 'the truce'. The truce is between teachers and pupils. Essentially it implies that 'the teachers will go easy on the pupils and the pupils will go easy on the teachers' (Reynolds, 1976, p. 133). The teachers will not try to exercise authority in relation to the non-pedagogic, expressive or character moulding goals of the school and in return pupils are cooperative in their classroom behaviour, showing most respect for those teachers who facilitate learning which is personally significant to them. Where such a truce does not exist — and Reynolds provides illustrations of such schools (Reynolds, 1976, pp. 134–7) — delinquency, truancy, academic failure, pupil violence and disruption are high. Whilst the form of the truce is similar between institutions, it clearly takes different forms in different schools. In some, it takes the form of having rules about smoking, uniform and chewing gum in class (for example) but rarely enforcing them. In others, it takes the form of project-based teaching which maximizes pupil involvement and their powers of negotiating what is to be studied and how it is to be studied. In others it takes the form of a large variety of extra-mural activities in which teachers stop playing the role of authority-expert and become more of themselves. This notion of truce highlights again the relationship between the nature of the school as an institution and the work of the teacher in the classroom. For when the truce is broken and, to use Reynold's phrase, a school 'goes to war' against its pupils and seeks to enforce its control over the non-pedagogic, expressive and character moulding behaviours of its pupils, the effects of this campaign are felt in the classroom.

Just as a decision to 'break' the truce taken by a group or an individual within the school at large can affect the experience of the classroom, so a decision to change the experience of the classroom can affect the school. Teachers who initiate new curriculum materials and create a new atmosphere in their classrooms can act as a focus for change or for increased pressure towards conformity: teachers seen to be 'deviant' can be incorporated and made to conform or can be used as models for development. In the latter case they often develop a leadership-initiation role. Leadership can thus be a description of the relationship between the teacher's role in the classroom *and* her role as a classroom teacher within the organization of the school. Leadership in these respects concerns acting as an examplar and in so doing encouraging followership. The effective school permits the individual to experiment in her classroom, enables the dissemination of classroom experiences and encourages, in an accepting climate, the evaluation of classroom processes. In short, it facilitates rather than hinders personal staff development. It is an organization willing to learn from the experience of any one of its members, irrespective of their status.

## Ineffective Leadership

These views of leadership derive as much from observations of schools that are clearly failing as from schools having effective interpersonal relationships. To illustrate some key points about the nature of interpersonal effectiveness and the role of leadership in its promotion this section describes some of the findings of an LEA advisory team's study of a school about which there had been much local concern. We shall call the school Leasehold Comprehensive.

There were local concerns about the school which precipitated the decision to investigate thoroughly. These included: (1) the number of parents opting to send their children to Leasehold as opposed to a nearby comprehensive was declining rapidly; (2) the failure of the school to attract an academic sixth form; (3) a high incidence of internal vandalism; (4) a high level of pupil truancy and staff absences; (5) an unusually high use of pupil suspension as a sanction — sixty-four pupils were suspended in one term, twenty-eight of them for a period in excess of five days; (6) the use of corporal punishment was also high and had recently featured in the local press; and (7) the low level of pupil achievement in the school.

In their investigation, the local advisory team talked with staff and pupils and explored as fully as possible a variety of issues. They issued a very full report (23 pages) and gave it a wide circulation. We are not able here to examine the report in full. What is possible is a review of their findings as they relate to leadership and the interpersonal qualities of the school. The following points are made in the report:

1  A feature of effective leadership is visibility. Leaders need to be seen. Ineffective leaders generally hide or remain unobserved. The advisors comment on senior staff at Leasehold that 'there is insufficient recognition of the fact that the observable presence, involvement and interest in the work of the school by those with ascribed status is of considerable importance in the generation of a corporate spirit and in the maintenance of a high level of morale.' They also note that 'the majority of teachers consider that the headteacher is too remote' and lacks empathy.

2  Leaders, to be effective, need to be able to communicate thoughts and feelings and describe behaviours to others. Ineffective leaders usually have poor communications skills. This was noted at Leasehold. The advisors say 'the quality of communication, whether written or oral, often leaves much to be desired ... most of the communication is downwards only and the appropriate machinery for effective dissemination has not been established. The result is that many members of staff feel ill-informed and isolated and there is a widespread sense of frustration with, and suspicion of, the leadership.' Having reviewed the written communications within the school, they conclude that 'the style of presentation does not encourage reading ... it is frequently turgid, dictatorial and patronizing' and it concludes that the leadership fail to 'recognize the teaching staff as professionally trained people.' Turning their attention to meetings held within the school, the advisors say 'instead of meetings enhancing the quality of communication, they tend to generate tension, frustration, suspicion and animosity' and they note that meetings chaired by the head are conducted in an atmosphere described as 'less than cordial'.

3  Leaders need to accept others, not reject them. At Leasehold meetings are held in a 'less than cordial' atmosphere since 'any points raised tend to be dealt with in a patronizing manner which tends to discourage further participation' and reduce feelings of mutuality.

4  One feature of acceptance displayed by effective leaders is openness and genuineness. Ineffective leaders tend to be secretive and not genuine. At Leasehold the advisors report 'an unwarranted degree of secrecy' about matters which all staff have a right to know about. In addition they note that the head 'presents a facade of democracy but frequently acts in an autocratic manner.'

5  To be able to follow a leader others need to know why it is they are following. Ineffective leaders rarely declare their intentions. At

Leasehold the advisors found that 'the headteacher had not presented nor explained his educational beliefs' and that major changes
in school policy were implemented without staff being informed of
the motives for the change or their rationale. This led to staff feeling
'abandoned to face the problems on their own' which has led some
to 'walk away from problems' preferring to 'pass by on the other
side'.

6 Ineffective leaders do not face problems but seek to avoid them.
Effective leaders face problems, share them and seek to learn from
them. The advisors at Leasehold note that 'major issues tend to be
discussed at far too late a stage because monitoring procedures in
the school are either inadequate or non-existent.'

7 Ineffective leaders resolve difficulties in a punitive fashion, effective
leaders seek appropriate responses to particular circumstances. At
Leasehold punitive responses are most commonly applied to pupils,
as the figures concerning suspension provided earlier show. As the
advisors observe, 'the school's use of the power to exclude from
school is symptomatic of the school's general approach to the
application of sanctions . . . positive, constructive use of counselling
is not undertaken as frequently as it could be, whereas resort to the
application of more serious sanctions is too readily taken.'

Leasehold Comprehensive School seems to lack leadership and to be a
failure in terms of many different measures of school effectiveness. At the
core of its problems, according to those who have studied the school, is the
lack of mutual respect, warmth, empathy and genuineness. It is a deper-
sonalized, punitive institution. The failures of Leasehold are not the failures
of a bold experiment with new curriculum or the weaknesses of a particular
teaching method; rather, its failure is intensely personal. There are few
personally significant relationships between working colleagues and real and
effective blocks to the development of these relationships.

## Training and Support for Leadership

Leadership, according to the analysis offered here, revolves around two key
features: (1) the degree of followership a leader can generate by means of the
personal qualities of empathy, warmth and genuineness; (2) the concrete
nature of the action the leader and her followers wish to take. Whilst
additional qualities have been examined briefly here, these two remain the
necessary and sufficient conditions for effective leadership in the school.
Our experience of educational organizations suggests that where these
qualities are present the organization is more likely to be effective in
achieving its aims and objectives. We have documented in the case study of
Leasehold Comprehensive the consequencès of ineffective leadership. They

are that the educational institution not only fails to achieve its educational objectives but also fails to provide satisfactory environments for the development of personally significant learning or personal relationships.

Given the importance attached in this paper to effective leadership for the achievement of educational objectives in schools, it is necessary to examine two questions. First, can the skills associated with leadership be developed through training? Secondly, what support do leaders require to enable them to maintain leadership in the school? Before it is possible to examine these two questions four essential points need to be made.

First, the analysis of leadership provided here does not relate to role. Leadership is a term used to describe a particular combination of personal qualities ('ways of being') which both encourage and enable others to follow. The idea of a person having a leadership role implies that leadership is a set of skills which can be learned and developed. Leadership is not about skills, rules or procedures but about the person and the quality of their relationships with others. Leadership training and support need therefore to focus upon the person and her relationship with others.

Secondly, leadership as described in this paper is not about power. Rather, leadership is here defined in the context of openness, acceptance, sharing and exchange. Yet notions like 'power' and 'authority' are often equated with leadership. Leaders who see themselves as organizer, decision-maker, arbiter or supreme authority will experience difficulty as leaders since they will both create dependency and find themselves increasingly isolated and the subject of criticism. Our experience of leaders who see themselves as reformers and agents of radical change in their schools is that they unduly intrude upon the natural development of the school, disturb carefully built relationships which are more likely to lead to change if they are allowed full expression, work too hard and have difficulty coping with the responsibilities they seize for themselves. A reforming leader who drops dead in her study will be replaced within twenty-four hours by another person who will undo some if not all of her work. Leadership training needs therefore to avoid normative prescriptions about how to achieve reform, how to administer staff, how to write job descriptions. Instead, it needs to maximize the individual talents and personal qualities of those who see themselves as leaders.

Thirdly, leaders may occupy any position in the school. Whilst many expect the head and her senior colleagues to display leadership, there is a sense in which leadership is an issue for those who teach and a possibility that leadership may, at a given time, come from any point in the school. Indeed, there are many schools which have innovated in their curriculum as a result of the curriculum ideas and practices of young, 'novice' teachers.

Finally, training for leadership cannot be normative, prescriptive, skill-based or problem-centred. Instead, it needs to focus upon the personal and interpersonal qualities of the person. It needs to develop and sustain openness, empathy and warmth and to encourage exchange, acceptance and exploration. Though the aims may be pursued by means of studying specific problems or issues or by exploring key concepts and research, such training needs to be person-centred.

Leadership training of the kind described here has recently begun at Huddersfield Polytechnic. The course — part-time over two years for a Diploma in Leadership in Educational Settings — has attracted people from schools and further education who wish to develop their own understanding of their behaviour in their own organizations. The methodology of the course is experiential. This means that the staff offering the course use sensitivity training, group-related and counselling skills to help the group of students following the course decide what the course should be, how it should develop, what methods it might use and how it should be assessed. The purpose of this approach is to sensitize participants to the dynamic processes of the training group and to provide them with some skills and support so that they can facilitate the discovery of tasks and the completion of work. Participants learn not to depend upon the course staff for guidance but to take on the task of leadership *in* the course. They experience leadership within the group.

This experiential model of training has two important merits. First, it does not involve simulation or role play. Rather than discussing the role of leader or the possible responses to imaginary problems, participants have real problems (what shall we do and how shall we do it?) in a real organization (the group) with a real time dimension. Leadership is experienced and developed through practice. Secondly, experiential learning is 'whole-person' learning: it involves thoughts, feelings and actions, not just cognitive processes. The difficulty with experiential learning is transferability: will participants be able to transfer their developing skills, values and insights to other organizations in which they work? The problem of transferability is not unique to experiential methods — it applies just as much to lecture-based or project-based management education. In experiential learning, however, transferability is often a focus for discussion and activity whereas it is often taken for granted in other course-forms.

At the end of the two-year course it is not expected that participants will be 'fully-fledged leaders'. Just as those who engage in counsellor training never become totally proficient counsellors, leadership training aims at sensitizing and resourcing those who see themselves as having a leadership role in their own organization. Participants may need ongoing support. At Huddersfield this is offered in the form of consultancy which uses counselling and sensitivity training as its rationale. The aim of such consultancy is to support the person not to directly 'solve problems'.

These are new developments, but are much in line with contemporary thinking about the nature of management education (Everett, 1981; Cooper, 1981a; 1981b). They aim to enable the person acting as leader to be change conscious, future-oriented, precedent-breaking and participative in their work. In short, the leadership education programme at Huddersfield aims to support individuals who wish to examine and develop their own thoughts, feelings and actions in the context of organizational development, change and evaluation. It aims to make the participants more effective in these areas so that they may help to create more effective schools and colleges.

## Conclusion

This paper has: (1) described the nature of leadership in educational organizations, (2) shown the importance of leadership to educational organizations in terms both of classroom activities and of the school as an organization, and (3) briefly described a programme aimed at facilitating leadership through training and support. One underlying assumption has been that effective organizations depend upon effective leadership.

Preston and Post (1973) describe three stages of management development which they refer to as the 'three managerial revolutions'. The first management revolution was the appearance within a hierachical organization of management itself. In schools, the period of comprehensivization saw the emergency of a variety of management roles (head, deputy head (academic), deputy head (pastoral), year tutors) which were recognized as such. The second management revolution is described as 'professionalization'. The development of comprehensive education in the 1970s saw an increased emphasis on the professional skills of managers, especially in the pastoral care and guidance sector. The third management revolution is described by Preston and Post as 'participation', which they define as 'the inclusion of persons and groups involved and concerned with the diverse outcomes of managerial activity as participants in the managerial process'. The concept of leadership and the programme of leadership education described here falls very much into the participative frame. Given the demands upon schools and their need to embrace change and development, the participatory nature of management activity and the importance of leadership in the development of participation will increasingly be realized. Schools, to be effective both in terms of managing change and enhancing the quality of interpersonal relationships, need leadership.

## References

ASPY, D.N. (1969) 'The effect of teacher offered conditions of empathy, positive regard and congruence upon student achievement', *Florida Journal of Educational Research*, 11, 1, pp. 39–48.

ASPY, D.N. (1972) *Towards a Technology of Humanizing Education*, Illinois, Research Press.

BATES, A.W. (1974) *Decision Making in Schools*, Milton Keynes, The Open University Press.

BARR-TELL, S. *et al.* (1980) 'Relationship of locus of control, achievement, anxiety and level of aspiration', *British Journal of Educational Psychology*, 50, pp. 53–60.

BROOKOVER, W.B., *et al.* (1967) *Self-Concept and Ability and School Achievement*, Final Report of the Co-operative Research Project No. 2831, Michigan State University Press.

CARKHUFF, R.R. (Ed.) (1967) *The Counselors Contribution to Facilitative Processes*, Urbana, Ill., Parkinson.

COOPER, C.L. (1981a) 'The challenge for management education in creating greater opportunities for participative management in the 1980's', in COOPER, C.L. (Ed.) *Developing Managers for the 1980's*, London, Methuen.

COOPER, C.L. (1981b) 'Social support at work and stress management', *Small Group Behaviour*, 12, 3, pp. 285–97.

DICKENSON, W.A. *et al.* (1970) 'A humanistic programme for change in a large inner-city school system', *Journal of Humanistic Psychology*, 10, 2.

EVERETT, R. (1981) 'Management education for the year 2000', in COOPER, C.L. (Ed.) *Management Education for the 1980's*, London, Methuen.

GRAY, H.L. (1979) *Change and Management in Schools*, Driffield, Nafferton Books.

HALPIN, A.W. (1966) *Theory and Research in Administration*, London, Collier-Macmillan.

HARGREAVES, D. (1967) *Social Relations in a Secondary School*, London, Routledge and Kegan Paul.

LIEBERMAN, M. *et al.* (1973) *Encounter Groups — First Facts*, New York, Basic Books.

MOON, S.F. (1966) 'Teaching the self', *Improving College and University Teaching*, 14, pp. 213–29.

MURGATROYD, S. (1976) 'Counselling and continuing education', *Teaching at a Distance*, 6, pp. 40–5.

PRESTON, L.E. and POST, J.E. (1973) 'The third managerial revolution', *Academy of Management Journal*, 3, 17, pp. 476–86.

ROGERS, C.R. (1957) 'The necessary and sufficient conditions of therapeutic personality change', *Journal of Consulting Psychology*, 21, pp. 95–103.

ROGERS, C.R. (1980) *A Way of Being*, Boston, Houghton-Mifflin.

REYNOLDS, D. (1976) 'When pupils and teachers refuse a truce: The secondary school and the creation of delinquency', in MUNGHAM, G. and PEARSON, G. (Eds.) *Working Class Youth Culture*, London, Routledge and Kegan Paul.

REYNOLDS, D. *et al.* (1980) 'School factors and truancy', in HERSOV, L. and BERG, I. (Eds.) *Out of School*, London, John Wiley.

SADLER, P.J. (1970) 'Leadership style, confidence in management and job-satisfaction', *Journal of Applied Behavioural Science*, 6, 1, pp. 3–19.

*Styles of Leadership* (1962) 16 mm. Film (3 reels), California, Round-Table Productions.

TAUSCH, R. (1978) 'Facilitative dimensions of inter-personal relations', *College Student Journal*, 12, 1, pp. 2–11.

WALLER, W. (1932) *The Sociology of Teaching*, New York, John Wiley.

WHITE, A.M. (1974) 'Humanistic mathematics', *Education (USA)*, 95, 2, pp. 128–33.

# 3
# The System

# Introduction

The choice of the eight papers in this section was dictated by the need to carefully define the leadership role of the administrators and overall policy-makers of the educational system. The biggest virtue of the Education Act 1944 and its recent 'replacement' has been that no single constituent organization has a monopoly of authority, power and leadership. We enjoy a system of dispersed responsibility which has avoided some of the problems found in other countries which have a centralized leadership, or in which the service is fragmented into parochial decision-making bodies.

The first three papers reintroduce the reader to the leadership function of that part of our system which is at the pinnacle of the traditional pyramidal structure of authority. They examine the extent to which leadership is effective at this level, and look at the types of constraints which are found in attempts to 'lead' the system towards its goals. Hunter's paper, for example, cogently examines the changing relationship between the central government and the local education authorities in the context of cuts in expenditure and falling rolls. It is a controversial paper, strenuously denying earlier views of the relationships and the level of involvement of the central authorities which have suggested an attitude of promotionalism and interest in educational goals. Instead he suggests, with numerous examples to support his views, that cooperation is now much less evident and that local education authorities are increasingly forced to adopt the role of 'conciliators' rather than 'educators'.

The second extract, by Sir William Pile, examines the way in which 'national policies' for education are originated, processed to the point of agreement as policies for the service as a whole, and communicated so that they can be effectively implemented. The problem for the reader is simply this: can you think of a better way?

A significant part of the staffing of the Department of Education and Science is the body of men and women known as Her Majesty's Inspectors. The contribution by Tim Brighouse has brought his great experience to bear in examining the problems and possibilities inherent in attempts by HM

Inspectorate to influence the schools. In 1979 the Inspectorate published a document entitled *Aspects of Secondary Education in England*, and the paper considers the way in which randomly selected paragraphs from the document might be received by the officers of an LEA seeking to examine its current practice. He points out that unless local education authorities respond positively to the evidence presented by HM Inspectorate, which is itself a reflection of classroom practice, then an opportunity to make use of their resources is lost. The need for cooperation and acceptance of the role and credibility of the other partners in the educational service is therefore emphasized.

The next two papers together constitute a remarkable analysis of leadership functions of the highest posts in a local education authority; those of the Chief Education Officer and the deputy. The paper by John Hornsby was specially commissioned for this book and reflects his long experience at all levels of local authority administration. He sees the leadership role as that of determining how things should be done and advocates, like Tim Brighouse, a significant measure of cooperation with both central authorities and the schools within his charge.

The paper by Robert Jennings is an exploration of the evolving role of the deputy director of education. At all levels of the educational system and in all sectors deputies seem to have a rough deal. Their position is difficult to define and their specific duties range from zero to virtually full control of their organization. Perhaps this paper will help reassure those who possess position, but lack duties, to play a more precise leadership role. It is certainly an enlightening paper in the search for the real foci of educational leadership and decision-making.

The article by Christopher Phillips and Michael Strain brings the discussion much nearer to the institutional level by its examination of the means of controlling the curriculum. The authors consider the current role of the LEA with regard to curriculum leadership and the changes to which it has been subjected during the last two decades; they go on to suggest a greatly expanded role for the LEA as a curriculum planner and coordinator for its schools. They suggest that the responsibility for data collection and assessment procedures would depend upon an expanded role for the local authority advisory service. Unfortunately this observation does not sit easily alongside the points made in the last two articles of this section, by Joan Dean, who wrote the paper specially for this volume, and Ray Bolam. Their descriptions and analyses of the leadership role of the LEA advisers indicate that the people involved are already overloaded with the impossible dual role as 'advisers', and therefore friends of the schools, *vis-à-vis* their task as 'inspectors', which implies a much more coercive and threatening role. On the other hand, the dual role may not be a bad feature of their work as educational 'leaders'. It is no worse than that borne by many other leaders in the educational system and in their particular situation could enhance the level of respect with which their words are heard.

All the contributions to this section emphasize the importance which must be attached to the human aspects of the educational organization. 'The System' is clearly much less a mindless machine than most people believe.

# Education and Local Government in the Light of Central Government Policy*

*Colin Hunter*
*Leeds Polytechnic*

## Introduction

The present contraction in pupil and student numbers and the squeezing of economic resources available, in nursery through to higher education, is particularly painful in a service which since the Second World War has experienced expansion in all areas.

This paper looks at the managerial and education problems which accrue in schools due to the effect of the cutbacks in public spending of Central Government policy. It particularly encompasses the effects of the changing power position and structure of Local Authorities. Theirs is an uncomfortable mediating position for, on the one hand, they try to absorb Central Government financial constraints while on the other they attempt to retain some autonomy in the level of services offered to their electorate. Their problem can be encapsulated in the fact that since 1974 their share of public expenditure has gone down by 16% while Central Government spending has risen by 7%.

Education is the major spending service of Local Authorities and it is at the forefront of being affected by decisions made at Whitehall or City Hall which, as resources become more scarce, are being based increasingly on political rather than educational criteria. Some of the possible positive and negative consequences of this trend are discussed at the end of the paper.

## Schools, Teachers and Cuts

I suggest elsewhere (Hunter, 1981) that 1974 is a suitable date to mark the commencement of a significant shift in the definition of the career of

* This is an edited version of Chapter 4 of Ahier J., and Flude M., (Eds) (1983) *Contemporary Education Policy* London, Croom Helm.

teaching and the place of the educational system in our society. Due to such events as the oil crisis and the rise in inflation, there slowly emerged in the Labour Government policy a shift to containing public expenditure and positive support for industry. The twin goals of justice and efficiency presented by Anthony Crosland in the previous Labour administration in his advocacy for comprehensive schooling became increasingly telescoped into the goal of efficiency in the Great Debate.

The present Conservative Government took this trend even further, spurred by its ideological commitment to monetarism and the need to regenerate the wealth-producing sector in order to finance more securely the public service expenditure. However, it could be argued that the present Government has reversed the post-war political consensus that there should be some positive attempt to make Britain a more equal society by redistributing wealth through a graded tax system and welfare state services, in that the balance of both has tilted to accentuate even more the difference between the richest and poorest in society.

The cutback in real terms of public expenditure has severely affected the education services to the extent that basic requirements are often at risk. In May 1981 Northamptonshire and Surrey parents challenged the Education Minister as to whether the education service offered to their children via the Local Authority was able to fulfil the requirements of the 1944 Education Act. In October later that year, a Peterborough Head advised parents that he believed the school was now operating illegally under the 1944 Act because it could not provide the books and equipment to maintain required educational standards.

While these may be celebrated media cases, they reflect a growing concern about the resources available to schools. It is also a reflection of the way that Local Authorities have approached the management of implementing the cuts. Even in the Comprehensive School debate there had been a broad political consensus between Labour and Tory Councillors that education was 'a good thing' and that changes in school organization under their jurisdiction was based on educational rather than political criteria. When the necessity for cuts came, there was no political basis for the prioritizing of where they should be located. There tended to be an incremental cutting back over the whole budget by officers, with the agreement of Councillors — a holding operation to maintain the whole service until better times re-emerged. However, except for a modest up-turn in the pre-election year of 1978, as the availability of funds became tighter and the room for manoeuvre more restricted, Local Authorities were forced to identify priorities for cuts on political rather than educational criteria. This process of education moving from a politically neutral managerial service to one being dependent on overt political decisions is clearly demonstrated in the Officer Service Plan, Bradford Directorate of Educational Services (December 1981).

Unlike most other services, educational services are used by practically everybody in the District — rich and poor, able and less able, theatre-goer and remedial learner, squash player and city teenager. What we have largely done over the past few years is simply to trim and prune, still trying to keep *all* the services going. The result is that practically *all* the services are worse and we are feeling the public pressure about the cuts from parents in economically advantaged areas as well as unemployed teenagers who cannot get good grants to do further education. . . . Some action can be taken within the Directorate itself. We are now, and will go on, re-directing our own resources and pursuing efficiency savings to release money for use in other areas. Re-direction takes time, but be under no illusions. A 're-direction' usually means a cut somewhere — in standards, or in a service, or in a part of the District. And internal re-direction can only go so far. Ultimately, there has to be an overall political decision by the Labour Group. An answer to the question 'What is your strategy for Educational Services in the future?'

Perhaps this appeal identifies the culmination of possible exercises that can be done with trimming the whole range of the budget, and shows the critical period education is entering into if cuts are to be extended further, for since 1974 there has been extensive surgery in both staffing and resources. With regard to staffing, there have been many ways found of slimming down the teaching force without resorting to compulsory redundancies, and incidentally avoiding large redundancy payments. This is often done by voluntary or compulsory redeployment and is closely connected with the issue of falling roles and a strict observance of pupil/teacher ratios. If a school is over-staffed then those willing to move are encouraged to do so, often with help with travelling expenses incurred because of the move and with undertakings of security in their new school. Where no one volunteers, there is the necessity in many Authorities for the Head with Governors and advisers to nominate who will become compulsorily redeployed. Having been involved as a Chairman of Governors in this exercise I can testify to its effect on the morale of staff rooms — particularly in smaller schools. There is also the problem that other schools look with some suspicion on those teachers who are asked to leave their previous school in that it is thought that they may be one of the weaker members of that school. There were some teachers who not only had the stigma of being asked to leave, but have not been accepted by any other schools where vacancies had occurred. Such a policy therefore may save money by making internal appointments within the Authority, though would cause great problems of insecurity and lack of morale among staff, and prevent new blood coming into the Authority.

Another policy for slimming down staff numbers and saving money is that of early retirement in that DES regulations allow Local Authorities to retire teachers over the age of 50, with up to 10 years' enhancement of their pension rights. In practice, because of the expense involved, few will allow teachers to retire until 55, or even 59 or 60. An aspect of financial gain to the administrators of this policy is that if the teachers are replaced by younger teachers then they are cheaper to employ.

Again, some Authorities have instituted large in-service schemes, particularly where there are schools which have over-establishment; nine-tenths of their salary is paid by the DES during their secondment, thereby saving the Local Authority some money. One Authority, for example, supplemented this policy by raising the First School pupil/teacher ratios from 28:1 to 29:1 in order to take out more teachers who are in service and not have to replace all of them because of the higher teacher/pupil ratio, thereby saving money. In this volatile financial climate, many Authorities have extended the temporary appointment policy so that if the need arises they could be shed from the staffing without redundancy payments being necessary. This in turn creates great problems in the management of schools and the pupils do not get the continuity of teaching, and Headmasters claim there is a lack of commitment in staff who do not see any long-term career prospects at the school.

The important point, however, is that all the above staff trimming policies can no longer be relied on to reduce the size of the teaching force as fast as the Government requires. The probability is that many teachers will have to be made compulsorily redundant given the present Government policy. Having exhausted the possibilities of the trimming mechanisms, education officers have now turned to the politicians to legitimize necessary but unpopular steps.

This process is mirrored in school closure policies. The Bradford Educational Service Plan says:

> We have all seen the reaction to, for instance, threatened school closures, from the public, parents and the Government and the feelings that changes in staff cutting policy has produced. If we are to face the problems and make even more radical decisions about the future of our services, it will call for strong nerve and not a little resolve, together with solid and sustained political backing for our officers. (1982)

The resources available to schools are also under pressure. Headteachers of upper schools in Bradford in a special report — Education Cuts, Financial Support, September 1981 — highlighted the declining purchasing power of capitation.

> The increase has been smallest over the last four years, from 1978 to 1981; for lower school pupils the rate has risen from £16 to £18.70, an annual increase of 4.2 per cent, and for post sixteen the increase

has been from £22.50 to £27.60 at an annual rate of 4.5 per cent. In real terms since 1975 there has been a decline of at least 27 per cent in spending capacity, with a higher figure over the last four years. Over the same period, general price inflation has been in the order of 200 per cent. (p. 1)

After specifying in detail problems that now accrue in the practical areas of teaching they conclude —

A 13 year old entering an Upper School now will find fewer adults, poor maintenance of the fabric, inadequate furniture and a restricted curriculum. There will be less practical work, fewer games activities, no books to take home, less stimulation in lessons and fewer contacts with the community. The examination courses to be encountered may well be inappropriate and the preparation for them less thorough than expected. This most unsatisfactory state of affairs is to be expected with the completely inadequate level of capitation averaging considerably less than 10p a day per pupil, and much of that diverted to non-class purposes. (p. 4)

Detailed information could be given regarding the difficulties of nursery education which remains a marginal service reaching only 20% of three to four year olds; or student grants (up 4% for 1982–83 which is 6% below the Government's own estimate of inflation for that time period); or universities (average cuts of 15% in 1982–83, though administered unequally between institutions, e.g. 34 per cent for Salford, 7 per cent for York); and the public sector higher education (cuts of 6½% in real terms 1982–83 on the 1980–81 actual expenditure).

All of these reductions are strains which the educational service is now experiencing and often can be directly linked to the present Conservative policy as reflected in their economic policy.

### Present Government Economic Policy under Department of the Environment

The reasoning behind the educational cuts is a reflection of the interpretation of Government policy by the Department of the Environment. Indeed, this is one of the key Government areas in which public expenditure has to be held back, to the extent that it could be argued that it is the Department of the Environment, not the DES, which is making the decisions with regard to education.

The Government has always had some degree of influence over Local Authority spending in that the greatest percentage of relevant expenditure has come from the Rate Support Grant. However, since the 1980 Local Government Planning and Land Act (No. 2), the trend of Government intervention in Local Authority spending has reached a quite different qualitative level which threatens the traditional constitutional relationship between Central and Local Government by transforming the financial framework and which directly affects education as the largest service spender.

The extent of the cuts has meant that Councillors are afraid that the Government's determination to curb local spending will soon mean that they will be no more than agents of Central Government and unable to put into practice local programmes on which they were elected. There is a conflict between Central Government's wishes and local democracy; an impasse between two elected bodies in which one has greater and growing power over the other. For example, since 1975–76 to 1981–82, the total Central Government spending has gone up by 8% while Local Authority spending has decreased by 21%. (See Association of County Councils, 1982)

It is a conflict which is being enacted at the centre of the political stage and is mirrored by diametrically opposing rhetorics. For example, the Minister of the Department of the Environment, Mr. Heseltine, described in the House of Commons (*Times*, 3.6.81) the new and projected legislation as creating 'an environment of freedom subject to national policy' and 'a vindication of the tradition of voluntary co-operation between Central and Local Government to ensure that Local Government expenditure as a whole remains within what the national economy can afford' (*Guardian*, 4.9.81).

These are countered by the Shadow Secretary for the Environment (Mr. Gerald Kaufman) claiming that 'all the 456 Councils will become the puppets dangling from the strings of Whitehall' (*Guardian*, 12.11.81) while Mr. Jack Smart, Chairman of the Association of Metropolitan Authorities talks of the shackling of Local Government (*Guardian*, 17.12.81).

The principle behind the new legislation is that Local Authorities must act reasonably — but the definition of reasonableness is shifted away from the concept of the rates being an element of the social wage which redistributes wealth through expenditure on services to that of efficiently administering those services in a cost effective way to a quite different level of adequacy than was envisaged in the post-war development of the welfare state.

Ken Livingstone, the GLC leader, put it succinctly after the loss in the House of Lords of the principle of the right to subsidise transport fares.

The decision shifts the whole balance of every decision in Local Government, massively, against expenditure. It takes us back to the '20s. Since the Second World War, both parties have accepted that Local Government is there to provide a substantial part of the services of the welfare state. Now the law lords have affirmed, in straight language, their primary duty is to the relationship like that between directors of a company and shareholders. It is to make the least expenditure and the best profit. Services are secondary. Now that changes the whole attitude of Local Government since I was born. (*Guardian*, 21.12.81)

This rationale is repeated in the knowledge of the Council house sale case where Mr. Heseltine, under the powers of the 1980 Housing Act, sent agents to sell the houses because the Council had been too slow in satisfying tenants' purchase rights. This action was upheld by Lord Denning (one of the bus fare law lords), though he described the intervention as 'a very drastic action' and went on to say that 'this default power enabled Central Government to interfere with a high hand over Local Authorities. Local Government is such an important part of the constitution that, to my mind, the Courts should see that the power of the Government is not overused' (*Guardian* 10.2.82). Jack Smart blames the lack of consultation between Central and Local Government leading to the intolerable situation of too many issues decided in the Court while Professor John Griffiths (1981) says that neither Judges nor Parliament has established the principle of administrative law regulating when Judges should not overturn the decision of bureaucrats and politicians so that the whole thing has become a disgraceful lottery and much may depend on which Judges happen to hear the cases. So we have the case of the Merseyside fares Court decision being different to the London one (a different interpretation of a different Act) and Camden successfully took the Department of the Environment to Court for clawing back grant under the 1980 Act without consultation.

These current events mirror the great tension and uncertainty in the Central and Local Government relations which is directly mirrored in the DES policy and in the cash limits that Local Authorities have to meet in educational spending. The greater control of the expenditure is encapsulated in the 1980 Local Government Planning and Land Act No. 2 and in the proposed Local Government Finance No. 2 Act currently at Committee stage (March 1982).

Basically, the 1980 Act defines in a more precise way than ever before what Local Authorities should spend. The total exchequer grant still includes (a) specific grants (13.2% of total 1981–82) for police services, urban programmes, Commonwealth immigrants, probation and after care, Magistrates' Courts and improvement grants; (b) supplementary grants (3.8% of total in 1981–82) for transport and national parks and (c) domestic rate relief grant (6.4% of 1981–82 total) which is a grant to relieve the burden on domestic ratepayers while allowing Local Government spending to increase. This element has been decreasing as a total of the Rate Support Grant from 9.4% in 1975–76 to 5.7% in 1982–83.

By far the largest element is the block grant (76.6%) and it is this around which most of the controversy lies, for one of the main aims is to control Local Government spending. There are four main concepts involved in understanding the block grant — grant related expenditure; grant related poundage; volume targets and penalties, and these are interlocked in a complicated system.

## Grant Related Expenditure

The basic building blocks are the assessments made by Civil Servants of what each Council needs to spend to provide a standard level of service. It is built up by analysing unit costs of each Local Authority service and the number of 'clients' receiving the service and making allowance for factors such as the size, type and sparsity of population.

Over half (53%) of the GRE is based on educational need calculations. These include —

1   *Nursery Education*: The number of children under 5 in the Authority × unit cost. The unit cost is derived by dividing the national assumed nursery expenditure by the national total of the children under 5. This favours such Authorities as Oxfordshire which has no nursery education provision.

2   *Schools — Primary and Secondary*: Based on the latest statistics of pupil numbers. The assessment assumes that 15% of pupils nationally will have such special educational needs. Of these 1.8% in each educational Authority are assumed to require education at a unit cost 4½ times the average ordinary school pupils. The number of the remaining 13.2% at 1.5 × the usual unit cost is related to a number of socio-economic factors, which is derived from the estimated number of children in each Authority who are — (i) born outside UK or belong to non-white ethnic groups; (ii) living in households whose head is a semi-skilled manual worker; (iii) living in a household lacking exclusive use of standard amenities or occupational density is greater than 1.5 persons per room; (iv) in one parent families with dependent children; (v) in families with four or more children, and (vi) receiving free school meals.

3   *Schools — pupils over school leaving age.*

4   *Adult Education.*

5   *Number having free school meals*: All of these are based on total numbers in the Authority.

6   *Non-advanced Further Education*: This is weighted according to whether the students are on laboratory or classroom based courses, under or over 19, from home or overseas.

7   *Advanced Further Education*: Equals the contribution to the AFE pool.

8   *Youth Service*: Half is determined by the total population 11–17 in each area and the other half allocated on the special needs indication used for the socio-economic factors in the GRE for schools.

The rest of the GRE total is calculated on Housing, Social Services and other services using similar indicators. It can be seen that the basis of the allocation is relatively crude and does not take into account the level of spending or priority given to services previously; nor to the extent of the particular, as opposed to broad, special needs of districts. When it is taken into account that the total GRE had already been formulated, based on what the Government felt they could afford in the present economic circumstances, i.e. the needs were retrospectively made to fit the total, it is not surprising that the GRE represented a cut for the majority of Local Authorities.

The relationship between the GRE and what an Authority actually decides to spend determines its *grant related poundage* (GRP). This increases as an Authority's total expenditure grows in relation to its GRE. For example, if an Authority decides to spend more than 10% above its GRE, the schedule of GRP becomes steeper. That is, ratepayers have to pay more towards each pound of spending beyond the 10% threshold. This is done to discourage spending. We therefore end up with an equation: block grant = total expenditure — (GRP × rateable value).

If this were the end of the story, it would be a great relief to many people (including, I am sure, the reader). An additional feature in the above are multipliers which when applied can (and do) penalise Authorities which overspend current expenditure targets. Another feature is the 'close ending' of the grant. If the total claims exceed the amount available as defined by the Government, it reduces the allocations to each Authority by a common percentage or a common rate poundage — another constraint on the Local Authorities concerned.

However, as the 1981/82 planned Authority spending became known, it was evident that this block grant system had failed to control Local Government spending. To add to the confusion; the Government introduced another target in January 1981, only one month after the Rate Support Grant settlement based on GREs. This was that Authorities should cut their current expenditure to 5.6% below its out-turn spending in 1978–79 (the inflation since that time was taken into account). This target was in many respects more achievable to many Councils than the first calculation of GREs. It was based on a different price base, a different definition of spending, and starting from a quite different point. Because Authorities overspent both GRE and volume target, some (notably GLC, Merseyside and West Midlands) had some of their grant held back although the total Council expenditure still remained above the Government's required level. In 1982–83, this hold back is calculated within the block grant so that Councils know what the shortfall will be from the beginning of the finance year; and again there are two targets — GRE and volume target, though it is the higher of the two that is the target accepted by the Government.

Added to this in 1982/83 budgeting is that the percentage of grant to

by 1986. Taking into consideration local variables and eventual up-turn in school population, 1.3 million should be removed by 1986. Sir Keith Joseph's revised plans however have fallen from 700,000 to 470,000 surplus places removed by March 1983 to make allowances for the fact that only 230,000 have been removed by March 1982.

This again mirrors some of the difficulties that Local Authorities experience in having to fulfil Central Government requirements which are mirrored in grants, though the fulfilling of the requirements are often very difficult at the local level in political and/or educational and/or community grounds. The Circular calculates that every 100,000 surplus school places should, on average, yield savings approaching £10 m. — excluding any savings on teachers' salaries. These savings are necessary in order that 'a better range of educational provision be made for the pupils ... and the money saved can be put to more effective use in meeting important educational needs' (page 2).

Both Education Secretaries, Mrs. Shirley Williams and Mr. Mark Carlisle, had followed the premise that if staffing follows precisely the fall in pupil numbers in the school there would be damage done to the curriculum and allowances were therefore made for this. As we have seen in the calculation of GRE, the latest calculations assume a pro-rata drop. In school terms, this means that as number drops there may not be sufficient class hours to provide for minority subjects — or that school numbers of staff adjust themselves by natural wastage, putting at risk a balanced curriculum. It is coming to the point in some schools that if the constraints on staff/pupil ratios continue then in order to keep a balanced or full curriculum vital specialist staff may have to be replaced at the same time as other members of the school staff are made to be redeployed — or made redundant.

There is too the great problem of a community backlash to the closing of schools which the Local Authority has to face. The Circular 2/81 states that:

> The Secretary of State recognises the problems, political and practical, involved in closing schools. He appreciates that proposals for closure almost invariably arouse opposition ... but he intends to play his part in the common task of bringing home to the general public the very real benefits that can arise from taking places out of use. (p. 2)

This has not always been reflected in any quickening of school closures being processed through the DES — and there are examples of the DES succumbing to influential pressure in refusing to close some schools Local Authorities had deemed necessary to fulfil the DES demands (Powys and Bradford are two examples which come immediately to mind).

There is, however, a more insidious contradiction within the recent DES policy decisions which give rise to some fears of greater central control over school policy which overrides the wish for savings due to surplus places being taken out of the system. It involves particularly the reorganization of the Secondary systems of Manchester and Croydon.

Manchester particularly was faced with rapidly falling rolls. In 1966 there were 12,600 children but by 1980 this had fallen to 5,400. The Authority calculated that in 1982 there would be surplus capacity amounting to 77 old forms of entry — equivalent to eight schools. So as to maximize the opportunities for all 16 year olds, they decided on one uniform system throughout the city, having to take into account that the staying-on rate had not grown as anticipated, and the size of most sixth forms had become worryingly small. Although some of the larger schools (11–18) would have been able to sustain their own sixth forms, many others would not and many were in fact borrowing from the lower school to sustain a range of options in the sixth form. After a great deal of public consultation, the final decision that there should be a break at 16 and an evolutionary solution of sixth form colleges consulting with the city's FE colleges was approved. This was in line with the 1980 Education Act (Sections 12–16) which suggests that, where possible, the determination of plans should be produced locally.

However, the Secretary of State for Education, Sir Keith Joseph, rejected the plan and supported a minority interest of some of the parents of three schools in the largely middle class south of the city. He wrote:

> The Secretary of State is not satisfied that on balance the potential educational advantages . . . for the majority of pupils are sufficiently certain to justify the damage which will be done to some schools which have proved their worth . . . only in exceptional circumstances can it be right to reduce good schools from 11–18 to 11–16.

This decision immediately had an impact on the Tory controlled Croydon Education Authority which was waiting for the Manchester proposals to be passed before submitting their own tertiary college system proposals to replace school sixth forms, which was subsequently also refused. It was argued by the DES that the new 11–16 schools proposed would be too small to offer an appropriate curriculum and sufficient teaching groups without much more generous pupil/teacher ratios, and a novel and untried tertiary system raised doubts about the ability of the Education Authority to maintain educational standards.

The immediate effect was that Croydon was faced with extra costs from September 1982 unless an alternative system could be rushed through. The longer term effects are more insidious. No specific criteria as a basis for reorganization to secure the withdrawal of surplus places had been given in Circular 2/81. David Hart, General Secretary of the National Association of Head Teachers, immediately commented (*Guardian* 8.2.82) 'Sir Keith is now proposing new ground rules which means that his personal views about the way schools should be organised would take preference over plans best suited to individual local circumstances'.

By siding with particular local interests against an elected Authority, the Secretary of State undermines that Authority and therefore it could be argued diminishes the responsibility of Local Government. It is an example of 'centralism' with the DES or Government taking on more responsibility and negating local decisions when it suits them. It could be argued that Local Authorities are being made publicly accountable, though it seems that public accountability and central political control need not be synonymous in a school system which, though publicly controlled, must be professionally operated at the local level.

Ransom & Walsh (1982) argue that the 'mushroom' system whereby some schools feed into the sixth forms of others is the most inequitable of all systems which seems to be favoured by the Secretary of State in that it could be interpreted to be an attempt to create first and second class schools.

> Clearly the Secretary of State ... believes that the whole enterprise of stratifying young people would be more securely achieved within separate institutions. It might be a little difficult for the same institution to encourage a minority to study the horizon (to be given expectations) while the majority were taught to be realistic, stare at their boots, and acquire the virtues of place (Ransom & Walsh, 1982).

This seems to fit in well with Sir Keith's own philosophy which he outlined in his January 1982 speech at Leeds.

> For those who are unsuited to an academic curriculum, whether they leave at 16 or 17, education will be effective only if it directly prepares for life.

This will involve for many a curriculum which will

> provide a broad programme of general education, but with a practical slant that will develop young people's personal attributes such as a sense of responsibility and the capacity for independent work, and help them to discover what kind of job they might expect to tackle with success.

This philosophy is directly in line with the thinking behind the MSC recent training initiative. Indeed, by going out of the educational system, the Government have strengthened their control of the process which is based on training for jobs as opposed to education in furthering the 'needs of the economy'. Sir Keith stated that:

> The more effective we make education at school, the more we ensure a firm grasp of basic skills, knowledge and understanding,

the better for the children concerned and the better for society and the economy. Norman Tebbit and the MSC are seeking to provide a wider network of training and the schools are one of the most important agencies in equipping their pupils to be ready for it.

Emphasis is here placed on the training, rather than a broader education, and the local authority associations are given definite boundaries within which they should work.

The MSC Pamphlet 'The Youth Opportunities Programme and the Local Education Authority' (May 1981) in Section 1.10 specifically states that 'The Head Office of Special Programmes Division is responsible for setting out the broad requirement of courses and for issuing guidelines within which the curricula and courses are approved and monitored by SPD and Training Service Division local staff'. The utilitarian emphasis of such requirements is mirrored in The Profile Report of a northern FE College whose courses began in September 1983. Attainment is recorded on the following skills only — reading, writing, listening/talking, calculations, measurement, graphs and tables, visual understanding, dexterity, problem solving, coping skills and learning skills.

A tightening of the entry into higher education by the slimming-down of both University and advanced HE places for lower expenditure; the mechanism for taking out and refusing new courses in the advanced higher education; and the possible growth of Government involvement in the curriculum are all ways in which centralism in education is becoming clearly seen as a trend. This extends also into the retraction of grants for research and in defining the incompetent teacher.

But while the accountability of the education system, and particularly Local Government, is emphasized, the Government do not acknowledge the consequences of the effects of their own decisions. When parent groups in Northamptonshire and Surrey tried to use Section 68 of the 1944 Act to fight off 'unreasonable cuts in education spending' the DES refused to accept the complaints for investigation on the ground that the Section was inapplicable to the circumstances, namely, whether or not the LEAs were being reasonable in not providing a sufficient educational service under the 1944 Act.

In referring to the Tameside judgement as to what amounted to unreasonableness, it was argued that the Secretary of State had to have all relevant information before him about an issue and that he had to adhere to a legal standard of reasonableness. He could not just act on whether he agreed or disagreed with the local policy.

So we have the current situation where a Minister can use legislation to act or not act against Local Authorities depending on how he uses his interpretation of powers. Whether on economic or legal criteria, there seems to have been a significant shift in Central and Local Government relationships which could have critical consequences for education in the future.

### Education and Corporateness

One other significant aspect needs to be taken into account concerning the present administrative and policy processes of education at the local level. This is the introduction of corporate planning management techniques. The theory of corporateness is based on a rational approach for attaining the most efficient workings of large scale organizations. It was first used in practice by private companies in the United States during the late 1950s and later it spread to the larger United Kingdom companies before being taken into account in the early 1960s by Central Government, particularly with regard to the approach towards the study of urban problems and the forward planning of public expenditure (Hambleton, 1978, p. 49–55). The approach also began to influence Local Government reorganization. The London Local Government reorganization of 1963 based on the findings of the Herbert Commission, the Maud Report (1967) on management of Local Authorities, and the Mallaby Report (1967) on staffing, set the scene for the Redcliffe-Maud Report of 1969. Although much of the detailed proposals of the last report were rejected by the Conservative Government of 1970, many of the broad principles were established in the Local Government Act 1972 which created the two tier system of Counties and Districts. The implementation of the Act on 1 April 1974 was guided to a great degree by the Bains Report (1972).

Basically, the ideas underlying the approach involved taking an overall view of a Local Authority's activities, i.e. it should consider its resources and activities as a whole and that it should plan and review them in relation to the changing needs and problems of its environment. It was argued that the problems facing Local Authorities were not conveniently divisible into the designated services as they were then organized and that issues such as unemployment, homelessness, community development, the elderly and the under-5s, needed to be approached from a more coherent and comprehensive combination of organizational structures and processes.

This directly attacks the traditional Local Government structures of separate specialized departments manned by specialist professionals, and the inefficiencies of deploying resources without overarching management systems. The new management structures, based on models from the Bains Report, centred therefore on the post of Chief Executive with the Management Team of chief officers who would secure overall co-ordination and control. They would service the main Policy and Resources Committees where elected Members would set Authority objectives and priorities, co-ordinate policy, allocate resources and review performance (see Jennings, 1979; Stewart, 1974). From this it can be seen that the traditional positions of the separated individual services, including education, would become less autonomous and would work to fit into the policy plans and action plans of total Authority objectives rather than initiating policy independently in their own sphere.

In practice, however, there were many problems and opposition to implementing the theory. Much of the Bains structure models were implemented on reorganization without the full commitment and the necessary skills of many of the main officers concerned — that is the chief officers who constituted the Management Team. The strength of their separatist professionalism was underestimated so that there was a clash between the co-ordination and integration of activities across the Authority and the vertical functions of separate service departments (see Jennings, 1979, p. 11; Hunter, 1982). Hence, tensions developed between the centre and the periphery of the Authorities.

Reorganization also took place in a time of cutbacks and financial stringency and the resultant crisis situations were not conducive to the orderly development of corporate approaches. Indeed, it seemed to many in education, the biggest spending service, that the new procedures were being used to cut its allocation, for decisions with regard to education's resources were now being made by Committees other than the traditional Education Committees. Indeed, the implementation of corporate structures (as opposed to processes) meant that many important decisions were being made by a small caucus of officers and members of the controlling party who may not have grasped the differing emphases of needs of services or taken into account the subtle factors of flexibility, pacing and differential support affecting the quality of education in particular.

Since reorganization, the position and style of the Chief Education Officer became more that of an implementer and administrator rather than that of policy initiator and formulator. Miriam David (1977), in a study of Local Authority Education Departments in the early 1970s, identified a useful analytical distinction of chief education officer styles, that of between 'conciliator' and 'educator'. The former tends to stress the mediator or brokerage role of the officers, to arbitrate between the conflicting interests and demands on the system: 'Essentially they are professionals, but predominantly in generalist administration' (p. 41). The educator is one who pursues educational objectives, chosen as a result of professional training and experience, and is the teachers' representative: 'Theirs is a commitment to the substance of the task rather than to its organisation. They are professional educators' (p. 41).

Since this study was researched, there has been a definite shift of emphasis in structure so that the 'conciliator' rather than the 'educator' is the more relevant style given the shift of the locus of power in Local Authorities towards the centre. Also, as has been argued earlier in this paper, in a situation of declining resources, decisions are being made by the more centralized administration using political values to differentiate between competing demands rather than professionally based criteria per se. Again, it needs to be stressed that these politicized decisions are essentially re-active rather than pro-active in that the context in which they are made is in response to decisions made elsewhere by Central Government. The new

Block Grant System for regularizing grant allocations involves the Department of the Environment in needing and receiving greater information of what the Local Authority is doing before it decides the level of rate support. John Cretton (1980) remarks: 'The more Central Government looks in detail at what each Authority is doing, the greater its capacity for control, and the direr the threat to local independence'.

It seems then that education is entangled in a changing system of loci of power within Local Government and between Local and Central Government so that increasingly priorities other than educational priorities are being used to condition and, in some respects, determine what should be done by and for education.

## Some Theoretical Considerations

Much of the evidence above of the changing emphasis of education policy making could be taken as vindicating the clear-cut view of Cockburn (1977) that Councils are expressions at a local level of the state.

> We need an analysis that sets Local Government in the context of the real economic situation of the period in which we live and ask what is its job? Such an approach involves stepping outside the conventional frame of reference and seeing Local Government, our old red brick town hall, for what it really is; a key part of the state in capitalist society. (p. 49)

The main function of the state according to Cockburn is to secure conditions favourable to capital accumulation by contributing to both capitalist production and capitalist reproduction. From this, it could be argued that the main task of the Local Authority is reproduction and that in a fiscal crisis the process of capital accumulation (mostly private accumulation) takes relative precedence over the social wage elements of public expenditure. This is facilitated by the growing extent of centralization of power and resources towards Central Government and mirrored in education by the growing utilitarianism of the Labour Party's Great Debate (1976–77) with its emphasis on accountability, needs of industry and standards (see Finn *et al.*, 1977; Hunter, 1981) to the direct cuts mentioned in the earlier part of this paper. The systems of corporate management and planning with their emphasis on the mechanics of efficient administration are most useful in implementing the actual cuts within the given parameters of cash limits.

Corrigan (1979) does not take such a pessimistic view and indeed sees a possible scenario where such savage attacks on the social wage and services could lead to erazing of class consciousness which could be the basis of a potent reaction in that the local state is

> an arena for class struggle in the locality. It provides the opportunity for organising pressure and change in the local area of struggle, at all

times recognising the influence of Central Government and the power of the multi-nationals in the struggle but underlining that the consciousness of the great mass of working people is around local issues. (p. 204)

He does not, however, see this as unproblematic for he argues that the growth in the social wage by an increasingly bureaucratic state has de-politicized sections of the working class in that they have become passive recipients of aid. Bassett (1980) describes this in that:

Insofar as the process of reform has failed to provide any continuing democratic experience for working people, it has proved difficult to mobilise mass support for the defence of these reforms now that they are under attack as part of the cutback in state expenditure. (p. 55)

Indeed, it could be argued further that the Thatcher Government has transferred the fiscal crisis of the state on to the local state in that much of the tension has been placed between services in Local Authorities in their fight to keep their own cuts to the minimum. Educationalists have been at the forefront of such infights with regard to school closures, trying to keep teachers' posts to the detriment of materials, and for the different sections of the educational services competing against each other for the shrinking resources. The Falklands dispute and the rise of the SDP cannot entirely account for the present popularity of the Government and the relatively poor showing of the Labour vote in the municipal elections of May 1982.

But perhaps Cockburn and Corrigan, with their theoretical clarity, have not taken into account the complexity, the ambiguity and confusion that still exists with regard to understanding the relationship between Central and Local Government. In education and other services, there remain wide variations in patterns of expenditure and the way in which Central Government policies are implemented between different Authorities, and while Central Government powers may have increased, it is still an empirical question as to how effective they are in practice.

I argue elsewhere (Hunter, 1981) that there are contradictions and unintended consequences which stem from the present Government's educational policies, for example with regard to the Education Bills of 1979 and 1980 and their policies of school closures, 16–19 year old education, curriculum development, and their defence of 'standards'. It is suggested that there are possible spaces for manoeuvre for meeting alternative goals within the broad parameters which are set by Central Government.

Saunders (1980) argues on a similar line that Local Authorities have some relative autonomy from state control and points out the different Local Authorities appear to enjoy different degrees of autonomy over different policies at different times. One example of this relative autonomy at the present time is the nuclear free zone policy of many Authorities in direct opposition to the official Government defence policy. Saunders identifies the tension between social and economic priorities (social need and private profit) as being institutionally insulated in the division between local and central state agencies.

> Local Government in Britain is typically concerned with provision of social consumption through competitive modes of political mediation and organised around the principle of citizenship rights and social need. Central and regional levels of government, on the other hand, are typically the agencies through which social investment and fiscal policies are developed within a relatively exclusive corporate sector of politics organised around the principle of private property rights and the need to maintain private sector profitability. (p. 31)

It is this same tension which exists in education between the irreconcilable goals of striving for greater efficiency and social justice. The present Government have considerably reduced this tension by strongly emphasizing the former almost to the exclusion of the latter.

However, it is perhaps constraining to tie these tensions to class struggles in that there is a distinction between the struggles relating to capital and labour (class) and those around distribution and consumption which is where local political struggles take place. It is to argue for a pluralistic theoretical model rather than an economically based model. This would be underlined by a Weberian rather than a Marxist approach. Weber denied the 'necessary' supremacy of the economic factors in any historical stage of development (Weber, 1948, p. 68). He does not maintain that economic considerations are unimportant, but he would not make a definite choice as to whether economic or non-economic factors were decisive in the last resort in any given situation or epoch. What he did was to underline the potential importance of political, religious, military or economic interests, and that historically all were bases of power which were significant in themselves.

If this is accepted, it should be possible to explore alternative processes involving education vis-a-vis the Local Authority and the increasing centralization of Central Government. The latter process involves both main parties for the Labour Party too has recently suggested that education expenditure should be removed from the control of Local Authorities and given over to a new Government body responsible for the allocation of specific grants (*Education*, 13.4.82). This is consistent with the Labour Party's growing emphasis since the Second World War of the role of a strong central state with regard to reform relative to the local community or 'local state'. It is argued here, though, that there is evidence of movements in society which involve a raising of consciousness which challenges accepted norms and institutions and which, if the present argument is correct, could effect structural changes in society. At the institutional level, Donald Schon (1971) believes:

We must become able not only to transform our institutions, in response to changing situations and requirements, we must invent and develop institutions which are 'learning systems', that is to say, capable of bringing about their own continuing transformation. (p. 30)

These would include schools, Local Authorities and Central Government organizations and would entail systems that can change as rapidly as the environment in which they operate while remaining internally stable. There is a need for this for, whether we are ready for it or not, the opportunities and the problems of the imminent technological revolution will radically alter the definition of work, the communication system and many aspects of every-day living. Technically, it would be possible for control to reside in the hands of a few, or for greater opportunities to be made available for participation in communal life with a more rigorous interpretation of democracy. These movements can be seen in the ways in which new definitions of communality are being highlighted in community politics, in various forms of industrial democracy, in the women's and anti-racialist organizations, in the conservation lobbies and in the agitation for peace. In some schools and parts of higher education it is present in the debate of what constitutes open education, with its emphasis on teaching 'how' rather than 'what' to think (Hunter, 1979).

At the present time, however, the weight of evidence suggests that it is a more centralized process that is in the ascendancy. Perhaps if alternatives are supported, especially with regard to education, this will involve committed political action rather than discussions of theoretical niceties.

### References

ASSOCIATION OF COUNTY COUNCILS *et al.*, (1982) *Rate Support Grant* 1982/83, County Hall, Chichester.

BAINS COMMITTEE (1972) *The New Local Government: Management and Structure*, London HMSO.

COCKBURN, C. (1977) *The Local State: Management of Cities and People*, London Pluto Press.

CORRIGAN, P. (1979) The Local State: The struggle for democracy, *Marxism Today* (July).

CRETTON, J. (1980) *Quantifying the dire threat to local independence*, Education, Nov. 11th, p. 441.

DAVID, M. (1977) *Reform, Reaction and Resources: the 3R's of Educational Planning*, Slough NFER.

FINN, D. *et al.* (1977) *Social Democracy, Education and the Crisis* in 'On Ideology', London Hutchinson.

GRIFFITHS, J. (1981) *Lord Denning rolls the dice against London*, New Society Vol. 58, No. 992 (19.11.81).

HAMBLETON, R. (1978) *Policy Planning and Local Government*, London Hutchinson.

HUNTER, C. (1979) *The Politics of Participation — with specific reference to Teacher-pupil relationships* in Teacher Strategies, ed. by WOOD, P., London Croom-Helm.

HUNTER, C. (1981) *Politicians Rule O.K.? Implications for Teacher Careers and School Management*, in Schools, Teachers and Teaching, ed. by BARTON, L. and WALKER, S. Lewes Falmer Press.

HUNTER, C. (1982) *Draft Discussion Document: Performance Review of Policy Unit*, Bradford Metropolitan City Council.

JENNINGS, R. (1980) *Corporateness and Education: Changing power relationships in local government*, Sheffield City Polytechnic Department of Education Management.

MALLABY REPORT (1967) *Report of the Committee on the staffing of local government*, London HMSO.

MAUD REPORT (1967) *Report of the Committee on the management of local government*, London HMSO.

REDCLIFFE-MAUD REPORT (1969) *Report of The Royal Commission on Local Government in England*, London HMSO.

SAUNDERS, P. (1981) *Notes on the Specificity of the Local State* in The Local State: Theory and Practice, ed. BODDY, M., FUDGE, C., School for Advanced Urban Studies, University of Bristol.

SCHON, D. (1971) *Beyond the Stable State*, London Temple Smith.

STEWART, J. (1974) Corporate Management and The Education Service, Educational Administration Bulletin, Vol. 3, No. 1.

WEBER, M. (1948) *The Methodology of the Social Sciences*, Glencoe. Free Press.

# National Policies for Education*

*Sir William Pile*

The previous extract, in giving an account of the legal framework of the relationship between the centre and the local education authorities (LEAs), drew attention to the role of the Department in formulating national policy for education — a role that was for the first time given explicit recognition in the Education Act 1944.

It is undoubtedly true to say that this Act, with its emphasis on the centrality of the Minister of Education's role in formulating 'national policy', and on securing its 'effective execution' by local authorities under his control and direction, began a new phase. Moreover, the circumstances of the post-war period favoured the development of this function, indeed made it inevitable.

The rapid growth of the system in this period, as a result both of deliberate policies and of the growth in numbers, combined with the continuing limitation of resources, of buildings, of teachers, as well as of public finance, have made it inevitable that the central authority should increasingly concentrate on the role of long-term planning of the system which it alone can perform, and on the task of relating resources to plans.

In view of the central importance of this policy-making function in the work of the Department, it may be useful here to make a few introductory remarks about what is meant by 'national policy' — or rather, 'national policies' — for education: what they consist of, how they originate, how they are processed to the point at which they become agreed policies for the service as a whole, and how they are communicated so that they can be effectively implemented on the ground.

### What Is Meant by 'National Policies' for Education?

There are of course no rules for determining what kinds of issues or objectives take shape as 'national policies' for education. At any given time

* This is an edited extract from Sir William Pile (1979) *The Department of Education and Science*, London, George Allen and Unwin.

this depends not only on the needs of the system and the development of educational thought but also on the interplay of politics.

Broadly it may be said that the major issues that feature in national policies for education are: first, certain basic aims or objectives of the system on which there is in practice a fair measure of consensus (expansion of educational opportunity, mitigation of underprivilege); secondly, issues concerning the framework and organization of the system (the duration of compulsory schooling, the availability of pre-school education, the organization of secondary or further education, and the development of higher education); and thirdly, issues concerning what may be called the logistics of the system (the supply and training of teachers, the scale and standards of educational building, and related issues about priorities in the use of resources).

For the benefit of readers familiar with the more centralized systems of many European countries, it may be remarked that there is one respect in which, in the English context, the concept of national policies for education is restricted. The debate is not, or at any rate until recently has not been, primarily concerned with issues about the school curriculum or the content of education generally. This limitation arises from a traditional feature of the English system, which gives responsibility for determining the curriculum of the schools to the LEAs and teachers and not to the central department. This limitation applies even more rigorously in the university sector, where individual institutions have virtually complete autonomy in academic matters.

### How National Policies for Education Are Evolved: The Role of Ministers and of the Department

It is ministers and ministers alone — that is, the Secretary of State and, where major issues of policy or resource allocation are involved, ministers collectively — who are ultimately responsible to Parliament for national policies for education. Any survey of the ways in which national policies are formulated needs to be prefaced with this remark.

It does not follow that all new national policies for education originate with ministers. In many instances they may do so. Individual ministers may come to office with their own considered ideas on policy. Moreover, it is increasingly common for new educational policies to feature in the election manifestos of the main political parties. It has been noted that the political parties that are the protagonists in national politics at Westminster are also active in local politics, where education is one of the main issues. The experience of party workers at local level, and their appreciation of local needs, are likely to be fed through to the central offices of the national parties, to emerge as new national policies for education.

The Department's senior permanent officials also have a role in policy-making. 'We should ignore the old saw about Ministers being concerned with policy and officials with administration. It is officials' business to advise their Ministers on policy (Clarke, 1971).[1] This applies particularly to the Department, which is essentially a 'policy-making' department with few 'administrative' functions (in the sense implied in this quotation). The Department's permanent staff has in recent years become increasingly equipped, through the departmental planning organization, to undertake systematic thinking about national policy objectives and their resource implications, and to identify longer-term issues that may require policy decisions by ministers. In this context the role of HM Inspectorate must also be referred to. HM Inspectors have in recent years come to be more closely associated with the formulation as well as the implementation of policy.

### Advisory Machinery

From the time when the creation of an effective central department with a Minister responsible to Parliament came to be seriously considered, it was recognized that there was a need for some form of national consultative machinery representative of the educational world to advise the Minister on national policy for education. The Bryce Commission of 1895 had emphasized the point, and the 1899 Act which created the Board of Education provided for a consultative committee.

This proved to be a valuable device. The Haldane Committee on the Machinery of Government, which reported in 1918,[2] commented favourably on the practice of the Board and of certain other central departments in this respect, and *Education 1900–1950*, the Ministry's annual report, probably did not say too much when it claimed that in this area the Board had made a special contribution to the art of government.

Some of the reports that this body produced during the forty or so years of its existence, notably its 1926 report which came to be known as the Hadow Report,[3] had a far-reaching influence on contemporary educational thought and policy. Both this and the Spens Report[4] of 1938 did much to shape the thinking that went into the Education Act 1944.

The 1944 Act both extended and modified this machinery. It provided for two central advisory councils for education, one for England and one for Wales. These were to be appointed by the Minister and were to include 'persons who have had experience of the statutory system of public education as well as persons who have had experience of educational institutions not forming part of that system'. The Secretariat was to be provided by the Department. Unlike the consultative committee, these councils were free to advise the Minister 'upon any matters connected with educational theory and practice as they thought fit'.

In practice the central advisory councils have not functioned as standing bodies, and they have not, except in the early years, chosen their own subjects for inquiry. Since the 1950s they have been given specific remits by ministers, and they have been reconstituted on each occasion to include members particularly suited to advise on those remits.

These councils have had an immense influence on educational policy and practice in this country — and far beyond it — and the names of the chairmen of some of the councils have become almost household words in the educational world: Crowther and Newsom for secondary education, Plowden for primary and pre-school education, Aaron and Gittins for education in Wales. Some of them have injected new concepts into the educational thinking of the time, such as that of the educational priority area which was formulated by the Plowden Council.

### Specialized Advisory Bodies

In this period there has also been a development of advisory bodies for particular sectors of education, and these have come to have growing influence. Of major importance have been: the National Advisory Council on Education for Industry and Commerce (until its demise in 1977); that on the training and supply of teachers; the National Advisory Council on Art Education; the Advisory Committee on Handicapped Children; the Secondary School Examinations Council up to 1964, its successor body, the Schools Council for the Curriculum and Examinations;[5] and *its* successor, which at this time is not fully constituted, the National Council for Educational Technology, reconstituted as the Council for Educational Technology for the United Kingdom.

All of these are standing committees, with varying constitutions which usually in various ways provide for representation of the local authorities and other educational bodies. In most cases (although not all) their secretariats are provided by the Department. Their main purpose has been to advise ministers on needs and policies for the sectors with which they are concerned. Their recommendations may in many cases also be addressed to LEAs, teachers and others concerned in implementing policies on the ground.

Besides advising ministers, these bodies serve another purpose which is of peculiar importance because of the decentralized nature of the service. They serve what may be called a parliamentary function, acting as a forum for bringing together the partners involved in operating the service: local authorities, teachers, churches, and so forth, as well as the Department. They thus help to ensure a measure of consensus amongst all concerned with the implementation of policies.

With the development of these more specialized bodies, and with the enlargement of the Department's responsibilities to include the university sector, ministers have tended to resort less frequently to the use of the general advisory machinery of the central advisory councils, which is not appropriate for examining issues involving the university sector, and to opt for special inquiries by *ad hoc* bodies. Familiar examples are the Robbins Committee on Higher Education[6], the James Committee on Teacher Education and Training,[7] the Taylor Committee on school government[8] and the Cockcroft Committee on mathematics teaching[9].

Moreover, invaluable though many of the reports of the central advisory councils have been, they sometimes have a disadvantage that is the obverse of their excellence: their period of gestation may be considerable. Some of the best-known reports of the 1950s and 1960s took upwards of three years to complete. In a society in which educational needs and the policies required to meet them are changing fast, the findings of a major committee are liable to be less relevant after three years than at the time when it began its work.

Ministers have thus come to see increasing advantage in *ad hoc* inquiries which can come to speedy conclusions. In the case of the James Committee members were invited to serve full-time (or in some cases part-time) so that they could complete their report within twelve months — an arrangement that is likely to prove attractive to ministers in the future.

## The Role of the Department's Partners in Policy Formation

It has been noted that one of the purposes served by these advisory bodies, both general and specialized, is to perform a 'parliamentary' function. It is worth enlarging on this point, because it draws attention to the part that LEAs and the other partners in the education service play in the process by which educational policies are formulated, and thus to the fact they are partners in the making of policy as well as in its implementation.

In the discussions that take place in these bodies in the preparation of a major report, it is frequently the representatives of the local authority or teachers' associations, or individual chief education officers or teachers, who make major contributions. 'If we look to the past,' a past president of the Society of Education Officers has remarked, 'we must certainly recognise that during the course of this century most of our major educational advances have been due to the initiative and experiment of individual Authorities.'[10] This is probably no exaggeration, and indeed is what might be expected, since it is individual chief education officers and individual teachers who have the experience that comes from working 'at the coal face'; and this experience is reflected in the contributions that their representatives make as members of advisory bodies.

The involvement of the local authority world and the teachers and their representatives by no means ends at the stage at which a major report is completed. When such a report — for example, a report of one of the central advisory councils — is presented to ministers, it is the Department's usual practice, before reaching conclusions on the government's attitude, to publish it, to allow opportunity for discussion in the press and the educational world, and to ask for formal comments from the associations.[11] These usually take the form of considered memoranda of evidence, which may have no small influence on the Department's policy for implementing the report.

Similarly, it is the almost invariable practice of the Department to consult the educational and teachers' associations, and in some cases other national bodies with more specialized interests, when new departmental policies are being prepared in the form of legislation, or new regulations, or departmental circulars, or in other ways.

This consultation of the bodies concerned may thus be said to be an integral part of the process by which educational policies are formed, and since the reasons for it are not always well understood, it may be useful to say something here about its rationale.

The existence of interest groups, and the part that they play in the formation of government policy, are familiar matters to students of government. It is common practice amongst departments of central government here and in other Western countries, in the process of evolving new policies, to consult with the interests that will be affected. 'Each Department's contact with the various bodies within its own fields of business must be one of its most important tasks. It is here also that Government can best refute the charge of "remoteness".'[12]

In education there are compelling reasons for the government to involve the bodies concerned in the framing of policies. The Department's partners in the education service are much more than 'interested' bodies, in the sense that, say, trade associations are interested bodies in relation to the activities of the Department of Trade. They exist not to pursue their own material interests but to operate an essential public service, which they have a statutory duty to provide.

The LEAs, which are the main providers of public education (except at university level), have a special status in that they are democratically elected bodies, relying for a substantial proportion of their resources on local rates for which they are answerable to local electors. Moreover, because the LEAs are local, they have experience at first hand of local needs, of what is possible in terms of the local situation and of what will be the problems of implementing new policies on the ground. They have the 'feel' of the locality.

The reasons for associating the teachers' organizations with national policy-making are essentially similar, although their role in the partnership is different. Even more directly than the LEAs, the teachers are working 'at the coal face'. An obvious reason for consulting them is that policies involving action by teachers are more likely to be effectively implemented if they have the teachers' understanding and goodwill. Moreover, they enjoy a considerable degree of autonomy in such matters as the organization and curriculum of schools and colleges, and they have a professional concern in all that happens in the educational world and thus rightly expect to be consulted on the broader issues of national policy for education.

There is of course, and no doubt always will be, criticism of the Department on the grounds that its consultations are not sufficiently wide or timely, or that it pays too little attention to the comments it receives; and fears of this kind have tended to grow in recent years, with the introduction of more systematic central planning of educational strategy associated with the Public Expenditure Survey Committee (PESC) and with Programme Analysis and Review (PAR). It is here relevant to quote from a memorandum that the Department submitted to the House of Commons Expenditure Committee (Education, Arts and Home Office Subcommittee) in November 1975:

> The Department ... recognises the importance of associating ... other parties and the local authority associations closely with the planning process, the results of which are often vital to their interests. There are difficulties about this — not least the fact that decisions arising from the need to reduce the rate of growth of public expenditure often have to be taken on a short time-scale. This points to the importance of developing further the process of consultation, whether formal (e.g. through the Consultative Council on Local Government Finance established in 1975, and the Council of Local Education Authorities), or informal (e.g. through involvement in the Rate Support Grant negotiations).[13]

It is probably fair to say that the Department is as conscious as any department of central government of the need to promote continuous consultation with its local authority and other partners on all major issues of policy and resource allocation.

## The Announcement and Communication of New Policies

Major new developments of policy involving legislation are of course first announced by ministers in Parliament. Even where legislation is not involved, ministers may in many cases think their plans of sufficient importance to justify the laying of a White or Green Paper, or a statement in the House of Commons. As a rule this is at the earliest opportunity sent to all LEAs and other educational bodies concerned. New policies may also be announced in ministerial speeches at conferences or on other occasions.

The traditional medium for communicating new policies that are for one reason or another not embodied in a White Paper or in draft legislation is the departmental circular. The Department's circulars are issued over the signature of the permanent secretary. They are not directives. They are statements of government policy on particular developments or aspects of education, usually containing explanations of the policies proposed and indications of what the LEAs and other organizations are expected to do about them. They carry an assumption, implicit if not explicit, that the Department will consent to the use by authorities of the resources needed to implement the policies. As already explained, these circulars are usually agreed statements, in the sense that they will have been the subject of consultations between the Department and the associations involved before issue. They are public, and in some cases priced, documents.*

There are other channels used by the Department for communicating guidance, advice or information of a more specialized character. There is the administrative memorandum, which is used for statements of a more technical nature. Some policy branches have their own media of communication for specialized policy statements or advice. Thus Further Education and Teachers' Branches issue 'circular letters' or 'college letters' on new policies affecting these sectors. The Department's Architects and Building Branch issues periodic Building Bulletins and Design Notes to inform LEAs of the best current practice and the results of the most recent research in educational building. HM Inspectorate issues pamphlets on various subjects including aspects of the curriculum. These are designed for individual teachers and parents as well as for LEAs.

Information about educational policies and the background to them is not something which is of concern only to members of parliament, LEAs and teachers. It has been remarked earlier that there has been in the last three decades something little short of an explosion in public interest in education, and that in consequence the media devote much more attention than ever before to educational matters.

To meet these needs the Department has built up a range of services through its Information and Statistics Divisions. In addition to its annual reports, which the Secretary of State is required by law to publish, the Department publishes an increasingly comprehensive range of statistics of education. Seven volumes of these, including one for the United Kingdom as a whole, are now published annually. These are supplemented from time to time by special series, and much further statistical material is available on request.

The Department's Information Division issues a range of publications, both for the general public and for the educational world. There are monthly Reports on Education which deal with particular developments or phases of education of topical interest. There was until recently a quarterly publica-

---

* Prior to 1944 these appeared as Board of Education Circulars; from 1944 to 1964 as Ministry of Education Circulars; and from 1964 onwards as Circulars of the Department of Education and Science. Since November 1970 they have as a rule been issued as Joint DES/Welsh Office Circulars. In referring to particular Circulars in the text it will normally be convenient to refer simply to 'Circulars' and (in the case of Circulars issued since November 1970) to give only the DES Circular number.

tion, *Trends in Education*, produced by an editorial board consisting of senior officials of the Department and HM Inspectorate. There are other periodical publications of a more specialized character. Within the last few years the Department has also published occasional Planning Papers, designed to provide a framework of facts and figures for public discussion of some important issue of educational policy.

Like other ministries, the Department through its Information Division keeps in close touch with the media, arranging ministerial conferences for the press, television and radio, issuing press notices, briefing correspondents and dealing with inquiries.

This information work is of particular importance in education. It helps to ensure that in educational policy-making all concerned — Parliament, LEAs, teachers, universities, as well as the general public — have available to them current statistical data and the results of recent research, so providing a common universe of discourse within which debates on national educational issues can be pursued.

## Notes

1 Sir RICHARD CLARKE, (1971) *New Trends in Government*, Civil Service College Studies, London, HMSO, p. 100.
2 MINISTRY OF RECONSTRUCTION, (1918) Report of the Committee on the Machinery of Government (Chairman: Viscount Haldane of Cloane), Cd 9230, London, HMSO, paras 34–7.
3 BOARD OF EDUCATION, (1926) *The Education of the Adolescent: Report of the Consultative Committee under the Chairmanship of Sir Henry Hadow* (Hadow Report), London, HMSO.
4 BOARD OF EDUCATION, (1938) *Secondary Education, with Special Reference to Grammar Schools and Technical High Schools: Report of the Consultative Committee on Secondary Education under the Chairmanship of Sir William Spens* (Spens Report), London, HMSO.
5 The Schools Council was more than an advisory body and was independent of the Department.
6 This was appointed by the Prime Minister, not the Minister of Education. The universities were not at that time the responsibility of the Minister of Education.
7 DES, (1972) *Teacher Training and Education*, Report by a Committee of Inquiry Appointed by the Secretary of State for Education and Science (Chairman: Lord James of Rusholme) (James Report), London, HMSO.
8 DES, (1977) *A New Partnership For Our Schools*. Report by a Committee of Enquiry appointed by the Secretary of State for Education and Science and the Secretary for Wales under the Chairmanship of Mr. TOM TAYLOR. London HMSO.
9 DES, (1982) *Mathematics Counts*, Report by a Committee of Enquiry appointed by the Secretary of State for Education and Science under the Chairmanship of Lord Cockcroft. London HMSO.
10 J.C. BROOKE, presidential address to the Society of Education Officers (January 1973); published in *Education*, 26 January 1973.
11 The bodies usually consulted are:
    1   The main local authority associations concerned with education: namely, the Council of Local Education Authorities, the Association of County Councils,

the Association of Metropolitan Authorities, the Association of Education Committees (until 1976) and (where matters affect Wales) the Welsh Joint Education Committee. Some of these have a statutory role in relation to rate support grant negotiations.

2 The national teachers' organizations: namely, the National Union of Teachers, the National Association of Schoolmasters/Union of Women Teachers, the 'Joint Four' Secondary Associations and the National Association of Head Teachers. (Further Education, Teacher Education and other bodies are brought into consultation where appropriate.)

12 CLARKE, *op. cit.*, p. 31.

13 HOUSE OF COMMONS EXPENDITURE COMMITTEE (Session 1975–6), (1976) *Policy Making in the Department of Education and Science*, 10th Report, HC 621, London, HMSO, memorandum by the DES.

# The Influence of Her Majesty's Inspectors*

Tim Brighouse
*Chief Education Officer, Oxfordshire LEA*

The influence of Her Majesty's Inspectors on our schools has not always been good. Nevertheless, the first instructions for inspectors by Dr. Kay of the Poor Law Commission in 1839 read like a brief for a modern adviser in an enlightened authority.

> It is of the utmost consequence that you should bear in mind that this inspection is not intended as a means of exercising control, but of affording assistance; that it is not to be regarded as operating for the restraint of local efforts, but for their encouragement and that its chief objects will not be attained without the cooperation of the school committees; the inspector having no power to interfere and being instructed not to offer any advice or information excepting where it is invited.

Interestingly the qualities sought of the early inspectors were university education, good manners and 'extensive acquirements'. They were consulted about educational matters and had soon built up a reputation of robust independence which they have never lost. Many of the early inspectors were priests.

It was after Kay's retirement that HMI moved into its more notorious phase under the baleful influence of the 'revised code' introduced by Robert Lowe, ironically the architect of universal education and the origins of the present state system. From the early 1860s until the turn of the century only the exceptional HMI could overcome the feeling of dread which must have been provoked in the minds of those inspected at each and every visit. It is interesting to reflect on the reasons that prompted Lowe to introduce this period of fear and unnecessarily slow educational progress.

> What happened was this: when I was at the Education Department, as my eyes hurt me a good deal, whenever I went into the country I

---

* This is an edited version of the article which appeared in *School Organization*, 1, 4, 1981, pp. 363–77.

used to send to the national school to ask them to let me have one or two boys and girls who could read well, and they were to come up to me and read in the evening. I found that few, if any, of these boys and girls could really read. They got over words of three syllables but five syllables completely stumped them. I therefore came to the conclusion that, as regards reading, writing and arithmetic, which are three subjects which can be definitely tested, each child should either read or write a passage, or do some simple sum of arithmetic, and the idiots who succeeded me have piled up on the top of the three R's a mass of class and specific subjects which they propose to test in the same way.

During this unfortunate period famous inspectors like Matthew Arnold, Fitch and Morell could and did speak out against the stupidities of the system, some fortified by a source of independent income in addition to their stipends. It is likely that even then the really brave inspectors encouraged the exceptional teacher to develop his or her potential but HMIs had forgotten their original brief and it was not until the early part of this century that inspectors accepted fully their role of encouraging and spreading good practice by frequent visits and pastoral support, often as the result of inspection of schools.

They may have been encouraged by E.G.A. Holmes, an HMI whose influence after retirement was more profound than during his career. In his two well-known works, *In Quest of an Ideal* and *What Is and What Might Be*, he harnessed the practice encountered in one or two schools during his career with the theories and practices of Montessori so that for the first time there was close examination of an education designed to meet the needs of the individual child. He reflected on the period of payment by results:

> I could not fail to see that far too much was being done for the children: that they were being drilled into passivity and automatism; that even in the more successful schools they were too often mere receptacles for information; that they spent much of their time in school in sitting still and writing to orders; that initiative individual effort and spontaneous activity were systematically discouraged; that the discipline, which in some schools was so 'perfect that when silence was enjoined you could hear a pin drop', was an artificial veneer, imposed on the children by Prussian methods and so uncongenial to them that they were expected to misbehave themselves whenever the teacher's back was turned. The general impression left on my mind was that the atmosphere of the average elementary school was formal, mechanical, repressive, devitalizing, charged with unreality and make-believe.

The way was open for the period of great educational progress encouraged by the inspectorate in this century. With few exceptions HMIs seem to have had the eyes to see and the sensitivity to know when to encourage and when to be critical. A band of young inspectors was appointed in the 1930s who subsequently had the most profound effect on the practice in the classrooms of our schools. Percy Williams, an inspector at 32, George Allen, Martin Roseveare, Robin Tanner and perhaps most significantly on the national scale, John Blackie, who was only 29 but who retired as chief inspector of primary schools, formed a group of young inspectors who together with others of even more exceptional personal influence, like Christian Schiller, transformed the work of many, especially primary, schools. For the first time it was accepted that good practice in the primary years could be to diagnose a child's needs and engage his interest with skill and affection.

Probably it is fair to say that this period concluded in 1968 when a select committee recommended the discontinuation of the general inspection of schools by the inspectorate on the grounds that our schools were so good that they no longer needed such regular general inspection on an individual basis. HMI entered a new and critical phase.

Three vital factors in the influence of the inspectorate have been the mode of operation, numerical strength and quality. Of these, the first two are inextricably linked to be effective. For example, in the era preceding the revised code (1840–60) there were sufficient inspectors that they could visit schools twice a year and have one day a week for writing their reports. During the period of the revised code there were sufficient to carry out their tests in all schools. Moreover they were extraordinarily effective during this period even if in a wholly unhelpful manner, as their findings of sterility and lack of imagination in the period after the code's abandonment when regular inspection as opposed to testing was established, will testify.

By 1950 there were nearly 600 HMIs and the school population bulge had not yet occurred. Now, as the school population plunges from a peak of nine million to something over six million the number of inspectors has been progressively reduced to 470. In 1968 with the abandonment of regular inspection HMI's role was uncertain. Somebody had to determine how to exercise influence by operating in a new mode with a substantially reduced number. Moreover the climate suddenly changed in a way reminiscent of the period which preceded the introduction of the revised code. There were the Black Papers and the William Tyndale affair; there was the Great Debate launched by the Callaghan speech at Ruskin in 1976 and the start of the work of the Assessment of Performance Unit. At this vital phase in the development of the educational system, HMI was under the direct influence of Sheila Browne. It may be assumed that she realized that the only way the Inspectorate's diminished numbers, faced with more schools and a greater number of teachers, could retain influence on the schools was by work of substance — but at a distance. Hence we have the two substantial HMI surveys already published, with others in train. It is not the purpose of this article to review the influence of the first of these, *Primary Education in*

*England.* On the secondary side, perhaps significantly, HMIs have been much more active during this period. Besides the major work, *Aspects of Secondary Education in England* (1979) there have been the working papers of the red book *Curriculum 11–16* (1977) *A View of the Curriculum* (1980) and other publications in the same HMI series, 'Matters for Discussion'.

The number of publications, especially if one detects the hand of HMI in *The School Curriculum* and its ministerial predecessor, *Framework* — and I think one must as I shall explain later — admits of two explanations. The first is that there are messages which require much emphasis, the second that such a flurry of activity may have been designed to avoid less welcome, over prescriptive, even damaging initiatives by politicians in the wake of the Great Debate. Both explanations may be true. Certainly the initiative for the primary and secondary surveys was under way before the Callaghan speech of 1976; indeed the Local Authority Associations and the other interest groups were consulted on the plans for them in 1974/75. On a purely political level it is interesting to note that the aims outlined by the Secretary of State in *Framework* had their origins precisely in preceding HMI documents. One has to conclude that the presence of the Senior Chief Inspector, not to mention her strong-willed adherence to principle, has been of enormous significance to the work of the schools during a period which seemed about to drive the schools in a wrong direction. She has been able to argue her case in a way that is perhaps unrivalled by any of her distinguished predecessors.

What are the messages of the secondary document? I confess to remaining entranced and troubled by the red book *Curriculum 11–16*: I still dip into it more frequently than other similar documents. It entrances because, like the Schools Council document, *The Practical Curriculum*, it begins to set out strategies of how schools might be improved so that they become places where youngsters are engaged by interest and skill development rather than by compulsion and the traditional examination-led diet of information. It troubles because it is unclear to me as an Education Officer how best to help facilitate that change. It seems that there are at least three prerequisites to secondary schools moving in those generally laudable directions. The first is good leadership in the school itself and a willingness on the part of staff to examine afresh their arrangements and attitudes; the second is time, probably involving the secondment of groups of like motivated staff so that they may examine the skill and conceptual content of the curriculum and the organizational possibilities of the school itself to underpin any change; the third is the courage to back the school with Burnham points in quiet support as they change. Of course, even without these conditions, some schools have moved substantially towards the consideration of whole school policies on many aspects of their work; however, they have done it despite difficulties and through exceptional professional effort. How far they can sustain the changes without the sort of support outlined above is questionable. The challenge therefore to local education authorities is how they can, through their advisory services, in-service training arrangements and use of the Burnham Report, support schools wishing to take the 'curriculum 11–16' publication of 1977 seriously.

The survey document, *Aspects of Secondary Education in England*, poses a number of different tactical, less strategic, issues. Again it would seem doubtful that action on these tactical points will secure lasting gains unless some of the more strategic issues outlined in the 11–16 curriculum document are tackled. Otherwise there may be no framework to sustain the gains.

Perhaps in order to illustrate some of the uncomfortable issues raised by the aspects document it will be helpful to reproduce a discussion paper which informed an advisers' meeting in one local education authority. It consists of random extracts from the aspects document together with some speculative questioning.

### Policy Issues/Present Practices: A Discussion Paper

*Curricular Provision* (Chapter 3)

1   Consultation on curricular choice

6.1   A disturbing feature however was that in nearly 20 per cent of the schools curricular choices were made without the benefit of advice from specialist careers teachers about the possible effects of such choices. Even where advice was sought, more than a quarter of the schools indicated that this did not involve the careers service provided by the local education authorities. Careers advice delayed until year 4 or 5 is too late to avoid the closing of certain opportunities to pupils who have made earlier subject choices.

What is our practice? How do we ensure that none of our schools falls into the 20 per cent — or even the 40+ per cent? What are the implications for the links between the advisory services, the careers advisory service and the schools?

2   The change in curriculum at 14

15.1   The evidence of the survey raises a number of issues and questions.... The first group relate to the nature of the curricular break at 14.... It is widely assumed ... that the opportunity to start some new subjects, to drop others, and possibly to spend more time on some studies, increases pupils' motivation. Young people in their fourth and fifth years at school may be developing more clearly defined interests as well as becoming more aware of their own strengths and limitations, and are likely to welcome a chance to express some preference. It is less commonly acknowledged that the prospect of being able to drop some subjects may constitute a disincentive to sustained effort well before the stage of choice is reached.

15.2 Too often pupils simply stop three-fifths of the way through a five year course, without much consideration apparently being given to the nature of the experience and the value of the attainment this represents.

15.3 ... it is at least worth asking what might be the effect on the content, rhythm and pace of work throughout the secondary school as a whole if fewer subjects disappeared from pupils' programmes during the period of compulsory education. There could still be positive options, related to a smaller number of subjects, ... choice also of type progression could be better secured.

What do we think of this proposition? 'X' is one school which has changed already in response; others are discussing it. It seems to me to be a fairly fundamental change that is suggested. What do *we* think? Does it conceal a larger question which is what is the appropriate length of any 'module' of the curriculum?

15.5 The recent National Primary Survey revealed that skills and ideas in science and in geography were given insufficient attention before the age of 11 and also that few primary schools had schemes of work and teachers responsible for planning courses in history. Study of these subjects may therefore for many pupils be effectively confined at present to the early secondary years.

Is this true of our county? If it is what action follows? What arrangements have we made to facilitate improvement?

3 Curriculum for less able pupils

16.5 ... but the programmes offered to them were seldom successfully pitched at a level which both retained interest and demanded worthwhile achievement.... For the greater and as yet largely unsolved problem for the schools is to devise and sustain a curricular programme for their less and least able pupils which satisfies their broad objectives for this education of all young people at this age, and to take account of particular learning difficulties through the teaching skills employed.

What are we going to do about this through our advisory and in-service training arrangement?

4   Knowledge of pupils

> 17.2   While individual teachers knew which pupils had chosen their subject, details of the programmes taken by individual pupils were generally kept centrally by heads, deputies or directors of studies. . . . What was extremely rare was the recognition that subject teachers needed easy access to it, or evidence that they actually used it.

This is symptomatic of relationships in some especially larger schools. But is it true of our schools? What are the strategies, especially in school timetabling and organization? How can we avoid this happening?

5   The subjects in the curriculum

> 17.6   The process has been one of aggregation rather than a revaluation of changing circumstances accompanying the growth of comprehensive education. The present position of many subjects gives cause for concern: religious education, foreign languages (classical and modern), science, history and commerce are notable examples. . . . Classical languages are not always available and there is a disquieting paradox that while many more pupils are starting French the numbers continuing its study to ordinary level and beyond are falling. Commerce is rarely studied by able pupils. . . . The restricted nature of science education in some schools for some pupils is discussed in Chapter 8.

Is this true of our schools? If it is, how can we encourage all schools to look at the balance of skill, information, ideas and attitudes which make up the curriculum rather than be blinded by 'subjects'?

*Language* (Chapter 6)

The chapter makes worrying reading.

> 6   2.7   Opportunities for reading in school time were limited. Most secondary school pupils were required to read in class for a very small part of every lesson period, mainly in short bursts. Reading records for older pupils were rare; nor were pupils themselves involved in maintaining a profile of their reading.

2.13 In general, where there had been such a move towards individualised learning, it had not been well managed, especially where worksheets, applied without discrimination of pupils' ability, had simply replaced the textbook, or where they had been used primarily as a means of class containment.

2.18 The main problem revealed, though, was not so much one of limitations of stock, staffing or accommodation, real as these difficulties were in some schools. In over a quarter of all schools, it was neglect of the library as a support for the curriculum and attitudes to the library during the examination years which gave serious cause for concern.

Are these comments true of any of our schools?

7 2.20 In one rural comprehensive school, for example, many of the books were in the school entrance hall, where reading was also promoted by the sign 'Reading is not just books'. A huge display board was covered with leaflets about everything from social security to travel guides, from Simcas to farm-safety rules. A real truth about the school underlay this display. Library records showed the usual fall-off in borrowing after the second year, but enquiries revealed that — very sensibly — these young people, having acquired literacy, some of them laboriously, had every intention of making good use of it. They still read books (paperbacks sold well here, especially about teenage predicaments and hobbies), and there was a vast consumption of manuals and technical journals. Motor bikes were much read about. The librarian had to hide *Farmers' Weekly* on its arrival, and the boys queued up for it during the lunch hour.

How many of our schools are like this? And do we have the commended bookshops and the properly used libraries set out in 2.21?

2.21 What is more important, greater staff use of the library would have a beneficial long-term effect on pupils' attitudes to books, libraries, and even teachers. They not only tell us to read and find out, they actually do it themselves.

8 3.5 Switch to writing if you find them turning restless.

3.10 Much time was spent on the production of 'notes'. . . . But more often, there seemed to be an assumption that pupils acquired this skill automatically, irrespective of their natural capacity, or alternatively that they were incapable of mastering it. Notes were even painstakingly copied from duplicated sheets. . . .

Such criticisms of notetaking are followed by similar reservations about marking policy.

3.18 The first impression was one of uneven and often sparse marking, perhaps in part a consequence of the increased volume of writing produced by fourth and fifth year classes.

3.19 The idiosyncratic nature of assessment could be illustrated by careful reading and constructive remarks in, say, one science and scant attention in another, or by wide variations between two teachers in the same department.

3.20 The failure to regard writing as part of the learning process was responsible for marking which was not only at times haphazard, casual or inconsistent, but at other times negative, censorious and possibly counterproductive.

Do we really know what all our schools are like in these respects?

9 4.4 Mutual consideration and courtesy were in evidence in the most successful oral work.

4.18 Talk often appeared to be seen as containing some elements of risk. One of these was that progress in the subject along prearranged lines might be impeded. A class of pupils presenting a range of views on an issue would usually take longer to arrive at a given conclusion than if the teacher had offered it and set out the arguments for it. There were certainly times when it was appropriate to instruct, and other times when a process of cooperative thinking made class discussion a proper alternative. Another anxiety was in the area of class control, and teachers who were insecure in their relationships with classes were less likely to adopt discussion methods. This was a very real problem for some teachers; yet the practice of occupying classes in alternative activities, usually in writing, for as much time as possible, was only deferring a proper solution.

4.20 The best talking and listening lessons were exhilarating occasions, in which teachers engaged with classes in exploring relevant aspects of the work, conveyed information lucidly and economically and responded to questions and comments.... Lessons in which the talk of pupils was directed towards learning occurred most frequently in schools where the general style of teaching took account of them as individuals and built on their experience inside and outside the classroom. Lively banter along corridors and, perhaps even more significant, the ease of silence between teachers and pupils, as well as — if too rarely — the personal

talk in tutor periods at the start of the day all contributed to
the intellectual, social and affective significance of talking as
a means of learning.

10    The chapter discusses 'language across the curriculum' policies and
supports the good practice of schools where heads and deputies spend time
in promoting thought on these issues.


*Mathematics* (Chapter 7)

11    2.9    At the present time there is much concern amongst the
public and the teaching profession about pupils' standards
of achievement in mathematics. It is unlikely that any
dramatic changes in syllabus content, or any attempt to
ensure greater uniformity of syllabuses could by themselves
eliminate the cause of the concern ... it is ultimately the
interpretation which the teacher gives to the subject matter
and the teaching approach used which are crucial.

This might be the perfect summary for various points in Mathematics,
Language or Science in the sense that it has implications for the thrust of our
In-service Training programme and the importance to us of the '4 Year
Report' process as a means of improving the quality of teaching.

12    3.12    LEAs could make more provision for able mathematicians
of a kind which is common in the arts or in sport.

An interesting point which revives our need to get ahead with enrichment
courses?

3.14    Mode 1. As one consequence of this it was very common to
find that the CSE syllabuses which schools were using had
been chosen as much for their compatibility with the GCE
syllabus as for any other reason. . . . On the other hand, the
choice of CSE syllabuses in this way does mean that
considerable numbers of pupils follow courses in which the
abstract intellectual content and the manipulational facility
demanded stretch them rather beyond their limits.

3.25    An examination syllabus is not usually intended to provide a
systematic teaching scheme; it provides a series of topics
which the teacher needs to coordinate. Teachers have a
major responsibility in interpreting the framework provided
by the examination boards. Too often the syllabus is given
as a reason for ignoring the 'why' in pursuit of the 'how', or
for leaving out interesting and natural developments which
are not in the syllabus, or for giving less emphasis to those
areas in the syllabus that are difficult to examine and rarely

tested. Correspondingly, where it is a simple matter to set repetitive exercises on a topic, these can be pursued to excess, although the idea may be much more important than the routine skill.

Is this the case of Maths in schools?

13 Are the reservations on Arithmetic, Algebra and Geometry well made about our schools?

14 The Chapter discusses further the importance of specialist rooms, the overuse of worksheets, the insufficiency of textbooks, the prevalence of calculators and the growth of computers. Most of these problems are known to us. The Chapter's concluding remarks about the lack of a 'whole school' policy on Mathematics reflect those about Language in Chapter 7. Again the 4 Yearly Report must be the occasion for our asking the pertinent questions. Do colleagues think we should do more (other than in-service training)?

15 We should be heartened by the sentence in 10.22:

> It is a task for LEAs and their partners in in-service training to identify such schools and to find ways of disseminating their excellence more widely.

One of our aims on the 'Diploma' front must be to achieve just this. But what of:

> No cases came to light in the survey of in-service training deriving from local radio or from such means as the circulation of video-tapes, but less conventional methods such as these might make a contribution. (10.25)?

*Science* (Chapter 8)

16　0.1　HM Inspectors intended to assess science education across the curriculum. In the great majority of schools, however, it was disappointing to find that little science appeared anywhere in the curriculum outside science subjects themselves. . . .

17　2.2　. . . Nevertheless, it is a matter for concern that in this sample of schools, 9 per cent of the boys and 17 per cent of the girls did no science in their fourth and fifth years, and about 50 per cent and 60 per cent respectively were studying only one science subject.

Of which schools in our county is this true?

18　3.1　Examination success was eagerly sought by a high proportion of both pupils and teachers but in a considerable

of sources, in particular as a result of doubts by many educationalists about the accuracy of the 11+ examination, opposition by parents to the limitation of opportunities in a bipartite system, and the concern of those who were anxious to promote an egalitarian society and who saw the bipartite system as socially divisive.

The emergence of the early comprehensive schools no doubt stemmed from the leadership of small groups or individuals amongst members and officers of the local education authorities concerned, for example, in London and Coventry. This movement gained increasingly strong support from the political left. By 1965 with the issue of Circular 10/65 the leadership of the comprehensive school lobby had passed to central government. The Chief Education Officer therefore had a duty at this stage to respond to the circular; no longer was he faced with the decision as to whether to advise his Committee to act for, or against, reorganization of the secondary schools, and although there were legal loopholes, these were closed in the 1976 Act. The story does not end here, because one of the first steps taken by the subsequent Conservative Government was to rescind the Labour Government's legislation on comprehensive schools. As a result of this the initiation of any proposals for reorganization is once again in the hands of local government and a matter on which the Chief Education Officer must advise.

This example of the swing in the balance of power in the education service is typical of the last 100 years. There has been a dynamic equilibrium which has resisted the emergence of any really dominant party. For some time the church was an important partner in education, but its power has gradually receded. In many countries central government control is paramount, and dictates the range and quality of the educational provision and the content of the curriculum. In England any attempt by the church, central or local government to dominate the education service has always been resisted by the longstanding tradition that schools must be free from outside control — academic freedom has been the watchword.

I propose to examine the way in which over the past thirty years the increase in size and complexity of the education service, and the change in the power and influence of the main participants have affected the pattern of the leadership of the Chief Education Officer, and finally to consider possible trends in the future.

### The Influence of Size

The professional staff of a small or medium-sized authority shortly after the 1939–45 war would probably have consisted of the Chief Education Officer, his deputy, an Assistant Education Officer and an administrative assistant, with a small group of Advisers mainly concerned with crafts, physical education and music. This size of establishment was indicative of the relative simplicity of the education service. The Chief Officer was expected to have detailed knowledge of the county, and his opportunities for leadership in developing the service were considerable, although the resources available in those immediate post-war years were very limited. It was assumed that he could, in his professional capacity, advise the authority on developments and innovation within the service. The main arguments over his advice usually centred on the availability of finance. He could devote a considerable amount of his time to identifying opportunities for development within the county and to formulating the schemes with which to implement them. It was a straightforward example of leadership by personal intervention. It was the more effective because the aims and objectives of education were on the whole clear to most people and accepted by them, being based very largely on tradition.

In most organizations, whether they are public services or industrial enterprises, increase in size has required new and more complex management structures. This has the effect of changing the emphasis of leadership from direct personal intervention to a more remote style, where contacts are channelled formally through widely ranging consultative and advisory machinery. This places a greater emphasis on good channels of communication and professional advice of a very high standard. It means that the Chief Education Officer must rely increasingly on an advisory team with specialist knowledge of their own particular field of the education service; he in turn assumes an increasingly managerial role. Definitions of 'management' could fill many volumes and their increasing complexity often does more to cloud, rather than clarify, the issue, but there is one which has always appealed to me for its directness and simplicity, and is attributed to Sir Charles Renold: 'Management is the process of getting things done through the agency of a Community.'

The Chief Education Officer has a complex service to manage; the range of individuals and organizations that have to be consulted has greatly increased, as well as government legislation and reports. The relatively simple days of direct contacts and a high level of personal involvement by the Chief Education Officer in the oversight of the maintenance and development of the service have given way to a more remote managerial role. Leadership is less a matter of personal influence and more a matter of leading a corporate team which itself has to draw on many sources for information and advice.

### Political Influence

What are these growing influences which have to be taken into account by a Chief Education Officer and which have changed his style of leadership whether he likes it or not? First, there has been the growth of politics in local government. Evidence of this could be seen firstly in the large towns and cities — the old county borough local education authorities. Within the shire

counties it was less obvious, and many county councillors stood as indepen-
dents. It was by no means uncommon in counties with a right wing majority
for such senior posts as Chairman of Finance and of Education Committees
to be held by Labour councillors. Proposals before the council on major
educational issues were debated on their merits with no identifiable political
division in the resultant voting. The Chief Education Officer's reports to his
Committee contained his recommendations which were based on educational considerations, and rarely conceded anything to political dogma. Committee agenda were prepared within the education department, and the
chairman was unlikely to go through the agenda with an officer until after
they had been sent out to committee members.

The importance of politics within local government was gathering pace
in the 1960s, and by the time of local government reorganization in 1973 was
in full flood. The political organization of the main parties became highly
structured and was a dominant factor in local government policy-making,
and probably no more so than in the Education Service. County councillors
in general and main committee chairmen in particular became more
involved and indeed more knowledgeable about the services they were
concerned with. Parties became highly organized and policies within the
LEAs were frequently formulated at the parties' national headquarters.
Increasingly therefore the line to be followed by an LEA on a particular
issue was identified not by the reports of the officials but by the party line. It
also became normal practice for all chairmen to be appointed from within
the ruling party. Not surprisingly, draft agenda for committees had to be
submitted for approval in advance of printing. Many officers were finding
for the first time that items were deleted from the agenda on political
grounds, or they were asked to amend their reports. When the amendments
were unacceptable to the Chief Officer he would withdraw his document.
Sometimes this would be replaced by a report under the name of the
chairman of the committee or the party leader.

The major intrusion of politics into the education service is frequently
regretted and prompts the comment 'Education should be free from political
interference' — idealistic possibly, but totally unrealistic. Many educationalists would like to see a greater degree of consensus thrashed out on
such major issues as the aims and objectives of the service, and indeed this
would go a long way towards providing continuity and stability in the
schools and colleges. The Chief Education Officer however is faced with the
fact that politics in education is a reality which is here to stay. This will have a
very considerable influence on the way in which he must approach his task
of persuading his authority to adopt policies which seem to offer the best
opportunities for healthy development.

Prior to 1970 a Chief Education Officer was often called upon to attend
meetings of the public, societies or local pressure groups, to explain and
account for the policies and their implementation adopted by the LEA.
These policies often stemmed from the officer's own proposals which had

been submitted to and approved by the LEA. It was logical that the professional who had initiated the policies should explain them to parents and to the general public. From the late 1960s onwards LEA policies were increasingly politically motivated and officers either found themselves less willing to try to explain a policy with a strong and overt political bias, or found that senior members of the council wished, as part of their political tactics to act as spokesmen for the LEA on such occasions.

In 1974 Lord Morris, in a paper entitled 'Acceptability: The new emphasis in educational administration', dealt with the problems of the political background against which an administrator has to operate. He referred to the politician's primary problem of finding acts of government which are acceptable

> ... it is hardly an exaggeration to say that, outside war-time, no democratic leader nowadays wastes much time on seeking to determine what is 'best' for his country or for humanity, certainly not in economic or technocratic or 'equity' terms. He does not even bother himself about the lessons of history — as he confines his thoughts and plans within what he takes to be realism and simply tries to work out some kind of action which will prove to be acceptable; acceptable in the short run within the requirement of maintaining unity among his supporters, and acceptable for the next two or three years in the wider field of the community where the proposed line of action has to be effectively carried out, and of course defended.

The emphasis of government on what is acceptable will not make the administrator's world an easy one to live in because 'a plan which has been acceptable and accepted at the level of national statesmanship will commonly look very different in the detail of implementation.' Anyone who has had to deal with the policy of 'freedom of parents to choose the school at which their children should attend' will know the truth of this statement. The politician in local government will therefore look to the officer to implement a policy in a manner which the politician can defend to the electorate.

It is interesting to note that Lord Morris assumed that the Chief Education Officer would become increasingly involved in explaining and defending his authority's decisions. I believe that in practice the councillor has become much more involved whilst the Chief Education Officer's contacts with the public have been of a more consultative and investigative nature.

Whatever the trends may be, it is clear that in the highly charged political atmosphere of local government today, his style of leadership has to be much more subtle. He must decide whether an officer-initiated proposal is likely to generate opposition from the controlling party and the extent to which compromises can be made without emasculating the scheme. He must learn to lobby, to introduce ideas slowly and informally during conversations with senior members of the council and particularly his own chairman. He must use the 'planted question' in committee, he must be 'politician' himself. The 'hung parliament' in local government adds a further dimension to this problem: persuasion of a minority group as well as the main party may be necessary.

The leadership that a Chief Education Officer can exert is less trammelled where he has been asked to produce his own report for a committee. Even if the contents are not acceptable politically, the controlling party might find it embarrassing to veto the report's inclusion on an agenda. These however are rare instances and a Chief Officer must continually walk the tightrope of what in his opinion is best for the education service and what he knows is likely to be politically acceptable. He must accept however that in a democratic society the elected representatives have the final responsibility for determining policies and, once the decision has been taken, he must plan and devise strategies designed to implement the plan. Even this may present problems as, for example, when one LEA responded to a government requirement to produce a plan for the reorganization of secondary education. Although the scheme submitted complied with the government's policy the LEA's intention was to delay implementation in the hope that the ensuing general election would result in a change of government, and with it the attitude towards reorganization. Any strategy by the Chief Education Officer to implement the official plan was therefore likely to run into opposition.

On many major policy issues the outcome has been decided before the item appears on an agenda, and certainly before the committee meets. The Chief Education Officer's last opportunity to influence decisions is often at a side meeting of the controlling party prior to the committee meeting. At these meetings there may be discussions on the tactics to be employed to discredit or outmanoeuvre the opposition. If, as often happens, a Chief Education Officer is present at such discussions he can be put in an invidious position by being privy to such information when it comes to presenting his advice at a public committee meeting. There is much to be said for an officer being present when any political group discusses its attitude to new policy; this ensures that at least all the correct and relevant facts are available, but when the meeting discusses tactics, his subsequent freedom to manoeuvre is greater if he is not present.

There is no doubt that the party political organization in local government can help a Chief Education Officer. He becomes increasingly aware of the general approach of the controlling party to educational issues, and this can clarify the parameters within which he can work. He can use his influence at the preparatory stage, but once the decision has been taken his task is to implement the policy with optimum effect. In this, he is now much more akin to a senior civil servant.

Even in the most politically well organized authorities the balance of power cannot always be predicted. Education Committees are statutory bodies, and their constitution is controlled by a scheme which has to be approved by the Secretary of State. This invariably requires that up to one third of the number should be co-opted from outside the County Council. The composition of the Education Committee is usually in direct proportion to the strength of the main parties on the Council; co-option has no regard in theory to the political persuasion of the individual. It is possible, and indeed it often happens, that co-opted members voting in what they see as an independent and objective manner find themselves ranged alongside the opposition whose voting strength as a result may exceed that of the main party. There have been cases where co-opted members of Education Committees have taken the party whip of their own political party. This is disturbing; they were co-opted as individuals or to represent an outside group of people and not a political party, and their freedom of action in the interests of the group they represent has as a result been restricted.

These are all matters which a Chief Education Officer must take into account, but they are all time consuming and reduce the time he is able to spend seeing the service at work. The fact that politics has entered increasingly into local government and has had an impact on the role of the Chief Education Officer may be a matter of regret to him as an individual: his freedom of action may be more circumscribed, but in democratic terms it means that elected representatives and the party to which they belong have greater opportunities for determining and implementing their politics at local level.

There is one aspect of politics which is to be regretted. The tactics of politicians rely heavily on trying to embarrass their opponents, and in this context all too often any stick is good enough to beat a dog. One very senior member of a County Council admitted to me, not without some pride, that 'one of the tools that I use as a politician is double talk.' In the political game of 'discomforting your opponents' education has become the victim. An example of this occurred in a large urban area where ethnic minorities were concentrated in one particular part of the town and in the schools that served it. The establishment of catchment areas for the town based on geographical convenience merely confirmed the trend. Staff of the schools were concerned at the problems they would face with the increase in the minority intake, and felt that steps should be taken to distribute the problems more equitably amongst all the secondary schools. Attempts elsewhere in the country to engineer a balanced social and racial mix within secondary schools had usually failed (indeed there are legal implications in the deliberate dispersal of ethnic minority pupils). Alternative offers of extra help with staffing and other resources appeared to be the only immediate solution. The staff of the schools however still pressed for some method of sharing the problem with all the schools rather than receiving extra help. It was at this stage that the problem was thrown into the political arena, and a witch hunt started with accusations of racial prejudice. Suddenly what had been a difficult but not unusual problem was submerged beneath a tide of political invective. Rational attempts to deal with the situation based on a study of the facts became impossible. Feelings ran high and press reports appeared with such headlines as 'Ghetto Schools' and 'Dumping Grounds'. Sufficient mud was thrown to ensure that some of it stuck. The publicity given to the situation convinced many members of the ethnic minorities that they were the victims of a campaign of prejudice, and that there was a positive attempt to discriminate against their children. No viable alternative remedy was found, but much bad feeling had been generated. The Commission for Racial Equality launched an extensive investigation and their report published several years later found no evidence of racial prejudice. Even they could not escape the accusation that their report was a whitewash. Although there was probably no deliberate distortion of the facts, the political emotion that was engendered had prevented otherwise rational people from behaving rationally.

The upsurge of politics within local government brings with it benefits and problems, but whichever way the balance is tilted, it will, in the future, have an increasing influence on the part a Chief Education Officer plays in educational leadership. His role will be much less overt and more closely allied to the influence exerted by senior civil servants. At the time of writing the ILEA has instructed its officers to carry out a survey of political education in schools. The intention is to ensure that politics is included in the school curriculum. It would be interesting to know whether the officers felt able to advise the authority on this matter, and if so what was their advice. Opposition to politics in the curriculum stems for some from a natural fear that this will open the way to indoctrination whether intentionally or not, and for others from the belief that the inherent idealism and enthusiasm of youth, coupled with lack of experience of the realities of life, predisposes them to favour the extremes in politics.

## Corporate Management

The individual services within local government have for many years developed separately and in relative isolation from one another. This was perhaps not surprising where the services were of a disparate nature, but cooperation evolved naturally between departments with interrelated functions such as Health, Social Services, Education and Planning, punctuated by modest disagreements where questions arose over the control of some overlapping areas. By the late 1960s the results of research into the theory and practice of management in industry, initiated mainly in USA, began to find their way into management within local government, particularly via the management courses run at universities and polytechnics. The proposed reorganization of local government presented the opportunity to look again at its management structure and to review the functions of elected members and officers.

The concept of corporate management and corporate planning was gaining in popularity, but the infrastructure of most local authorities was hardly conducive to this approach. The Maud Committee on Management of Local Government suggested a substantial restructuring of the traditional pattern of committees, and a redistribution of executive functions. Although these proposals were generally considered to be too radical by the traditionalists, and by others as more relevant to industry than the variety and type of services offered by local government, a subsequent report on 'the New Local Authorities: Management and Structure' (The Bains Committee) advocated more moderate changes which were generally accepted. Not only were committee structures and powers reconsidered, but also the operation of local authorities' Chief Officers — corporate planning would require corporate management. Whilst this was universally adopted (because, as one Chief Education Officer put it, consultation and co-ordination between a Chief Executive and the principal officers is of inarguable benefit) the manner and extent of adoption varied enormously. Some Chief Education Officers found that their corporate work took up a major part of their time, and one colleague admitted that 'in effect my deputy is now running the education service'. In other authorities corporate management became corporate interference and resulted in a situation where letters from three different departments of the same authority were sent to the Chief Education Officer of another county asking for the same information which was in any case already in the possession of the Education Department. The misuse of corporate management was once described as 'the process whereby the Chief Executive tries to run the education service whilst the chief education officer is busily engaged in planning to lay a sewer uphill.'

The uncritical acceptance by many of corporate management as the solution to improve local authority services is reminiscent of the attitude to programmed learning in the 1960s. The Skinnerian approach to reinforcement of success which taught pigeons to play table tennis was applied to the preparation of educational programmes which would resolve the problems of motivation and improve the process of learning. Today programmed learning has found its place as another useful technique rather than the touchstone of success. The same is happening with corporate management.

Much has already been written and spoken on this subject, but its relevance to this chapter is that it represents another dimension that affects educational leadership within an LEA. The Chief Education Officer is now involved in the wider field of management, namely helping to advise on the goals and objectives of a local authority. He is required to present the case for education within the corporate plan and to be prepared to monitor progress as part of the exercise. He may eventually find himself supporting a policy which in some areas gives greater priority to another service rather than his own.

The management approach is described by George Baron as embracing the concern for the efficient use of resources for specified ends shared by the planner and the economist and the interest in individual and collective behaviour characteristic of the social scientist and the organization analyst. But above all it emphasizes the need for the clear statement of objectives for a rational sequence of operations, for the measurement of 'inputs' and 'outputs' and for built in feedback mechanisms. In its crudest forms it works on the assumption that operational theories developed in industry, in the public services and the armed forces can be generalized and applied to educational systems and educational institutions.

It is in this area that the Chief Education Officer has a difficult but very positive path to tread. The application of corporate management by those who do not understand it carries with it an inflexible desire for uniformity among services which are widely divergent in nature. In some cases this appears to stem from a desire to eliminate what many people feel is the unduly privileged position of education within local government. He must therefore within the corporate setting be prepared to check carefully the relevance of any proposal for the education service. The real work and the real needs of education can be masked by spurious measurements of efficiency and trite use of management jargon. R. Glatter expresses the position clearly in his book, *Management Development for the Education Profession*: '... it is scarcely possible to conceive of administrative training without substantial borrowing from studies of management in other contexts — particularly the industrial, since this is where most of the research work has been done. This work must be reinterpreted for its relevance to education and, where appropriate, studies to test such relevance should be mounted.'

This approach may bring criticism that education is expecting special treatment. This is a naive misunderstanding of the position. Each service in local government should expect and receive objective treatment based on individual needs. The careful study of the way in which management techniques can be used effectively in education has been of substantial benefit. It has resulted in greater freedom in the allocation and use of resources within schools and at the same time an insistence on greater accountability to the public in defining aims and objectives and in the formulation of the curriculum. It is in this context that accountability is not just a measurement of end products; more importantly it is an understanding of who is responsible for what and to whom.

### Conclusions and Trends

The framework within which the Chief Education Officer can exercise educational leadership has changed from the relatively free and personalized style of the immediate post-war years to the much more complex situation of today. He must pay much greater attention to the committee members and to their political organization, whilst as a member of the management team he has a commitment to the work of the authority's corporate planning. There is therefore a much greater emphasis on his managerial role. If it can be shown that he has a more complex task within the local authority, it can be argued even more forcibly that external influences and pressures have increased greatly. Quite apart from the change in relationships with elected members and colleagues in other departments, there are other increasing demands on the educational administrator. Education is vastly greater in size and complexity: sheer numbers have increased in terms of the length of schooling and the development of further and higher education, but even these are of less significance than the greater reliance on specialized knowledge and the improvements required to meet the needs of the individual. The movement has been away from the individual being required to adapt to the educational machine toward a more personalized service centred on attempts to provide for the development of the individual according to his needs and talents. The service is an instrument for social reform as well as for educational advance. In the last two decades vast strides have been made in ascertaining the needs of children with physical, mental and emotional handicaps, and in making provision for them. In addition, increasing attention has been paid to the needs of children who, by suffering some form of social deprivation, are unable to achieve their full potential. Equality of opportunity in the mechanical sense may be easy to achieve — the elimination of inequality is more deeply rooted in society and much more difficult to deal with.

A Chief Education Officer's professional and advisory staff is many times greater than in the early post-war years and reflects the wider range of educational expertise and administrative complexity of the service he now has to control. His own experience as a teacher represents a smaller proportion of the task he has to perform compared with his predecessors thirty or forty years ago. This re-emphasizes the reliance he must place on his managerial role as against his own personal experience and expertise as a teacher. This must not be interpreted as lessening the need for a Chief Education Officer to be drawn from the ranks of the teaching profession; his educational background will make him a more effective manager of the service. His leadership is exercised through a corporate approach within his own department.

Consultation has extended in recent years far beyond the confines of the staff of a local authority. Parents and the public at large as well as individual pressure groups and organizations expect to be consulted. Consultation with teachers' organizations is essential and is reflected in the inclusion of teachers' representatives on the Education Committee. It is of paramount importance to the work of an LEA that there should be mutual respect and trust between the Chief Education Officer and the teachers' professional organizations.

Any proposals which are likely to affect the future education of children must be the subject of careful and sympathetic consultation with the public. In recent years, in their plans for the reorganization of secondary schools, many LEAs have mounted massive schemes of consultation, consuming an inordinate amount of officers' time. Very careful thought needs to be given to the extent and level of any consultation. There is a simple belief that by initiating this process, the public will be satisfied that democracy is truly at work and any criticism of closed government will be forestalled. The purpose of consultation needs to be clearly established. Is it to consult in order to gauge public opinion, or is it to explain a scheme already agreed? How widely should the process be spread, and to what extent is there a danger that the omission of certain groups will offend and antagonize? Can all the information necessary to reach a balanced judgement be disseminated to the public?

The purpose of drawing attention to the increase in the number of people and organizations who wish to be involved in any developments in the education service is neither to encourage nor to decry their activities, but to stress the increasing influence that they bring to bear on the way in which the educational administrator can exercise the function of leadership. He ignores them at his peril, but he must not allow them to assume control. There are times when outside opinions must play a major part in his own decision-making, and conversely when it is his job to persuade and convert them to his own way of thinking.

Professor Eric Hoyle, in a paper on 'Leadership and decision-making in education', identified two fundamental models of organization:

|  | MODEL A | MODEL B |
|---|---|---|
| Boundary Relationships | Closed | Open |
| Internal Relationships | Mechanistic | Organismic |
| Role Prescriptions | High Specificity | Low Specificity |

Clearly leadership and decision making are conceptualized differently in each model. In Model A leadership is a function of formal position in the hierarchy with its prescribed range and scope of decision making. In Model B leadership is seen as informal, achieved, and related to task, whilst decisions are made collectively by the group who will be affected by the decisions made. Generally speaking greater moral value and practical efficacy has been attributed to concepts of organisation which approximate to Model B — often implicitly, sometimes explicitly.

The pattern of leadership for the Chief Education Officer has in the post-war years moved from Model A (the bureaucratic model) to Model B. The relationship between central government and local government recently however seems to show signs that the swing has halted or perhaps that elements of Model A are beginning to re-emerge.

Any service which expands in size and complexity makes demands on the structure and skills of management. If at the same time the organization moves increasingly towards Model B, good management becomes critical. It is therefore essential that a Chief Education Officer places great importance on management training for himself and his staff not only through courses at outside establishments but also within his own department. Schools and education departments have in the past been rightly criticized for promoting education for others whilst ignoring their own management training. It has been noticed in recent years that more functions of administration which were previously expected to be dealt with by a common sense or pragmatic approach can now be improved by study, training and research. The day of the British 'enthusiastic amateur' in management is over — no longer can the teacher or the educational administrator with a good degree rely on experience 'on the job' to become a good manager.

So far I have indicated the way in which the increase in size, extent and complexity of the education service has emphasized the managerial role of Chief Education Officers; how the growth of politics in local government and the concept of corporate management has changed his relationship with councillors and involved him in the corporate plans of the authority; how in the identification and analysis of problems and the synthesis of solutions he must rely increasingly on specialist expertise from within his own staff, from teachers' organizations, and research and development units in universities and elsewhere. None of this however absolves him from his final responsibility to the LEA for keeping them fully informed of the progress and requirements of the service. He must ensure that the case for the provision of sufficient human and material resources is clearly presented to the committee.

Leadership has too often been preoccupied with obtaining resources rather than ensuring that they are used effectively towards achieving objectives. The argument about the level of resources to be provided obscures the infinitely more important task of determining the aims and objectives of the service and where the responsibility for taking major policy decisions should rest — decisions on what schools should be setting out to achieve, rather than how they achieve it.

The Chief Education Officer is very much involved in tactics which help or hinder the outcome of educational strategies — but what of the strategies themselves? The remainder of this chapter is devoted to the role of the Chief Education Officer in the all-important task of setting aims and objectives for the education service and identifying specific targets to be achieved within a given timetable.

Education in England is constantly referred to as a national service administered locally; in the same breath we extol the virtues of our tradition of 'freedom for the schools' from outside interference. The curriculum over the last 100 years has evolved from a nineteenth century idea of liberal studies suited to the education of gentlemen. It has been based on the concept of the training of the mind through a system which was not related to the problems of day-to-day living. This approach was centred on the acquisition of information and knowledge, criticism and analysis — often to a very high level. The Royal Society of Arts in their promotion of Education for Capability, described the position: 'They gain knowledge of a particular area of study but not ways of thinking and working which are appropriate for use outside the education system.'

This rarified approach to the education system coincided with the possession of a worldwide empire which provided the nation with an outlet for almost anything it could manufacture, distributed by a vast mercantile fleet. Wealth and prosperity flowed from commercial and industrial links with the colonies. Schools and universities could remain detached from industry and commerce; indeed it was argued that the very strength of the nation stemmed from this freedom of the education system. With the disappearance of the empire as a closed trading system, we have been faced with the need to be competitive in the open market place. The industrial decline from the 1960s may be attributed to a number of factors but schools must take their share of the blame. The tradition which isolated the schools from the real world resulted in the evolution of a system which is not geared to changing conditions. Attempts to redefine the aims and objectives of the service nationally are met with cries of 'academic freedom' and teacher suspicion that their professional competence might be impugned. Local education authorities, jealous of their powers, resist what they feel is an attempt by government to centralize the service.

It is critical to our future well-being that the aims and objectives of our education system should be clearly defined, and that the machinery for achieving this must be able to respond quickly to changing demands. How is this to be achieved?

I do not believe that the present system for control of education has been effective; nor will it be in the future. The law gives substantial powers to the Secretary of State, but they are rarely used. LEAs have major responsibilities for schools, but where the curriculum is concerned the responsibility is delegated to school governors who in turn assign the task to the head, and the teaching staff, on the assumption that since they are the professionals they ought to decide not only what is taught but also how it is taught.

Central and local government have been preoccupied with the structure and organization of education, and have neglected the curriculum which has remained very much the province of the schools. Many teachers would claim that schools have suffered enough from changes, and what is now required is a period of stability. Changes in the 1960s and 70s had little to do with the purpose and content of education; they were concerned with such measures as the organization of secondary schools, the age range, the establishment of middle schools, the pastoral care of pupils, mixed ability classes, the integrated day and new teaching methods. It was not until 1976 when the Great Debate on education was started by the Prime Minister, Mr. Callaghan, that attention was focussed on what the schools were in fact teaching. Only then did people begin to accept that the nation must decide what was expected of its schools.

There are many countries where central governments have virtually total control over the schools, not only over organization and structure but also, and more importantly, over what is taught, and even how it is taught. Government control of education however is one of the first steps taken by dictators. It is used as an instrument of indoctrination and of power. It is unlikely that highly centralized control of education in this country would be acceptable. Indeed any attempt by central government to encroach upon what the LEAs consider to be their freedom to run the education service is strenuously resisted. The love-hate relationship of many authorities with their education service alternates between resentment toward major demands on local government finance, and their concern over the emaciated condition in which they would be left if the service were removed from local government.

Is it however realistic or rational to assume that 101 LEAs in England can identify what the nation requires from its schools and implement their findings? There is already a vast waste of time and resources amongst LEAs, each researching ways of developing its service. The resources and expertise available for such work at the LEA level may be inadequate for the task and the findings may become superficial and parochial. Too often the government has failed to give a lead in identifying what the nation needs from its education service, with clear targets of what should be achieved. An example can be seen in the recent recession which has highlighted our poor performance in export markets compared with other European countries. It is more than a coincidence that of two of our more successful rivals, France trains twice as many people in the 20–44 year age-group whilst in Germany two-thirds of the labour force have vocational qualifications (compared with one-third in Britain). The response of LEAs to the recession was to reduce expenditure in many areas of further education, whilst the task of promoting the training of young people has been taken up by the Manpower Services Commission. The tenuous and dispersed control of education was too slow to identify what was necessary for the training of the nation's labour force, and when the needs became all too clear the response was inadequate.

The teaching profession must rightly have the main say in what can be taught and how it should be taught. It also has a contribution to make in any decisions on aims and objectives of schools and the content of the curriculum, but there are other wider influences which must play a major role. Must we then look to a major reorganization of the education service? The outcome of the 1973 reorganization of local government must have effectively disillusioned too many people for them to put their faith in new or rehashed structures. The existing machinery for running the education service in England is basically suited to the size of the country, the distribution of the population and the traditions of government. What is required is a reappraisal of the roles of the respective partners in education.

There have been signs in recent years that the Department of Education and Science is prepared to play a more positive role in leadership in education. It has shown increasing interest in the goals at which primary and secondary schools should aim, and in the design of the curriculum. It has shown more willingness to initiate, rather than passively waiting to see whether LEAs are responding adequately to the changing pattern of the nation's needs. It is in the context of this development that the Chief Education Officer must review his role and that of the LEA. The early attempts of the Department of Education and Science to become more involved in what was being taught in schools and to analyze the extent to which LEAs exerted positive influence were met with active and passive resistance. The climate however is changing and it is likely that the concern of the nation about its schools has encouraged the Department of Education and Science, and reduced the opposition of LEAs. The Chief Education Officer in this situation is faced with the decision as to how he exerts his leadership and his influence. He must decide whether he will support parochial attitudes towards the distribution of power and decision-making roles or whether central government should increasingly identify what the nation needs from its schools, and provide positive leadership and support to LEAs to help them achieve their targets.

Teachers and LEAs would be important partners in this process, but the Chief Education Officer's task and that of the LEA would be concentrated upon adapting the national policies to the individual needs of their areas. Their energies would be concentrated less on what should be done, and more on how it should be done. It is in this area that the Chief Education Officer should be able to make a very positive contribution. There is no reason why local initiative should be stifled by the emergence of more clearly defined national policies, indeed it might transpire that LEAs with a different political complexion from the central government would devote less time to political manoeuvring and more time to the development of their schools.

The real danger is obvious. Would this not be the road that leads to total centralization with all the inherent dangers of political misuse of such powers? The traditions of democracy in this country and the vigilance of all those involved in the education service would have to counter any attempt to usurp powers by political extremists. There is no denying this danger, but so long as we are conscious of the problem it will be more apparent than real. But what is the alternative? A service too decentralized, too divorced from the needs of the nation, and too slow to react when those needs can no longer be ignored.

The Chief Education Officer should welcome this move of positive leadership by central government, and use his influence to ensure that it is promoted swiftly and effectively. It would not in any way constitute a limitation of his own sphere of leadership, but rather it would enable him to concentrate his energies on those areas where he could be most effective, namely the adaptation of national policies to local conditions and the promotion of local initiatives.

# The Deputy Director of Education: The Phoenix of LEA Administration*

Robert E. Jennings
State University of New York at Buffalo

One of the recurring questions in the administration of education is that of professional participation in decision-making vs. political/managerial control of the decision system. This paper explores an aspect of that contest during the period of local government reorganization, using the concept of system politics. The evolution of the role of the deputy director of education may illustrate responses to change and some strategies in the struggle over who will shape the decision processes.

## System Politics

Four types of politics can be identified which bear on policy-making and the implementation of policy. These are, borrowing from Wildavsky: policy politics concerned with the question of which policy will be adopted; partisan politics concerned with which party will win a contest over policy alternatives, as in a legislature; system politics concerned with the contest over what structures and procedures will be instituted and used in producing policy decisions; and patronage politics or who gets what jobs in the policy-making system (Wildavsky, 1966). In the paper in which he sketched these ideas, Wildavsky was pointing out that the installation of technological systems of cost-benefit analysis such as PPBS could bend the political system away from its true purposes, the sorting out of values and goals. These, he noted, are the province of elected politicians, not managerial or efficiency experts. Clearly, who won in any conflict over structures and procedures to be adopted for making policy, system politics, would have a great deal of control over policy and its administration.

Similar concerns for control of the system are evident in education, in

---

* This is an edited version of the article which appeared in *Educational Management and Administration*, 11, 1983, pp. 29–40.

terms of professional vs. political/managerial control. Bailey, in his study of the US Office of Education as it set about to administer the Elementary and Secondary Education Act of 1965, noted that the objectives of the act would be most difficult to attain if the old line specialist-in-education structure of USOE were left in place. Education was no longer to be dealt with in parts by specializations but as a totality which integrated social concerns and basic skills. The new processes and procedures which would be installed had to recognize that education was to become an instrument of social policy, reaching out to the disadvantaged. Control of the structures and procedures was shifted from educationists to administrators to bring this about at USOE (Bailey, 1965).

The problem which faced English local government in the 1970s was that of becoming more effective in the delivery of services. Its structures and processes had been developed for serving rural populations in a nation which had become urbanized. Each service tended to operate in a compart-mentalized fashion, serving its particular clientele. There was a lack of coordination between services so that while a service might be efficient in meeting the needs of its clients, the authority might not be effective in meeting the needs of the whole community.

Two concepts on which the improvement of effectiveness were to rest were corporate planning and corporate management. Both are ways of looking at processes in the setting of objectives and the implementation of policy. Essentially, the authority defines its objectives as an entity, plans policies to achieve them and, through the combined activities of its service departments, carries out the policies using available resources. Viewed as a problem-solving scheme, the emphasis is on processes rather than hier-archies and on systems of service delivery rather than separate services. In operation, the local council's policy and resources committee would oversee the setting of objectives. Policy-making could then be delegated to the service committees or sub-committees of policy and resources. The administration of policy would rest with the service committees and the departments. To aid in the coordination of administration, the council would establish a board of chief officers under a chief executive, the officers' management team. This team would also be used to review department plans and the management techniques of departments (Stewart, 1974, pp. 15–18).

The change from a vertical integration of activities within departments to a horizontal integration of services across several departments, the creation of the chief executive's office to coordinate policy administration and resource use as well as to monitor results, set the stage for a struggle over the structures and uses of the new system. The reforms as instituted in local authorities appeared to strike particularly hard at the education service, reducing its traditional autonomy within local government and its control over its decision processes (Fiske, 1975; Harrison, 1976; Ranson, 1978). The original study reported in this paper was undertaken to examine those problems. The study and its conclusions are summarized in the next section.

## The Study and Its Implications

The 1978–79 study examined corporate planning/corporate management and its impact on education policy-making in four local authorities.[1] The conclusions focussed on the system at the top: the majority party leadership, the chief executive, the director of education and the officers' management team. Three main factors were identified which accounted for many of the difficulties that the education service was experiencing in facing the new decision-making system. What is more critical for this paper are the implications which arose out of the conclusions.

First, what was observed in the four authorities studied was a centralization of decision-making in local government which came with corporateness but which was reinforced as it favoured party political control. This centralization also benefitted the chief executive in the power struggles to establish this new post. Party leaders and the CE created a closed, political-administrative system in a new corporate hierarchy. The education service suffered because centralization had broken in on the closed politics of education as previously practised in local authorities. Attempting to use the older ways of educational policy-making became dysfunctional for the service because access to political leaders had become severely limited. The analysis did not reveal in any depth how directors of education were moving to counter centralization or to assert the claims of education through the redevelopment of access. What was observed was a continuing defensive posture on the part of the education professionals, actions designed largely to hold on to what the service had in the way of resources and decision-making autonomy.

Second, it was concluded that the chief executive had become potentially the single most powerful appointed officer in local government. This came about, not through formal assigned responsibilities, but more through being privy to the aims and intentions of the controlling party leadership. Where such political arrangements had come into being, as they had in three of the four authorities, they were buttressed by the chief executive exercising control over the flow and interpretation of information as well as having a firm hold on the personnel function, in close cooperation with other central services officers such as the treasurer, corporate planning head and the personnel director.

The rise of the chief executive to a position of 'first among equals' was characterized as a premier example of system politics. Originally conceived as a post without a department, it became the centre for the two critical functions of information and personnel. The first meant control of intelligence-gathering and processing as well as interposing on the communications lines used for policy planning and budget-making. The second meant taking charge of or overseeing the assessment of need, hiring and assignment of personnel for all departments. In so far as the chief executive could control information and personnel, he had the power to compel directors of services to deal with him within the management structure.

Third, the command and control powers of the CE had been used to make decisions rather than to manage the decisions process. This was the perception of chief officers and it was not denied by CEs. The question was not specifically tested in the study but it is observable that when chief officers are defensive and set about buying time through consensus decisions, say, in the officers' management team, the CE just might make final determinations based on his assessments of the majority party's political aims or on his perceptions of what a sound management choice would be. That is to say, a political or managerially desirable end, e.g., reduction of costs, may override a professionally determined need, e.g., the broadening of school offerings.

There were many implications for the future development of local services, given the new concentration of political and managerial power in local authorities. Education could be the most affected as it had been the largest, most autonomous and professionally staffed of all the services. Additionally, having developed a dependence on a now defunct system of closed politics, it became more vulnerable because the ability to protect its 'sacred cow' posture had been removed.

For the education service and directors of education, the question became one of determining what parts of the new decision system were most useful and which might be irrelevant in maintaining education's place and influence within local government. Should education try to use the machinery of corporate management to outmanoeuvre the manager or strike out for a new political arrangement of its own? Should education seek to establish its own research and intelligence unit? If so, should it be integrated with any central unit? Should the department personnel section (for teaching staff only) be fully coordinated with the personnel officer's operations or should it make cases for differential treatment? Could the officers' management team be used to review and promote education and its plans or could it be ignored? What other fora might be used to interact with the chief executive and central services officers?

Having found out what wasn't working well in the new system, from the perspective of the education service, it seemed useful to try to find out what the service was doing to ameliorate its situation. After all, decisions were still being made and implemented, and, perhaps, the education service was exerting influence on them at other places than those observed. Out of that re-examination the changed role of the deputy director of education began to emerge.

## The Evolving Role of the Deputy Director of Education

A question about the role of the deputy director of education arose in the 1978–79 study when it appeared that the deputy didn't have much to do, compared with pre-reorganization days. It had been assumed that the role would continue to be organizationally defined and internal to the education department while the director bore the brunt of the external political struggle for a place of influence in the new decision system. If there were major changes in what the deputy did, these would come out of document search. However, what began to appear in interview data was that the deputy's role was evolving around new functions and ongoing, regularized interdepartmental relationships. The deputy was doing a great deal of work which wasn't always reflected in the job descriptions or lists of duties and responsibilities in the education department. What adds a dramatic note is the fact that a decade earlier there had been strong suggestions from the national committees on reorganization and reform to eliminate the post of deputy in all services.

The next questions after the discovery of possible new dimensions to the deputy's role were: Why was this happening? What was the role becoming and how might the changes which were taking place be explained? In turn, might these findings help explain the larger results of the study? The next several pages explore the changing role of the deputy director of education by looking back over a ten-year period and tracing what was observed into what was discovered in the 1978–79 study.

The post of deputy director of education is one which the director can use to delegate a number of duties or none at all. About the only set task is to deputise for the director when he is out of the authority. But the deputy has experience in educational administration on which the director can draw in assigning responsibilities to the number two officer in the department. In a career of eight to ten years, the deputy has probably served in two or more authorities, has most likely worked in several divisions as a fourth-tier officer and headed at least one division as an assistant officer (Birley, 1970; Jennings, 1977). The capstone of that career comes with advancement to director. Indeed, in the late 1950s and early 1960s four-fifths of all directors of education had been the 'sitting' deputy in the authority where they became director.

There were several conventional ways in which directors and deputies divided department responsibilities. The two main ones were organizational, dividing up the divisions or units of the department, or functional, each taking up activities and tasks which cut across several divisions and units. Often the two were mixed, with each officer responsible for a division and several functions. To illustrate:

**Organizational**
Director: schools, further education
Deputy: careers, youth service,
     buildings

**Functional**
Director: development and finance
Deputy: advisory services,
     curriculum development,
     staffing, catering

**Mixed**
Director: schools, development
Deputy: further education,
     curriculum, staffing

The director made these decisions based on the structure of the department, his own interests and expertness as well as some assessment of the political saliency of issues likely to arise, e.g., going comprehensive in the 1960s. Another factor for consideration was the external relationships, dealing with other departments: who might get on best with the treasurer, the town clerk or the director of works in the conduct of department business and who should sit on various consultative or review panels of the authority?

In the tables which follow the duties of deputy directors of education are reported. They illustrate a decade of change in the role through the period of reorganization and reform in local government, pointing up the effects of various recommendations. However, there are limitations of the data which should be borne in mind. It has all been put together *post hoc*, using interview results and documents from a variety of authorities in three different studies. Also, for convenience, the conventional duties of deputising and special assignments have been omitted as categories. Special assignments might include everything from preparation of the directorate meeting agendas through to leading a working party on ROSLA and from the clerking of committees on to drafting a brief on the impact of the latest DES circular.

Table 1, based on a 1969 survey of the large Outer London Boroughs, shows that deputies usually had at least one division to administer and a functional task, reaching across several divisions. If the deputy had line responsibility for two divisions, there was usually an assistant officer for each reporting to him. In two authorities where the deputy was in charge of the building programme, the importance of going comprehensive was reflected in a specification to those duties. The functional duties of coordinating advisers and curriculum development, seen in six authorities, reflects the shift from quasi-independent local inspectorates to school level and subject matter advisers as well as the addition of Mode 3 courses. These were the results of educational changes fostered by the Schools' Council and Nuffield studies of school offerings. Several authorities were also developing sixth-form centres and colleges as a part of secondary reorganization.

The duties in finance, establishment and buildings meant that these deputies were representing the department with the treasurer, town clerk, and the director of works. This was largely a liaison or consultative role at this time as the departments did most of their own planning, hiring and monitoring of expenditures. In OLB 11, there was a centralization of the personnel function in the office of the town clerk *cum* chief executive, and the deputy had direct responsibility only in the matter of teaching staff.

The origin of Table 1 is interesting in itself. As national committees on local government management began to report, there was a threat that the post of deputy in all local services might be abolished. The Maud Committee (Committee on the Management of Local Government, 1967) recommended in 1967 that every principal officer have responsibility for a division or unit and that all officers, as a team, were responsible for the functional tasks of

Table 1.   Duties of Deputy Chief Education Officers in Twelve Outer London Boroughs, 1969–70[2]

| | Organizational | | Functional | | | | |
|---|---|---|---|---|---|---|---|
| Authority | Finance and establishment | Buildings, projections and plans, development schemes | Cross-divisional matters, e.g., staffing, school meals, grounds | Coordination of advisers curriculum development | Liaison with teacher organizations | Representation at social and ceremonial events | Representation on a regional development board |
| OLB 1 | X | X** | | | | | |
| OLB 2 | | | | | | | X |
| OLB 3 | | | | X | | | |
| OLB 4 | X | | X | | | | |
| OLB 5 | | X** | | | | | |
| OLB 6 | | X | | | | | |
| OLB 7 | X | | | X | | X | |
| OLB 8 | X* | | | X | | | |
| OLB 9 | | | | X | | | |
| OLB 10 | X | | | | | | |
| OLB 11 | X* | | | X | X | | |
| OLB 12 | X* | X | | X | | | |

Notes:  * Finance handled by the administrative officer, supervised by the deputy.
       ** Mainly responsible for ensuring that schemes aid and abet secondary reorganization.

department management and coordination. The objective was reduction of the span of control and greater efficiency. The Bains Committee in 1972, noting that a number of authorities had eliminated deputy posts, recommended that the question be given hard scrutiny in every new authority. In short, the Committee (Study Group on Local Management and Structures, 1972) did not see a need for a deputy to every director. The chart data and an accompanying brief were prepared as evidence for the Bains Committee by the Society of Education Officers. The brief attempted to head off abolition of the deputy's post by noting that corporate schemes, aimed at authority-wide planning and management coordination, would increasingly take the director away from the day-to-day affairs of the department. Thus the deputy would have to become the one contact point for elected members and officers and would also have to take on more responsibility for the overall supervision of the service.

The influence of these debates is evident in Table 2, which uses data from a 1973–74 study of educational policy-making. Each deputy in the six authorities was in charge of two or more divisions. In County A three deputies were in charge of the three main divisions. In OLB 4 the deputy has added buildings and development to his finance division responsibility. In

Table 2.  Duties of Deputy Directors of Education in Three Shire Counties and Three Outer London Boroughs, 1973–74[3]

| | Organizational | | | | Functional | | | | |
|---|---|---|---|---|---|---|---|---|---|
| Authority | Finance and establishment | Buildings, projections and plans, development schemes | Schools Division | FE Division | FE, Careers, Youth Service Divisions | Coordination of department management | Research and evaluation | Coordination of advisers | Liaison with teacher organizations |
| County A 1 | X | X | | | | | X | | |
| 2 | | X | | | | | | | |
| 3 | | | | X | | | | | |
| County B | | X | | | | | | | |
| County C | | | | X | | | | | |
| OLB 4 | X | X | | | | X | | | |
| OLB 5 | | X** | | | | | | | X |
| OLB 11 | X* | | | | X | | X | X | X |

Note: * Finance handled by the administrative officer, supervised by the deputy.
** Mainly responsible for seeing that plans aid and abet secondary school reorganization.

OLB 11 the director and the deputy have split the department down the middle with further education, careers and youth services being added to the duties of the deputy. Two new terms appear under functional duties, coordination of department management and research and evaluation. In County A deputy 1 was linked to the chief executive's research unit, more or less as its 'education branch'. In OLB 11, however, this function was internal to the department and results were shared with the chief executive at the discretion of the director.

When reorganization became fact in 1974 a number of deputies were shaken out of local government either through individuals taking advantage of special retirement options or by the abolition of posts. Deputies in education fared better than some, contrary to earlier fears. According to two past presidents of the Society of Education Officers (1974 and 1979), some five or six deputies rose to director in the new authorities while between eight and twelve took retirement. A few metropolitan districts and non-metropolitan counties abolished all deputy posts (one such district is included in Table 3). Others did away with selected posts in smaller departments but the size and complexity of education was a useful rationale for retaining the deputy in most places (Greenwood *et al.*, 1976).

Table 3 is based on data from the 1978–79 study. It was the observable sparcity of specified duties which raised the original question. In the two counties neither deputy has any line responsibility, only functional duties.

Table 3. Duties of Deputy Directors of Education in Two Metropolitan Districts and Two Non-metropolitan Counties, 1978–79[4]

| Authority | Organizational | | | | Functional | | | | |
|---|---|---|---|---|---|---|---|---|---|
| | Finance, buildings, staff training, catering | Management planning and coordination | Non-teaching staff | Press and publicity | Research and evaluation | Personnel | Curriculum development, evaluation, advisers | Enrolments and resources | Maintenance and repair of facilities and equipment |
| County D | | | | | X | X | | | |
| County E | | | | | | | X | X | |
| County Y* | X | | | | | | | | X |
| District Z** | | X | X | X | | | | | |

Notes: * There are no deputy posts in this authority. The administrative officers in education and several other departments deputise for their directors.

** The deputy in this authority resigned in 1978 and was not replaced until late 1979. Duties reported here are from 1977 documents.

These focus on information: research and evaluation, enrolment and resources. Both are internal to the department but, as can be seen in Table 4, most useful in the interface with the planning and budget-making processes of the authority. In County D the personnel responsibility was carried out in very close coordination with a central services officer, the deputy county secretary. Districts Y and Z retained the deputy as head of only one division. It should be noted, however, that in Y the title is administrative officer but the role is *de facto* a deputy role. In District Z even the type of division is new: management and planning coordination was constituted as a unit of the department, reflecting a rising emphasis on this kind of work. (The unit was never fully staffed or completely operational from its inception in 1976 through to the time of the study.)

The last row in Table 4 summarizes the discoveries made about what deputies do. These functional activities, further described as cooperative, provide evidence about the changing nature of the decision process. A brief look at the developments in each authority follows.

In County D the deputy county secretary brought the deputies of several departments together to create a semi-centralized personnel system after the officers' management team rejected the idea of establishing a personnel department. When the national Health and Safety at Work Act had to be implemented, the OMT called on the deputies' group to do it. These two tasks resulted in the formalization of the deputies' team which now has the duties listed and takes items on remit from the OMT.

In County E the deputies meet with the assistant chief executive. The

Table 4.   Duties of Deputy Directors of Education in Two Metropolitan Districts and Two
Non-metropolitan Counties, 1978–79, with Detail of Functional Duties

| Duties | Authority: County D | County E | District Y | District Z |
|---|---|---|---|---|
| Organizational | | | Finance, buildings, staff training and catering | Management planning and coordination |
| Functional (Department) | Research and evaluation; personnel* | Curriculum development and resources | Maintenance and repair of facilities and equipment* | Non-teaching staff; press and publicity |
| Functional (Special) | | Fuel emergency | | Committee relationships, Roman Catholic School Reorganization; Area redevelopment* |
| Functional** (Cooperative) | Personnel system,* capital projects, coordination, health and safety, management reviews, fuel efficiency, other items on remit from Officers' Management Team | Facilities and equipment needs,* fuel efficiency, other items on remit from Officers' Management Team | Management reviews,* finance advisory,* transportation, items on remit from General Purposes Subcommittee of Policy and Resources | Local government reorganization,*** capital projects*** |

Notes:   * Carried out in coordination with a central services officer.
   ** Carried out as representative of the department on a deputies' group or team.
   *** Carried out as department representative in chief executive's projects unit.

group began by looking into building and equipment needs of the authority and making recommendations to the chief executive. It has continued as a development committee concerned with resource needs and planning projections which are sent to OMT as part of the budget-making process.

In District Y the administrative officers of the several departments act as an advisory committee to the treasurer. The general purposes subcommittee of policy and resources sends questions of finance and facilities to the administrative officers' group through the treasurer. Most of this work is concerned with adjustment of allocations and seeking equitable distribution of surpluses and savings. They also undertake management reviews and oversee authority transport needs, working to the director of management services.

In District Z the chief executive's capital projects unit, charged with keeping building construction on time and on budget, is the only continuing deputies' group. The local government reorganization group of the CE was more *ad hoc*, involving directors on some questions, deputies on others. Area redevelopment began with one project involving the deputies of several services. Neither of the last two groups appeared to be active at the time of the study.

In sum, reviewing the information and accepting the limitations of the data, three trends are observable in the evolving role of the deputy director of education.

1   There is a movement away from organizational duties, line administration, toward more functional duties and tasks reaching across the several divisions and units of the education department.
2   There is a broadening of responsibilities beyond education and uniquely professional functions, e.g., curriculum development, to include more general managerial activities, e.g., personnel, management planning and coordination, resource development and use.
3   There is a shift from *ad hoc* tasks in the external relationships of the department, e.g., consultation on facilities and finance, to more regularized, authority-wide activities, e.g., resource needs and uses, managerial efficiency, personnel processes, in well defined, continuing groups or teams.

Under the third trend it should be noted that the remit of these groups or teams often originates with a central services officer or the officers' management team rather than with departments. The significance of these trends is discussed below.

## Discussion

In answer to the questions posed earlier in terms of system politics, the contest over the structures and procedures to be adopted and used in decision-making, it seems clear that the evolving role of the deputy in education has become a part of it. The conclusions of the 1978–79 study pointed up the fact that the director of education was heavily involved in the political tasks of maintaining the place and influence of the education service in the new system. He was working out how to face a more centralized decision system, attempting to make it more predictable and, at the same time, defending the service from unwarranted encroachment by the chief executive and others, especially in those areas where professional judgement was required. But, regardless of those outcomes, education could not be left out or just choose to take part in only those issues in which it felt a vital concern. Whatever happened in the way of decisions, the department had to be represented in, and be a part of, implementation.

This created a need for someone in the department to take on a series of tasks which would keep the service connected with the ongoing management routines of the authority and who could express its views in working out the details after policy had been decided or when consensus had been reached in lieu of policy. The deputy director was an obvious choice. When freed of day-to-day divisional responsibilities, with broad experience in several aspects of the service as well as knowledge in finance, personnel and management, the deputy could easily step into these tasks. At the same time, as a professional, the deputy carried into this work an understanding of the chief's attitude and assessments of the educational questions involved in any issue.

Directors of education may have initiated the new external role of the deputy in many areas, not only to effect the decision system but also, perhaps, to reduce their own workload or to free more of their own time for departmental supervision and coordination. Whether or not they envisioned or helped to promote the creation of ongoing deputies' groups, working to OMT or central services officers, is not clear. Nevertheless, continued participation by a deputy had to have the acquiescence of the director. The further assumption has to be made that such participation was beneficial from the point of view of the education department because the tasks of deputies' teams appear to have become a part of the regular duties of deputy directors of education.

Several examples show that central services officers instigated or convened the deputies' teams to respond to particular questions which might affect departments or as a staff group working to the officers' management team on some authority-wide concern. While this may indicate some progress toward corporate integration, some matters seem to have gone to the deputies because the OMT couldn't reach a decision or develop an agreed plan for administration and coordination. This could mean that the OMT had manoeuvred itself, and the chief executive, into a position where it seemed that more information was needed from departments to clarify decision alternatives or to get on with implementation. It could also mean that the OMT might prefer to give certain tasks to their deputies as a group, rather than have the chief executive or a central services officer alone make the determinations. Thus, if the education service, or any other service, didn't achieve what it wanted in the initial discussions of policy alternatives, there was another opportunity to shape decisions for further consideration or as they were being implemented. Then, too, there is the question of buying time by deferring decisions or to prepare departmental responses to projects and plans by sending them to the deputies for study. Thus, the deputies' group provides another avenue for the expression of department viewpoints or for making the argument that certain decisions ought to be reserved to departments. All of this serves to blunt the effects of centralization and to moderate the powers of central services officers.

On the more positive note, deputies' groups working to OMT or a central services officer might be getting on with corporate working and achieving that desired balance between authority needs and department perogatives. They may be finding ways through the impasses which chief officers and chief executives have created. Compromises might be more easily reached when those in the group making the decisions or selecting the alternatives for decision are not perceived as seeking power or abandoning their professional principles. The exchange of ideas may be more open and wider ranging. Perhaps, too, decisions at this level are less subject to concerns for defending the service and more subject to the immediacy of getting on with particular activities. Those who are closer to the implementation of a decision may be more concerned with how to do it than with who will give up what to get it done.

This is an interesting area for further examination, not only from the perspective of the evolving role of the deputy but also in the appearance and use of deputies' teams, working to central services officers and taking items on remit from OMT. The struggles of chief officers against corporateness and its concomitant centralization of decision-making may have changed the role of the deputy. But certain deputies' groups, while currently useful to chief officers in further exerting department and professional influence on the system, may be a rational step in the further development of corporate structures. If deputies, functioning as managers, become more attuned to corporateness than directors who feel they must carry on from their professional value base, these deputies' groups may begin to succeed where OMT has failed in achieving greater effectiveness through authority-wide coordination of services.

## Notes

1  The preliminary results of this study, supported by the Leverhulme Trust Fund, are reported in ROBERT E. JENNINGS, (1980) *Corporateness and Education: Changing Power Relationships in Local Government*, Sheffield Papers in Education Management, No. 11, Sheffield Polytechnic.
2  Survey conducted by Society of Education Officers (London Region), 1969, unpublished.
3  From a study of educational policy-making, general findings published in R.E. JENNINGS (1977) *Education and Politics: Policy Making in Local Education Authorities*, London, B.T. Batsford.
4  From data gathered for R.E. JENNINGS (1980) *Corporateness and Education: Changing Power Relationships in Local Government*, Sheffield Papers in Education Management, No. 11, Sheffield Polytechnic.

## References

BAILEY, S.K. (1966) *The Office of Education and the Education Act of 1965*, New York, Bobbs-Merrill.
BIRLEY, D. (1970) *The Education Officer and His World*. London, Routledge and Kegan Paul.
COMMITTEE ON THE MANAGEMENT OF LOCAL GOVERNMENT (1967) 'Report of the Committee', Vol. 1 of *The Management of Local Government*. London, HMSO, pp. 43–7.
FISKE, D. (1975) 'Education: The cuckoo in the local government nest', *Lady Simon of*

*Wythenshawe Memorial Lectures*, Manchester.

GREENWOOD, *et al.* (ca. 1976) *In Pursuit of Corporate Rationality*, Birmingham, IN-LOGOV, pp. 225–6.

HARRISON, G.M.A. (1976) *Forum*. 19, 1, Autumn, pp. 12–14.

JENNINGS, R.E. (1977) *Education and Politics*, London, B.T. Batsford, pp. 117–18.

RANSON, S. (1978) 'Notes on a conference: Education and corporate management', *Local Government Studies*, 4, 2, April.

STEWART, J.D. (1974) *The Responsive Local Government*, Tonbridge, Chas. Knight.

STUDY GROUP ON LOCAL MANAGEMENT STRUCTURES (1972) *The New Local Authorities: Management and Structure*, London, HMSO, pp. 54–5.

WILDAVSKY, A. (1966) 'The political economy of efficiency', *Public Administration Review*, 26, pp. 292–310.

# Planning and Sustaining the School Curriculum: Questions of Coordination and Control*

*Christopher Phillips*
*Formerly Chief Education Officer, Derbyshire*
*and*
*Michael Strain*
*Lecturer, Worcester College of Higher Education*

Teachers and schools are used to facing public criticism; more recently local government has been the subject of general criticism for its alleged extravagance and inefficiency. It is surprising, therefore, that these same criticisms do not appear to have been directed specifically at the administration of the education service. Recent concern about the school curriculum, its proper scope, function and associated questions regarding its management and control suggests that these general criticisms of local government should now be considered in the context of its management of the education service. The purpose of this article is to examine present arrangements for control of the curriculum and how it has been subjected to change in the past two decades by various agencies. Attention will be paid to the degree to which the agencies sought to collaborate with each other in making proposals for change and to assess the general effectiveness of their efforts. Finally, the possible need for improved arrangements to be devised for the future will be discussed.

The legal position on responsibility for the school curriculum needs no more than a brief restatement. Section 23 of the Education Act (1944) provides that secular instruction to be given to pupils shall, subject to the school's rules of management or articles of government, be under the control of the local education authority. The practice has been for the general direction of the curriculum to be passed to managers and governors. Over the years the predominant influence has been exercised by the head and the school staff and so widespread has the acceptance of this working arrangement become that teachers' professional associations have claimed that the determination of the school curriculum belongs, as of right, to the teaching

* This is an edited version of the article which appeared in *School Organization*, 2, 1, 1982, pp. 75–84.

profession. This assertion has never gone completely unchallenged and the issue has been raised afresh for public debate with the publication of the Taylor Report.[1] To say that the head and school staff decide, in large measure, the school curriculum does not tell us how decisions on the curriculum come to be made because the statement, by itself, does not reveal the various influences at work which affect the professional judgement of teachers in making changes to the school curriculum, either in terms of broad objectives or in detail.

'Schools exist above all else to carry out a curriculum.'[2] The curriculum is the central pivot round which the life of the school revolves and yet it is difficult to find agreement on a definition. The DES paper, *Getting Ready for Work*, which appeared in 1976, listed the broad aims towards which schools should strive and this expresses fairly accurately the current consensus. Schools, however, being complex and organic institutions, translate broad educational aims into a curriculum in significantly different ways. In one sense the curriculum covers the formal programme of courses organized by a school, embodying those areas of educational experience felt to be essential to pupils during this period of compulsory schooling. The meaning of the term 'curriculum' can be, and often has been, extended to include other school-based activities, such as clubs and societies, the nature and quality of pupil/teacher relationships and the norms of conduct through which the school conveys implicit values. 'The curriculum, in other words, is that which the school intends as its educational policy and is the public expression of its educational thinking.'[3]

The curriculum at present followed in schools still appears to adhere with surprising tenacity to a traditional pattern. This pattern owes much to the persistency of the liberal model encoded in Morant's 1907 regulations and to the reinforcing effect of the examination structure. In addition, the enlarged autonomy conferred upon teachers following the 1944 Education Act may well have introduced, paradoxically, a conservative tendency into the control of the curriculum. The HMI report on primary education in England (1976) confirmed that the acquisition of the skills of literacy and numeracy are still given pride of place in the curriculum of the primary school; even in the 'secret garden' of the secondary curriculum, stigmatized by its detractors as a labyrinthine maze, a similar pattern of traditional practice was recorded by HMI in recent surveys.[4]

Nevertheless, the movement for curriculum change, or development as it is more popularly described, has run strongly over the past two decades. Changes were both inevitable and appropriate. The winds of change in twentieth-century industrial societies never cease to blow, even if with varying force. Developments in science and technology, for example, call for a constant reassessment of what is taught in schools and how knowledge is presented and skills imparted. Changes in the structure and composition of the labour force and its technological base stimulate fresh endeavours to bridge the gap between school, industry and working life by some rearrangement of curriculum or through some different approach to it.

A continuing interaction can be demonstrated between the social and economic context of education and attempts by providers to conceptualize the educational process afresh and to reformulate its appropriate scope and content. Anxiety about relevance in education is not new;[5] it is indeed older than state secondary schools themselves. What is new is the extent to which contemporary economic and social circumstances lend an acutely political significance to this general anxiety. Moreover, the rate of economic and structural change makes it more and more difficult for conceptual 'retooling' in education to keep pace with the perception of fresh needs, expressed in the form of economic and political discontents. It is clear that the very notion of a 'working life' will need to be reformulated before the current initiatives to forge new and more productive schools/industry links have reached the stage of general implementation.

In response to social forces within society at large, structural changes within the educational system itself have had a significant impact on the curriculum. The compulsory school leaving age has been raised twice since the end of the Second World War. To raise the school leaving age from 15 to 16 involved redesigning, not merely extending, the curriculum to be offered to older pupils, for some of whom neither old nor new style examinations were likely to be appropriate. The second major change was the development of the comprehensive secondary school in its various forms of organization. Teaching in comprehensive schools brought teachers face to face with educational issues which it was possible to avoid in bipartite systems; the presence of pupils in one school with so wide a span of interests and ability raised curricular questions for which an answer had to be found. Merely dovetailing the curriculum of the grammar school with that of the secondary modern school may have been a short-term expedient but it was certainly no long-term solution. As part of the movement towards comprehensive education, there was a growing awareness of the role of the school in promoting the general welfare of pupils and a belief in the school as an agency for social justice. Only in the latter part of the past decade has disillusionment begun to set in.

Throughout this period, the relevance of what is taught, the interrelation of the different areas of educational experience and the devising of new methods of presentation have absorbed the energies of practising teachers and academic educationalists. The list of agencies is impressive: the Department of Education and Science, including the work of HM Inspectorate, the universities and colleges of higher education, research organizations, such as the National Foundation for Educational Research, the Schools Council, the examining bodies, and the teachers' professional associations. All these bodies have contributed to the movement for curriculum change and development; the energies expended and the expenditure involved have been far from insignificant.

The question, however, has only recently been asked whether the achievements have been commensurate with the outlay of money or the labours of so many people. The answer will depend on the objectives which were set, whether consciously or implicitly. If the intention was to create a consensus on what the curriculum might consist of, at least in broad terms, then the recent national debate on curriculum and standards gives little hope that the objective was in process of being realized. If, on the other hand, the aim has been to improve educational standards by providing more enlightened approaches to teaching or to devise more imaginative and relevant syllabuses for pupils generally, the verdict is no more encouraging, as is clear from the published evidence. The HMI survey on primary education in England (1978),[6] to the surprise of many within the profession, indicated this concern about the quality and range of science teaching, commented on the lack of progression and the amount of repetition in history and geography, and was not complimentary about the use of craft in the curriculum. Likewise special HMI papers on the quality of teaching in modern languages, mathematics and science could only have been received with general dismay. The NFER research project on the teaching of French in primary schools[7] certainly gave support to those who were critical of the varied success of sustained and expensive initiatives undertaken by local education authorities and their teachers.

Another disappointing aspect of curriculum development has been the apparent neglect of certain areas of the curriculum now recognized as important. The Warnock Report[8] was critical of the curriculum of special schools and the educational standards achieved. Two reports on multi-ethnic education[9] have expressed grave disappointment that so little has been achieved in schools to provide a curriculum relevant in a multi-cultural, multi-racial society. Part of this failure — though only part, since the profession has itself been slow to respond — can be attributed to the lack of attention from those engaged in curriculum development. It is significant that only one of the GCE and CSE Boards has reviewed its syllabuses in the light of its relevance to a multi-ethnic society. As one aspect of the national debate on the curriculum, a sharper thrust has been given to the whole question of the relationships between school and industry. What has emerged is the need to develop a pattern of more organized and systematic relationships between schools and industry and commerce. Lack of systematic enquiry into this aspect of the curriculum must bear some of the responsibility for the shortcomings which have been revealed.

Much has been achieved, as John Tomlinson emphasized unequivocally in his address to the British Association.[10] Many schools have adapted successfully to changing circumstances; new syllabuses have been devised to encourage pupils to develop their interests and to set them on the path towards achieving higher standards. Yet the general realization of these separate achievements awaits fulfilment. Professional energies have at times been misapplied; some experiments have been embarked upon and left unfinished; often there has been a lack of consistency in approach and solidity in achievement. Even where the development has been judged worthwhile in scope and conception, the actual teaching in some schools does not appear to have benefitted as it should. What is needed for the fuller realization of these gains is sensitive but effective machinery of planning and coordination.

Certain of the curricular experiments can be dissected in retrospect and reasons for the partial failure discovered with some accuracy. The introduction of a foreign language into the curriculum of primary schools has been well documented, and the story is in many ways familiar. Schools responded too readily without understanding the operational need to define their practical purposes in terms of appropriate objectives. Nor did they estimate accurately the demands which the introduction of a foreign language would make on school staff and general resources. The timing was often inappropriate; many schools did not have a sufficiently stable staff to enable the experiment to be more than short-lived. In a number of instances schools worked in collaboration with their LEAs which helped with equipment, books and materials and the training of staffs. That in itself was not sufficient to guarantee success. Some LEAs found the continuing cost of training too expensive; teachers in primary schools often discovered the professional demands of teaching a foreign language too exacting, while it has been said that some of their colleagues in secondary schools gave little encouragement to them to persevere by being openly sceptical of the value of the innovation. So the professional commitment was by no means uniform or wholehearted.

If reasons for the uneven impact of curriculum development are to be sought in a broader context, then three factors need to be considered: first, ways in which the education service has evolved in the post-war period; secondly, professional attitudes which have developed during the same period; and thirdly, the distribution of authority and responsibility within the education service itself. Each of these elements has a separate identity and yet they interact; some would argue that it is the failure to link them together coherently which has contributed significantly to the failures already mentioned.

Commentators have often not appreciated the scale and pace of development of the educational service in the post-war period. A new educational edifice has been constructed on the basis of a rising school population, a lengthening of the period of compulsory schooling and an entrenched belief, accepted almost without question until recently, that through education lay the gateway to equality of opportunity and social justice. So the contemporary structure has grown, brick by brick as it were, responding with resilience to external and internal demands but without the benefit of an over-arching rationale or coherent framework. Extending from nursery schools through colleges of further education to universities and colleges of higher education, an institutional system, virtually unrecognizable to those whose education stretched back to pre-war years, has been erected since 1944. The concomitant has been the increasing share of gross national product devoted to education. Significant also has been the emergence of a new order of institutional hierarchies, particularly in higher education with their own claims for a stake in the in-service training of teachers and the promotion of curriculum development.

What is surprising has been the persistent strength of the interest in curriculum development generated as part of the general development of the education service and the idealistic confidence with which so much has been attempted. At a time when the educational service was expanding rapidly it would not have been unreasonable to have expected the emphasis to have been on a cautious approach, on a careful selection of those areas of the curriculum where, in rapidly changing circumstances, a considered review might have been judged appropriate. In reality the reverse appears to have happened; piecemeal adaptation and radical changes in subject matter and approach went forward so that the overall consequences for the curriculum have rarely been fully considered. In extenuation it should also be admitted that models of the management of learning (i.e., the teacher as resource allocator, and classroom entrepreneur) and a systematic identification of the implications of managing innovation have only fairly recently been developed.

Neither central nor local government has made a systematic attempt to control or direct the pace or direction of curriculum development. This was not unexpected; the ideology of partnership precluded such positive direction in territory so recently conceded to the profession. Support for the 'laissez-faire' approach may be found in the tradition of academic freedom in higher education. The result was a strengthened conviction among the teaching profession that they were the guardians of the curriculum and that it was their responsibility to preside over its structure and content.[11] This gradual and informal extension of autonomy was to some extent confirmed by the recommendation of the Beloe Committee in respect of 'teacher controlled examinations'.[12] Individual schools embarked on their own syllabuses for the Mode 3 examinations of the CSE Boards. The work of the Schools Council proliferated, using individual schools and LEAs as agencies for the projects. The colleges of education and the institutes of education ensured their own stake in the field of curriculum development and devoted a proportion of their teaching resources to this work. These agencies did not, however, establish a monopoly, for LEAs have played their part as well. They have sponsored projects of the Schools Council and, in collaboration with teachers, have initiated their own developments, some of which proved to be highly successful. The establishment of Teachers Centres has had a generally valuable and supportive function in this context. All the evidence indicates, however, that they were never in a position to monitor the whole process or to determine priorities throughout the service within their areas. Neither did the DES seek to convey an overall view; it chose selected areas in which to sponsor research or to conduct an investigation. It prodded and sometimes stimulated, but never appeared to provide direction or general oversight.[13]

One regrettable feature of curriculum development, certainly as far as individual schools have been concerned, has been that much of it has been undertaken without an awareness of what was required for success in terms of resources of staff, materials and equipment. LEAs have delegated control of the curriculum to schools yet, through annual budgets, they have retained control of resources. The financial system did not mean that it was impossible to match resources to the needs of projects but in practice schools often embarked on curriculum development without gaining assurances that extra staff, or other resources, where needed, would be available to sustain it. The point deserves emphasis. Key instruments of financial control are retained by LEAs yet the power to make important decisions about the curriculum has been delegated to schools. In particular, in the deployment of staff, schools have sometimes pursued aims which have proved to be mutually incompatible. There is evidence from surveys conducted by LEAs that staff employed in maintaining or increasing sixth form options could have been more beneficially used in sustaining the range of curricular choices available to the rest of the school. Curriculum development is often a casualty in schools for the same reason.

One of the most serious obstacles to maintaining support for schools on curriculum development arises from the financial procedures operated by both local and national government. Local budgets are presented annually; they reach an advanced stage before the Rate Support Grant for the year in question is known and it is difficult for LEAs to formulate a rolling programme of recurrent expenditure, largely due to the reluctance of central government to enter into forward commitments on expenditure in the form of Rate Support Grant. Such procedure deters, if not prevents, the LEA from giving a financial commitment to individual schools for several years ahead. This in turn precludes the establishment of a sound basis for making decisions about the curriculum which frequently need to be part of a broad strategy to be pursued over an extended period. The problem is exacerbated by the narrowing margins within which local decisions on the allocation of resources are possible. Objectivity is obtained at a price which bears heavily on the scope of local autonomy and the LEA's potential for adaptive change. In consequence the first victim of a national decision to reduce the volume of local government expenditure is often an area of educational innovation or development which the government itself might have wished to protect. Instead, the inherited pattern of resource use, which was itself the intended target of government retrenchment, survives unscathed and the cycle of unplanned development in education continues under its own momentum.[14]

Other factors also contribute. There appears to be an almost innate tendency for the educational system to breed agencies which succeed in developing an independent life and set their own objectives. If to this is added the entrenched belief in academic freedom and teacher autonomy, it is a matter of no great surprise that the activities of all who have been involved in curriculum development over the past two decades have been far less effective than they might have been.

If ways are to be sought of making curriculum development of more lasting benefit to schools and avoiding the past misdirection of energies, where are they to be found? Root and branch solutions are not likely to command much assent. The structure of the educational service, and in particular the nexus of influence and power within it, exhibit a complexity and robustness which suggest a course of pragmatic rather than radical modification. In respect of the curriculum, the DES has now made it clear in general terms that it expects local government, under the aegis of its existing legal powers, to review more frequently and more systematically the curriculum of the schools within its jurisdiction.[15] Yet whatever steps are taken to encourage this, they are likely to fall far short of any overt, centralizing process, a general conclusion which seems to be borne out by the recommendations of *The School Curriculum*.[16] Undoubtedly the school itself will continue to remain the most influential single agency in determining and modifying the school curriculum. Of all the elements of which the school consists — governors, parents, pupils and staff — there is no reason to doubt, despite changing attitudes, that the school staff, given its professional expertise and its central place in the life of the school, will not continue to exercise the preponderant influence.

Any review of the ways in which changes, or improvements, in the curriculum ought to be brought about, should start from an acceptance of this position. In our view there is no doubt that the staffs of schools need to become more aware of the professional commitment involved in these responsibilities for the curriculum, and they should be ready to devise new forms of organization within the school which could assist systematic planning and review. Changes in the curriculum should be considered in accordance with the prescribed aims which the school has set itself and their effectiveness assessed over a reasonable period of time. There is merit in schools cooperating with each other in curriculum development, particularly in areas where communications present little difficulty. In both primary and secondary schools, staff development, fuller utilization of shared resources, the more equitable provision of minority subjects, could all be facilitated by the establishment of a framework of cooperation based on the need for a coherent curricular planning. Pre- and in-service teacher education could also acquire a more sharply focussed and supportive function, with opportunities for fruitful school and college interaction within such a local framework.

Having accepted the school as the originating base for curriculum development, a qualification ought immediately to be entered to the effect that such development cannot be wholly school sponsored or promoted. It has been unfashionable to consider LEAs as playing a comprehensive and positive role in curriculum development. The teaching professions in general, and schools in particular, have tended to keep LEAs at arm's length on curriculum matters; dialogue at this level has been mainly on the quantity of resources available or on the expansion of the educational structure rather than on curriculum content. By and large, LEAs have accepted this role and elected members in their Council Chambers have seldom concerned themselves with educational debates on the curriculum. This may partly explain why the advisory service in many LEAs has been insufficiently equipped or encouraged to exercise direct responsibility for curriculum development, and why advisers as a group have accepted a limited concept of their function.

However, if the argument up to this point is accepted, which envisages the school continuing to be an important initiating base for curriculum development and at the same time identifies the need to bring to bear on this development an influence wider than that of the individual school,[17] then the LEA becomes the logically appropriate agency to exercise a pivotal role in the future. To make this possible and effective, changes would undoubtedly be necessary not just in the attitude of the teaching profession but within LEAs themselves. As one example, the advisory service would need to be expanded and restructured so as to fit it for the more positively managerial role which, it is advocated, LEAs should play. Likewise the teaching profession would have to accept willingly the demands of a new partnership with the LEA in curriculum development, at the same time as it sought to utilize more fully its acknowledged expertise in this field.

In our view this would entail a new approach to the planning of curriculum development in that it would give LEAs, in association with their schools, a more decisive influence than in the past. The intention would be to ensure that whatever curriculum development is undertaken will be of lasting benefit to the schools. Appropriate formal machinery to make the new approach work would have to be devised. This might well provide for the establishment of a committee, representative of the teachers and all other educational bodies within a single authority, to have direct responsibility for all in-service training and curriculum development. As well as elected members, teachers and the professional staff of LEAs would be represented, along with universities and colleges of higher education within the area, members of HMI and, where appropriate, regional officers of the Schools Council or other national bodies. The professional interests involved should be such that the committee would be in a position to make a comprehensive and effective review of curriculum development.

A secondary but important function of such a body would be the systematic gathering of information on what is happening in schools by way of curriculum changes, sadly lacking up till now. From this basis of knowledge the new body would be able to take decisions on priorities for future curriculum development. In this way resources could be both more closely matched with development about to be undertaken and deployed more sensitively in relation to the known effectiveness of existing projects, since the machinery of assessment would be an integral part of the democratic machinery of planning and resource allocation. From the professional point of view, the possibility would be created of a more fruitful interaction amongst interested parties and of a greater balance between the zeal of universities and colleges for sponsoring research and development and the practical needs of schools. The advisory service would also have a more clearly focussed role, acting as a Taylorian[18] liaison officer between the head and governors of the school, concerned as they are with the specific implementation of local policy in a particular school, and the curriculum management committee with its broader strategic responsibility for planning and the allocation of resources. The adviser would also be the most important element in the data collection and assessment procedures referred to above. With the development of a strong corporate identity, a common framework of objectives within the broad parameters of the authority's policy, and the realization of a clearly defined and pivotal function, the status, influence and effectiveness of such a committee would quickly become established.

Finally, if such a pattern of curriculum planning were established throughout the education service, the long term national benefits to the quality and coherence of educational planning would be considerable. The aggregate of information and detailed knowledge available to the DES would enable education policy to contribute to the public expenditure decision process instead of largely responding to it passively in an annual succession of adjustments to its imposed constraints. The nature of planning in any field is just such a reciprocal process as has been outlined here, not merely the extrapolation and selection of 'targets' which have preoccupied the DES for too long. The far-reaching criticisms of two committees of the House of Commons are highly apposite here. The Price Committee[19] stated emphatically that 'the whole question of linking the output from higher education courses to any kind of manpower policy is far more complex than the DES appears to realise.' Accordingly the Department is recommended to assume a 'partnership' role in policy planning, improving its informational and liaison services. Direction is regarded as an inappropriate role in such a complex process; in any case it is a function in which 'the DES seems not to have been effective'.[20] The difficulties attached to curriculum planning in the school sector are no less complex. If this is recognized, a more positive and pragmatic approach to national education planning will be set in motion by implementing these kinds of prudent and cooperative arrangements for managing the curriculum at the local level. The advantages to schools and their pupils are evident.

## Notes

1 DES (1977) *A New Partnership for Our Schools: Report by a Committee of Enquiry* (Taylor Report), London, HMSO.
2 DES (1977) *Curriculum 11–16: A Contribution to the Current Debate*, London, HMSO, p. 4.
3 *Ibid.*, p. 5.
4 DES (1979) *Aspects of Secondary Education in England*, London, HMSO, p. 260.
5 See W.E. FORSTER's remarks during the Second Reading of the Endowed Schools Bill (Hansard, 15 March 1869, col. 1358): 'but we found generally that there was great difficulty in obtaining a good scientific education, such as might be obtained in Germany and France and that there were not many schools in the kingdom in which such an education could be procured.'
6 DES (1978) *Primary Education in England*, London, HMSO.
7 CLARE BURSTALL (1970) *French in the Primary Schools: Attitudes and Achievement*, Slough, NFER; (1974) *Primary French in the Balance*, Slough NFER.
8 DES (1978) *Special Educational Needs: Report of the Committee of Enquiry* (Warnock Report).
9 A. LITTLE and R.L. WILLIS (1981) *Multi-Ethnic Education: The Way Forward*, Schools Council Pamphlet, No. 18, and DES (1981) *West Indian Children in Our Schools: Interim Report of the Committee of Inquiry into the Education of Children from Ethnic Minority Groups*, Cmnd, 8273, London, HMSO.
10 J.G.R. TOMLINSON (1981) *The Schools' Council: A Chairman's Salute and Envoi*, address given to the British Association for the Advancement of Science, York, 1 September 1981.
11 It is instructive to consider the address of D.H. MORRELL at the annual meeting of the NFER on 24 October 1962. As joint head of the newly formed Curriculum Study Group in the Ministry of Education he proposed 'the active participation in some form or other of agencies other than the teachers, including central and local government' in order to achieve a more productive relation between society's 'vital interest in the content and purposes of education' and the teachers' 'individual responsibilities as trustees for the natural rights of individual children and their parents'. Sir William Alexander in his reply advocated a reconstituted SSEC in which the Ministry, LEAs and teachers would 'work in the fullest cooperation'. Cf. *Educational Research*, 5, 2, February 1963, pp. 83–103.
12 MINISTRY OF EDUCATION (1960) *Secondary Schools Examinations Other Than the GCE* (Beloe Report), pp. 33–5.
13 The diffuseness of research initiatives by the DES is still apparent in the *List of Current Educational Research Projects* issued by the DES in January 1982.
14 Reference here is to the penalty powers conferred upon the Secretary of State for the Environment by the Local Government, Planning and Land Act, 1980. Their restrictiveness will inhibit novelty, even more severely than existing features of the grant distribution system. Indeed, any objective measurement of needs, whether calculated by multiple regression analysis or upon whatever assumptions underlie Grant Related Expenditure (GRE), will necessarily be insensitive to expenditure plans arising from locally determined initiatives except in so far as they are already reflected in historic patterns of spending. To employ such calculation as a ceiling rather than a base for local spending decisions erects an additional barrier to change. Local discretion is a necessary condition of local initiative.
15 DES (1981) *The School Curriculum*, Circular 6/81, October.
16 DES (1981) *The School Curriculum*, March.
17 The Taylor Committee considered the views of a 'widely assorted group' of witnesses who were 'regarded as representative of the communities and wider society served by

the schools' and evidently sympathized with their claims 'to take some part in decisions about the school curriculum' (cf. paras 6.10, 6.14). Nor was the committee oblivious to the proper interests and increased responsibilities of LEAs which would result from the extension of participation in curricular decisions. 'Education departments may expect to have to treat the aims of the school curriculum, and the means to help schools to achieve them, as a priority' (para. 6.51).

18 Taylor Report, *op. cit*, para. 6.54.
19 'The Funding and Organization of Courses in Higher Education, Education, Science and Arts Committee' (1980) Vol. 1, Report, (HC 787–1), para. 36.
20 *Ibid.*, para. 48.

# Local Education Authority Advisers: Their Role and Future*

Ray Bolam
University of Bristol

This article sets out to review some of the main factors influencing the roles of advisers currently, and those which are likely to do so in the future. The article falls into five parts. First, some previous work in the field is briefly referred to and a guiding framework is outlined. Second, the inspectorial aspects of the role are considered. Third, the advisory aspects of the role are discussed. Fourth, some issues associated with the size and structure of advisory teams are explored. Finally, some of the implications of these developments are considered.

A 1979 study broadly confirmed the accounts of the adviser's role given by their professional association but also provided some additional, detailed information.[1] The majority of advisers in the fourteen LEAs studied were involved in staff appointments, advising individual teachers, advising on school-wide innovations, in-service training, advising on LEA-wide curriculum development work, the design of school buildings and equipment, teacher evaluation, school inspections and advising LEA administrators and various education committees and sub-committees.

About three-quarters of the advisers interviewed regarded a 'defender' strategy as relevant to their role in relation to educational change. Many instances were cited of advisers acting as a check to over-hasty innovation whether at subject, school or LEA level.

With some qualifications, most advisers in the sample saw themselves as facilitators of innovation but about one in three felt constrained from carrying out this role. Many examples were found of advisers playing a vital and multi-directional linkage role within their LEA to promote innovation. Area advisers were more likely than others to facilitate direct contact between schools as a strategy of innovation; advisers in 'low density' LEAs more likely to support innovation by provision of funds or facilities; advisers

---

* This is an edited version of the article which appeared in *Education 3–13*, 7., 1, 1979, pp. 37–42.

in 'high density' LEAs, chief and area advisers were more likely to innovate by influencing staff appointments. The existence of two clear strands in the work of advisers was also confirmed by the study. These strands may be represented diagrammatically (see Figure 1).

In the advisory or professional aspect of the role, the adviser draws upon his professional expertise to give advice to teachers and heads in schools. It is in this capacity that he also acts as the professional representative or even advocate of the teachers and schools in relation to the administration and policy makers at the local authority offices. In addition, however, the adviser also has an inspectorial or administrative aspect to his role. On the one hand, this involves him in interpreting, transmitting and implementing local authority policy decision relating to teachers and schools. On the other hand, it involves him in making evaluative judgements on the performance of teachers, heads and schools and in transmitting these judgments to the LEA.

This function is well-known but the views of advisers about the aspect which they most prefer to emphasize was less clear prior to this study. A comparison was made between the responses to four questionnaire items, two of which dealt with what were essentially advisory tasks and two of which dealt with inspectorial tasks.

> The contrast is very striking; 75% and 60% said that they actually spent a fair amount of time on, respectively, in-service training and advising individual teachers; whereas only 12% and 21% said so for school inspections and evaluation of teachers respectively. The contrast is even sharper when these figures are set alongside those for what the respondents would prefer to spend more time on: 38% want to spend more time on the two advisory tasks, on which so many of them were already spending a fair amount of time; but only 24% said so for the two inspectorial tasks. The principal exceptions were the chiefs and coordinators, both of whom were more likely than their junior colleagues to emphasise inspectorial tasks.

> On the basis of this evidence it seems reasonable to conclude that many of the advisers at present in post are likely to react unfavourably to demands that they should extend their inspectorial work. This conclusion also finds support in the reasons given by many respondents for joining the advisory service in the first place: these were largely to do with a desire to improve the system through the advisory role.

### The Inspectorial Aspects of the Role

The principal factors which influenced the inspectorial, administrative and policy-interpretation aspects of the advisory role in recent years may be summed up in one word: accountability. The reasons for the increased demands for accountability are broadly twofold: first, what may be regarded as a temporary reason, the need for economies and retrenchment following the 1973 financial crisis and the consequent demands from local politicians that severe cuts should be made in local authority spending on education. As far as advisers are concerned, this has often meant that they are asked to evaluate teachers, schools, teachers' centres, etc. using cost effectiveness criteria which they themselves consider inappropriate.

However, the longer-term reasons for demands for accountability are rooted in a concern about standards of teaching and learning as expressed for example in the Department of Education's 'Yellow Book', written to brief the Prime Minister before his major speech on education at Ruskin College in 1976.

At national level there have been a number of developments since the Ruskin speech. First there was the so-called 'Great Debate'. Second, and of more importance to primary teachers, was the publication of a report from HMIs who carried out a national survey of primary schools. Amongst other things this survey was severely critical of standards of achievement in science, geography and history although it did refute some of the criticism which had previously been levelled at the teaching of basic numeracy and literacy. Incidentally, it is worth noting that this survey also represents a shift in role, for HMI: they are now far more involved in the review of national educational standards than was the case some years ago. One of the principal problems about the role of advisers — their relationship to HMI — is being clarified because HMI seem now to be adopting a more distinctively inspectorial role.

The third national response to the concern over standards has been the establishment of the Assessment of Performance Unit. In an article in the spring 1978 issue of the advisers' professional association journal, Mr. D.T.E. Marjoram, Head of the Unit, said:

> The first APU survey reports will provide necessarily coarse-grain snapshots of national performance at 11 and 15 ... APU monitoring procedure is so designed that it will not be possible to identify the performances of individuals, schools or even LEAs — that is not the business of the Unit.

Figure 1

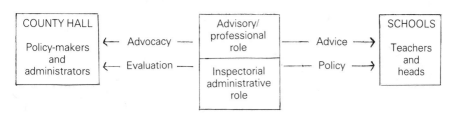

He went on to explore the implications of the APU for local authority advisers:

> In this task of developing a multi-level assessment system which coheres, inter-relates and produces the right information when and where it is needed anywhere in the education system, the role of inspectors and advisers could be a crucial one. There are local education authority inspectors and advisers on all the working groups of the APU — and on each of the exploratory working groups as well. The APU has already begun to receive helpful advice and views about its science discussion document from science advisers. But in spite of the APU's efforts to publicise its activities and to operate as openly as possible, there are still some teachers who are unaware of its existence. Indeed the leaflets provided for all schools have not yet reached some. Local advisers and inspectors are in a good position, if they so wish, to disseminate information of this kind and to coordinate the kind of constructive reactions from schools which could help to improve the monitoring programme over time.

There have also been responses to the concern over standards at local level. Perhaps the most dramatic example of this was the William Tyndale Junior School affair, in response to which the ILEA expressed a much clearer commitment to using its advisory team to inspect schools and teachers:

> The inspecting and reporting function is still an important one; historically the inspection function came first and members and officers have a right to expect sound advice and information so that they may do their own work properly. It is now proposed to maintain a basic annual programme of full inspections of about ten schools with one or two establishments of further and higher education. To this could be added extra full inspections or visitations as required. In addition it is intended to increase the number of occasions when a team of inspectors moves into a school to give it sustained attention over a period.

This local trend is confirmed by reports in *The Times Educational Supplement*. For example, in the outer London Borough of Hillingdon, two-week inspections of every school are reported as being carried out as part of a comprehensive scheme to monitor schools' work.

Other trends and factors connected with the administrative or policy interpretation role of advisers are also evident. First and foremost perhaps is the problem of managing the contraction of the teaching profession — a time-consuming, difficult and painful task. The second policy-oriented factor is the probable implementation of national policy arising from the Taylor Committee report on the government and management of schools.

This is bound to be a complex and protracted business, again involving a great deal of adviser time and calling for sensitive skills. A third policy development is really a continuation of one which has now been with us for some time: the problem of making all aspects of LEA work more accountable to the elected representatives. This is an inherently important political task which has, however, been thrown into sharper focus by the recent economic crisis and has been further complicated by the introduction of corporate management in many local authorities. This in turn has led to demands for cost effectiveness (for instance, of teacher centres) by departments outside education which, according to many advisers, do not understand the particular needs of education. These pressures are not likely to diminish and will no doubt continue to take up a great deal of advisers' time.

## The Advisory Aspects of the Role

The policy developments referred to in the previous section have been, on the whole, ones with distasteful and unpleasant consequences for teachers and thus have not been likely to improve adviser/teacher relationships. Other policy developments will be equally demanding in terms of time and energy but are less likely to have these less pleasant aspects. The principal ones at national level may well be mainly contextual developments as far as primary schools are concerned. For example, the introduction of a single examination at 16+ is likely following the Waddell Report and over the next five years the coordination of this innovation will involve a great deal of adviser time especially with respect to in-service training. Similar demands are likely to arise from the increasing attention now being paid to the 16–19 age-range and especially the transition from school to work.

However, there are also some policy developments which have more direct implications for primary advisers and primary schools. An obvious one is the implementation of the Warnock Report on Special Education. It is not yet entirely clear what this will actually involve for primary schools but there will be undoubtedly an impact and advisers will be directly involved.

What is quite clear is that the HMI Report on primary schools mentioned above will have direct consequences for primary schools and for advisers.

Thus, much will be expected of local advisers by way of generating enthusiasm and action at the local and school level, in response to the findings of HMI's survey.

All these developments, particularly the last, have considerable implications for in-service training. But in-service training is in itself a major development area in education, and, since many advisers see this as their principal contribution to the education service, they are bound to be in the forefront of this work.

It is certain that they will be centrally involved in developing induction

advisers in an authority is that there should be one to every 20,000 of the population. The research indicated that this was an unsatisfactory criterion: it takes no account of the differing problems of the adviser in a large rural area with difficult access to schools and it begs the question of what it is that an adviser does that requires this kind of numbers in a team. One alternative is to adopt the analogy of the teacher/pupil ratio and relate the number of advisers directly to the number of teachers in the LEA with an appropriate weighting for rural LEAs. We may reasonably argue that each adviser needs to make at least one contact per term of, say, one hour with each teacher for whom he has a responsibility. If we further assume that in a school year of about forty weeks, an adviser should spend half of his time on such contacts with teachers, then each adviser would have approximately 100 days available. If we further assume that the urban adviser can make approximately four and a half visits or contacts a day this argues that he should have a maximum loading of about 150 teachers. The equivalent calculation for a rural adviser leads to the conclusion that he should have a 100 teacher loading.

The precise assumptions and figures are of less importance here than the method adopted: i.e., to argue that a meaningful adviser role involves certain kinds of contacts, that only so many of these contacts are possible in a school year and that therefore the number of advisers required in an authority should be calculated accordingly. Although authorities differ considerably in the extent to which they provide advisory teams, this adviser/teacher formula would not necessarily lead to a dramatic increase in the number of advisers, at least in urban authorities.

Another aspect of advisory team organization which remains to be clarified is the increase in the numbers of people with related jobs. Advisory teachers, who are usually seconded for two or three years to the authority, teachers' centre wardens, college lecturers working on in-service training and most recently teacher tutors, are all working on the same broad tasks as advisers. The most effective contributions to be made by each of these are far from clear as yet. Another aspect which requires clarification is the most effective relative contributions of specialist subject advisers and general/subject advisers. The latter have a major responsibility for a group of schools in an area while the former usually do not.

### Conclusions

Most of what has been said earlier confirms the adviser's duality of role which was identified in the opening sections and also the dilemmas which this duality creates. The preference for advising over inspecting is also confirmed in the description above of advisers responding to demands for accountability and evaluation in terms of staff development and in-service training. Of course the advisers' central dilemma must not be exaggerated.

Most supervisory and managerial roles have this built-in conflict and advisers cope with it as well as any. Indeed many advisers argue that their administrative/inspectorial role is on balance a good thing because it means that their advice is listened to with greater respect.

The discussion on team size is not simply a logistic one. Impressionistic evidence suggests strongly that many teachers are either quite ignorant about LEA advisers (and are frequently unable to distinguish them from HMI) or are sceptical about their value. The provision of an advisory team based on the teacher-contact assumptions outlined above would surely strengthen the professional bonds of advisers and teachers by enabling them to meet and work together more meaningfully. In any case we lack adequate research knowledge about what teachers really do think of advisers and this should be put right as a matter of urgency.

Finally, it is worth noting one further trend of importance. The majority of advisers in the research sample had not had any formal preparatory or in-service training, yet they were unanimous in recommending that such training should be provided. Increasingly, advisers are taking in-service training as seriously for themselves as they are for teachers. Numerous examples could be quoted but one will suffice. In Liverpool an exercise in self-appraisal, which took as its initial focus the work of teachers and schools, developed into an intensive self-appraisal of the roles and training needs of the advisory team. Teachers should welcome this both because of its inherent importance and also because of what it indicates about the way advisers see their place in the profession.

## Notes

1 BOLAM, R. *et al.* (1979) *LEA Advisers and the Mechanisms of Innovation*, Slough, NFER Publishing Company.
2 SAVILLE, C. (1978) 'A local education authority's evaluation of in-service work', in McCABE, C. (Ed.), *The Evaluation of In-Service Education and Training in the UK*, Paris, OECD.
3 BIRCHENOUGH, M. (1976) 'The authority inspectorate: The present position and future developments', *Appendix to the ILEA Education Committee Agenda: Tuesday, 18 May*, London, ILEA.

# The LEA Adviser: Developing Roles

*Joan Dean*
*Surrey County Council*
*Advisory Service*

> A leader is best
> When people barely know that he exists,
> Not so good when people obey and acclaim him
> Worst when they despise him,
> Fail to honour people
> They fail to honour you
> But of a good leader who talks little,
> When his work is done, his aims fulfilled,
> They will say, 'We did it ourselves.'
> > Lao Tze, *The Way of life*

Jim Johnson left his home at 7.30 a.m., bound for a school at the most distant end of the county, where a new head was reputed to be making heavy weather of her first headship in a three-teacher school. Jim arrived as he had planned in time to have a word with the head and staff before school started and to watch the school day beginning. He noted an improvement in the appearance of the school, with children's work much in evidence and after morning assembly, to which children contributed a good deal, he was able to see the teachers at work and have a brief word with each. He then talked with the head over a mid-morning coffee about the parental complaints which had come to the education office.

The head, who had clearly done a good deal in the term she had been in the school and was anxious to do well, was upset about the complaints. Jim did his best to reassure her and suggested that it was not unusual for parents to be worried about changes which they did not understand. He commented on how much she had achieved in the short time she had been in the school and went on to discuss possible ways of explaining what was happening to parents.

In the course of the visit, Jim noted a number of pointers to the way the head saw herself working and was able to make some suggestions which seemed to be useful. He promised to arrange some visits to other schools for the staff and to come to talk to parents about more up-to-date approaches in the not too distant future. He managed to leave the head feeling that here was a friend who would be willing to help when things got difficult.

He left the school at about 11.15 and went on to the county's largest comprehensive to have lunch with the head and the head of the intake year to discuss plans for liaison with local middle schools. Jim was able to speak with fairly close knowledge of the four main contributory schools and could draw on experience of a number of patterns of liaison between primary and secondary schools in different parts of the county. He was thus able to add other ideas to those put forward, extend some of the school's ideas and help them to work out in practical terms how they would implement them.

The rest of the afternoon was spent in a neighbouring first and middle school where the governors were interviewing candidates for a scale 2 appointment of a teacher to be responsible for the first school section. The field was a poor one and, after helping the governors and head to interview the three candidates, Jim suggested that the post should be readvertized. The head, whose strength was with older children, was worried about the interregnum and felt he would rather have the best of those interviewed than wait. After a good deal of discussion it was agreed that there should be another attempt to get the right person. Jim promised to try to find a suitable supply teacher for the following term. He also had a word with each of the candidates, offering some feedback on the interview performance of each and making appropriate suggestions about preparing for appointment to a post of this kind.

His next call was the area office, where he was based. Here he spent half an hour looking at post and messages which had come in. He managed to deal with some of the letters and left a note to his part-time secretary about what to do with some of the others. He noted that the piles in his filing tray and in-tray were getting uncomfortably high and he hoped there was nothing urgent at the bottom.

At 6 he was due to run a course at the Teachers' Centre for teachers in middle schools who were coordinating work in language. This was the third meeting of this group which was to be devoted to formulating a school language policy. He had a number of examples to show them and had copies of a paper suggesting areas which a language policy might be expected to cover. After a brief introduction the course members divided into small groups, each working on a different aspect of the list Jim had prepared. At the end of the evening there was enough work from each group to make the basis of a statement for all the members of the group. Jim agreed to tidy the work up and get it typed and duplicated for distribution.

This is not untypical of a day in the life of many advisers, and it gives a clear indication of some of the ways in which advisers may be leading and influencing. In the first school he visited Jim was seeking ways of supporting and helping a new head and his main aim was to create a good relationship between himself and the head, making her feel that she could turn to him in difficult situations.

His role in the secondary school was somewhat different. Here he was mainly helping the teachers concerned to develop their thinking by listening, commenting on the viability of their ideas and adding to and extending them. His influence in this context was likely to be very subtle, exercised by the way he reacted and responded to the teachers involved and the emphasis he placed on the different ideas discussed.

At the interviews he was able to bring a wider experience of the state of the job market and the possibility of finding better candidates for a particular job. This eventually convinced the others involved that it would be worth waiting. They might have continued to disagree with him however, and in that situation he would need to abide by their decision unless it was likely to be quite disastrous. He also probably exercised some influence in what he said to the candidates. What is said in the emotional aftermath of an interview is often important to those concerned.

What kind of leadership is appropriate to the advisory role? A leader's ability to lead must be judged by the extent to which other people have acted as a result of his leadership. It is sometimes possible to see a very direct result of the leadership role of a particular adviser in some of the things happening in classrooms in a particular authority, much as one can sometimes see what programmes are being put out in school broadcasting from the material around in primary classrooms at any given time. This is only of lasting value, however, if it actually enables a teacher to think things through for him or herself and see where what is being offered fits into his or her own thinking.

Advisers, like teachers and headteachers, have different working styles. A few depend on a charismatic personality to stimulate enthusiasm. This can have a tremendous impact on those in contact with such an adviser, and may make a lasting impression. It carries the danger that teachers simply imitate a style which is not their own. A rather different style is to try to offer a variety of approaches and ideas and to try to help teachers to select from them. This is less dramatic, although it still demands enthusiasm in putting over ideas, but the approach in the end may have a lasting effect because each teacher chooses and makes his own what seems to him to be appropriate. Both of these approaches and all those in between can be used effectively. Each adviser, like each teacher, has to decide on the best way of working for him or herself.

There are many odd things about the advisory role. Teachers are understandably ambivalent about advisers. Sometimes they complain that they never see an adviser, and in the next breath complain that there are too many advisers. While they are aware in theory that advisers have a role *vis-à-vis* administrative officers and councillors in an authority, they often talk as if the work of the adviser were only that which is visible in schools. Administrators occasionally take this view in reverse. A teacher's or an administrator's opinion of the value of advisers depends considerably on the advisers he has met and worked with.

There is an element of conflict built into the advisory role in being at once the friendly neighbourhood adviser and at the same time being involved in inspection, dealing with failure and with interviews and promotion. Yet if advisers are not involved in these activities the good work done by teachers in classrooms seems less likely to be recognized and there is also value for a teacher in having someone in addition to the head who knows his work. Even when the pressure on the advisory service is such that advisers have very little time to spend with teachers in classrooms the alternatives to involving advisers seem to be even less satisfactory. The important thing is that the adviser is aware of the problems of his role and makes allowances for them.

Being an adviser is an impossible job. No one ever does it to anywhere near his own satisfaction. You need to be able to live with a permanently guilty conscience about what you haven't time to do. In addition, each group of people with whom you work, teachers, heads, administrators and others, sees only part of your work and when you are unable to do what they request is inclined to blame you.

The view of the leadership role of the adviser from the school or classroom is often somewhat different from the reality. It sometimes comes as a surprise to someone entering the service, especially if he comes from a headship, to realize that not only is he likely to have to work in poor conditions with fewer holidays, longer hours, a shared secretary, if there is one at all, a shared office and a scramble for a place to park, but that he is really what the title implies — an adviser, even if he is called an inspector. He is not a decision-maker. He advises others to make wise decisions but they are perfectly within their rights to ignore his advice and indeed they sometimes do, although there are situations where the adviser comes with the full strength of the employer behind him, where he is making demands which must be met. These are comparatively rare, however, and for most of his time an adviser must work by persuasion, and his power to influence has to be won. It isn't until you have been in the post sometime that you begin to see that the influence of an adviser is a subtle one and much nearer the view put forward in the poem quoted at the beginning of this paper, although perhaps not quite so self-effacing.

When you first become an adviser, you establish your credibility on the basis of the experience you bring to the job and this may determine initially how teachers respond to what you say. Unless you go on from this point, however, recognizing that there are skills peculiar to advisory work and many good ways of teaching a class, running a department or a school, you will cease to maintain your credibility and will have little influence on what is happening. You may be a superb teacher and initially teachers may be impressed if you demonstrate your ability to handle 4Z, but unless you can help a teacher with a quite different style to develop ways of working which are suitable for him, you are doing no more than establishing that you know what you are talking about. You still have to demonstrate that you have something to say.

The adviser's task is to assess what he finds and to seek ideas and suggestions which fit the situation and the style of the teachers with whom he is working. He needs to be able to see with their eyes, recognize the validity of goals other than his own and build knowledge of varied ways of doing things. He then begins to have something to offer and may be able to influence people towards new or extended goals which they hadn't previously considered.

When an adviser can do this, teachers begin to listen to him and take seriously what he has to say. Some of the best advisers can identify with each teacher to the point where the teacher sees the adviser's thinking as an extension of his own and may not recognize the help that he is receiving.

Advisers influence what happens through the responsibilities they carry. While the role differs somewhat from one LEA to another and individual advisers interpret their role differently, most services are concerned with advising, on the one hand, the Chief Education Officer and his administrative colleagues and through them the education committee and, on the other hand, the schools and other educational establishments of the authority. Advice to the LEA normally covers the following:

1 The quality of the education being offered in the educational establishments for which the authority is responsible, including aspects of the service of teachers;
2 Relevant aspects of the organization of education within the area covered by the authority, e.g., the viability of schools of different sizes, the effects of alternative ways of making provision, etc.;
3 The service and deployment of teachers. This normally includes making recommendations about the termination of the probationary period, advice on teachers who are candidates for promotion, and advice on teachers who are failing. It also normally includes some involvement in making appointments, both in advising on short lists and in helping to interview candidates;
4 The building, furnishing and equipping of schools. This is now a much smaller part of the work of most advisers but there is still work to be done in deciding on the best way of using the money available;
5 Curriculum development and in-service education;
6 Advice on a range of specific problems. Many of the complaints and difficulties of an educational nature, which come to the notice of the authority, are likely to be referred to the advisory service.

The implications of these demands for advisers are considerable. If the LEA is to have a proper picture of the state of its establishments, the advisory service needs to have an overview of what is happening which is seen to be valid. This means that advisers must spend time collecting and studying evidence of what is happening. For example, many LEAs are now collecting evidence of the curriculum followed by each school and the way in which it is deploying staff. While the process of collection may be done by others, the advisory service has an important role in helping to interpret this information. Statistics are rarely what they seem in so complex an activity as education and they need to be assessed by someone with a wide knowledge of the schools to which they refer.

Curriculum information and information about deployment of staff says nothing about the quality of education. Yet at present concern with quality is going hand in hand with cuts in provision. The advisory service has a much more important role here than is sometimes recognized. It is the adviser who can be at hand when such decisions are being made, although the problems may be such that his or her advice cannot be sufficiently heeded. Nevertheless, if an adviser has succeeded in convincing his administrative colleagues and councillors of his knowledge and integrity, his advice is likely to be influential.

In a number of LEAs advisers have made studies of different aspects of curriculum, looking at the overall quality of work, at some of the effects of policy and budget decisions and at where the problems are most worrying. Such studies not only provide administrators and councillors with information, but also provide the advisory service itself with information which can help to determine its priorities.

Most advisory teams also have a role as inspectors. This is in most places fairly limited because the demands of the follow-up work from any one inspection are such that few services have the manpower to cope with it. In this the differences between the role of advisers and HMI are evident, since HMI have no responsibility to follow up inspection with plans for action; indeed, recent legislation places this responsibility on the LEA. Self-evaluation may go some way towards replacing inspection, although there must still be a place for moderating and monitoring self-assessment reports, and there will always be situations where an authority needs an expert view on the state of a school. It must also be said that you cannot really advise without inspecting, since your advice must relate to what is already happening.

The education service in many places is once again concerned with reorganization. This time falling school rolls are making many schools much smaller than before and advisers are not only concerned with offering advice to the LEA on school size, but are often concerned with helping to deal with the effects of reorganization, bringing schools together, interviewing teachers for newly created amalgamated schools and trying to arrange redeployment for others.

Advisory services in nearly all authorities are involved with head-teachers in assessing whether teachers have completed their probationary period satisfactorily and with doing what they can to support probationers.

In most LEAs the advisory service is involved with headteachers in providing professional assessment of teachers applying for promotion. Advisers are also normally present at interviews for senior posts in schools, including headships, and are very often present at other interviews, depending on the time they have available and their own priorities. At head of department level, the specialist adviser should be able to complement the contribution of the head in the specialist area. At the headship and deputy headship level, the adviser will probably work more closely with whoever is appointed than anyone else and should also know the school as an educational institution. His knowledge should thus be complementary to that of governors and administrators.

An advisory service normally advises heads and teachers on the following:

1 The internal organization of schools and other establishments, including advice and help on staff deployment and other management issues;

2 Curriculum. This may be the responsibility of the general or the phase adviser who will be concerned with the overall view or with the specialist subject adviser, who will be concerned with the work of teachers and departments;

3 Resources. An advisory service should be able to offer advice to heads and teachers on the use of resources and on books, materials and equipment relevant to different aspects of work. He should know the market in his own area of work and be able to discuss the merits of different materials often from experience of having seen them in use elsewhere;

4 Staff development. The development of the work of all teachers is a major responsibility which advisers share with heads and senior staff. The adviser's responsibility may be exercised through development within the individual school or college or through formal provision of in-service courses and other opportunities;

5 Advice on specific problems. These are likely to be largely educational problems and very often concern relationships or problems of teacher performance;

6 Community relationships. This includes help in making liaison with contributory schools and institutions and schools to which pupils transfer. It also includes relationships with parents and with employers and with the wider community.

The advice offered will depend on the experience, knowledge and skill of the individual adviser and also on his particular view of education, his goals and objectives and ideas about how these are best achieved. It should also depend on his ability to see from the point of view of those he is trying to advise. In the end his effectiveness will depend on the extent to which teachers find his advice acceptable.

An advisory service exercises leadership and influence in various ways. Advisers work to some extent in isolation and need to be self-starters. Even where there are many pressures an adviser has a good deal of freedom to work as seems best to him. There is therefore a subtle and hidden form of leadership in the choices an adviser makes about his priorities and the way he uses his time. Some of these choices are to do with an adviser's style and some are to do with his own underlying aims and objectives.

An adviser influences through his activities. Probably the most important of these are his visits to schools and other establishments. At schools level, the adviser's influence may be exercised through observation of teachers at work, advice on curriculum, organization, resources, through discussion with teachers and headteachers, through working parties and study groups, through in-service provision and in many other ways. He may be able to influence probationers, especially where he is able to spend time with them, and he may have an important role in helping teachers who are failing in some way. An adviser is often asked for career advice by teachers and he has undoubted influence in his role as adviser to heads and governors on appointments and promotions.

Advisers exercise leadership through their involvement in teacher education of all kinds, including both school-based and other in-service work, publications and papers for teachers, and development through working parties and study groups, as well as through work in classrooms with individual teachers.

Attendance at courses is only a small part of what is normally involved in professional development. The most important development for a teacher is very often through his or her experience in the classroom and through involvement with colleagues within the school. Courses and other in-service activities make a major contribution to this school-based development, but their value depends a good deal on how far the teacher who has attended a course is able to use what has been learned back in school.

The adviser plays a part in teacher development at many levels. He sees teachers at work in the classroom and reflects their performance for them, perhaps asking questions and offering comment which may help a teacher to extend what he is doing or see it from a new perspective. The adviser may simply encourage a teacher and reassure him. Or he may be able to provide ideas and developments and suggest schools where they may be seen in action. Where the advisory service is sufficiently well-staffed for teacher and adviser to know each other well, this reflection on performance becomes a dialogue, with the teacher using the adviser as a sounding board for ideas and someone to help with evaluating the success of particular activities. It is important for this kind of relationship not to be seen as threatening but as dialogue between professional partners. It is a relationship which is particularly important at a time when teacher morale is low. Encouraging comments by an adviser may be very important to a teacher who is finding life depressing and difficult.

The adviser works with the head and senior staff of the school, providing in a similar way a sounding board and an opportunity for them to reflect on performance and talk over problems. In this context the adviser may be seen as someone not personally involved, who may therefore be able to discuss difficulties in a disinterested way.

Part of the contribution of the adviser at school level may be advice on management. Training for senior staff in school is much discussed at the present time and in a number of LEAs opportunities are offered, sometimes involving providers of in-service training from colleges of further or higher education, as well as making provision from within the service using experienced heads and advisers.

Whatever the training offered, there is still a need to help senior staff in schools to apply their knowledge and skill to the particular situation in the particular school, and a good advisory service should be able to help with this. This is not a matter of saying 'this is how to do it' but of talking through the various aspects of the job under consideration and examining together some of the alternative ways in which something can be done. In this situation the adviser should bring knowledge of how things are done in many schools to add to the in-depth knowledge of the particular school which is the province of the particular head or senior member of staff.

Another important role for the adviser is in helping schools to recognize the learning and development possibilities for teachers in dealing with day-to-day tasks and plans and problems. Almost any aspect of school life offers learning opportunities for teachers as well as children. One way of providing this is to spread responsibilities very widely, with some offered on a temporary basis to give a teacher an opportunity to learn about another job for development.

Similar opportunities are often available in tackling particular developments or problems. The choice of new materials, the tackling of a new curriculum topic or the problem of helping children to make better use of the library, and many similar topics, provide the opportunity for the inexperienced teacher to work with the experienced teacher to consider what is needed. An adviser may sometimes be able to help a school to see such opportunities.

Advisers may also lead thinking and at the same time provide in-service opportunities of a rather different kind by involving experienced teachers in working and study groups, with the group perhaps providing ideas and material for use across the schools of an authority or studying areas of work where more knowledge and information is needed. Such groups may, of course, form within a school, but the adviser has the benefit of knowing people from a number of schools and can bring them together and, in a sense, orchestrate the group.

The adviser also has a leadership role in the provision of in-service education per se, and his influence on the in-service programme and the way a particular course is run is very important. He can complement the

167

knowledge of in-service needs which a group of teachers may have with knowledge of the needs of a wider group. He may also see needs which teachers haven't yet recognized for themselves because they only become evident when one sees many schools.

To undertake this work the adviser needs knowledge and skills. He needs to know a great deal about the education service and become familiar with work in schools at all levels. Even where he is a phase specialist, he should know about other phases and where the work of his own phase fits in. An adviser, particularly when he is new in post, needs to recognize the importance of learning not only from advisory colleagues but also from heads and teachers and children.

Over the last twenty years or so the advisory teams have changed radically. They have become larger and more representative of the curriculum. Many now have much more structure, with designated leadership and advisers as far as possible for most subjects of the curriculum and all phases. Cuts have made some inroads into advisory staffing, but there is still the view that main subjects need to be represented.

One important development is the recognition in some LEAs that just as heads are not fully prepared for their headship role by the experience which has gone before, so advisers do not come into the service knowing all they need to know. They need skills in observing the interaction between teachers and pupils and between head and staff; they need a rather different view of the current state of knowledge in their specialism, whether subject or phase or other, and a working knowledge of the rest of the curriculum at each stage; they may need knowledge of school design and building, and need not only the ability to read and use plans but must be able to relate this to what they know about schools. They need to know what is involved in the different skills of managing a school, whether as head or senior member of staff, as well as knowing a great deal about possible ways of doing things in the classroom.

Most advisers have a good deal to learn about the way local government works and how to get things done in the particular office in which they find themselves. They often have to learn about the attitudes of elected members and the way to present reports and ideas in the rather different context of the education office and committee room.

There is also learning about the way the law works in education, about what conforms with LEA policy and about how to deal with problems of many kinds. It is easier to acquire this kind of knowledge in a situation where your professional colleagues have a responsibility to help you to learn and are ready to help you to think through problems and plan for action.

Perhaps the most difficult thing about advisory work is that results are not always easy to recognize and it is very slow coming to fruition. Much of the adviser's work is hidden. No one except those concerned sees the counselling offered to a head or teacher with a problem and no one except those concerned can make a judgement about how useful it was.

Advisers contribute differently from the head or the administrator. They have a knowledge of what goes on inside classrooms which is unique and which is an essential background for many aspects of work at LEA and at school level. We need to make the most of this.

A good adviser needs to be an enthusiast of a particular kind and he needs to be optimistic enough to go on being enthusiastic when progress is slow. He should be a source of inspiration for many teachers, finding good things in unlikely places and stirring and stimulating and enlarging the experience of the teacher.

# 4
## The Schools

# Introduction

While effective leadership in the administrative, system-wide sectors of the educational system of England and Wales is important, there can be no doubt that effective leadership of the implementation sector is crucial to the survival, maintenance and development of educational provision. Therefore within this section papers have been commissioned and chosen which fully reflect the trends in leadership action and thought in this sector during the last few years.

The broad scene is set in an original paper by Lynton Gray and Nigel Bennett, who apply themselves to examining the likely role of the governing bodies of our schools in the light of recent central government initiatives. They suggest three scenarios. First, schools may become increasingly politicized and heads will be required to take on the role of power-brokers and conciliators. Secondly, governing bodies could become analogous to a council, with the head as chief executive, a measure which would encourage centralization of power and influence. Thirdly, they suggest that the governing bodies become the agents of the local authority, planted firmly within the structure of the school and therefore able to enforce LEA policy decisions with greater vigour than at present. Only time will tell which one, or more, becomes the archetype.

The next two papers attempt to tease out some of the leadership functions of a headteacher. The contribution by V. McGeown is the result of an extensive research study. Among other things it highlights the discrepancies between the reported actual behaviour of heads and the expectations expressed by teachers. Combined with the clear wish of teachers to be involved in decision-making, school leadership is therefore shown to require much more subtle behaviour than might at first sight be expected. This point is reiterated in the original contribution by David Winkley which shows how the concept of school leadership has changed with changing political circumstances. He advocates an increase in the autonomy of schools, based on the already greatly developed professionalism of teachers.

The other seven papers in this section examine specific leadership characteristics, roles and functions within schools. Paul Harling considers the pressures from inside and outside the school which have forced the primary school headteacher, for better or worse, into a position of great power and responsibility, which he can choose to delegate, or not, as the case may be.

Delegation within a carefully structured framework is the theme of Colin King's contribution concerning the secondary headteacher's leadership of the school. The problems of a deputy are again highlighted in the paper by P.R. Owen, M. Davies and A. Wayment in their search for a role for the deputy during a series of recent vacancies for such posts.

The responsibilities which are delegated to a head of department form the substance of the two papers by Nicholas Tyldesley and R.G. Bloomer. The first of these attempts to redefine the role of the head of department in terms of interpersonal relationships. The author sheds great light on the difficulties inherent in the traditional form of job specification and suggests that such formalistic lists hide a large number of equally important, but difficult to measure, activities which are of benefit to self, staff and school.

As a corollary to this original paper, the article by R.G. Bloomer reports the results of a workshop which attempted to summarize some of the characteristics of departmental leadership which are desirable in a thinking, developing school.

However, leadership is not always in the hands of designated leaders, as the original article by David Reynolds and Steve Murgatroyd and the supplementary one by Simon Pratt clearly show. Both examine ways in which the 'chalk-face' workers of our profession are able to influence and 'lead' designated decision-makers along paths which may be more suitable reflections of the real needs of the school.

# Educational Leadership and the School Governing Body

*Lynton Gray*
*and*
*Nigel Bennett*
*Anglian Regional Management Centre*

A book on educational leadership written a decade ago would have been most unlikely to have included a chapter on governing bodies. However, recent changes in the composition and duties of governing bodies as a result of legislation and government circulars have created expectations that school governors should begin to exercise a leadership function in primary and secondary education, and a new educational industry has emerged producing handbooks, manuals, courses of study and other forms of training to help school governors perform effectively in this new role. It is, perhaps, a little premature to seek to demonstrate the impact of these changes on the education service. It is certainly too soon to be able to explore the patterns of leadership behaviour and leadership style which it is appropriate for school governors to adopt.

The changes of the last ten years, designed to clarify and extend the role and authority of governing bodies, have paradoxically succeeded in confusing the source and legitimation of their authority by laying on them tasks which they cannot perform without making it difficult, if not impossible, for LEA and central government to discharge the duties and powers created by statute. This chapter will therefore attempt to trace the development of this paradox, and then explore some of the potential consequences of attempts by governing bodies to exercise this nascent leadership function.

Governing bodies, like so many aspects of British public life, can be traced back to the Victorian era. They began as a means of channelling state aid into schools when government grants were introduced in the 1830s. As state investment in elementary education increased through the nineteenth century, other bodies and organizations were created to raise, disburse and receive accounts for the spending of public money on the education of children during the years of compulsory schooling. The Acts of Parliament under which these developments occurred laid down the roles of governing bodies and boards in very general terms, and there was therefore great scope for the development of variety between sectors and districts. It was the 1944 Act which sought to create some form of standard practice through the five clauses on managing and governing bodies, and this thrust of ministry policy was continued in the subsequent Model Instruments and Articles by which LEA practice was influenced for the next thirty years. These did not iron out all the variations, however. One major difference was between those authorities which established governing bodies for each school and those which worked with one central body to govern all schools. Baron and Howell (1974) have charted the variations to be found, and they have pointed out that the political colour of the authority was not a major determinant of such variations.

A further development of governing bodies occurred as a result of the wholesale reorganization of local government which followed the Bains Report (1972). New LEAs required new instruments and articles for their governing bodies, and opportunities were taken to make some alterations. Most common was the inclusion of parent representatives, in response to the growing visibility and vociferousness of pressure-groups such as CASE (the Campaign for State Education) and NAGM (the National Association of Governors and Managers). It was at the same time that a small number of local authorities embraced a far more democratic approach to the appointment of governing bodies (for a discussion of Sheffield's experience, which is probably the best known, see Bacon, 1978), in line with views on participatory democracy fashionable at the time. This pressure to create greater participation in government was a major contributor to the decision in 1975 to establish the Taylor Committee to review the arrangements for managing and governing schools, and influenced strongly its final Report (DES, 1977), with its radical proposals for restructuring and changing the responsibilities of governing bodies.

The Taylor Report's recommendations rested on the belief that governing bodies should 'stand in the direct line of formal responsibility' between LEA and school (Taylor Report, 3.15), so that governing bodies could determine the lines on which individual schools would be run. This was seen, in the words of the Report's title, as a 'new partnership' for schools. It was too radical for either major political party to swallow whole, and those parts of the Report which have become government policy have done so piecemeal. Primary school 'managers' have been transmogrified; LEAs are to end grouped governing bodies; provision is made for parent and teacher representatives to sit on governing bodies; and DES Circular 6/81 has made more explicit the responsibilities of governing bodies in the field of the curriculum and in reviewing school policy. In the wake of the 1980 Education Act, a new round of revision for instruments and articles of government has commenced.

The articles of government under which governing bodies of the late 1970s were operating provided extensive if unspecified and normally unused powers. The revisions required by the 1980 Education Act have provided an opportunity to extend and specify those powers more precisely. As indicated above, one direction in which that extension could be taken is signposted by DES Circular 6/81, which provides direct encouragement for governing bodies to take a more active leadership role in school affairs.

At the same time as these changes have been made in the governance provisions, other significant developments have occurred in society at large. The basis of accountability upon which the Taylor Report was predicated was in all essentials supportive of schools, teachers and the education service. However, a speech by James Callaghan at Ruskin College, Oxford, in 1976 had launched a new spirit of criticism of schools and teachers in which the 'de facto' autonomy of teachers over the curriculum was challenged, and the ability of schools as currently constituted to meet the demands of industrial (or post-industrial) society questioned. Economic stagnation followed by recession and slump produced unprecedentedly high levels of unemployment, including very high levels of youth unemployment: schools were blamed for the unemployability of their products. This new climate led observers of the education scene away from the rhetoric of participatory democracy towards other ways of restricting and controlling the 'professional autonomy' which the teachers had captured after the Second World War. New ways were sought of making schools' provision more 'relevant'. Resources were cut severely, partly under the excuse of demographic contraction, and partly as a consequence of a government wish to 'roll back the frontiers' of government spending. Education vouchers have surfaced intermittently, but with growing frequency, as a possible means of enhancing the schools' responsiveness to parental pressure — and of increasing central control over the education service (Bennett and Gray, 1983). While the Department of the Environment and the Treasury tighten Whitehall's control over local authority spending, the Department of Employment and its Manpower Services Commission are intervening increasingly openly in schools, providing additional resources, including computers, and establishing pilot schemes for vocational education in schools. Meanwhile, the entire thrust of DES policy has been towards a more centralized control of curriculum planning.

It is not easy to determine where governing bodies fit in to these developments, nor indeed to be sure where they are intended by central government's policy-makers to fit in. It is clear that what has been in many respects a remarkable era in state education in England and Wales is drawing to a close — an era in which the teachers captured control of decision-making about the central activities of schools, the curriculum. It was the intention of the creators of the 1944 Act to discourage close local authority control of the curriculum through the clauses and subsequent model articles concerning governing bodies (Baron and Howell, 1974). Central government control had been discredited since the days of payment by results. Now the Ministry of Education's White Paper (Cmnd 6523/1944) explained that under the forthcoming Act 'the governors would have general direction of the conduct and curriculum of the school' within the local education authority's responsibility for the 'general educational character' of the school. This statement was repeated in the Ministry's Model Articles and in LEA articles of government and management up and down the country. In practice, the teachers took advantage of the vacuum thus accidentally created, and hijacked curriculum control. Governors' interests were channelled into 'towels and toilets' or, once parent and teacher representatives joined governing bodies, into the pseudo-participation described dismissively by Sallis (1977) as 'playing mothers and fathers'. Any attempt by non-educators, including civil servants and LEA administrators, to enter the curriculum's 'secret garden' was strenuously resisted by teacher associations. Thus the DES attempt to introduce a curriculum body in the early 1960s was transformed into the teacher union-controlled Schools Council as the price of its not being aborted altogether (Lawton, 1980). Consequently, the next major foray of the DES into the curriculum field, in the wake of Callaghan's Ruskin speech, asked LEAs what controls and policies they had over their schools' curricula (Circular 14/77), and found, not unexpectedly, few or none. The DES report (DES, 1979) makes only a brief reference to governing bodies (para. 7), recognizing that their curricular responsibilities 'are often in practice devolved upon the headteacher and staff.' We would wonder how many governing bodies knew they had exercised such devolution — indeed, if this is devolution, could not the transfer of funds from a bank vault into the robbers' swag-bag be interpreted similarly?

Since 1979 the DES has made a number of attempts to redress what it sees as an imbalance of power over the curriculum; these have revealed the wide variety of attitudes of distrust which characterize all parties' perceptions of each other. Thus the initial takeover bid by the civil servants (DES, 1980) was howled down by teachers and their associations and local councillors and their associations in a rare show of unanimity. Subsequent central government effusions have included the HMI's more reasoned *A View of the Curriculum*, and DES Circular 6/81 (of which more below). These and their responses leave the impression that each group — DES, LEAs and teachers — regards itself as the only group appropriate to exercise control over the school curriculum. Teachers claim to have an exclusive understanding of its full complexity, and argue that it is their 'professional' preserve, just as medical practice is the 'professional' preserve of the doctor. Local authorities resist any notion of central government dictation, while central government seems to fear the development of excessive local variations, especially those which derive from 'political extremism' — always of the other political colour, of course! But just as teachers and LEAs united against the DES in 1980, so central and local government appear united in their unwillingness to allow unfettered teacher control of the curriculum to continue. Alternative forms of control are therefore being sought. Circular 6/81 has already been referred to. Its eight brief paragraphs declare that governing bodies 'have a valuable role to play in bringing together the views of teachers, parents and the local community', and, in partnership with the head and other teachers, parents and the local community, 'securing a planned and coherent curriculum within the schools' (para. 4). LEAs are enjoined to consult governors and teachers about their policy-making and review procedures as they affect the curriculum (para. 5), while the Secretary of State 'looks to governors to encourage their schools ... to develop their curricula ... and to cooperate with the local education authorities in the action which they take' to introduce curriculum planning.

However, even as the DES offered this encouragement to governing bodies on the one hand, it complicated the situation on the other through further provisions of the 1980 Act. This altered the composition of governing bodies of all schools, while not establishing the line-management relationship between governing bodies and local authority advocated by the Taylor Report. Consequently, it is by no means clear to whom governing bodies are answerable. Working on minimum numbers of governors as laid down by the provisions of Section 2 of the 1980 Act, the LEA will nominate two out of a minimum of five and a maximum of eight, depending on size of school, sector and the decision of the headteacher, who has the option of being a governor. Thus Parliament clearly intended that local authorities should not be able to dictate terms to school governing bodies. However, while articles of government typically make governing bodies responsible to the authority for the exercise of the school curriculum, it is the authority which is charged with control of the curriculum under section 23 of the 1944 Education Act. As long as membership of governing bodies was controlled by the local authority, there was no problem. Now, however, members of the governing body owe their position to other sources of influence, as elected representatives of the school staff or of the parent body. There may also be a representative of the local district council, which can be of a different political complexion from the LEA.

In other ways, too, the responsibilities of school governing bodies are both clear and confusing. Articles of government will typically require governing bodies to submit special requests for funds to the authority on behalf of the school. This allows the authority to carry out its duty of providing sufficient education under section 8 of the 1944 Act. But does this mean that the prime responsibility of the governors is to the authority, whose money they seek to spend, or to the school, whose provision they seek to maintain and improve?

Once again, the diverse sources of legitimacy which underpin individual governors' membership of the governing body make the answer far from clear-cut. There is no obvious answer to the question, on whose behalf governing bodies should exercise educational leadership.

So although governing bodies are being enjoined to exercise educational leadership, it is not clear on whose behalf or in what direction they should do so. Examination of the membership and composition of governing bodies reveals other obstacles to the exercise of effective leadership. Who are the LEA representatives? Traditionally, they are appointed by the ruling political group. Commonly they are elected members or aspiring party workers who are acquiring some public body experience prior to gaining nomination for a ward seat. In most cases, these will be the only governors who will have experience of sitting on other schools' bodies, an experience which can give them an edge over their governor colleagues when discussing appropriate forms of action in response to most educational circumstances. However, it would be naive to look to ambitious local politicians for active leadership in circumstances where this involved going beyond the simple endorsement and implementation of council policies. While the presence on a governing body of a cadre of senior councillors, with political 'pull' and the consequent ability to make a forceful case for recognizing a particular school's needs, could gain for a school some relative advantage over others, the number of such councillors is limited. Frequently restrictions are placed upon the number of governorships an individual can hold. Politicians have, in any case, recognized the tensions which could be generated between council and governing bodies if the latter flex their muscles, and the controlling political party of most local councils take steps to ensure majority group representation on governing bodies. The optimism of the Society of Education Officers, that not only is there no provision that LEA governors shall constitute a majority of the body, but 'it is very unlikely that they would ever do so' (Brooksbank and Revell, 1981) does not seem borne out by events.

Nor is it likely that teacher and parent representatives on governing bodies can normally establish decisive leadership. Teachers will usually represent professional opinions in supporting the headteacher and in explaining educational policies and terminologies to lay members. Parent representatives have few opportunities of gaining knowledge of schools other than the one for which they are elected as governor, and the prospects for drawing on support of those they represent is limited. LEA officials, acting as clerks for governing bodies, can establish firm control over those bodies, nipping firmly in the bud any attempts at establishing forms of educational leadership. On the other hand, where the clerk has no more than clerical responsibilities as a very junior official from the education office, governing bodies can be very conscious of their distance from the LEA, and lines of communication become extremely tenuous. This becomes even more pronounced when LEAs, for financial reasons, withdraw clerking facilities, leaving governing bodies to make their own arrangements. Packwood (1982) has recorded the problems that can then ensue.

Such obstacles are not, however, insuperable. The various pressure groups for educational consumers have not only recorded successful examples of educational leadership by governing bodies, but have also provided a number of the proliferating guides for successful governorship, which offer several forms of assertiveness training for governors. These have been usefully summarized by Locke (1982).

The Advisory Centre for Education provides not only governors' handbooks, but* regular commentary and up-dating on issues likely to be discussed (or to be deliberately avoided) at governors' meetings. The National Association for Governors and Managers offers a national support system for governors, including information leaflets and training courses. Training is also available through the multi-media Open University courses, and the programmes provided, sometimes in association with university extra-mural departments, by individual local authorities. There is less excuse than ever before for governors to plead ignorance of the educational issues on which, in theory, they are expected to provide leadership.

Governing bodies' opportunities for leadership will derive from the articles and instruments of government under which they operate. With the changes in the 1980 Act and the model articles of DES Circular 4/81 still working through into LEA practice, there is probably more diversity between LEAs at the moment than ever before.

In their handbook of guidance for governors, Brooksbank and Revell (1981) identify four areas of responsibility wherein leadership opportunities might be found: conduct and curriculum; finance; premises; and appointments. We would add a fifth: school organization. We turn now to a consideration of possible opportunities in each, with some comments on the implications for the school where such opportunities are seized.

Responsibility for making appointments of teaching and non-teaching staff to a school are likely to be circumscribed by LEA policies, particularly where LEA-wide redeployment policies are operated, and where all but senior teaching staff are appointed not to the school but to the local authority. It is in the appointment of senior staff, and particularly headteachers, that governors probably have the greatest potential for influencing their school. But this of course is also the area where local authority officers, inspectors or advisers and the headteacher (for appointments at deputy head and other senior levels) also recognize the opportunities for reshaping and developing the school. The establishment of the selection process might itself, therefore, be a highly political process, with the setting up of selection sub-committees from which some categories of governor — notably teacher governors and members of the minority political parties — are arbitrarily excluded. The shortlisting process and the final selection interviews provide powerful opportunities for intelligent leadership in which the criteria for selection are both clearly drawn up and rigorously adhered to. The general contempt in which selection procedures are held by the teaching profession arises mainly from the absence of such criteria and of effective educational leadership during the appointment process, and the opportunities which are taken therein for political manipulation and the demonstration of ignorance and incompetence. While the articles usually reserve the final appointment to the CEO or a sub-committee of the Education Committee, in practice

181

governors' selections are hardly ever overturned, but it is common practice for the final interview panel to be comprised both of governors and of Education Committee members, with the latter in the majority. Dismissal procedures, circumscribed as they are by employment protection legislation, are closely controlled and monitored by LEA officials — and hence provide few opportunities for imaginative educational leadership by governors, however desirable this might be thought to be.

Appointments of senior staff are likely to be rare in a time of contraction such as the education service is experiencing. Influencing the curriculum is likely to be a more fruitful field of leadership opportunities for governors, notwithstanding the widespread belief of teachers that this is properly their private property. However, recent interest in the curriculum has tended to show that broad curriculum content, in terms of areas of study to be available, is not a source of major controversy. This statement may become inaccurate as stands are taken over the provision of religious or political education, and it is possible that the Manpower Services Commission may be awakening sleeping dogs with its Technical and Vocational Education Initiative. However, curriculum policies, such as have been demanded of LEAs by DES Circular 6/81, will need to involve more than pious statements of general content if they are to influence practice (Bennett, 1983). They will need to focus on the aspects of the curriculum which do provoke controversy, and here governors will have a role to play.

Such controversial aspects are less concerned with content, and more concerned with the ways the content is taught, the differential access to the subjects created by the school's pupil-grouping policies, the specific re-sources and textbooks employed, and the effectiveness of the teaching as measured by examination results. Governors are likely to have views on all these matters, but they will be one group among many. Although this field is susceptible to their leadership it is the one in which the questions of responsibility and authority which we discussed above (pp. 179–80) become most pressing.

Where governing bodies take up their responsibilities for curriculum policy and curriculum review they are not, however, likely to do this realistically without coming to terms with these issues. Many governing bodies may continue to devolve these responsibilities to the staff and the headteacher, either as a deliberate decision or without realizing it. Others, perhaps with the encouragement and support of the local authority, a political party or an educational pressure group, or in consequence of governor training programmes, might attempt to undertake the responsibilities enjoined of them by Circular 6/81 and their articles. In such a situation the head and teacher governors will at the least be forced to articulate and defend existing policies and practices. If this in turn stimulates a debate concerning those policies and practices within the school it can only be to its benefit. Regardless of the groups on whose behalf they are acting, the clear expression by a governing body of its expectations within these curricular territories would provide powerfully the educational leadership some are looking for from governing bodies. There are some significant dangers in such developments and these are discussed below. However, there are also benefits, where a school is demonstrably responsive to community, parent and local authority views concerning the central tasks expected of the school as expressed by an informed governing body. Teachers, through their involvement on such bodies, have the responsibility for ensuring that they are appropriately informed.

Governing body policies on school premises are the traditional territory explored in governors' meetings. This is not to disparage them. At a time of serious resource constraints, the maintenance of properly furbished school premises is becoming a national scandal, and governing bodies can (and many do) make a significant contribution to the educational and financial arguments in favour of sensible maintenance policies. In some authorities and in voluntary aided schools governors already have powers to approve minor repairs and developments, although increasingly tight LEA financial controls have restricted and even removed the powers of many governing bodies to permit use of the premises by non-school-based groups, etc. Finances and other resources tend similarly to be under tight LEA control. In the internal allocation of resources within the school it is possible for governing bodies to express their views, although it would seem that at present very few do so. Finally, in areas of school organization there is not a great deal of scope for governing body initiatives. Pupil admission and holiday policies tend to be controlled quite carefully by the local authority, and most administrative issues are clearly within the area of responsibility of the headteacher.

What are the prospects for governing bodies as they prepare to take on significant leadership responsibilities in the education service? Three possible scenarios can be discerned. One is that governing bodies might become politicized policy-making arenas, in which groups representing different political parties, parents and teachers compete, bargain and make coalitions. Political skills and leadership would become paramount. The extent to which they encompassed educational leadership would depend very much on the experience, training and personal qualities of those implementing such leadership. The role of the headteacher would change dramatically in such a situation. Some would use their influence as expert witnesses and information sources in order to become power-brokers and conciliators, and thus maintain their own educational leadership. Others could become servants of the governing body's dominant group.

A rather different scenario sees the development of a working relationship between headteacher and governing body, modelled on the local government system. Governing bodies would be the policy-makers, analogous to the council, while headteachers, as chief executives, would provide expert service and information before policies were made. They would then ensure loyally that the policies were implemented. This could accentuate centralized power and decision-making within the schools, with the strengthening of the internal authority of the headteacher with more scrutiny and appraisal of individual teachers, in order to ascertain whether declared policies were in fact being implemented.

A third scenario is perhaps closest to existing situations, with the governing body as the agent of the local authority. The Taylor Committee's recommendations for reducing local authority representation on governing bodies to a minority seem irretrievably lost. Recent DES restrictions on councillors to hold no more than five governorships could, paradoxically, have the effect of tightening party political control of governing bodies. The majority party on the education committee is likely to seek to ensure that its views are expressed at governors' meetings, once governors begin to make and review educational policies for individual schools. Party political nominees are more likely to attend such meetings if unburdened by large numbers of governorships. Control of curriculum and other policies would in this way become wholly politicized. Education Committee policies would be enforced in individual schools by pliant governing bodies.

In a democratic society, it is surely appropriate that schools should be responsive to democratic wishes. If governing bodies are able to offer to headteachers and their staffs capable leadership which represents the democratic will then this is a role which they should be asked to undertake. But the key determinant of effective leadership is the extent to which the lead is followed, and this is in turn determined by the extent to which those whom it is sought to lead are prepared to concede the legitimacy of those who seek to lead them. Notwithstanding the examples of success to which advocates of strong governing bodies can point, the obstacles to accepting a leadership role for governors are considerable. If they go too far ahead of the LEA, their leadership will be called into question by their paymasters. If they go too far ahead of the teachers, they will encounter resistance akin to mutiny, which can be deeply effective. If they claim to represent 'the community', they are open to close questioning as to how they have achieved that role. At best, school governing bodies will be able to act as a focus of information, receiving opinions and transmitting them to authority and school, ensuring that both paymasters and practitioners receive the feelings of the community, and building a trust and sense of partnership between teachers, parents, the school's social environment and the decision-makers in the local authority. At worst, as agencies of LEA control and direction, they will become the machinery through which centralization of the education service will occur.

The problem for governing bodies is that the scenario which emerges depends on forces outside their control. Their first task must be to establish unambiguously, both to those they govern and to those who lay down the rules under which they govern, that they represent a mix of constituencies. Each possesses a right to an independent voice and a right to guide and criticize. Collectively, these voices cannot be expected as a matter of course to sing in harmony, and the guidance and criticism will commonly be both vociferous and incompatible. In these circumstances, the task of providing educational leadership would make demands that few forms of assertiveness training can meet. For the moment, the alliance of headteacher and chairperson of governors is likely to remain a mainspring of school leadership, and our crystal ball is still too cloudy for us to discern which scenario will emerge as tomorrow's norm. In all possibility, all the scenarios we have indicated will come to pass in different parts of the country, and the role of the headteacher will become one of considerable variation, defined by the personnel involved and the particular combination of circumstances affecting school and LEA. A more unpredictable situation could in itself make headteachers presume on their governors even less than they have cause to already, and that would alter the balance of influence away from the teaching profession.

Yet the heightened uncertainty in which both governors and heads will have to work could provide precisely the circumstances in which they are thrown together, to defend themselves against encroachment by central office or town hall. In a state of uncertainty, coalitions can develop to fill the void. For two of the three groups on every governing body it will not be in their interests for the vacuum of school policy-making to be filled by the local authority. Perhaps, then, school heads, staff and governors might after all be able to come to a working arrangement which creates decentralized locations of power to set against the centre. If this is to happen, then staff and parent governors may have to see themselves as part of an alliance against the councillors, and a major figure in creating such a perception must surely be the headteacher. Whichever way things develop, there can be no question that the school's head will play a pivotal part in the development of satisfactory working relations among LEA, governors and the school, and that the leadership to be exercised by a governing body would be exercised through the head as chief executive. For all the shifting of public support away from education in the 1970s, senior staff in schools will continue to seek to repel central and local government incursions into territories they regard as inviolable, and may succeed in negotiating powerful support from their governors in manning the barricades.

### References

BACON, W. (1978) *School Accountability and the Schooling System*, London, Harper and Row.

BAINS REPORT (1972) *The New Local Authorities: Management and Structure*, London, HMSO.

BARON, G. and HOWELL, D. (1974) *The Government and Management of Schools*, London Athlone Press.

BENNETT, N. (1983) 'Seeking effectiveness in curriculum policy', in *Curriculum*, 4, 1.

BENNETT, N. and GRAY, L. (1983) 'Voucher power — for whom'? in *The Times Educational Supplement*, 4 March.

BROOKSBANK, K. and REVELL, J. (1981) *School Governors*, London Councils and Education Press.

DES (1977) *A New Partnership for our Schools* (Taylor Report), London, HMSO.

DES (1979) *Local Authority Arrangements for the School Curriculum*, London, HMSO.

DES (1980) *A Framework for the Curriculum*, London, HMSO.

DES (1981) *A View of the Curriculum*, London, HMSO.

DES Circulars 14/77; 4/81; 6/81, London, HMSO.

LAWTON, D. (1980) *The Politics of the School Curriculum*; London, Routledge and Kegan Paul.

LOCKE, M. (1982) 'What the law and guidebooks say', in *The Times Educational Supplement*, 15 October.

PACKWOOD, T. (1982) 'A high price to pay for clerking governing bodies', *Education*, 8 October.

SALLIS, J. (1977) *School Managers and Governors: Taylor and After*, London Ward Lock.

# Selected Leadership Functions of the School Principal*

*V. McGeown*
*The New University of Ulster*

The study of organizational leadership in professional settings is a relatively neglected area of research in the social sciences. This study examines a special case of organizational leadership, the leadership functions and processes associated with the school principal as the formally designated leader of a professionally staffed organization.

That principal's role conceptions and the expectations held by teachers for the principal's leadership are characterized by considerable haziness, dissensus and potentialities for conflict is well-documented in the literature. Kelsall and Kelsall (1969) argue that: 'As yet in Britain no agreement exists either among heads themselves, or more widely, about the different aspects of the headteacher's role and the relative importance to be attached to each of them.' Goldhammer *et al.* (1970, p. 1), commenting on the confusing conceptions and expectations surrounding the role of the elementary school principal in the United States, arrive at a similar conclusion.

In the UK, apart from a handful of empirical studies (Hughes, 1972; Cohen, 1970; Bates, 1971; Lyons, 1976; Bernbaum, 1973; Coulson, 1974; Richardson, 1973), there has been little systematic research on the principal's role behaviours and conceptions, the role expectations held by teachers and the potentialities for conflict between behaviour, conception, perception and expectation. The literature on school administration, with some exceptions (e.g., Hughes, 1974; Baron and Taylor, 1969; Barry and Tye, 1975; Allen, 1968; Peters, 1976), has tended to be anecdotal, prescriptive and hortatory. Typically it is asserted or assumed that the successful principal may be identified by the possession of certain personal qualities of leadership and by the exercise of certain techniques of control, which allegedly are generalizable across various school settings. It will be argued here that there is little empirical support for such generalizations and that effective leadership is likely to be contingent on complex interactions among varying

* This is an edited version of the article which appeared in *Educational Administration*, 8, 1, 1979, pp. 153–79.

personal qualities of the principal and varying characteristics of teachers, tasks, schools and environments.

The study briefly reported here is part of an extended study of leadership and organizational change in schools, which is partially reported in four papers (McGeown, 1979a; 1979b; 1979c; 1979d). Specifically it examines the role behaviours and conceptions of principals in terms of selected leadership functions and processes, differences between principals' conceptions and behaviours and the perceptions and expectations held by teachers for principals' leadership behaviour, the degree of consensus existing among principals and among teachers and the potentialities for conflict between conceptions, behaviours perceptions and expectations. Additionally the study explores relationships between principals' leadership behaviour, principals' values and attitudes, school innovativeness and organizational climate for change and teachers' innovativeness.

For this purpose three versions of an instrument were designed to describe selected leadership functions and processes. There is nothing prescriptive or normative about the list of functions chosen for study, nor do they imply any particular value orientation. It is not suggested that the principal's role is reducible to any list of functions. The activities in which he may engage, the manner in which he performs such activities, his values, motives and leadership style are likely to vary, depending conjointly on the person, the job and the situation. Taylor (1968) observes that the way in which a principal allocates personal time and resources may be of symbolic rather than direct significance in describing his role performance. An excessive concern for the minutiae of the stock book and the attendance register, he argues, may indicate a value orientation permeating a head's entire administrative style.

The instruments developed by the author were administered to three pilot study groups and three main study groups, comprising a total of 96 principals and 954 teachers.

## Theories of Leadership

Half a century of research on leadership has produced little consensus on the nature of leadership, its determinants, processes and consequences (Stogdill, 1975). It is beyond the scope of a brief paper to attempt more than a resume of a small portion of the literature on which the present study was based. Hencley (1973) identifies a number of developmental trends in the emergence of new images or conceptions of the 'leader' viewed as 'the efficiency expert' (Taylor, 1911), as a 'social engineer' (Mayo, 1946), as an 'organisational engineer' (Gulick and Urwick, 1973) and as 'clinician' (Schutz, 1958). Two contemporary conceptualizations are particularly relevant to this study — the view of the leader as 'change agent' and as 'politician'. The change agent perspective asserts that the distinctive function of leadership is effecting organizational change and formulating the goals of the organization (Lipham, 1964; McCleary and Hencley, 1965). Viewed as a politician the leader's primary institutional function is the determination of policy (Hencley *et al.*, 1970).

Another clear trend may be seen in the shift from narrowly focussed 'trait' and 'situational' theories to more complex behavioural theories. Comprehensive critiques of the trait-based literature by Stogdill (1948; 1974) and Gibb (1969) tends to support the conclusion that, without depreciating the importance of certain leader qualities in certain situations, there are very few generalizable traits which are consistently associated with effective leadership. 'Situational' approaches examined relationships in various group settings and regarded leadership as relative and reciprocal to the behaviour of other group members and determined by members' perceptions of the forces operative in the situation (Hencley, 1973). Situational approaches may be criticized as adopting a deterministic perspective, which takes too little account of the salience of the leader's personality in influencing the situation. 'Behavioural' theories are concerned primarily with the study of observed behaviour rather than a capacity for leadership which may be inferred from behaviour. Rigidly situational perspectives are being supplanted by structural functional approaches and by phenomenological approaches, which take account of the individual's 'construction of reality'. Greenfield (1968), Cunningham and Gephart (1973), Stogdill (1974), Hughes (1972) and Cohen (1970) provide excellent critical reviews of the present state of the art in leadership theory and research.

While there has been an increase in studies of organizational leadership, the study of leader behaviour in professionally staffed organizations such as schools has been relatively neglected. It may also be argued that the predominantly managerialist orientation of administrative theories has resulted in a failure to study the interdependence of leader behaviour and followers' perceptions. Typically leader behaviour is measured by means of followers' perceptions of the frequency of occurrence of specified leader behaviours, as defined by instruments such as the ubiquitous Leader Behaviour Description Questionnaire (LBDQ). Gouldner (1965) detects in LBDQ-based research evidence of a trait approach peering through the cracks of an ostensibly system-oriented approach. The LBDQ takes little account of the nature of the group or its interaction with its environment. There is a danger of regarding the pattern of behaviour so defined as attributes of the individual leader, which he brings independently to the group and which determine the leadership functions performed within it (Greenfield, 1968).

Charters (1964) criticizes what he calls the 'leadership phantasm', 'our culturally derived inclination to glorify the power of the individual human agent'. Leadership is more appropriately defined as a social influence process in which leader and followers interact to achieve the tasks of the organization and to satisfy the needs of individuals and groups within it. To this end there is a need to develop instruments which take more account of the interaction of person, task, process and system.

It is also open to serious question whether leader behaviour may be described adequately in terms of two supposedly unidimensional factors, generally labelled 'initiating structure' and 'consideration', which may be described respectively in terms of behaviours indicative of concern for achieving the tasks of the organization and behaviour indicating concern for staff motivation, morale, commitment and interpersonal effectiveness. A review of the evidence reveals a remarkable convergence, notwithstanding the semantic ingenuity of researchers in devising alternative labels, in identifying these two basic constructs. Yukl (1971) usefully postulates a further independent dimension labelled 'decision-centralisation'. Of particular relevance to this study is the dearth of research on the 'change agent' image of leadership, relating leader behaviours to various processes and strategies of change. We know very little about the kinds of leader behaviour which may be appropriate for different kinds of change-related tasks.

### Rationale of the Study

The school principal is the formally designated leader of a professionally staffed organization. His leader behaviour is viewed as a transactional phenomenon determined by the interaction of leader, individuals, groups and tasks within the organizational context of a school, which is conceptualized as an open socio-technical system. The study of leadership in systematic terms focusses attention on the interdependence of the elements of the system, on the ways in which individuals influence and are influenced by the elements of the system and on the dynamic interaction of the system and its environment. How the principal as leader influences staff members is only one of many relationships existing among organizational variables which are interrelated in a complex manner.

The proposition that one of the major expectations held for the principal is that he will provide leadership for his staff has a long tradition in the literature on school administration (Gross and Herriott, 1965). Reavis (1953, p. 303) argues that: 'There is no greater test of leadership on the part of the principal than his positive influence on the professional growth of his teachers. If he is accepted by his teachers merely as a school executive and not as a professional leader he cannot be regarded as a successful principal.' It would be mistaken, however, to conclude that teachers do not hold an expectation that the principal will discharge his routine management functions effectively. In any event the long-standing debate regarding alleged distinctions between leadership and administration is in the author's view sterile and misleading. Hughes (1972) developed a dual model, which defines the principal's behaviour as 'leading professional' and as 'chief executive' and provides evidence of the importance of and interaction of both roles. Gross and Herriott (1965), using a measure of principals' 'Executive Professional Leadership', found that teachers rated more highly those principals who discharged their executive functions more effectively. Principal's EPL, which somewhat strangely combines 'professional' and 'executive' in an ostensibly unidimensional measure, was found to be related to teachers' morale, teachers' work performance and pupil learning. The potential danger, however, is that an excessive preoccupation with the minutiae of administration may result in the operation of a kind of Gresham's law of administration whereby routine activities drive out creative leadership acts (Thomason, 1974). This is likely particularly to inhibit the principal's performance of those 'change agent' functions which have been found in several studies to exert a critical influence on a school's responsiveness to change. The point may be illustrated by reference to two large-scale case-study projects conducted by OECD/CERI (1973) and by the Rand Corporation (Berman *et al.*, 1975), which found that principal's leadership is a major determinant of the successful adoption and implementation of innovation.

To develop a conceptual schema for the classification of principals' leadership functions, the author adapted Argyris's formulation of the 'core activities' of an organization (Argyris, 1962; 1964). The principal's organizational leadership is examined functionally in terms of three core activities of the school — task achievement or the school's ability to achieve its primary operational tasks, group maintenance or the school's ability to maintain itself internally in terms of staff motivation, morale commitment and interpersonal relationships, and organizational change or the school's ability to grow and to adapt to its external environment. Within each of these three core activities a number of constituent functions are defined. The principal's conception of these functions and his behavioural response are likely to be influenced critically not only by his personality but also by his perception of the needs and expectations of staff members and the nature and tasks of the school in its environment.

## Methodology

A review of the literature on leadership, organization theory and the school principalship was conducted to identify the main observed and ascribed leadership functions of the school principal. The author's experience as principal of a primary school and a post-primary school provided additional insights. Two further major sources for the generation of relevant questionnaire items were employed. The author interviewed seventy-eight principals and teachers to elicit conceptions of and expectations for the roles of head, deputy head and senior staff. Additionally some 104 principals and teachers wrote case studies of administrative processes employed by their schools, using a structured schedule devised for the purpose. Content analyses of the case studies and interviews together with the literature review provided a basis for writing an initial pool of 249 items describing leadership functions and processes. Items were initially assigned to one of the three categories described as 'core activities' — functions associated primarily with school processes oriented towards task achievement, functions associated primarily with school processes oriented towards group maintenance, and functions associated primarily with school processes oriented towards organizational change.

Within each area items were further classified in terms of a number of postulated constituent processes and functions.

1 Task Achievement was taken to include Planning, Organizing, Communicating, Coordinating and Evaluating.
2 Group Maintenance was operationalized in terms of Promoting Staff Development, Developing Staff Participation, Fostering Staff Motivation, Optimizing Staff Utilization, Fostering Staff Cohesiveness.
3 Organizational Change was taken to comprise four constituent processes designated Initiating Change, Adopting Change, Implementing Change and Assessing Change.

The items within each of the fourteen functional areas thus hypothesized were carefully scrutinized for face validity, relevance, meaningfulness and acceptability. Additionally the opinions of a panel of experienced principals and teachers were sought. In the light of this scrutiny sixty-six items were discarded. Some of the remaining items were reworded or assigned to different sub-categories. From the resulting set of 183 items forty were chosen to define each of the three core activities and their constituent processes, by selecting those items, which, on the basis of the review of the literature and subsequent scrutiny and consultation, appeared to define each area most adequately. The resulting 120 items were systematically distributed to form a questionnaire, which was designated the Principal's Behaviour Description Questionnaire (PBDQ).

Four forms of the PBDQ were developed, two for completion by principals and two for use with teachers. On Form PA (Principal's Actual) principals rate the degree of importance relative to their other functions which in practice they perceive themselves as actually assigning to each function and on Form PI (Principal's Ideal) the degree of importance which they think they should assign to each. Form TA (Teachers' Actual) is a measure of teachers' perception of the degree of importance which the principal appears to assign in practice to each function, and Form TE (Teachers' Expectation) measures their expectations regarding the importance which they think he should assign to each. Additional forms of the PBDQ were designed to ascertain principals, self-reported commitment of time to each function, their self-assessed evaluation of their effectiveness in performing each function, their degree of delegation to staff members, their perception of superordinate support and their degree of professional interest and satisfaction in relation to each function.

On each form respondents rate each of the 120 items on a scale of relative importance by assigning a value from 7 representing a function 'of the utmost importance' to 1 indicating a function considered to be 'of no importance'. Each of the fourteen sub-scales yields a Likert-type summated rating scale, by summing the values for each of the items assigned to the sub-scale.

### Pilot Studies

The questionnaire was administered to two pilot groups, one comprising fifty principals and one comprising fifty-five experienced teachers. The principals' pilot group consisted of thirty principals of secondary schools drawn randomly from four of the original eight LEAs (Co. Londonderry, Co. Tyrone, Co. Antrim and Derry City), and twenty principals of comprehensive and community schools in the Republic, who attended a course on school management conducted by the author. Both groups completed Form PA and Form PI. The pilot group of teachers, composed of fifty-five experienced teachers reading for the Diploma in Advanced Studies in Education at The New University of Ulster, completed Form TA and Form TE.

Modified T tests revealed that principals' Actual scores differed significantly ($p < 0.05$) from their Ideal scores, and teachers' Expected scores differed significantly from their Actual scores ($p < 0.05$).

The reliability of each of the fourteen sub-scales of each of the four forms of the PBDQ was calculated by means of Cronbach's coefficient alpha, a measure of internal consistency reliability. The mean obtained reliability coefficients for all sub-scales was 0.86, none falling below 0.73. Each item correlated more highly with its own sub-scale total than with that of any of the remaining sub-scales. Reliabilities for the forty items in each of the three functional categories averaged 0.94. Correlational and factor analyses were used to examine the relationships among the fourteen sub-scales in each form. The factor analyses yielded three factors for each form of the PBDQ, which indicated a more complex interactive relationship among the fourteen sub-scales than that posited in the priori allocation of sub-scales to three functional areas. For analytical purposes task achievement, group maintenance and organizational change might be regarded as conceptually independent but phenomenally interactive variables. In practice there was strong evidence of subtle interrelationships across the three categories. The most parsimonious factor solution revealed that Factor I was defined by the four organizational change sub-scales, together with staff development and staff utilization, Factor II predominantly defined task achievement and Factor III clearly defined interpersonal effectiveness. The evidence of sub-scale reliability, independence and discrimination was taken to justify further use of the PBDQ.

## Main Study

In the main study two groups were employed to investigate two separate but related research questions. The first study (Study A) was designed to examine differences between principals' self-reported actual behaviour and teachers' reported expectations for the principal's behaviour and to explore inter-school differences in teachers' expectations. The second study (Study B) was designed to explore relationships among principals' self-reported actual behaviour, principals' values and attitudes, school innovativeness and organizational climate for change and teachers' innovativeness.

In study A twelve secondary schools were randomly selected in Northern Ireland. In each school the principal completed Form PA and a simple random sample of seven teachers completed Form TE. One-way analysis of variance and multiple discriminant analysis entering the fourteen sub-scales simultaneously revealed highly significant differences between the twelve schools ($p < 0.001$) in terms of the expectations held by staff members for the principal's leadership behaviour. The variations between schools of the same type provide some support for the hypothesis that varying characteristics of schools and teachers are likely to be important determinants of effective leadership. The successful principal is likely to be more aware of such variations and to consider the extent which he may influence and be influenced by such variations. As the differences between schools exceeded the differences among teachers, it may be inferred that the PBDQ was tapping some set of organization-level variables, characteristics of schools in addition to characteristics of teachers within them. This may be taken as a crude index of the concurrent validity of the PBDQ. Within each of the twelve schools a mean score for the teachers was computed. The twelve obtained teacher means were compared with the principals' score for self-reported actual behaviour. Teachers' scores for expected behaviour differed significantly from principals' scores for actual behaviour ($p < 0.05$). To the extent that the principals perceive such discrepancies and for any reason are constrained from diminishing or alleviating them it may be assumed that there exists a possibility that principals may experience a degree of role conflict or cognitive dissonance and that teachers may experience some diminution of needs satisfaction.

The sample used in study B comprised a non-random group of thirty-four principals of primary schools ($N = 12$) and secondary schools ($N = 22$) distributed throughout Northern Ireland. The group, who were reading for the Diploma in Advanced Studies in Education Administration at The New University of Ulster, completed Form PA of the PBDQ measuring principals' self-reported allocation of time to each function (PT), their self-assessed evaluation of their effectiveness in performing each function (PE), their degree of delegation to staff (PD), their perception of superordinate support (PS), and their expressed professional satisfaction and interest in each function (PI). A composite score for each of the 120 items was computed by converting raw item scores to normalized T scores and summing the obtained scores for each item across forms PA, PT and PI of the questionnaire. Sub-scale totals were calculated and again converted to normalized T scores to provide a composite measure of principal's actual leadership behaviour. The group also completed Stogdill's LBDQ, Form XII (1963), Gordon's Survey of Interpersonal Values (1960), Oliver and Butcher's 'Attitudes to Education' (1962), and a number of instruments developed by the author to measure school Organisational Climate for Change (OCCQ) (McGeown, 1979c), School Adoption and Implementation of Innovations (McGeown, 1979a), Principals' Change-related Values (PCRV) (McGeown, 1979b) and Principals' Innovation Decision-Making Behaviour (McGeown, 1979d). Each principal also administered to the entire staff of his/her school (teacher N = 671) four measures designed by the author (McGeown, 1979a) to measure teachers' predisposition to adopt specific innovations, their general change-related values and their behavioural orientation to adopt a hypothetical innovation, as influenced by their perception of selected characteristics of the innovation and by their perception of selected characteristics of the process of innovation in their school. Each teacher's scores from the four measures were combined by summing normalized T scores to form a composite measure of Teachers' Innovativeness. For subsequent analyses three schools with a staff of less than ten members were omitted from the study.

Analysis of variance and multiple discriminant analysis of the teacher data revealed significant inter-school differences on each of the four measures of teacher innovativeness ($p < 0.001$). As found in Study A, this suggested that the instrument was measuring certain organization-level characteristics of individual schools. Schools appeared to exert a significant influence on teachers' receptivity to change. It seemed defensible, therefore, to compute for each of the thirty-one schools a mean composite score for teachers' innovativeness by averaging the scores of teachers within each school.

The composite measure of principals' actual behaviour (Form PA + PT + PE) was correlated with each of the variables under study and the mean correlations for the three functional categories were computed. Principals' behaviour was found to be significantly related ($p < 0.05$) to the school's mean score for teachers' innovativeness ($r = 0.38$) and to the school's score for innovation adoption ($r = 0.45$) and implementation ($r = 0.44$), to the school's organizational climate for change ($r = 0.46$), to the principal's innovation decision-making behaviour ($r = 0.41$). Actual behaviour was also significantly related to LBDQ structure ($r = 0.47$), and consideration (r = 0.51), to Oliver and Butcher's tendermindedness (r = 0.42), to principal's dogmatism (r = 0.37), conservatism (r = 0.40), traditionalism (r = −0.40), progressivism (r = 0.38), venturesomeness (r = 0.37), and change-proneness (r = 0.41). Stepwise regression and factor analysis entering scores for the six forms of the PBDQ (importance, time, evaluation, delegation, support, interest) showed that the PBDQ was internally consistent and that PBDQ scores were most significantly related to school and teacher-level innovativeness, to principal's innovation decision-making behaviour, to LBDQ consideration and structure and to school organizational climate for change. PBDQ degree of delegation was most significantly and positively related to teacher-level and school-level innovativeness. It was also significantly related to PBDQ perception of superordinate support. There were significant interrelationships between PBDQ importance, evaluation, time commitment and interest.

The reliabilities of all measures used in study A and B were again computed using Cronbach's coefficient alpha. Average coefficients of internal consistency reliability for all measures were in excess of 0.80 ranging from 0.71 to 0.93. Several crude indices of validity were also calculated. In study A the PBDQ discriminated between the twelve schools studied. In study B evidence of concurrent, convergent and discriminant validity was found in the correlations reported above.

## Item Analysis

Each of the items on Form PA and Form TE was examined to study differences within and between each of the three postulated functional categories, task achievement, group maintenance, growth and adaptation. The mean score recorded by the entire group of principals (N = 96) for each item was computed. To discriminate between items considered most important and least important the means were transformed to normalized T scores. Items falling more than 1.S.D. above and below the mean were regarded as most important and least important respectively. Thirty-six items were identified in this way, the remaining eighty-four items being considered to be moderately important. A similar analysis was performed on the scores by all teachers who completed Form TE (N − 139), to determine the relative strength of teachers' expectations for all items.

In general, principals rated task achievement functions more highly than those relating to group maintenance and organizational change. More specifically, the most highly rated items all related to the planning function: 'formulating the goals of the school', 'formulating the policies on which the school runs', 'formulating the objectives of the school curriculum', 'reviewing the needs and priorities of the school', 'planning for balance and coordination in the school curriculum'. Also in the task achievement category items describing communicating, organizing and coordinating were highly rated: 'communicating and clarifying school objectives to staff members', 'seeing that the principal's attitudes are clearly understood by staff', 'managing the school budget'. A second cluster of highly rated items dealt with fostering organizational cohesiveness: 'creating an atmosphere of sharing and trust among staff members', 'welding the staff into a unit with clear goals', 'developing cooperative teacher-pupil relationships', 'giving a clear sense of direction to staff members'. Staff participation and motivation are rated highly on four items: 'giving staff members support and backing on professional matters', 'seeking the advice of staff members on important issues', 'consulting staff members on proposed changes in the school', 'inspiring confidence and a sense of security in staff members'. Significantly only two of the forty items relating to organizational change were rated highly: 'encouraging staff members to develop their own ideas' and 'discussing educational innovations with other principals'. None of the items defining the implementation of changes which had been adopted was rated highly. Significant, too, is the omission of all items defining the control function of leadership, evaluating organizational effectiveness and assessing changes which have been introduced. Nor are any of the items describing the professional development of staff rated highly.

Among the items which are rated as being least important the dominant cluster relates to the control function of leadership, evaluating and coordinating: 'assessing the outcomes of innovations which have been adopted', 'assessing with staff members the effects of innovations which have been implemented', 'monitoring the implementation of policy decisions which have been taken', 'encouraging the use of standard practices by staff', 'supervising the efficient use of school resources by staff members', 'making effective use of non-teaching staff', 'evaluating and revising staff personnel policies'.

In the analysis of teachers' expectations for principal's leadership behaviour the most striking feature of the items which were rated highly was the predominance of items dealing with teacher participation: 'seeking the opinions of staff about changes which affect them', 'involving staff members in decision-making on important issues', 'seeking the advice of staff members on important issues', 'encouraging staff to participate in decision-making on issues that affect them', 'evaluating with staff members the effectiveness of the school', 'consulting staff members on proposed changes in the school'. Only two of these items appeared in the principals' list and those items dealt with consultation rather than full participation. Interpersonal relationships are represented by three items: 'maintaining good personal and professional relationships with staff', 'creating an atmosphere of sharing and trust among staff members', 'providing staff members with support and backing on professional matters'. It is significant, however, that certain items describing interpersonal relations between principal and teachers were assigned a relatively low rating: 'helping staff to settle their personal differences', 'dealing with disagreements among staff members', 'devising procedures for the management of conflict among staff members', 'dealing with disagreements between teachers and pupils', 'helping staff with their personal and social problems'. The literature on teachers' aspirations for professional autonomy would suggest that insensitive or excessive engagement in certain behaviours which have been described as 'consideration' might, however well-intentioned, be perceived as an encroachment upon that autonomy.

Teachers assigned high importance to three items in the area of organizational change: 'securing resources needed for proposed innovations', 'encouraging staff members to develop their own new ideas', and 'keeping abreast of reading about educational change'. The most highly rated items in the category of task achievement relate to communication and evaluation: 'improving the transmission and sharing of information with staff members', 'conducting regular staff and group meetings', 'evaluating the overall effectiveness of the school', 'evaluating the goals and objectives of the school'. Within the same area, however, seven items describing close supervision and control received low ratings: 'devising effective methods of organizing the school tasks of staff members', 'supervising the efficient use of school resources by staff members', 'encouraging the use of standard practices by staff members', 'coordinating the roles and tasks of staff members', 'supervising the use and maintenance of school plant and equipment by staff', 'assessing the classroom teaching performances of staff members', 'evaluating and revising staff personnel policies'.

Of the 120 items only six were rated highly by both principals and teachers. Four of these related to group maintenance and two to task achievement needs: 'creating an atmosphere of sharing and trust among staff members', 'encouraging staff members to develop their own new ideas', 'giving staff members support and backing on professional matters', 'consulting staff members on proposed changes in the school', 'formulating the goals of the school', and 'seeing that the principal's attitudes are clearly understood by staff'. Ten items were assigned low ratings by both principals and teachers, five dealing with task achievement, four with group maintenance and one with organizational change: 'supervising the efficient use of school resources by staff members', 'encouraging the use of standard practices by staff', 'supervising the use and maintenance of school plant and equipment', 'evaluating and revising staff personnel policies', 'appraising and selecting new teaching aids', 'experimenting with alternative methods of staff development', 'making effective use of non-teaching staff', 'helping staff to settle their personal differences', 'devising strategies for the management of conflict among staff members', 'helping teachers to use new teaching aids effectively'. Viewed in terms of the three 'core activities', principals rated most highly items describing task achievement, followed by group maintenance and organizational change respectively. Teachers assigned most importance to items relating to group maintenance, followed by organizational change and task achievement. It is beyond the scope of a brief paper to report in detail the degree of consensus which existed within the group of principals and within the group of teachers. Summarily, this was tested by computing the standard deviation for each of the 120 items for all principals (N = 96) and for all teachers (N = 139). A small S.D. was taken to indicate a relatively high degree of consensus and a high S.D. low consensus. Consistent with the evidence of the literature (Kelsall and Kelsall, 1969; Goldhammer *et al.*, 1970) there were wide variations in consensus. In general principals showed high consensus on items relating to task achievement and relatively low consensus on items relating to group maintenance and organizational change. Teachers indicated relatively high consensus on group maintenance items and relatively low consensus on task achievement and organizational change items.

### Modified Versions of PBDQ

Space permits no more than a brief account of the development of two modified versions of the PBDQ. The second version of PBDQ embodies two major changes. On the basis of observed reliability and reported significance twenty-six items were discarded. To test item discrimination, twelve items describing overtly administrative functions were incorporated. The 106 items were randomly distributed to form four sub-scales measuring task achievement, group maintenance, organizational change and administration. More significantly the PBDQ was modified to explore concurrently teachers' expectations for the role behaviour of the principal, the vice-principal and heads of department in relation to the same 106 functions. Previous studies (Bernbaum, 1973; Coulson, 1974; Lambert 1975) tended to treat the roles of vice principal and heads of department in isolation from the role of the principal or examined the delegation or sharing of responsibilities as a dichotomous variable. The revised PBDQ was designed to explore the participation or delegation hypothesis, using a continuous seven-point scale.

The revised PBDQ was piloted by administration to thirty-one post-graduate students. Cronbach's internal consistency reliability for each of the four sub-scales exceeded 0.80. For the main study a 50 per cent random sample of teachers (N = 126) in six randomly selected secondary schools in Belfast completed the PBDQ and an inventory of biographical data. Reliabilities for the four sub-scales was found to be in excess of 0.80, with a total scale reliability of 0.96. Pair-wise T tests using a modified formula for a repeated measures design revealed highly significant differences between teachers' expectations for the roles of principal, vice-principal and heads of department. Analysis of variance showed that there were significant differences between the six schools but few significant differences were found to exist between teachers partitioned on the basis of the biographical data. The finding provides further evidence of the influences of the school upon teachers' expectations.

Mean item scores for each of the four sub-scales for principals, vice-principals and heads of departments were computed to ascertain the rank order of importance assigned by all teachers to each category of functions. The mean and rank of functional categories were respectively, for principals group maintenance (5.87), task achievement (5.73), organizational change (5.63) and administration (5.63), for vice-principals group maintenance (4.80), task achievement (4.63), administration (4.55) and organizational change (4.35), for heads of department organizational change (5.52), group maintenance (4.67), administration (4.55) and task achievement (4.21). All the means exceed 4, indicating a value above average importance.

The fifteen sub-scales were examined to identify the most important and least important functions in terms of teachers' expectations for the principal, the vice-principal and heads of department. For principals the most important functions were staff participation (6.36), planning (6.16), staff motivation (6.01) and adopting change (6.05). The most important functions for vice-principals were staff participation (5.48), organizing (5.12), staff cohesiveness (4.96) and staff motivation (4.96). For heads of department the most important functions were implementing change (5.98), evaluating change (5.66), adopting change (5.32) and staff development (5.26). Teachers indicated that they expected the principal to assign importance to implementing change (4.95), administration (5.02), staff development (5.27) and evaluation (5.39). The corresponding expectation scores for vice-principals were evaluation (4.04), initiating change (4.14), implementing change (4.19) and assessing change (4.25). The least important functions for heads of department were organizing (3.52), administration (3.54), staff cohesiveness (3.96), and planning (4.17). The overall means for all sub-scales for principals, vice-principals and heads of department were respectively 5.62, 4.55, and 4.55. Teachers in this sample, therefore, expect that the principal should share significantly with the vice-principal and heads of department responsibility for the functions described in the PBDQ.

The data suggest that in general the principal should be concerned primarily with formulating goals and policies, fostering participation and motivation and facilitating the adoption of change. The vice-principal's primary functions relate to group maintenance and to organizing and coordinating staff activities. Heads of departments are seen primarily as agents of change, growth and development in contrast with the vice-principal whose major role is seen as providing stability and continuity. Analysis of the 106 items, however, reveals several interesting differences in role expectations. While teachers expect the principal to assume major responsibility for most functions, they assign significantly ($p < 0.05$) higher scores to the vice-principal and heads of department for fifteen of the 106 items. In general primary importance is attributed to the vice-principal for the organization and coordination of staff activities, for pupil discipline and pastoral care and for routine administration. Teachers assigned higher scores to heads of department than they did to either the principal or vice-principal for staff induction, assessment and development and pastoral welfare, for assisting teachers with professional problems and for the adoption and implementation of innovations. Although the items defining each sub-scale were randomly distributed throughout the questionnaire the analyses revealed a clear and consistent set of core expectations for the principal, vice-principal and heads of department, which challenge widely held assumptions regarding the role of the head and senior staff in secondary schools. More specifically vice-principals' expectation scores for forty-four items and heads of department scores for twenty-seven items do not differ significantly ($p < 0.05$) from expectation scores for the principal. The data from this sample provide some support for the proposition that teachers express a strong aspiration for a greater degree of participation and the wider diffusion of leadership functions.

## Conclusions

Conclusions from an exploratory study using relatively small and unrepresentative samples are bound to be tentative. Nor can they be generalized beyond the groups used in the study. They do, however, suggest a number of potentially fruitful areas for further investigation with larger and more representative samples.

Within the samples of principals and teachers used the evidence provides some support for several findings in American studies. Of the significant differences observed between role conceptions, behaviours, perceptions and expectations the most striking finding was the magnitude of the discrepancies between principals' reported actual behaviour and the expectations expressed by teachers. It cannot be asserted that principals can or should necessarily conform with all expectations held by teachers. The principal is constrained by the conflicting expectations held by significant others in his role set, pupils, parents and superiors, for example. The evidence suggests, however, that the existence of extreme differences between principals and teachers may be dysfunctional. To the extent that a principal accurately perceives such difference and is inhibited from modifying either his behaviour or teachers' expectations it may create for the principal a degree of role strain or cognitive dissonance or result in a diminution of teacher morale and needs satisfaction. Either outcome may reduce the effectiveness of the principal's leadership behaviour. Of special interest in the item analysis of teachers' expectations is the strongly expressed aspiration for greater participation in the decision-making process. This accords with the findings of several studies of teachers' demand for professional autonomy and collegial decision-making (Belasco and Alutto, 1972; Sharma, 1963).

The finding of significant differences in teachers' expectations between schools of similar type calls attention to important variations in the organizational context of leadership behaviour. A newly appointed principal from outside the school might well take account of such variations and make such accommodation as may be consistent with his priorities and values. The evidence of significant relationships between leadership behaviour on the one hand and selected characteristics of principals' values, school-level and teacher-level innovativeness provides support for the proposition that effective leadership is more appropriately conceptualized not in terms of personal qualities or situational attributes acting independently but in terms of the subtle interactions of the person, the job and the situation. Correlations, however, do not warrant the inference of any simple cause and effect relationships.

The danger inherent in implying that behaviour may be explained and understood by analyzing an arbitrary list of principals' functions has already been adumbrated. Nonetheless, some interesting questions are suggested by the item analysis of principals' self-reported behaviour, which indicates wide variations in the degree of importance assigned to individual functions and to the three functional categories and in the degree of dissensus that appears to exist among principals. Whether such variations are adventitious or may be explained in terms of self-conscious personal choices by principals based on professional socialization, their internalization of certain norms and their perception of situational characteristics is not known. We need to know much about the values, assumptions and criteria which inform principals' decision-making behaviour. Principals receive little practical guidance from nebulous job specifications and vaguely articulated role expectations held by competing constituencies. It would be inconsistent with the logic of this paper to suggest that principals can be provided with a detailed itinerary to guide them through the tricky terrain of administration. Until research and experience can provide a clearer understanding of the complex determinants and consequences of organizational behaviour in schools we cannot pretend to do more than suggest a kind of diagnostic orienteering kit and a rather blurred road map which locates potential hazards and havens and the likely consequences of following alternative routes, depending on one's destination and one's travelling companions.

## References

ALLEN, B. (1968) *Headship in the 1970s*, Oxford, Basil Blackwell.

ARGYRIS, C. (1962) *Interpersonal Competence and Organisational Effectiveness*, Homewood, Ill., Dorsey Press.

ARGYRIS, C. (1964) *Integrating the Individual and Organisation*, New York, Wiley.

BARON, G. and TAYLOR, W. (1969) *Educational Administration and the Social Sciences*, London, Athlone Press.

BARRY, C.H. and TYE, F. (1975) *Running a School*, London, Temple Smith.

BATES, A.W. (1971) *The Administration of Comprehensive Schools*, PhD. Thesis, University of London.

BELASCO, J. and ALUTTO, J. (1972) 'Decisional participation and teacher satisfaction', *Educational Administration Quarterly*, Winter.

BERMAN, P. *et al.* (1975) *Federal Programmes Supporting Educational Change*, Rand Corporation, Vols. 1–IV.

BERNBAUM, G. (1973) 'Headmasters and schools: Some preliminary findings', *Sociological Review*, 21, 3, pp. 463–84.

BRIDGES, E.M. (1965) 'Bureaucratic role and socialisation: The impact of experience on the elementary principal', *Educational Administration Quarterly*, 1, pp. 18–28.

CHARTERS, W.W. Jr. (1968), cited in GREENFIELD (1968).

COHEN, L. (1970) *Conceptions of Head Teachers Concerning Their Role*, PhD Thesis, University of Keele.

COULSON, A.A. (1974) *The Deputy Head in the Primary School: Role Conceptions of Heads and Deputy Heads*, MEd Dissertation, University of Hull.

CUNNINGHAM, L.L. and GEPHART, W.S., (Eds) (1973) *Leadership: The Science and the Art Today*, New York Peacock Publishers.

GIBB, C.A. (1969) 'Leadership', in LINDZEY, G. and ARONSON, E. (Eds) *The Handbook of Social Psychology*, Reading, Mass. Addison Wesley.

GOLDHAMMER, K. *et al.* (1970) *Issues and Problems in Elementary School Administration*, Centre for Educational Research and Service, Oregon State University.

GOULDNER, A.W. (1968) cited in GREENFIELD, (1968).

GREENFIELD, T.B. (1968) 'Research on the behaviour of educational leaders: Critique of a tradition', *Alberta Journal of Educational Research*, 14, 1, pp. 55–76.

GROSS, N. *et al.* (1958) *Explorations in Role Analyses: Studies of the School Superintendency Role*, New York John Wiley.

GROSS, N. and HERRIOTT, R.E. (1965) *Staff Leadership in Public Schools: A Sociological Inquiry*, New York John Wiley.

GULICK, L. and URWICK, L. (Eds) (1937) *Papers on the Science of Administration*, New York, Institute of Public Administration.

HENCLEY, S.P. (1973) 'Situational behavioural approach to the study of educational leadership' in CUNNINGHAM and GEPHART (1973).

HENCLEY, S.P. *et al.* (1970) *The Elementary School Principalship*, New York Dodd, Mead and Co.

HOLLANDER, E. and JULIAN, J.W. (1969) 'Contemporary trends in the analysis of leadership process', *Psychological Bulletin*, 71, pp. 387–97.

HUGHES, M.G. (1972) *The Role of the Secondary School Head*, PhD Thesis, University College, Cardiff.

HUGHES, M.G. (1974) *Secondary School Administration: A Management Approach*, 2nd ed., Oxford, Pergamon.

JENNINGS, A. (Ed.) (1977) *Management and Headship in the Secondary School*, London Ward Lock Educational.

KELSALL, R.K. and KELSALL, H.M. (1969) *The School Teacher in England and the United States*, Oxford, Pergamon.

LAIDIG, E.L. (1967) *The Influence of Situational Factors on the Administrative Behaviour of Selected Elementary School Principals*, EdD Thesis, University of Texas.

LAMBERT, K. (1975) 'The role of head of department in schools', *BEAS Bulletin*, 3, 2.

LIPHAM, J. (1964) 'Leadership and administration', in GRIFFITHS, D.E. (Ed.) *Behavioural Science and Educational Administration*, 63rd Yearbook, NSSE, Pt. II, Chicago.

LYONS, G. (1976) *Heads' Tasks: A Handbook of Secondary School Administration*, Windsor NFER. Pub. Co.

McCLEARY, L.E. and HENCLEY, S.P. (1965) *Secondary School Administration*, New York Dodd, Mead and Co.

McGEOWN, V. (1979a) 'School Innovativeness as Process and Product', New University of Ulster.

McGEOWN, V. (1979b) 'Dimensions of Teacher Innovativeness', New University of Ulster.

McGEOWN, V. (1979c) 'Organisational Climate for Change in Schools', New University of Ulster.

McGEOWN, V. (1979d) 'Principals' Decision Making Behaviour in The Management of Innovation', New University of Ulster.

MAYO, E. (1946) *The Human Problems of an Industrial Civilisation*, Graduate School of Business Administration, Harvard University.

MEARY, J. (1967) *Differential Perceptions of the Leader Behaviour of Secondary School Principals*, EdD Thesis, University of Maryland.

MORIN, L.H. (1965) 'Role perception and principals', *Canadian Administrator*, 4, pp. 17–20.

OECD/CERI (1973) *Case Studies of Educational Innovations: IV, Strategies for Innovation in Education*, Paris, OECD.

PETERS, R. (Ed.) (1976) *The Role of the Head*, London, Routledge and Kegan Paul.

REAVIS, W.C. (1953) *Administering the Elementary School*, Englewood Cliffs Prentice-Hall.

RICHARDSON, E. (1973) *The Teacher, the School and the Task of Management*, London, Heinemann.

SCHUTZ, W.C. (1958) 'The interpersonal underworld', *Harvard Business Review*, 36, pp. 123–35.

SHARMA, G.L. (1963) *A Comparative Study of the Process of Making and Taking Decisions within Schools in the UK and USA*, PhD Thesis, University of London.

STOGDILL, R.M. (1948) 'Personal factors associated with leadership: A survey of the literature', *Journal of Psychology*, 25, pp. 35–71.

STOGDILL, R.M. (1974) *Handbook of Leadership: A Survey of Theory and Research*, Glencoe Free Press.

TAYLOR, F.W. (1911) *Principles of Scientific Management*, London Harper and Row.

TAYLOR, W. (1968) in ALLEN, (1968).

THOMASON, G.F. (1974) 'Organisation and management', in HUGHES, (1974).

WILLOWER, D.J. (1960) '"Leadership styles and leaders": Perceptions of subordinates', *Journal of Educational Psychology*, 34, pp. 58–64.

YUKL, G. (1971) 'Toward a behavioural theory of leadership' *Organisational Behaviour and Human Performance*, 6, pp. 414–40.

# Educational Management and School Leadership: An Evolutionary Perspective

*David Winkley*
*Grove School, Birmingham*

It would be a mistake to think of school leadership as wholly separate from the contingent political and administrative system that manages it and controls its context. From the first the behaviour of headteachers in state schools was linked to the management expectations of the school boards or LEAs. Writers such as Tropp[1] and Grace[2] describe the struggle of teachers to take command of their professional lives in a state education system which was from its inception highly directive and obsessed at all levels with discipline. The early school managements controlled the service in the Benthamite tradition of public administration with the twin powers of legal authority — especially authority over teacher tenure — and bureaucratic controls. Control was enforced with varying degrees of ferocity through an ever-expanding inspectorial and administrative system. In Birmingham in the 1880s schools were visited up to fifty times a year.[3] In Leeds teachers were instructed to give demonstration lessons to all colleagues, formally annotated by the head. School leadership was inescapably enmeshed in a systematic process of control, the managerial equivalent of the PE lesson in the yard, rigid and enforced by use of the stick. The authority which the inspector had over the head was mirrored in the head's control of his staff and of the teachers' enforced control of the children. 'The crux of the matter', claimed a report of the Board of Education in 1906/7, 'was that some authorities had not learnt to distinguish between control and management.'[4] In 1910 the President of the Board of Education, in a speech in the House, said: 'I should like to refer to the position of the headteachers in secondary schools. I fear they are too much under the control of officials.'[5]

As the twentieth century has progressed there have been considerable modifications of these authority structures. Nonetheless, some fundamental aspects of the control relationship between LEAs and schools have remained. The managerial powers of the LEA are enshrined in the 1944 Education Act. In series of interviews I undertook recently with senior administrators, more than one Chief Officer pointed out that 'I am ultimately *responsible* for the *control* of my schools.' These two key words, like electric contacts, continue to energize questions of who in the end determines the style of school leadership and the manner of school accountability. In a recent publication the NUT Education Department writes: 'The head of the school, under the articles of government or rules of management is *responsible* for internal organisation, management and discipline, and by virtue of his or her position *controls* the teaching and the non-teaching staff.'[6]

Here again the key words 'controls' and 'responsible' are confidently blandished; it is, as it stands, a statement which would have stood in 1880. On the other hand of course, in the 1980s the *actual* meanings — as expressed in practice in head/staff relationships — have changed, and indeed the gap between legalistic and actual meanings is part of the problem of present-day heads. Notions of control in their most blatant authoritarian sense are viewed with considerable distaste, and even those who espouse them have to take into account the *realpolitik* that people, including teachers, cannot be instructed what to do with quite the directive vigour of the past.

It is also true that there is a consistent thread in the managerial nature of school accountability which, whilst it periodically weakens or sharpens in emphasis, is still a key determinant of school leadership. It is not possible for the 1980s head to forget that he is part of a wider controlling managerial system.

This managerial tradition is not, however, the only source of modern school leadership style. Another important influence has come from the evolution of schools themselves, and in particular from two strands of the independent school tradition. Much of our notion of the 'powerful headmaster' myth derives from the exemplar of the public schools' leadership which was, as Badley says of Devine, head of Claysmore, 'a curious combination of sound educational ideals, great ambitions, boundless self confidence, and an artless egoism.'[7] The public schools and their headmasters clung ferociously to their freedoms, and the state secondary school headmasters, especially in the new twentieth century grammar schools, set out to continue an inherited tradition of autonomy. From the turn of the century onwards there was some concern that, following this tradition, state secondary school heads should be entrusted with a large amount of responsibility for, and control over, teaching, organization and discipline.[8] This growing autonomy was tacitly recognized by LEA inspectors, who up to the 1960s in many authorities had the policy of visiting grammar schools only by invitation, informed secondary modern schools that a visit was on the way, and arrived at primary schools uninvited (the primary school being seen in this context as a true inheritor of the elementary school). There is a thread of the tradition of the charismatic and controlling head still alive in state schools — the man who talks about 'his' school and commands respect not so much for his managerial or bureaucratic skills, as for the authority of position, as assertion of personal style.

A concomitant to this is the second and no less important tradition of the much smaller experimental school of the first half of the century — which once again arises almost entirely from the independent school sector. In Stewart's elaborate study of educational innovation in English education, his first reference to an innovatory state school is on page 358 of Volume 2, Prestolee Primary School, in the 1960s.[9] The development of the liberalism of primary education, formally authorized in the Hadow Report of 1931, and later by the Plowden Report, 1968, has its origins in the development of small, radical and sometimes highly eccentric schools of which the most important, in Stewart's view, are Susan Isaac's influential infant school in Cambridge, and A.S. Neill's Summerhill. Such schools represented 'an opposition to the kind of poverty in the education offered in the public and grammar school, and to another kind of poverty in the Revised Code of the elementary school.'[10] They offered a new style of leadership based upon attention to personal relationships as a central value, and undermined the notion of the head as charismatic autocrat, or management/authority representative. Susan Isaacs in particular shifted the attention of the school to the importance of the link between teaching and parenting, and to the family as the fundamental educative institution — one of the most fruitful and interesting ideas to have grown out of English education this century. The model of the school having a family role led to the inescapable consideration of the importance of the child's parents in school, to school/parent liaison, and to broader considerations of the role of the school in the child's community.

This new style of leadership implied, above all, a change of emphasis from the head as an autocratic patriarch to the leader as a consultative figure. It shifted attention from the brutal externals of measurable performance to a sense of the emotional needs of the child. Above all, it complicated the simple line-management model which characterized so strongly the dominant pre-war state elementary school tradition. It complicated the sense of what a good school and good teaching is about, identifying links between motivation, emotional security, enthusiasm, relevance and objective attainments; it put a new emphasis on the role of art and the imagination. This sense has been supported subsequently by growing evidence focussing on the value of 'ethos', and detecting links between personal relationships and academic achievement (Cf. Rutter).[11] It was strengthened in the education system as a whole in part by changing social attitudes towards children, and in part by the recognition of its value by powerful administrative figures from Henry Morris to Alec Clegg.

The present leader/manager role of the headteacher is a complicated amalgamation of elements drawn from these very different traditions. The oft-repeated assumption that it is the head who makes the school is in itself far too simple — as is the notion that the problem with the educational

system is 'bad teachers'. It presumes that heads and teachers act inspir-
ationally with a kind of autonomous control over events which is far from
the truth. This simplified view of the head-as-master is reflected in *Ten Good
Schools* (DES, 1977).[12] It is, as Heller says,[13] a naive and anecdotal interpretation based on a view of the head as historically king of his castle, a mono-
chromic view of the head in the charismatic/autonomous tradition.

It is clear that the 1980s headship, while retaining some of the vestigial
elements of the much simpler management control features of the 1880s, is a
much more complicated phenomenon. The head's power resides not so
much — or not only — in his formal status of appointed middle manager, as
in choosing a style amongst a number of options. Like an organist he has a
variety of stops to play upon in restless combination; he can manipulate each
within its own constraints. These can be divided into two groups, broadly
reflecting two strands of the contrasting traditions: the *managerial* and the
*consultative*.

### Managerial

1 Legal: the head has both *in loco parentis* common law and the 1944
Education Act to support his position; the head can claim responsibility in law, and can make unilateral decisions according to his
judgement of appropriateness.
2 Hierarchical: like all managers in the upper/middle echelons of the
hierarchy, the head can take advantage of LEA 'authority' when it
suits him. He has particular influence over teachers' promotional
prospects.
3 Bureaucratic: the head has considerable control of the information
system.
4 Financial: via 2 and 3 the head can claim (if he so wishes) control
over financial allocations to the school.

### Consultative

5 Professional: as the appointed 'professional' leader, the head has
considerable powers to define the parameters of the teaching world.
6 Psychological: the head is the appointed group leader of the staff,
and has powers to manipulate events to develop, or influence, the
staff group.
7 Parental: the head has a very special role in relation to parents,
being in law the person to whom the parents ultimately delegate
responsibility for their children during school hours: he thus acts as
a quasi-father figure, the most crucial point of contact for parents.
8 Strategic: the head has access to a diverse number of support/power

references outside the formally established ones of the LEA. These may include the Governing Body, local politicians, community representatives — as well as parents — any of whom may be used as a means of blocking, shifting, countering, urging, or otherwise confronting the LEA managerial system itself.

This is strategically a formidable array of choices, and part of the success of successful headteachers lies in the subtlety, efficiency and cunning to which they are mutually exploited. The drawback is that each of these potential areas of authority is also potentially a constraint. The complexity of the modern headship derives not only from the multiplicity of choices from the authority-matrix he is able to make, but the fact that each mode of authority has a negative as well as a positive capability.

I can't be sure my local authority is going to support me. . . .

Our LEA is increasingly using money on resources which are outside the schools' direct control. . . .

I get very little more than a vaguely interested support from the Governing Body. . . .

Our Governing Body is highly political — it's trying to force peace studies into our curriculum. . . .

There are people on our staff who have created a kind of subversive group leadership to the head. . . .

Clearly the head is not necessarily going to have things all his own way. Moreover, these different 'authorities' are by no means necessarily compatible with each other. From the LEA perspective the head is expected to ensure accountability and efficiency from his staff. Officers looking for the conventionally definable tend to attend to measurable and visible elements of performance. As one chief adviser said to me, 'we look for neatness and good display work, the kind of school you can take a visitor round . . . it always gives away what's going on. . . .' The staff on the other hand may expect the head to protect their autonomy, and look for good working conditions. The parents expect the head to ensure that the school responds to their expectations, and to the needs of their particular child. The children — the silent majority — probably have the sharpest awareness of all of how well the head has steered an effective course between these pressures, an awareness intuited, as it were, in their daily lives in school. The head may feel uneasily that the various power groups that confirm his authority may not be at all responsive to the child's actual needs. This is a lonely and disorienting perception when it occurs, and he might icily conclude, with the character in Thomas Keneally's *Gossip from the Forest*, that 'in battle the moral stature of the commander is the deciding issue.' Yet, of course, with heads as with generals, moral stature does not live easily with the need for cunning strategic sleights of hand, or the thick skin and lack of humility that successful leadership behaviour often demands.

The result is a job not only of complexity but also of unusual stress. The head above all is highly exposed, representing authority in a world in which traditional formal authority is decreasingly respected. His strengths lie increasingly in his skills as a negotiator of stamina or sheer awkwardness. As Rhodes Boyson once wrote, an authority will leave the head alone if he is reasonably successful and if he attains a reputation for being awkward.[14]

It is hard to know how many heads succeed in this enterprise, or even what success means precisely by these criteria. There are certainly many confusions that result from such evident role strain. So many different loyalties can lead to a kind of intellectual paralysis — and to endless confusing compromises. What is a 'good school' (cries the compromising voice of the negotiator) but the creation of impressions and images in the minds of your clients — teachers, LEA, parents? As there is no necessary consortium of agreement — except within the broadest terms — between what the different client groups expect of you, the head is in danger of taking the crudest of external criteria as his value: there are many pressures on him to present a 'face' to the world of visitors and scrutineers. All interested parties have vested interests and limited perspectives, and the head is under pressure to run a course down the middle of the various expectations, putting a particularly high priority on external image-making.

The vulnerability of school heads, bewildering to outsiders and often to officers in the LEA itself (whose place in the leadership/management nexus is more precisely defined), is often accompanied by a sense of isolation. This isolation is caused by the insecurity of his objectives, and the general uncertainty of his management role. The loneliness is emphasized by the fact that heads feel their schools are peculiarly special (as well as peculiarly vulnerable to criticism from all directions). Defensiveness in this state of isolation can result in a rigidity bordering on arrogance, and a determination to exploit all possible managerial/legalistic artillery, together with self-assertiveness and remorseless use of power over the staff group. This develops into a modified version of old-fashioned authoritarianism which only survives because of the strategic weakness of class teachers in the system. Authoritarianism in this context is, above all, an attempt to *simplify*. Sometimes of course, teachers resist, like children against a father figure. 'We've withdrawn our goodwill. We do no dinner duties and all go home at 3.30. The LEA have tried to intervene ... but we're keeping this up until the head either leaves or changes....' The LEA in this case is uneasy about responding to such demands, and the situation, which looks suspiciously like the sulking of a slapped (or possibly oppressed) child, is currently entering its second year, the head resolute on his lonely pinnacle.

At its worst, heads have been known to retreat entirely into their rooms, or occupy themselves on strange and obsessively mundane tasks. In one school the staff used to organize a sweepstake on who saw the head first during the school week. Another head of a large comprehensive school recently spent a whole day looking for a small boy's lost pump.

We might go on to argue that this curious complexity of modern school leadership is obviously unsatisfactory. If so, one rational form of improvement might be to reaffirm the management tradition in order to simplify the role of the head as middle manager in a better structured and more precisely accountable system. The Secretary of State's recent White Paper on teaching quality is a step in that direction.[15] There is no doubt that many LEAs on both sides of the political spectrum are sympathetic to his view that bad schools — perhaps all schools — can be improved by managerial attentiveness and the discipline of poor teachers.

This approach is distinguished by increasing inspection, direction from the centre (the DES or county/city hall), tightening and strengthening the administrative (as opposed to the professional) policy-making caucus. It is relatively easy for administrators to take hold of the reins by virtue of their prime influence in decision-making in LEAs. As Kogan puts it: 'Organisation constraints ... inevitably make CEOs sensitive to what can be done with existing policies and law. . . . No teacher need worry himself about such things.'[16] Thus, the teachers, administratively naive, and locked away in their classrooms, are quietly dismissed from the scene. Administrators have considerable power, in particular, over monitoring the performance of schools, and control of teacher promotion. Pateman[17] is amongst a number of commentators who have argued that in the 1980s the debate has been structured in such a way to weaken the teacher's voice.

Bergen, in an impressive analysis of the development of teaching into a quasi-profession controlled by a managerial elite over the period 1870–1910, notes the way the move to professional unity was from the first controlled by segregating the different groups of teachers, isolating secondary from elementary teachers, and women from men.[18] Segregation of teachers in the 1980 model is to be achieved by *training*: the idea is that, as at the turn of the century, movement from one part of the system to another should be discouraged on the grounds of a need for an increasing definition of subject and age specialism. In practice this is a case of the mis-use of common sense arguments in the cause of greater managerial control of educational events.

From the head's point of view, this process seems to strengthen his hand by marking out in a thoroughly nineteenth century fashion the managerial responsibilities of the head as middle manager. Increased definition of role in a well ordered hierarchy, together with increasing precision of objectives in the system as a whole, gives clarity to administrative and managerial impulses. It is somehow easier and more purposeful to be a manager than a leader.

The problem is that this particular version of managerialism, despite its apparent administrative elegance, does not simplify the complexities of school leadership, and fails to tackle the central question of how to convincingly improve schools. This is for a number of reasons. First, it pays attention to only one strand in the historical evolution of school leadership. Pandora's box has been opened. Regression to the simple notion of a directorial system with a directorial headmaster is now an unconvincing option. The complicating voices will not go away. It fails to recognize how much the evolution of the educational system into its present state is related to the historical development of different voices competing for control. Musgrave has argued that developments in the education system have taken place over the years, not so much out of clear managerial or political initiatives, as from struggles among disparate interest groups competing for control — periods of struggle punctuated by periods of bargaining, ending in truce situations.[19] Power balances and negotiated stances are now seen as unavoidable ways to proceed. Managerial purpose based upon a reassertion of unnegotiable authority is fighting a hard, and probably an ineffective, battle against the tendency for all kinds of authorities — including educational ideologies — to diversify.

Secondly, it is not possible to ignore the powerful decentralist tendencies in the present educational system. The educational philosophy of radical conservatism (the main thrust behind the shift to managerial accountability) embraces what seem to be incompatible opposites — the centralist managerial will to control and improve the services, and the decentralist demands of the consumer to have a say in the process. The radical left have a curiously similar dilemma. For them the attraction of imposing change from a directive political impulse consorts uneasily with recognition of the desirability of shifting power to ordinary individuals and communities over events which affect their lives — over the way schools are run, for instance. It is, moreover, as we have already argued, at the crossroads of these paradoxes that the school head stands.

There is a third reason why 'managerialism' in its historical form fails to clarify the debate as to how best to lead (and thus by implication, improve) schools. This is because it fails to take into account the autonomous nature of teaching itself. There is a good deal of evidence that teachers can successfully isolate themselves in their classrooms, and remove themselves largely from the storm of the debate. Boyan argues that schools exhibit much more structural looseness than is usual in bureaucratic institutions, and that this effectively serves to protect the teacher's autonomy.[20] Mary Lee Smith is one amongst many who have noted how curriculum innovation can become attenuated to the point of extinction by unsympathetic class teachers.[21]

Teaching is a very isolated and isolating job in which persuasion and goodwill are at a premium. Children, their motivation and their performance, are happily not — or not entirely — a statistically analyzable product, which accounts in part for the fact that schools as institutions are extremely hard to manage along precisely directive principles.

We are left with the question of which way the system in the long run will, and ought to, develop. It is possible that despite pressures to the contrary, we shall have a splintering of different management styles and approaches in different local authorities, an administrative pluralism of a peculiarly localized kind reflecting the different perceptions of LEAs and Chief Officers, some of whom are suspicious of the naivety of the managerial cult of efficiency and of centralistic accountability tendencies, and have a very realistic awareness of the nature and difficulties of school leadership in the present climate.

Another possibility is that the system as a whole is simply not in its present form susceptible to long-term planning of any kind. Derr and Delong, amongst others, have argued that 'schools exist in a decreasing market and generally have very few economic resources. They are unable to diversify their markets because of their legal mandates.'[22] There is thus the question of whether school systems can support long-term organizational plans. Most administrators are aware of the nightmare of continual political and economic shifts in planning, which give no hope to anything beyond short-term objectives, and make keeping the show on the road the most important thing. The point has been equally forcefully made by head-teachers, and Marland has undoubtedly reflected the opinion of many heads that pressures of school life as it works at present preclude any proper planning for long-term strategies.[23]

Nonetheless, schools and school systems inevitably *will* evolve and we have some responsibility to set compass bearings, and fight against arbitrariness and the pressure always to plan (if that is the right word) for the short term. So what do we do?

Our central argument has been that the present system as it has evolved encourages above all a *vis inertiae*, a psychology of compromise and conformity in its leadership. This uneasy observation, once recognized, presents particular difficulties to management, simply because it is not possible to respond by directive managerial strategies without either making matters worse, or only making peripheral improvements. The problem with schools is not that they are full of bad teachers who ought to be disciplined, or hopeless schools which can be easily improved by managerial direction, but that they lack the confidence, skills or insight to make themselves a whole lot better. A lack of understanding of the skills and processes required for the development of excellence begins with senior administration, and continues into the school leadership itself.

If we ask what kinds of initiative need to be taken, we may begin with the proposition that we need, above all, a leadership — which includes a school leadership — process which will convincingly identify excellence and effectively nurture and generalize it. This has to be the *prima mobile*, the point of reference to which all other principles, and activities, ought to be subservient.

We shall be accused here of going in circles: it all depends what we mean by excellence. It is certainly true that excellence in schools may develop in many different ways. The present Secretary of State has one particular view of excellence that goes back to the tradition of radical toryism of people like Sir John Gorst,[24] expecting the school system to respond as a first principle to the requirements of an academic elite to which the rather different education of the many is made subservient. Another, and quite different view of excellence, is described by Musgrave who proposes (and anticipates) 'the death of the school as a community, and on its grave must rise a fundamentally different kind of organisation, voluntary in character, sensitive to the needs of clients and consumers....'[25] This firmly places the school in a further education setting, in which the head would become something like a college principal, or the chairman of an academic board. Hargreaves presents yet another strikingly different model of the excellent school, which is much closer to the tradition of the best primary schools.[26] The Hargreaves secondary school would retain an organizational identity and ethos of the kind the comprehensive school has at present, but he opposes the tradition of hierarchical management; it would have a more liberal and radically different curriculum, and would (like Musgrave's) shift authority to the community. In the Hargreaves model the head will require developmental skills — an understanding of how the ethos of the school can be facilitated to evolve a responsiveness to individual needs. It is possible in this model that the head as formally appointed manager might eventually disappear altogether.

The problem with all utopian perceptions of excellence, whatever their ideological background, is how we might successfully achieve them. The argument as I have developed it requires — most of all — a process of long-term sophisticated planning. This planning needs to be based upon two fundamental principles:

1   that in the end it is the school leaders and teachers in a relationship with parents and local communities who enact the *meanings* of excellence (whatever they are), and without excellent and committed teachers no model will actually work and
2   that schools and communities require freedom to work out these qualitative meanings for themselves — not without data, support, analysis, recommendations and the like, but none the less with an ultimate autonomy to explore the needs of their children, as they see them.

This is to acknowledge the viable claims of different theoretical views as to the nature of excellence. But it is a realistic and unpompous kind of acknowledgement. It represents a shift to a recognition of the consumer as the ultimate arbiter or (put more nobly) a perception of education in a democracy as a *service* as opposed to a centrally imposed purpose. Both these principles can be encouraged within the powers of the present system, and are, indeed, a logical response to one part of its historical evolution — its decentralist and consumer-oriented tendencies.

We know remarkably little about how good schools of any kind evolve, and we are in urgent need of detailed descriptive accounts. It can be argued that good schools develop above all from responsive and precise identifications of working examples of excellence by intelligent leadership. The head needs to consider primarily his role as facilitator of a carefully observed practice of teacher excellence leading to the generalization of this good practice to the larger group. Thus the teacher practitioner becomes the main focus of attention and value. This evolutionary process may demand in the long run the weakening of the formal managerial powers of the head, and a shifting to a more democratic notion of leadership, in which the teachers, and particularly the best teachers, share more formal authority over decisions than they have at present. I have argued elsewhere[27] that the developmental process where the facilitating head achieves such changes of focus and authority is a function of slow and careful planning.

It is the same process that needs to be extended beyond schools to the administrative system as a whole. The failures of the present system to build from perceptive understanding and encouragement of the excellence of actual teachers and schools can be illustrated by one example. One head described 'a head of department for art in my school who is a teacher of the highest quality of anyone I have seen. His achievements are acknowledged by everyone who has seen his work.' The head has developed the facilitating/ generalizing process in his own school, by using this teacher as the focus of good practice. 'I've managed to get him to influence the art work of all the teachers in the school ... he has really built up their confidence in the subject ... the standard of art has gone up amazingly.' Yet the teacher remained almost totally unrecognized outside the school: 'He's never been used by the LEA on courses, or to develop work in the Authority.' Why not? 'I don't think the recognition of quality extends to the use of teachers in the process of development of the authority here. I've invited art advisers to come and see his work ... so far, no-one has come. . . .' How long has he been with you? 'Eight years. . . .' In another authority a head wrote to his LEA and the DES to get some acknowledgement, some dialogue, about the quality of the work he felt his school was engaged in. It wasn't that his LEA didn't appreciate the work of his school (they were, on investigation, really rather proud of it); it was that they were uninterested in setting up the kind of dialogue that would move this outstanding head's thoughts onwards. He felt a kind of intellectual isolation. The DES were no help either. They were certainly not interested in using the school as a model. It was left to another organization,[28] outside the conventional management system, to put the head in touch with colleagues in other parts of the country, working in similarly inventive ways.

There is no convincing evidence that teachers are adequately consulted, or used, either as a central focus of management purpose or in INSET, or in teacher training. In a survey of 200 teacher opinions about administration which I recently completed, over 90 per cent of all teachers at all levels, in each of the (very different) authorities examined, considered that they were not adequately drawn into the decision-making process; of the seventy questions to which they responded on many aspects of advising, inspection, accountability and administration, this was the most strongly and decisively expressed response.

The truth is that very largely policy-makers exclude the teachers, and the class teachers are the most devalued and ignored members of the service, in which the most powerful and best-paid members are an administrative elite. We need to draw brilliant practitioners more convincingly into the decision-making process, thus giving new status to the practice of teaching. Teachers need to be given more time to talk together — across schools, across authorities.

There should be a rolling programme of teacher-directed discussions, greater freedom for schools to develop new possibilities, and a close and rigorous scrutiny of success — as well as endless, and precise, search for excellence wherever it may be. It would require teachers speaking out much more, and a dramatic rethinking of management priorities, consultative procedures, decision-making strategies, finance allocations, communication methods, and even salary scales. INSET and release of teachers to develop and think about their work with colleagues should be expanded on a huge scale.

There are, of course, places where authorities are moving towards these quite radically different approaches to developing excellence. The Cleveland developmental model touches upon this kind of process,[20] as do some of the recent developments in Oxfordshire. Most authorities, like most schools, have positive features and points of growth, but in the main LEA attempts to tackle the development of excellence convincingly have been on the margin, piecemeal, lacking the central force and impetus and management energy that is required. Most of all, they are excessively dominated by controlling management hierarchies, who have all too successfully put vested interests before the business of facilitating good teaching, committed to control as a value in itself (Salter and Tapper).[30]

It should be added finally that there is a role too for the DES in this development process, which is to examine with much greater precision the workings of LEAs — and to use excellence as a model here. It is through the LEAs that the DES needs to work, just as the LEAs need to work through the schools, and the heads through the teachers. The system itself requires more clear thinking, more listening, and more humility in the presence of those who actually make the good things work.

The kinds of changes which I have described would require from the teachers as an epiphenomenon of their new sense of value and authority, a kind of self-criticism and openmindedness that gives more say to those most influenced by the system — the parents and children. Halsey has suggested the need for a radical shift in the present accountability structures to the community itself who ought in his view to have much greater power over the development of schools.[31] In his view LEAs constrain rather than advance such developments, and he puts forward the idea of a nationwide network of direct-grant schools funded from the centre. As a potential model, he describes the schools of Yugoslavia. There is also the example of the Australian Capital Territory, a local education system run by the teachers and parents, who control everything from teacher promotion appointment to curriculum and administrative activities.[32] It appears to be academically respectable, as well as pedagogically imaginative: the fears of take-over by reactionary parents and self-protective teachers have not been realized.

The important fact here for the school leader is the potential autonomy he, and the community, would have to develop a school responsive to particular local needs, and parental and community values. Such a shift to increased autonomy (which I would accompany with long-term detailed analysis of progress) is not without supportive evidence from surprising quarters. At least one LEA was recently taken aback by the outcome of an independent financial analysis by management consultants who concluded that it would be more cost efficient to greatly decentralize the LEA's financial procedures.

Business consultants who have analyzed the educational system closely have come up with more gloomy conclusions that schools ought to learn ways of protecting themselves against the insensitive and tough-minded behaviour of central offices. Schools, they argue, must fight against being made management directed business-style enterprises.[33] Decentralizing would, however, mean that 'the LEA would no longer occupy the role they like to retain as social validators for the assumptions which teachers use as guides in their work.'[34] The logical development of the process might be (as would actually happen in the Halsey model) for the management to facilitate its own extinction. There is no place, he argues, for the complicating voices of the middle men. The good manager in education, like the good head (indeed, like the good father), quietly removes himself from the scene as the children grow older, stronger and more independently minded — and retires discreetly to his garden.

These are radical alternatives to centralist thinking and the increase in managerial powers of control. They have many attractions. They offer alternatives to the short-term superficial (or very sketchy) planning and philosophizing which pass for educational planning and decision-making at the moment. They offer alternatives to the obfuscating (as opposed to creative) complexity and the lack of intellectual motivation and inventiveness that bedevil the present job of being a school head. They are responsive to the argument that 'excellence' is the province of excellent class teachers — is by definition, *what good teachers do* — whilst aiso accepting the values of parents and local communities. They respond, too, to important evolutionary elements in the growth of teaching towards fully fledged professional status, as well as to an increasing public demand for a meaningful voice in a decentralized service. They offer a developmental model, a way of moving on to improve the service as a whole; moreover they develop perfectly well *from where we are now*. They focus, above all, on what is already being well done — and there is plenty of good practice hiding under stones in schools and LEAs all over the country. Finally, they take up the best elements of the educational traditions which have developed over the years, and they leave the nineteenth century back where it belongs — to rest in peace.

## References

1  TROPP, A. (1957) *The School Teachers*, London, Heinemann.
2  GRACE, G.R. (1978) *Teachers, Ideology and Control*, London, Routledge and Kegan Paul.
3  *Birmingham Daily Post*, Report, 6 November 1894.
4  Report of the Board of Education, 1906/7.
5  Speech of the President of the Board of Education in the House of Commons, Parliamentary Debates, Fifth Series, XIX, Cols. 393–4, 13 July 1910.
6  NUT Memorandum of Guidance to Heads No. 16 (1982) 'Students on Teaching Practice'.
7  BADLEY, J.H. (1955) *Memories and Reflections*, London, p. 202.
8  Cf. EDMONDS, E.L. (1962) *The School Inspector*, London, Routledge and Kegan Paul, p. 141.
9  STEWART, W.A.C. (1968) *The Educational Innovators*, London, Macmillan.
10 *Ibid.*, Vol. 2, p. 35.
11 RUTTER, M. *et al.* (1979) *Fifteen Thousand Hours*, London, Open Books.
12 HMI (1977) *Ten Good Schools*, Matters for Discussion, No. 1.
13 HELLER, H. (1982) 'Management development for headteachers', in GRAY, H.L. (Ed.) *The Management of Educational Institutions*, Lewes, Falmer Press, pp. 225–6.
14 BOYSON, R. (1974) *Oversubscribed*, Ward Lock, p. 108.
15 DES (1983) *Teaching Quality*, London, HMSO, March.
16 KOGAN, M. and VAN DER EYKEN, W. (1973) *County Hall; the Role of the CEO*, Harmondsworth Penguin pp. 65–6.
17 PATEMAN, T. (1980) 'The great accountability debate', *The Times Educational Supplement*, 22 February 1980, p. 18.
18 BERGEN, B.H. (1982) 'Gender, class and the effort to professionalize elementary teaching in England 1870–1910', *History of Education Quarterly*, 22, 1. pp. 1–21.
19 MUSGRAVE, P.W. (1970) 'A model for the analysis of the English education system', *Transaction of the 6th World Congress of Sociology*, Vol. 4, pp. 65–82; reprinted in MUSGRAVE, P.W. (Ed.) (1970) *Sociology, History and Education*, London, Methuen.
20 BOYAN, N.J. (1969) 'The emergent role of the teacher in the authority structure of the school', in CARVER, F. and SERGIOVANNI, T. (Eds) *Organisation and Human Behaviour*, New York, McGraw Hill, p. 203.
21 LEE SMITH, M.L. (1978) in STAKE, R. *et al.*, *Case Studies in Science Education*, Centre for Instructional Research and Curriculum Evaluation, University of Illinois, Booklet 2, p. 23.
22 DERR C.B. and DELONG T.J. (1982) 'What business management can teach schools', in GRAY, H.L., *op. cit.*, p. 129.
23 MARLAND, M. (1982) 'The politics of improvement in schools', in *Educational*

*Management and Administration*, Proceedings of the 10th Annual Conference, No. 2, June, p. 120.

24  Cf. SIMON, B. (1965) *Education and the Labour Movement, 1870–1920*, London, p. 238.

25  MUSGRAVE, F. (1980) *School and the Social Order*, Wiley.

26  HARGREAVES, D. (1982) *The Challenge for the Comprehensive School*, London, Routledge and Kegan Paul.

27  WINKLEY, D.R. (1983) 'An analytical view of primary school leadership', *School Organization*, 3, 1.

28  The Centre for the Study of the Comprehensive School, York.

29  Cf. HELLER, H., *op. cit.*

30  SALTER, B. and TAPPER, T. (1981) *Education, Politics and the State*, London, Grant McIntyre, p. 212.

31  HALSEY, A.H., Speech to the North of England Education Conference, 1981.

32  Cf. *The Guiding Principles and Aims of the A.C.T. Schools Authority*, Interim A.C.T. Schools Authority Report, 1973; *Primary Children in the A.C.T.*, Report of the Committee to Review Primary Education in A.C.T. Schools (1980); and *Senior Secondary Education, A.C.T.* (1980).

33  DERR C.B. and DELONG, T.J., *op. cit.*

34  EGGLESTON, S.J. (Ed.) (1979) *Teacher Decision Making in the Classroom*, London, Routledge and Kegan Paul, p. 60.

# School Decision-Making and the Primary Headteacher*

*Paul Harling*
*All Saints' CE School, Chorley*

Arthur Razzell has suggested that 'it is the concentration of decision-making in the hands of headteachers'[1] which prevents the emergence and development of professionalism in too many schools. He pleads for greater staff participation in decision-making if we are to avoid 'staleness and ossification'[2] in the years to come.

Without doubt such participation is an admirable aim for any organization in which people constitute both the staff and the clientele. Unfortunately it seems likely that the concentration of decision-making in the hands of the head will be maintained and could possibly be increased during the late 1980s, particularly if there are no specific legal measures introduced to change the current management structure in schools. This proposition is based on the contrary suggestion, to be examined here, that it is mainly *because of* the development of professionalism in what is basically a bureaucratically structured organization that primary school headteachers have maintained and could enhance their autonomy in decision-making relative to both the staff of the school and to the 'outsiders' who have an official interest in the conduct of the school, namely the school governors and the LEA and its officers. It seems likely, therefore, that the future direction of primary education is firmly in the hands of the twenty-odd thousand primary school headteachers because of circumstances both within and beyond their control.

## A Model of School Decision-Making

Hanson developed a model of school decision-making applicable to the United States.[3] This model has been adapted and extended here in an effort to find those fundamental features which will help in understanding the

* This is an edited version of the article which appeared in *Education 3–13*, 8, 2, 1980, pp. 44–8.

complex processes of control and decision-making in a primary school and local school system caused by the interaction of professionalism and bureaucracy.

It is suggested that the following features in the educational system shape decision-making in English primary schools:

1 *three* spheres of influence on decision-making with decision being (a) formally zoned to the 'outsiders' as defined above, or (b) informally zoned to classroom teachers, or (c) formally *and* informally zoned to the headteacher. These spheres together form a local sub-system of the wider educational system;

2 various degrees of autonomy in decision-making within each sphere, the amount depending mainly on participants' knowledge and use of the possible bases of authority and power;

3 identifiable constraints placing limits on the decision-making auton- omy of each of the three spheres;

4 areas of overlap of the spheres within which there are processes of interaction, negotiation and accommodation which serve to reduce conflict;

5 direct and indirect strategies used by members of each sphere to attempt to manage the behaviour of members of the other two spheres;

6 defensive strategies used by members of each sphere to protect their own sphere from influence by the other two.

This article examines the model and its implications under three broad headings. First, it considers the range of characteristics of, and the justification for the existence of, the three spheres of influence. Secondly, it considers the limits to autonomy of decision-making within the three spheres. Thirdly, it considers the interaction system; that is, the attempts to manage behaviour across spheres, and the counter-strategies to defend spheres from influence by others.

### The Spheres of Influence

#### 1  *That of the School Governors, the LEA and Its Officers*

LEAs are required by law to provide 'efficient' and 'suitable' education for their areas. But as the Auld Report points out, 'The authority does not and could not, meet these fundamental obligations simply by providing or financing school premises and resources and providing teachers to man the schools. There is also the responsibility to control the conduct and curriculum of each school'.[4] Various Acts of Parliament have therefore given the LEA a wide range of responsibilities and powers in such broad matters as the provision and allocation of physical, financial and human resources, as well as in the conduct of the whole sub-system to encourage a degree of uniformity of provision and to allow for the handling of developments and contingencies.

However, the important point for this discussion is that the LEA has a choice[5] whether to control the conduct and curriculum itself or to transfer such control in whole or in part to other persons under the articles of governance it is obliged to make for the school. In effect each LEA has exercised its statutory power to divest itself of the control of the conduct and curriculum of each primary school. This has been done by drawing up articles of management based on the DES model articles which have stated that, 'the LEA shall determine the general educational character of the school. . . . The managers, subject to this, shall have the general direction of the conduct and curriculum of the school . . . *the headteacher shall control the internal organisation, management and discipline of the school*' (my emphasis).

## 2   That of the Classroom Teachers

Even casual observation of an English primary school day will show that certain decisions are being made independently of the head or the 'outsiders'. Hanson refers to these decisions as being in 'protected pockets of autonomy'.[6] They tend to involve the day-to-day running of a classroom and to surround the processes of teaching and learning — the 'chalk-face'. It must be stressed here that the autonomy of a class teacher has no formal basis in law. It rests instead upon non-formal power justified by the ideology of the teaching profession and the expertise of teachers, it is one of the ways of attempting to reconcile the problems of professional people working in bureaucratic organizations and involves the setting up of personal, flexible rules based on knowledge of a particular class and the subject matter to be taught. But the non-formal nature of such rules must be emphasized: in law teachers are assistants to the head.

## 3   That of the Headteacher

The headteacher of an English primary school has been granted considerable formal power by the law of the land. But in addition he is always a teacher by training and thereby possesses a base of informal power, justified by the ideology of the teaching profession and his expertise as a teacher. As such he possesses both a direct action role, being involved in the day-to-day mission of the school as an agency for the promotion of pupil learning and a managerial, or administrative, role. He is therefore in a unique position in the school system, wearing the dual labels of 'chief executive' and 'leading professional'.[7] The head has legal, moral, or professional responsibility for five broad areas, each of which can involve colleagues but never be handed over completely since the head remains legally accountable for all internal school matters.

First, the head tends to make final decisions concerning the overall aims of the school, usually because he is regarded by both teachers and 'outsiders' as the one possessing the overall view.

Secondly, heads usually make final decisions concerning the allocation of human and material resources within the school. He has almost total power over the form and range of equipment which comes into school because he, or a delegate, are the only members of staff who can sign orders and invoices. There is no prior division by the LEA before the allowance is notified to the school.

Thirdly, the head is concerned with boundary decisions. To a large extent he controls both internal and external communications, monitoring and filtering attitudes and flows of information.

Fourthly, he is concerned with security, discipline and the like, formulating rules based on memoranda from the LEA and his own knowledge of the situation. It is necessary for them to be rules for which he is prepared to be legally responsible and so they are usually his rules.

Fifthly, and a very important point in this discusion, is the head's concern with evaluation and monitoring of staff and pupil progress. Teachers, as professionals or at least semi-professionals, do not readily allow their work to be evaluated in public, while at the same time the 'outsiders' accept to some extent the need for professionals to be evaluated by other professionals. The head is seen as the most satisfactory agent of evaluation. In combination particularly with his role regarding boundary decisions he is a powerful figure both in fact and in potential.

## The Limits to Autonomy

No person's autonomy can be without limits. In the case of a local educational system and school the limits of decision-making autonomy are shaped by several forces, some rigid, others allowing for considerable interpretation to suit circumstances.

For example, the law affects the behaviour of the participants within the three spheres at practically every point, whether we are considering common law, statutory law, or ministerial regulation. It is the law which shapes and limits LEA autonomy *vis-à-vis* central government. It is the law which places the task of running the school in the hands of the head, even allowing his personal school rules, whether written or implied, to have the force of law. His decisions, therefore, can have significant legal implications for the participants in the other spheres, and can therefore limit their autonomy without necessarily infringing his own.

The head is also very favourably placed relative to other participants if we consider constraints imposed by the characteristics and availability of educational resources. 'Outsider' control of schools is limited by, for example, the philosophy of equality of provision, which limits resource influence on particular schools, and by the relatively remote, infrequent and impersonal decision-making of 'the office'. Teachers' pay is nationally determined, the organization of primary school staffing is relatively 'flat' and national agreements tend to award extra pay for experience and education rather than for specific skill shortages. Sanctions and incentives available to outsiders are therefore limited. The headteacher is the man on the spot. His is the sphere from which the most effective direction and influence can emanate.

His pivotal position in relation to political influences on school control and decision-making also seems clear. Because of his legally defined responsibilities and discretionary powers a head is able to fend off attempted political influences on the conduct and curriculum of the school. LEAs are subject to party political changes and therefore policy changes. Individual teachers have individual views on various policies.But in the midst of it all the headteacher still retains formal responsibility for the internal organization, management and discipline of the school and possesses discretionary powers which to a large extent allow him to determine the limits of autonomy of others. It is his responsibility, and his alone, to interpret higher order policy and to manage the day-to-day school-community relationship. It is his role to mediate between the school and the community it serves, and the words that he chooses to use can determine the attitudes of other participants towards him and towards each other.

Therefore, given that there are constraints on the autonomy of the participants in school decision-making, the head would seem to be the participant most likely to be able to influence the limits of his own autonomy. Any personal constraints will therefore be from the head's own choice to *allow* others to participate in any particular decision. Indeed it seems valid to extend this to the suggestion that the autonomy of 'outsiders' and 'teachers', relative to headteachers and with regard to decision-making in schools, depends upon the management, administrative and leadership style of the headteacher and the climate which is developed. The relative extent to which the head is 'concerned for people' or 'concerned for getting the job done' can determine the environment for future development, and changes in the head's beliefs would seem likely to alter the scope and intensity of the constraints on others.

The fundamental point is that decision-making is an ongoing process, depending on present circumstances for future development, and a long-serving head has usually determined the climate to an extent which is difficult for others to change and influence. Meanwhile his own unique combination of formal and informal authority will minimize the effectiveness of attempts to influence his decisions while allowing him to influence others.

## The Interaction System

The decision-making process in schools is more complex than is suggested by the existence of three clear spheres. There also exist areas of overlap where extensive negotiation or collaboration or bargaining takes place, and within which the participants develop and use strategies for influence over other spheres, if possible without direct intervention, and also for protection of the participants' own spheres.

A superordinate can manage and influence subordinate behaviour by a number of means. He can motivate the individual to pursue overall organizational goals by harnessing and satisfying the subordinate's own goals and needs through granting, for example, security and facilities for social interaction, esteem and achievement of 'self-realization'. He can learn and utilize psychological techniques of persuasion and negotiation. He can retrain subordinates to fulfil organization goals more effectively. He can reinforce positively any good work, perhaps by suggesting that it is 'good for the children'. He can manipulate the subordinate's sense of professionalism by granting at least a sense of independence of action. Conversely, it is possible to imply that a particular action is 'unprofessional' — the point being that it is usually the superordinate who is defining 'professionalism' in order to influence the subordinate.

Superordinates legally control all appointments and the allowance and status structure, this being a prime example of the actual influence of the headteacher. His is the dominant voice in the appointment and promotion of subordinates. In the long run, a headteacher can make serious inroads into the class teachers' sphere of control by judicious appointments and promotions of cooperative teachers. In addition, when he needs to defend his sphere he can 'pass the buck', form a committee to play for time, or simply invoke the law and refuse to cooperate.

Fundamentally, the chance of someone taking a leading role in decision-making is considerably influenced by his position regarding lines of communication; the more access you have to information, the more prominent your role is likely to be. The primary school headteacher, by being at the apex of both the formal and informal internal structure, and by being the major filter for outside information, has more chance of being centrally placed with respect to information flows both up and down, and also of manipulating the organizational structure to ensure that in the longer term his position is maintained and indeed enhanced.

This is not to say that subordinate influence is negligible. Indeed, as Lane, Corwin and Monahan write, 'Because subordinates are personally affected by their superior's decisions, they seek to influence them'.[8] Thus teachers seek to influence headteachers, and both spheres seek to influence outsiders. Following Bridges,[9] some strategies can be discerned, such as flattery, which may be open or disguised by being transmitted through an influential third party. Also, information about children or curriculum can be distorted to encourage decisions in the required direction. Elements of bluff, threat, threat fulfilment, sabotage, ritual insubordination, or working to rule may be used. In this way the views and goals of a teaching staff may become part of the environmental influences affecting superordinate's decisions.

Clearly a strong personality within the subordinate body may become a major influence as an informal leader. But the important point for this discussion is the fact that in an English primary school the head, as both a teacher and an administrator, can be both the formal and informal leader. The headteacher, with both *de jure* and *de facto* power and the ability to be both superordinate and subordinate depending on the chosen role of the moment, can, with skill and knowledge of possible plays from above and below, manipulate (in the sociological rather than the pejorative sense of the word) the educational progress of the school in the direction he wishes. It is the unique combination of bureaucracy and professionalism which both initiates and sustains the power of the primary head.

### Conclusions

It was suggested at the beginning that the primary school head is in a unique power situation and that Razzell's plea for greater teacher participation is noble but unlikely to be realized. It would seem that this has been confirmed by the brief details given in this article.

Clearly, whichever of the three spheres we choose, the participants do possess a degree of discretion in making certain decisions. But if they are to act on these decisions they must possess a degree of autonomy from outside intervention. This autonomy is sometimes granted and sometimes carved out and held by the use of 'pocket veto'[10] strategies by the participants. Examples are non-cooperation, working to rule and the like. The sources of power which teachers and heads possess appear to be a mixture of academic expertise, the ideologies of teaching and the support of colleagues. In actuality, classroom teachers do possess a degree of autonomy surrounding the conduct of affairs in the classroom, as well as discretion to make curriculum decisions within well defined limits. Their power to act, however, represents a very low level of power, drawn basically from superordinates and directed mostly at the teaching-learning process and behaviour of children. However, when superordinates attempt to withdraw the limited autonomy of teachers and intervene directly in school or classroom events teachers (and heads) can use informal power to block the interference.

Conversely, similar powers and constraints mark out and maintain the administrative sphere, a sphere which would appear, on formal analysis, to be large and all consuming. But there is in addition one uniquely placed participant in the decision-making process, the headteacher. As the senior official and administrator within the school he has been shown to have the capacity and need to exercise significant control of policy, finance and staff allocation in both the short and long run in order to fulfil his legal obligations. He is the hub around which the school-outside interaction takes place and there are few ways in which he can be bypassed without serious repercussions.

Without doubt the headteacher's decisions can vitally affect teachers' working conditions. His position as the real and symbolic head identifies the school as his school. He assigns teachers to classrooms and children to teachers. He is the ultimate authority on disciplinary matters and parents turn to him for redress of alleged grievances. Teachers tend to collide with headteachers rather than outsiders if they wish to enhance their autonomy but at the same time they need his unique power to intercede in relationships with parents and to cope with difficult children. As the instructional leader of a school he is both the 'Leading teacher' and the major source of information to outsiders. He can symbolize professional purpose and competence and is in the unique position to reassure teachers about the quality of their work *vis-à-vis* their own perceptions of it and *vis-à-vis* the perceptions of outsiders.

The head, as both administrator and teacher, is therefore in a pivotal position in relation to both the outsiders' interest in system-wide affairs and to teachers' interest in pedagogical affairs. The former preoccupation tends to encourage rational, centrally controlled procedures to control events. The latter requires flexibility and a degree of autonomy to respond to unexpected events and happenings. This juxtaposition of bureaucracy and professionalism in education is mediated by the formal and informal position and function of headship.

The facts are as follows. His sphere contains superior scope and depth of autonomy of *school* decision-making, relative to the other spheres. Also, not only does he possess very considerable formal authority and power, but in addition the other participants' perceptions and use of his power as a mediator would seem to enhance his official power. Finally, the evidence would seem to suggest that, relative to other participants, the constraints on a head's autonomy are no greater, and are possibly less. Indeed, he alone is probably the major cause of constraints on other participants, in his superior capability for using formal and informal authority and power to influence the behaviour of others. For better or worse, future changes in primary educational practice are likely increasingly to depend on the characteristics and methods of headteachers. Can participation really be valid if its existence depends on the beneficence of the head, as indeed it must given the present structure of primary education?

## Notes

1 RAZZELL, A. (1979) 'Teacher participation in school decision making', *Education 3–13*, 7, 1, p. 4.
2 *Ibid.*, p. 7.
3 HANSON, M. (1976–77) 'Beyond the bureaucratic model: A study of power and autonomy in educational decision making', *Interchange*, 7, 2.
4 AULD, R. (1976) *William Tyndale Junior and Infants Schools Public Inquiry*, p. 268, London HMSO.
5 EDUCATION ACT (1944), Section 17 (3)(a).
6 HANSON, M., *op. cit.*, p. 29.
7 HUGHES, M.G., in PETERS, R.S. (Ed.) (1973) *The Role of the Head*, London, Routledge and Kegan Paul, Ch. 3.
8 LANE, W.R. *et al.* (1966) *Foundations of Educational Administration: A Behavioural Analysis*, New York Macmillan, p. 135.
9 BRIDGES, E. (1970) 'Administrative man, origin or pawn in decision making?', *Educational Administration Quarterly*, 6, 1, p. 12.
10 HANSON, M., *op. cit.*

# The Secondary School Head As Leader

*Colin King*
*Lancashire County Council Advisory Service, formerly*
*Headmaster, Darwen Moorland High School*

Asked his opinion of Antony Eden's speeches, Ernest Bevin is said to have replied, 'Clitch, clitch, clitch.' Churchill apparently could not resist a more literary form of criticism, noting that the same speeches consisted '. . . entirely of cliches — cliches old and new — everything from "God is love" to "Please adjust your dress before leaving".' The task of writing about leadership in the secondary school runs a grave risk of attracting similar — and well-deserved — criticism. The literature in recent years has expanded, extending from that originating as external observation interpreted in sociological or behavioural terms to realistic and practical descriptions. It is perhaps appropriate to marry the two approaches.

*Ten Good Schools*[1] indicated evidence to support the need for effective leadership, to outline its related functions, and to propose the likely attitudes and philosophies that will underpin it. Providing a general analysis of current perceptions and understanding of leadership, John related these to the nature of authority. He noted the dysfunctional effects of alternative and often contradictory assumptions about leadership function and individual authority,[2] and claimed with some justification, in view of recently published HMI school inspections, that 'The absence of a coherent view about leadership and authority not only handicaps institutional relations but also confuses and frustrates the individual member by undermining his sense of "one-ness" or "integrity".' His criticism goes to a fundamental problem of leadership in exposing how far it is seen as synonymous with direction. It could also be taken much further. Lack of conceptual underpinning for the approaches of senior staff to their daily tasks not only handicaps the relationships but results in systems, techniques and styles of management that are either inadequate or inappropriate. One framework might well be provided by an analysis of the relationships between leadership, power and authority.[3] Another, and possibly more pragmatic approach, would be to consider what leadership is, what it does, and how it might most effectively achieve these ends within actual circumstances indicated within a definition. Further, there is a need to examine the relationship between function and style.[4]

Gibb pointed out that leadership was '. . . not an attribute of personality but a quality of his role within a particular and specified social system. Viewed in relation to the group leadership is a quality of its structure' (p. 205).[5] Functions and styles would therefore properly reflect in some part the purposes and perceived needs of the group, as well as the organizational ends which the group serves. For the sixty or so teachers of the thousand pupil comprehensive school, the purposes and appropriate styles of leadership would be a concomitant of that school's intellectual, social and ethical goals; its organizational needs; and the needs of its staff as professionals. School leadership which would influence staff positively would have functions interpreting those defined by Halpin as

> To initiate structure in the form of systems for interactive curriculum, organizational and professional developments; and
> To exercise consideration in the forms of encouraging and maintaining cohesive, interlocking teams or groups; and of motivating, developing and supporting individual colleagues.[6]

Because followership behaviour tends to be a mirror image of leadership style,[7] it can be argued that while directive styles based simplistically upon authority endowed by Articles of Government may initiate early forms of structure, the function of consideration can only be achieved by movement towards a participatory approach. Consequently there is some consensus in favour of 'consultative' or 'democratic' leadership.[8] Such a style, because it consciously recognizes, accepts and undertakes the function of consideration, is likely to be more effective through fulfilling individual professional needs to develop the extended professionality considered necessary for constructive response to change through means of curriculum and organizational adaptation.[9] A prospective and proactive model for leadership in secondary schools should therefore recognize the duality of function and the interaction of function and style. This recognition would take the form of adopting what has been conceptualized as 'appropriate style.'[10] There is growing evidence from schools that the need to get things done is met more effectively by a style which manifests consideration than it is by a more prescriptive approach.[11] How consideration can be exercised contiguously with initiating structure is therefore worthy of analysis.

Individual aspects are likely to be covered by conscious selection on the part of senior staff of what circumstances, events or opportunities demonstrably attract high levels of teacher commitment. Sergiovanni found that Australian teachers were motivated by work-centred activity,[12] and as yet there are no grounds for assuming that his conclusions would not apply to their English counterparts. Such activity provided them with a sense of achievement, of recognition and of bestowed responsibility. Leadership by senior and middle level staff should therefore be exercised through systems designed to produce circumstances that would result in these feelings. In this way they would conceptualize the interaction of the technicalities of their management systems with the activities, purposes and feelings of their staff.[13]

Therefore, in designing and setting up, modifying or revitalizing the school management systems in terms of both procedures and outcomes, the head could move towards the adoption of an appropriate style. This could be described generally as defining the limits within which both he and his staff jointly made decisions, for which all shared responsibility and which all would in some part implement and monitor.[14]

To apply such a proposition embodying an interactive relationship between management systems, organizational behaviour and teacher motivation[15] to the routine management of the school, reference may be made to key tasks,[16] or preferably areas of key results[17] derived from models suggested for industry.[18]

First, as required by DES Circular 6/81,[19] most schools have undertaken a review of the school curriculum, and this has inevitable implications for scrutiny of the management system which produces it. Many heads have realized that this task is a specific stage in a particular model of management which requires the leadership of an ongoing process of redefinition of procedures, resources and evaluation.[20] In practice a large staff could be arranged into a series of cross-function, cross-hierarchy working groups, of temporary duration but necessarily tied into the main management system.[21] Their potential for modifying the school system is evident in the amount of information they could bring to bear upon their tasks, so long as the assumed style of leadership allowed them to do this. Their tasks could also be defined to provide the involved staff with those oppoortunities for achievement, for recognition of use of self-valued skills and experience, and by bestowed responsibility to capitalize on their competence. Such tasks might well relate to the statement of overall school aims and goals, how far they were seen to be relevant to present circumstances, and in what ways they needed to be modified to meet changing expectations. Professional need for a sense of bestowed responsibility could be met and individual consideration and team-building effectively exercised by using this definition of aims and goals as a basis for following stages. Each group could contribute to the refining of these goals into school objectives,[22] and thus lay a foundation through their involvement for the subsequent design of consistent and coherent, contributory activity at department and classroom level. The leadership function of senior staff would adjust to devise means whereby group propositions could be collated and coordinated in ways which by involvement would attract staff consensus. Such occasions as a day staff conference have been used successfully to achieve these ends,[23] complementing while stimulating the maintenance of the normal, after-school meeting.

An updated and relevant statement of school intent provides the basis for refining long- and medium-term purposes into key results.[24] By reconstituting staff into groups representing their general functional areas, such as areas of pupils' learning experiences,[25] senior staff could initiate or reinforce an 'interactive-influence system'.[26] This would bring about participation in evolving the school's systems by means that would simultaneously provide consideration of individuals and teams. Further, the range and depth of analysis and synthesis of the information which they were required to generate in order to translate the school's hierarchy of purposes into a pattern of key results across a variety of functional areas and at a number of operational levels would enable '. . . a participative management program which meets the needs of those particular teachers. . . . Such a differential strategy is necessary if the educational organisation is to effectively retain and ensure high quality performance of its most critical resource — the classroom teacher.'[27] Setting up means to provide resources of time, INSET, space and occasion; and introduction of outside expertise when required which would fuel discussion, would increase the probability of constructive professional relationships, as well as meeting recognition needs for individual contributions. There would be an attendant organizational benefit in that there would be incentive to routinize feedback. In this way there would integrated into the school systems some of the parameters of good communication which have been noted as an element of effective leadership.[28]

The definition of key results by these groups of teachers concerned with areas of pupils' learning experiences could be further developed by an appropriate, participative leadership style. School level objectives relating to pupils' development could be stated in operational terms[29] as department or unit goals and objectives. Some of these would already have been attained, and this would be opportunity to support the groups by recognizing such achievement, as well as to reinforce and develop structure by indicating modified or future targets. Teachers' competence in subject and methodology could be systematized by the statement of cognitive, affective and social objectives[30] which would form the framework for classroom activities.[31] While there might continue to be functional emphases which would still be termed 'pastoral' or 'academic', the personal-social curriculum would become an integral part of the academic curriculum, and the former would inform, extend and support the latter. The curriculum would regain an integrity which it appears to have lost in the guise of the 'pastoral-academic dichotomy',[32] for the operational links between the school's detailed objectives and the functional units' goals would be clearly defined. Consequently it could be claimed that it would be not only possible but practical to examine the relationship between the '. . . organisation of the curriculum and in the teaching programmes . . .' and the school's '. . . stated aims'. Further, as suggested by the Circular, schools through their staffs would then be able to '. . . assess regularly how far the curriculum — in the schools as a whole and for individual pupils — matches the stated aims.'[33] By designing and providing such opportunities, providing the resources to maintain their progress, the senior staff would be also providing for professional needs. By developing teachers at this stage they would also be structuring a framework for routine classroom work. The teachers who would be planning and implementing this would be likely to understand and accept it because of their involvement in its definition at each stage. This development would enable some indication of the relative priorities within the statement of the school's key results and associated tasks that individual teachers were expected to achieve. A further benefit would be that teachers would — as in many schools they already have — shape their own perceptions of their roles with characteristics and purposes that were congruent with school aims and role expectations. Organizational integrity could therefore be achieved through a necessary reduction in human variability[34] by channelling and guiding individual creativity and initiative rather than by inhibiting or constraining it.[35] Encouraging the institution or development of feedback systems at unit level similar to those at school level and developing the corporate will to act on such feedback would again integrate the development and consideration functions. For '... each person searches for positive recognition of his worth, and he comes to view himself as adequate in those areas where he receives assurance of his competence or success.'[36] The sequential definition of practical and realistic annual and termly targets, at both school and unit levels, together with routine evidence on how far they had been met would generate powerful and acceptable leadership images. 'The essence of the task of constructive leadership is to foster a climate of security and openness which enables identity and corporate commitment to flourish without the need for scapegoats and adversaries.'[37] Involved in such a process, teachers feel not only that their school is doing things, but that they are part of this through senior staff support for their immediate team; that their teaching and organizational skills are being more fully utilized; and that other professional qualities are being fostered and developed. Organizational benefits would arise from the multiplicative process of refining school purposes into unit aims, goals and objectives which would allow realistic and practical coordination among the different levels. An example would be class teachers being closely involved in defining and agreeing the medium-term results to which their daily and weekly efforts contributed.

The resourcing of the actions by which such results could be achieved would be another occasion for the interactive operation of initiating structure and consideration. How the school capitation should be allocated and spent; how teaching staff were to be deployed; how space should be shared and utilized could become realistic issues for analysis, discussion and decision by functional and task-specific groups. Senior staff would develop the system by which such decisions would be made, defining means which would ensure the necessary levels of coordination and control. Sharing the definition of their own targets and opportunity to understand how these aggregate to the achievement of school purposes provides a logical preparation for sharing in resource decisions; it would also produce the anticipation of the latter, and reinforce the tendency towards a participative style.[38] In some schools that have adopted this approach there has been a considerable modification of procedures for resource allocation; a perceived improvement in resource use; and a reduction in factional envy and conflict. It is difficult to avoid concluding that scarce resources are being used more effectively and that there is an understanding that more no longer necessarily means better.

As members of each unit planned into their assigned lessons and activities the defined targets, and agreed resources for which individually and collectively they had assumed responsibility, a logical development for senior staff would be to control and coordinate each phase by applying the concept of key results to the observed outcomes. Evolution of this part of the system under participative leadership would require continued collaboration on the part of all staff, by the pooling of ideas and the sharing of information and resources, while creating or redirecting what was additionally required.[39] Consideration would be manifest as a systematized, practical opportunity for job enlargement and professional development.

Contribution to curricular review and regeneration could be matched by similar strategies to enable staff participation in organizational development.[40] Concern with school policy and procedures has been noted as a factor in teachers' attitudes to their jobs.[41] The relationship between participation in decision-making on curriculum policy and procedure with organizational and professional development is an evident area for leadership functions. Their interaction would take effect where those colleagues seeking further satisfaction from closer involvement in decisions contingent upon their daily tasks or for those seeking promotion were given the structured opportunity to take part in decision-making groups which improved effectiveness at school, unit and classroom levels. These teachers could in their future tasks manifestly demonstrate having had and used such occasions to acquire valuable insights, experience and skills. These could be described as attributes of management wider and deeper than those previously used at classroom or unit levels, and would consist of interpersonal and intergroup skills and the attitudes attendant upon them. As these functions became convention, individual contribution through a participatory system of school management could become an accepted part of job definitions. Senior staff would have attained a close correlation between the two major functions of leadership. Using this improved form of job definition, recognition of contributions at school and unit management levels would form an obvious part of any appraisal of individual performance. 'This discussion [on annual career development] should relate to the job description which, if not already in existence, should be prepared in consultation with the teacher concerned.'[42] The value would be signalled not only by programmed use of senior staff time to provide these interviews. Most staff by regularly provided, positive feedback and recognition are likely to be encouraged to anticipate favourably such outcomes. The regular featuring of these working parties on the school calendar would indicate the probability of such opportunities. The school system would be further developed by the delegation of real power that would be encouraged as a result of the application of this concept of leadership function.[43]

Frequent reference to working groups indicates the need to consider interpretations of the leadership functions which both set up and maintain them. Approaches to problem-solving and decision-making could embrace initiating structure, team-building and individual consideration. Bennis assessed the health of any organization — and by implication the quality of its leadership — through the effectiveness of its problem-solving approach.[44] If such mechanisms did not exist within the school, overtly and consciously used, then adoption of the suggested cross-function, cross-hierarchy working groups, interacting with the routine school and unit management systems, could be one practical and realistic way of introducing them. Considerable literature exists on techniques and systems of organizational problem-solving,[45] and much of it indicates the effectiveness of group approaches within an agreed procedural framework. Not only would the school system be developed by such an adoption, but consideration would be exercised as opportunities were presented for teachers to be introduced to and acquire systematic and procedural forms of the necessary technical skills. Team-building could be enhanced by recognition of group products, and the assigning by school management committees of the required power and resources to implement the subsequent decisions. The school's approach to problem-solving would thereby become a practical expression of 'influence-interaction' in which senior staff continue to exert overall leadership through their structuring of the system and their response to their colleagues' activities. Middle level staff, too, could demonstrate leadership potential within the problem-solving sequences by the quality of information their group generated, by the accuracy of problem definition, and by the appropriateness and feasibility of their solutions. Recognized and acted upon, these would be further forms of professional and organizational development. Fiedler argued that this latter situation could be a more practical way of training effective leaders with attributes appropriate to their location within the system.[46] McConnell demonstrated that in schools the adoption of a participative approach by a pattern of leaders at various points had the added benefit of generating understanding among a staff of the need for the exercise of ultimate authority by senior staff if the school were to progress.[47]

Exercise of the 'initiating structure-consideration' functions in an interactive approach would, through problem-solving by interlinked groups, clarify and subsequently internalize the need for different qualities of authority to be exercised at different points within the system. In this way a realistic association of levels of leadership with extent of authority which had concerned John could be achieved. There would also be the realization that power need not necessarily be an executive expression of authority. For power in the form of information, in the sense that 'knowledge itself is power' (Bacon), would be generated and used in the group problem-solving approach. Consequently, another attribute of leadership functions in the secondary school would be to design systems of decision-making that patently got things done while maintaining groups and motivating individuals.

There is evidence to support the participatory approach to decision-making in English schools which reinforces the argument for balancing consideration against initiating structure.[48] Autocratic and oligarchic styles of deciding as one interpretation of leadership are likely to preclude use of other colleagues' self-valued skills, undermine their anticipation of autonomy, yet also inhibit a desired, extended professionality.[49] While things get done to a limited degree, particularly those which do not require a high level of commitment for their execution, consideration is neglected and that which calls for enthusiasm remains unadopted. Both Georgiades and Sikes found demotivated teachers resulting from the use of such autocratic or paternalist styles.[50] Models of decision-making which accord with the proposed participatory style are required. The constitution of short-term working parties which complement an effective routine system of participation could be extended by realistic delegation to individuals. Areas of delegation should be a product of the translation of school key results into individual priorities of targets and associated tasks, which are then undertaken by agreement within each functional unit. During preliminary briefing by senior staff of groups or individuals, such targets could be agreed in ways which exercised consideration while defining acceptable or expected procedures. For example, in time, anticipation by involved staff of probable achievement, recognition and bestowed responsibility for delegated tasks could be generated. In normal routines, by creating a rational empirical structure in which teachers were involved in decisions they would implement, senior staff could delineate overall strategies; discuss, agree and develop these with middle level colleagues into tactics; which they in turn would discuss, develop and agree into action plans with their unit members. That such approaches will need to be taken into account in the future by senior staff has been indicated by Conway, who concluded that '... there has been development towards participative management.... While [teachers] have indicated that they are presently reasonably satisfied with the intensity of their involvement, as they continue to participate and taste the fruits of power, it is likely that their demands for more visible, formal or frequent participation will intensify.'[51] Both John and Sikes confirm this proposition.[52] Practical guidance on the forms of participatory decision-making as an aspect of appropriate leadership style can be found in Watts' consideration of the role of the head in participative government, where he focussed on this issue of relating style to emerging staff expectations and needs.[53] From external observation, Nias confirmed Yukl's findings by stating that 'positively' seen heads in primary schools were those who were good at getting things done while maintaining positive individual and team feelings without over-centralizing decisions; '... maximum job satisfaction went hand-in-hand with humane but positive leadership....'[54] General acceptance of a participatory leadership style within a system of interlinked problem-solving/decision-making groups would also provide realistic occasions for a clearer definition and extension of the deputy head's role, a development seen as both desirable and inevitable on professional, organizational and economic grounds.[55]

Establishing a participative leadership style to fulfil structure and consideration functions through group activities would require a necessary preliminary of defining and applying appropriate technical skills. Communication as an organizational task should be seen as operating in ways which are congruent with the adopted leadership styles. It is one of the major means whereby leadership functions become events or conditions. Schmuck *et al.* claimed that '... clarity of communication is essential to all the techniques and sub-goals ...' of the school, and such clarity depends upon adoption of a two-way mode.[56] The latter's transactional nature would reinforce participative leadership. By routinizing the frequency and regularity of occasions for two-way communication, understanding and internalizing of policy and procedure could be improved. Their regular event and 'open' nature would provide another occasion to fulfil the consideration function, while developing and improving the system. A conscious acceptance of the need for more effective communication skills would indicate areas with potential for staff development. For example, the constitution of different communication networks have been found to influence group performance,[57] and such conclusions would support the argument that effective leadership would be that which prepared for and set up networks of a size, constitution and operational style that transmitted in addition to information, some further indications. These would include individual and group achievements as well as recognition and fulfilment of bestowed responsibility. Networks could be seen as another dimension of the functional units, school committees or task-specific groups that solved problems and took decisions, one of which would be to ensure the transmission of information and the receipt of meaning by other staff. Implicit within such a system and a further aspect of communication is the need for reporting. Two issues need to be considered.

Means of generating information are inherent, and therefore could be easily activated within the 'review-aims-objectives-key results/tasks-action plan' model,[58] for the hierarchy of purposes delineates the approaches to monitoring, assessment and evaluation at school, unit and classroom levels. If participatory leadership style, by relating development of the organizational system to means of meeting the developmental needs of staff, produces high levels of staff involvement and commitment to making and implementing decisions, it would follow that this style should continue by devolving responsibility for the evaluation and improvement of those decisions. Staff needs could be met by instituting means for staff to present their own findings and relate them to the overall school context. Groups could report in a commonly used format and vocabulary to each other or to the staff. Reports to the governors, now required termly, would be opportunity to puncture the threat of accountability and make its undertaking a professional exercise. Heads of units would be asked to draft reports on their current activities in consultation with their colleagues and according to a format defined and agreed by the routine management system which was appropriate to the purposes in hand. Chairmen of working parties could use similar approaches. Deputy heads would share in the initiation, compilation, coordination and ultimate presentation of such reports.

The evolution of such a more widely-based system of representing and validating the school's purposes, procedures and products would provide further benefits. Present circumstances could be described to indicate attainment and future intention, which would again demonstrate the effective interaction of organizational and professional development. Feedback would be generated from recipients, and Governors in particular would have opportunity to acquire a more detailed and realistic impression of the school of which they were a part. For, sharing in the description of and accounting for the execution of one's own responsibilities as a member of a staff team would contribute not only to increased commitment through perceived job enlargement and professional development, but by its application to the process of curricular and organizational improvement. Bestowed responsibility would be exposed and because such reports were 'open' there would be opportunity for coordination by senior staff and recognition from Governors and colleagues. In one school in the author's experience, over a period of eight years which involved three Boards of Governors, such a system brought a marked increase in Governor interest, understanding, support and constructive criticism. Of the thirty-two staff of a total of seventy who were directly involved, only one made a token attempt when asked to take part; three of the five heads of faculties requested similar opportunities for members of their faculty who were undertaking routine or innovative responsibilities; and three staff who had gained external promotion during the latter part of the period remarked during de-briefing that they had described their part in the system with favourable results.

Leadership style has considerable influence on the effectiveness of delegation, which is seen in this context as part of the wider issue of role negotiation and role adaptation. A capable school system depends to an extent on clear role definition, for roles are the dynamic whereby the school's purposes are turned into effective actions and outcomes. Understanding and acceptance of the defined roles relates directly to how successfully the staff translate ideals into practice in classroom, corridor, office and playground; hence the practicality of analyzing by participative means the desired key results, refined from aims and goals, into individual priorities at the various points of action and then devising means whereby these become the goals and objectives of individual jobs. Developing the latter into roles can be achieved by detailed job specifications, a task which again integrates leadership functions. These specifications should define the organizational context as a background to stating job goals, and each goal or long-term task could be developed into a series of action statements, not necessarily discrete but probably overlapping or expressing different emphases or outcomes for common patterns of activities. Potential for future organizational growth can be mapped in ways which build upon individual professional development. To design and then through subsequent discussion to improve this system, the head could achieve an effective management system which patently matched curricular, organizational and professional needs. Opportunity to fulfil the latter, while detailing the means towards organizational growth, would emerge in such documents as targets of actual or potential participation at group, unit or school levels; as scope for desired forms of job enlargement by defining the outcomes of present tasks but indicating probability of future areas; as bestowed responsibility by lines of communication and reporting; and by leaving opportunity for the incumbent to extend his role. At selection or staff development interviews, parts of these job specifications could form the basis for evaluating the school's present system and the individual's present or potential contribution to it. During staff development interviews the scope offered by the existence of a range of action statements would allow forms of role adaptation such as alternative or substitute functions. Within such a structure there would be the mutual confidence to achieve firm but absolute delegation. As each job could be seen as a necessary part of an overall pattern defined by the analysis of aims into key results, the need for directive leadership — antipathetic to the effective exercise of consideration for a body of self-perceived professionals — would be reduced. A functional balance between individual professional needs and organizational requirements of coordination and control could be achieved. Bolam claimed that there has been a consistent demonstration over a ten-year period of the need for schools to design and implement some such programme of staff development, which of necessity would relate to organizational growth.[59] The NUT advocated the use of 'a system of self-appraisal with an exchange of observations on how far objectives are being reached, and an examination of the constraints and other factors influencing that achievement . . . .' Such a system as this would be a more likely outcome from the operating of a staff development programme within a participatory leadership style founded upon cognition of both leadership functions. Prescriptive staff appraisal has been shown as ineffective, in circumstances relevant to teachers;[60] and Maier has asserted that change in incumbent performance would only result from the use by the superordinate of a problem-solving approach within a participative environment.[61] It would follow that where the individual is given responsibility by the structure in which he works for defining his own performance towards agreed and accepted goals, he is likely to generate information that can be realistically used to define his problems and indicate solutions he will be able to put into effect. Such solutions might well take a form which contributed to organizational growth, such as job enlargement or rotation and consultancy. Effective leadership would foresee the need for required resources to implement such propositions; would prepare a school system that could produce these; and, by sharing responsibility not only for an individual's present performance but through provision of resources towards future performance, the head would demonstrate recognition of the individual and his potential for facilitating the school's continued growth. Appraisal and development would be a systematic means towards joint development planning in which superordinate and subordinate — head and head of department; head, head of department and teacher — could balance individual and organizational needs. 'Such aspects as school-based or school-focused in-service training and development of staff could become an integral part of the on-going structure of the school.'[62]

In some schools such approaches are already working; others demonstrate the need for their initiation. That they are effective and do meet a real need is because '. . . humans are very adaptable; almost *anyone* can contribute a valuable element to a goal that most others in a group want to pursue and almost everyone can find gratification in doing so. . . .'[63] However, an essential prerequisite to producing changed perceptions would be that of adequate, planned and appropriately occupied time. Considerable patience, coupled with sensitivity, insight and a willingness to learn and adapt would be required to modify the forces analyzed by Tannenbaum and Schmidt which influence choice of style.[64] However, consideration of those forces indicates the need to start along a path whose destination is clearly defined. The steps along the route can be marked by measures taken to modify leader and follower values and beliefs; the degree of mutual confidence and trust which can only be engendered by properly executed delegation and accountability; the amount of security perceived by participants and their freedom from mutually originated threat. The means which allow these steps to be taken will include the introduction or development towards a logical, self-checking model of school management; explicit and detailed job specifications which relate to that model; the evolution of problem-solving and decision-making techniques which develop towards higher levels of integration of effort; the design of an underpinning communication process that acts as an effective organizational nervous system; and the provision of means of integrated development. Consequently, staff groups will become more cohesive and effective as they learn to travel together. People do change; participative leadership in the large school of the 1980s and 1990s will coordinate and guide those changes in directions which satisfy the needs of both school and staff.

## Summary

If leadership is the effective influence of one person's behaviour upon that of others within a group towards desired ends, then that influence operates through two major functions.

The functions of leadership are initiating structure or the designing, setting up, maintaining and improving of systems whereby group members achieve the purposes of the school. It is not the function of initiating structure for the head to run the school; his responsibility is for the 'internal organization, management and discipline' of the school. Rather should he devise the means whereby all major plans, the definition of all important procedures, the allocation of resources into overall categories, the taking of overall decisions, the monitoring of activity and the evaluation of the school's effectiveness, are achieved by the school system to an optimum level.

There is an associated function equivalent to and interacting with initiating structure. Consideration describes the encouraging and maintaining of interlocking cohesive teams or groups, and the motivating, developing and supporting of individual teachers so that the prime resource of a school — its staff — is so influenced that there is understanding, involvement and commitment to make the structure produce the desired outcomes, and then to evaluate and improve it so that it continues to do so within changing circumstances.

Such functions manifest themselves in behaviours of the head and staff with responsibilities for the work of others, and can be categorized as styles. Within the constraints of a school there will be a limited variation of appropriate style. It has been argued with conviction and from experience that to be appropriate for the work of a school such a style has to, and can, achieve a balance of these functions. Other field evidence suggests that structure only becomes effective where consideration operates; consideration is only functional where there is a complementary and supporting system. The operation of consideration indicates movement towards a style which may be defined as participative, so that there are opportunities for individuals to fulfil their professional needs as their actions and achievements meet school purposes and procedures. Means of participation can be applied to the normal management of a school in a variety of ways, both within the routine decision-making structure, and by short-term, task-specific groups engaged in solving particular problems.

These two dimensions of participatory opportunity can be implemented in any management model that accepts the ongoing nature of a people-centred organization. Such a model is likely to include review, planning, organizing, resourcing, implementing, evaluating and improving. As the school develops, the staff develops; in turn their professional growth is the means for the school's continued evolution.

Individual creativity and contributions can therefore find a legitimate outlet within the developing system, in whose definition the individual has shared. The necessary reduction of human variability can be achieved to result in an acceptable level of organizational coordination and control by means which not merely avoid the individual's alienation but through his involvement increase his commitment to making school purposes and procedures effective. Heads and senior staff who adopt this style can be readily detected — 'Emphasis is laid on consultation, team work and participation, but, without exception, the most important single factor in the success of these schools is the quality of leadership of the Head ... though ready to take final responsibility they have made power-sharing the key-note of their organisation and administration. Such leadership is crucial for success and these schools are what their Heads and staffs have made them.'[65]

## Notes

1 HMI (1977) *Ten Good Schools, a Secondary School Enquiry*, Matters for Discussion Series, London HMSO, section 8.
2 JOHN, D. (1980) *Leadership in Schools*, London, Heinemann, pp. 4ff.
3 KING, R. (1968) 'The headteacher and his authority', in ALLEN, B. (Ed.) *Headship in the '70s*, Oxford, Blackwell; WATSON, L.E. (1975) 'Office and expertise in the secondary school', in HOUGHTON, *et al. Management in Education: The Management of Organisations and Individuals*, London, Ward Lock Educational.
4 SADLER P.J. 'Leadership style, confidence in management and job satisfaction', in HOUGHTON *et al.* (1975) *ibid.*
5 GIBB C.A. (1947) 'The principles and traits of leadership', (1958) 'An interactional view of the emergence of leadership', in GIBB C.A. (1970) *Leadership*, Harmondsworth, Penguin.
6 HALPIN A.W. (1966) 'How leaders behave', in CARVER, F.D. and SERGIOVANNI, T.J. (1969). *Organisations and Human Behavior: Focus on Schools*, McGraw-Hill.
7 TANNENBAUM, R. and SCHMIDT, W.H. (1973) 'How to choose a leadership pattern', in *Harvard Business Review*, May/June; SCHMIDT, W.H. and BUCHANAN, P.C. (1954) *Techniques That Produce Team Work*, New London, Arthur C. Croft Publications; VROOM, V.H. and DECI, E.L. (1972) *Management and Motivation*, Harmondsworth, Penguin.
8 SADLER (1970) *op. cit.*; JENNINGS, A. (1977) *Management and Headship in the Secondary School*, London, Ward Lock Educational, pp. 23ff.
9 DES (1979) *Aspects of Secondary Education in England*, London HMSO, pp. 223–4.
10 TANNENBAUM and SCHMIDT (1973), *op. cit.*
11 DES (1979), *op. cit.*
12 SERGIOVANNI, T.J. (1973) 'Factors which affect the satisfaction and dissatisfaction of teachers', in WALKER, W.G. *et al. Explorations in Educational Administration*, University of Queensland Press, p. 205.
13 HOYLE, E. (1975) 'Leadership and decision-making in education', in HUGHES, M. *Administering Education — International Challenge*, Athlone Press.
14 TANNENBAUM and SCHMIDT (1973), *op. cit.*
15 BARR GREENFIELD, T. (1973) 'Theory about organisations — a new perspective', in HUGHES (1975) *ibid.*

16  MORGAN, C. and HALL, J. (1982) 'Managerial tasks of the secondary school head', in *Education*, 18 June.
17  NEWELL, T. (1973) 'Organisation development in schools', in HOUGHTON *et al.* (1975), *op. cit.*; 'A framework for educational management courses' (1982), *North West Area Education Authorities, Discussion Paper*.
18  HUMBLE, J.W. (1969) *Improving Management Performance: A Dynamic Approach to Management by Objectives*, Management Publications for BIM.
19  DES (1981) *The School Curriculum*, Circular 6/81, October.
20  HUMBLE (1969), *op. cit.*
21  *Curriculum 11–16: A Review of Progress*, (1981) London, HMSO, pp. 76–8.
22  *Ibid.*
23  *Ibid.*
24  HUMBLE (1969), *op. cit.*
25  SCHMUCK, R.A. *et al.* (1972) *Handbook of Organisational Development in Schools*, Mayfield, p. 101.
26  LIKERT, R. (1961) *New Patterns of Management*, McGraw Hill, pp. 178–83, 188–91.
27  BELASCO, J.A. and ALUTTO, J.A. (1975) 'Decisional participation and teacher satisfaction', in HOUGHTON *et al.*, (1975) *op. cit.*
28  HMI (1977), *op. cit.*, p. 11.
29  SCHOOLS COUNCIL (1981) *The Practical Curriculum*, Working Paper 70, London, Methuen.
30  BLOOM, B.S. (Ed.), (1956) *Taxonomy of Educational Objectives: The Classification of Educational Goals, 1. The Cognitive Domain*; KRATHWOLD, D.R. *et al.* (1964) *Taxonomy of educational objectives, 2. The Affective Domain*, Mackay, N.Y.
31  TYLER, R.W. (1949) *Basic Principles of Curriculum and Instruction*, University of Chicago Press.
32  HAMBLIN, D.H. (1978) *The Teacher and Pastoral Care*, Oxford, Blackwell, pp. 3ff.
33  DES (1981), *op. cit.*
34  KATZ, D. and KAHN, R.L. (1966) *The Social Psychology of Organisations*, Wiley, p. 70.
35  JOHN (1980), *op. cit.*
36  BLOOM, B.S. *et al.* (1971) *Handbook of Formative and Summative Evaluation of Student Learning*, McGraw Hill, p. 56.
37  JOHN (1980), *op. cit.* p. 171.
38  TANNENBAUM and SCHMIDT (1973), *op. cit.*
39  HOYLE, E. (1975) 'Professionality, professionalism and control in teaching', in HOUGHTON *et al.* (1975), *op. cit.*
40  SCHMUCK *et al.* (1972), *op. cit.*
41  'Happiness is ... job satisfaction for staff', *The Times Educational Supplement*, 18 November 1977, p. 3; HILSUM, S. and START, K.B. (1974) *Promotion and Careers in Teaching*, NFER.
42  NUT (1981) *A Fair Way Forward*, p. 23.
43  COCH, L. and FRENCH, J.R.P. (1948) *Overcoming Resistance to Change: Human Relations*, Vol. 1, pp. 512–32; CONWAY, J.A. (1978) 'Power and participatory decision-making in selected English schools', *Journal of Educational Administration*, 16, 1, May, p. 94.
44  BENNIS, W.G. (1966) *Changing Organisations*, McGraw Hill.
45  SCHMUCK *et al.* (1972) *op. cit.* pp. 233ff.
    W.G. BENNIS, K. BENNE, R. CHIN; Dynamics of planned change; Holt, Rinehart and Winston, 1968.
46  FIEDLER, F.E. (1973) 'The trouble with leadership training is that it doesn't train leaders', *Psychology Today*, 6, 9, February.
47  McCONNELL, T.R. (1968) 'The function of leadership in academic institutions', in

LASSEY, W.R. and FERNANDEZ, R.R. (1976) *Leadership and Social Change*, University Associates, pp. 276–94.

48  GIBB, J.R. (1967) 'Dynamics of leadership and communication', in LASSEY *et al.* (1976) *op. cit.*

49  HOYLE (1975), *op. cit.*

50  SIKES, P. (1982) *Teacher Motivation and Promotion*, unpub. research thesis, University of Leeds; TES (1977) *op. cit.*

51  CONWAY, J.A. (1978) *op. cit.*

52  JOHN (1980), *op. cit.*, p. 168; SIKES (1982), *op. cit.*

53  WATTS, J. (1976) 'Shoring it out — the role of the Head in participatory government' in PETERS, R.S. *The Role of the Head*, London, Routledge and Kegan Paul p. 127.

54  T. *et al.* (Eds) *Approaches to School Management*, Harper and Row, pp. 270ff. YUKL, G. (1971) 'Towards a behavioural theory of leadership', in HOUGHTON *et al.*, (1975) *op. cit.*, p. 272.

55  TODD, R. and DENNISON, W.F. (1978) 'The changing role of the deputy headmaster in English secondary schools', *Education Review*, 30, 3, pp. 209–20.

56  SCHMUCK *et al.* (1972), *op. cit.*, p. 34.

57  LEAVITT, H.J. (1951) 'Some effects of certain communication patterns on group performance', *Journal of Abnormal and Social Psychology*, 46, pp. 38–50.

58  HUMBLE (1969), *op. cit.*

59  BOLAM, R. (1982) *School Focussed In-service Training*, London, Heinemann.

60  HUNTER, C. and HEIGHWAY, P. (1980) 'Morale, motivation and management in middle schools', in BUSH, J. *et al.*

61  MAIER, N.R.F. (1976) *The Appraisal Interview*, University Associates, pp. 21–65.

62  HUNTER, C. and HEIGHWAY, P. (1980) *op. cit.*, p. 485.

63  SCHMUCK *et al.* (1972), *op. cit.*, p. xiv.

64  TANNENBAUM and SCHMIDT (1973), *op. cit.*

65  HMI (1977), *op. cit.*

# The Role of the Deputy Head in Secondary Schools*

*P.R. Owen, Orton Longueville School, Peterborough*
*M. Davies, Bretton Woods School, Peterborough*
*and*
*A. Wayment, Orton Rushfield School, Peterborough*

To many staff, the deputy headteacher is the person appointed to the school staff to understudy and deputize for the headteacher whenever necessary. Our perception is coloured by experiences in our own schools, but most would agree with this basic assumption. But what of the reality?

From the 'other side of the fence' the practising deputy headteacher often finds a very different situation, fulfilling a large number of tasks varying from school management to mundane clerical work. An analysis of the range of duties expected of prospective deputy headteachers has enabled the authors to attempt a classification of roles and the identification of deputy headship 'types'. It revealed that a wide range of 'types' was looked for by prospective employing authorities.

In addition to the deputy head 'identikit' constructed, the case study below illustrates the dichotomy faced by the newly appointed deputy in terms of employer requirements compared to the actual demands of the job. An attempt is made to separate the rhetoric from the reality.

During February and March 1982 details were obtained of thirty secondary deputy headship posts that appeared in *The Times Educational Supplement*. They were from a wide geographical area, both urban and rural schools, from Northumberland to Kent, including the London Boroughs, and from Gloucestershire and the West Midlands to Salop. In size the schools ranged from Group 9 to 12. The sample incorporated single-sex schools, co-educational schools, comprehensive, grammar and modern schools.

Advertizing for any post is a matter of communicating a message to the target populations, hoping that it will provoke the desired response. Following that stage the receiver has to decode the messages to enable an

* This is an edited version of the article which appeared in *Educational Management and Administration*, 11, 1983, pp. 51–6.

appropriate response to be made. Interest centred on what was expected of the deputy head — the personal qualities and skills that were being sought: a possible check list against which the potential deputies could gauge their potential. Could there, in fact, be such a well-defined job description offered, given the breadth of tasks often expected to be undertaken by the deputy head? Could one generalize about the requirements necessary for the amorphous job of deputy head? Can the unsuspecting candidate interpret the clues being offered or is it simply a case of blind man's buff?

## The Job Description

The messages from some schools were loud and clear, stemming from either a prescriptive starkness or political nuance. There was little need to use one's experience of schools to read between the lines of some job descriptions.

The telling phase often appeared on the second page of a job description but it coloured all else about that job and the type of person being sought. All the skills and attitudes asked for elsewhere in a job were subsumed by that one overriding requirement. The following example illustrates the point: '... the new appointment will undertake a responsibility for the timetable construction.' In others, the deputy needed to be a particular type, irrespective of specifically held skills: '... someone is required with a concern for the needs of really able girls. Some experience outside grammar and independent schools could prove beneficial' and '... the governors are hoping to appoint a graduate teacher.'

The essential nature of some jobs became all too clear upon a first reading: '... a concern for the interests of girls — in the curriculum provided, in access to the choice available and in day to day pastoral matters', or, put more directly: '... responsibility for the welfare and discipline of the girls of the school'. Another group of job descriptions was non-specific: '... expected to take a keen interest in both curriculum and pastoral matters in the school.' Some descriptions stressed that specific tasks could not be given for the post of a deputy: '... anybody feeling ready to apply for such a major position would already have a clear knowledge of the complex range of jobs and responsibilities that exist', and, '... all else we do depends on ability, interest and availability and negotiation between colleagues.' Having said that, most of the posts advertized were prescriptive enough for a check list of skill requirements and essential qualities to be drawn up. These are shown in Table 1 together with the frequency with which they appear in the thirty job descriptions.

Table 1.  *Responsibilities, Qualities and Skills Specifically Requested*

| | |
|---|---|
| Administrative (dinner arrangements, duties, buses, covers . . .) | 24 |
| Curriculum (policy and development, options . . .) | 20 |
| Outside links ('feeders', post-16, PTA, governors) | 16 |
| Personal qualities (ambitious, leadership, dynamic, energetic, self-confident) | 14 |
| Flexibility (role arranged upon appointment) | 14 |
| To be part of a team | 11 |
| Pupil welfare and discipline | 9 |
| Arrange public occasions and functions | 9 |
| Teaching load (between 35–60 per cent timetable) | 9 |
| Staff welfare and support | 9 |
| Professional tutoring (INSET, probationers, students) | 8 |
| Examinations Officer | 7 |
| Deputize for head | 6 |
| Chair meetings | 5 |
| Fabric of school (caretaker, furniture, groundstaff . . .) | 4 |

## Job Description Analysis

Table 1 shows the commonest skills requested, but others quoted included the ability to appoint staff, make demands on staff, have computer experience, take responsibilities for school reports, resources and reprographics and take assemblies.

Is it now possible to think in terms of a deputy head 'identikit'? From the list you might imagine a potential deputy being a 'person of considerable presence, self-confident and energetic, a proven administrator who can timetable, chair meetings, teach successfully, work in a team and have a flair for public occasions!' Perhaps there are deputy head *types*, combining a variety of strengths and qualities but existing within a school essentially to fulfil one specific role.

There is the nuts and bolts deputy or the *oiler*: the mechanic who maintains, services and patches up the system (staff duties, fire drill, school calendar, invigilation . . .), he might be the timetabler. The *linker* is the deputy who liaises with outside agencies, the facilitator who contacts the EWO, teacher's centre, etc. Who has staff and pupil welfare at heart . . . The *auntie* or *uncle* who had broad shoulders and an open door (probationers, girls' welfare . . .). The *front man* or *woman* is the public relations officer who gains the confidence of all (press officer, liaison with feeders . . .), while the *chameleon* responds to the tone and environment of the school. The *teamster* operates as part of a team and believes totally in the exclusive brethren of senior management. The *action man* is the innovator, the ideas person initiating change, a visionary who has what it takes to get there; he can be the timetabler. An important post is held by the *buffer* who acts as a shield for 'the boss' and is a secondary target for the staff. Finally, there is the *knight*, in white satin and a shining example to all. But possibly ideal types are born of those who sit in armchairs and reflect upon an unreal world, making sense of it through a reified set of typifications.

*P.R. Owen, M. Davies and A. Wayment*

## A Case Study

It was fortunate that at the time of this investigation a deputy head appointment was made to one of our schools. The job description for the post is shown below:

*Senior Staff Responsibilities*

Each member of the senior management, the headmaster and the three deputies, shares a variety of duties including:

1 overall responsibility for the organisation and curriculum of certain departments.
2 responsibility for coordinating the work of the year tutors, with headmaster responsible overall for policy decisions.
3 a share of day to day activities.

There is no pastoral/academic division among the deputy heads, each having responsibilities in both areas.

In a team situation it is not possible to observe rigid boundaries, and the following tasks are shared, depending on the availability of individuals: briefing and assemblies, disciplinary matters, pupil welfare, staff welfare, seeing parents, chairing meetings, carrying out policy, dealing with emergencies.

*Individual Responsibilities*

*Pastoral* Responsibility overall for years 3 and 4, option course design and implementation, production of guidance booklet, advising parents and pupils, careers programme, tutorial time.

*Departmental* Careers Education, links with careers service, Project Trident (jobs), school/industry links.
Mathematics and computer studies, games, physical education and outdoor pursuits, including Project Trident outward bound type courses.
Economics, sociology, commercial subjects.

*Other Areas* Timetable — general curricular policy, timetable planning and construction, day-to-day amendments.
External examinations — overall organization and policy decisions.
Community–Parent's Association, leisure centre management, leisure and community association.
Duties — preparation of all duty schedules.
Minibus — maintenance, balance of use, financing, replacements.
Forward planning — annual calendar of events.

What was the school looking for? An all rounder? Quite obviously somebody with a proven skill in timetable construction. Did the very prescriptive nature of the job description help explain why out of the 210 application forms requested only seventy-nine were actually returned? Those seventy-nine applications revealed a broad spectrum of experience, talent, skills and potential (see Table 2).

Table 2.   *Analysis of Applications for Post As Deputy Head*

| | | | |
|---|---|---|---|
| Age range: | 30–46 | | |
| Average age: | 35.6 | | |
| Sex: | 77 male | 2 female | |
| *Qualifications* | | | |
| Two degrees | | 13 | |
| One degree + Advanced Diploma or similar | | 4 | |
| CertEd. + two degrees | | 2 | |
| CertEd. + one degree | | 21 | |
| One degree | | 36 | |
| CertEd. | | 3 | |
| *Teaching Subjects* | | | |
| Art | 2 | Mathematics | 19 |
| Biology/Botany | 2 | Modern Languages | 5 |
| Chemistry | 7 | PE | 4 |
| Craft | 4 | Physics | 4 |
| English | 2 | Politics | 1 |
| Geography | 14 | Psychology | 1 |
| History | 8 | Social Studies | 3 |
| Humanities | 1 | Theology | 2 |
| *Teaching Experience* | | | |
| Average number of posts held: | 3.64 (range 2–7) | | |
| Present post: | Deputy head | | 4 |
| | Head of upper/middle/lower school | | 8 |
| | Director of studies | | 4 |
| | Head of year | | 16 |
| | Head of department or faculty | | 45 |
| | Subject or part time | | 2 |
| (Total applicants: 79) | | | |

Does the 'new' deputy fit any of the nine types presented earlier? He thinks not, seeing himself as a mix of most of them. Certainly the diary he kept for fourteen days shows an astonishing variety of jobs tackled with some completed and others ongoing. Wednesday and Thursday the 3rd and 4th are typical entries:

3.3.82   Periods 1 and 2 teach. Then read Schools Council document. Ordered 'Litterpack'. Contacted RSA board regarding typing exam. Met Head and Deputies regarding duties, prefects and pupil access to buildings. Finalised option booklet.

Taught all afternoon. After school Tutorial meeting. Evening — marked 1st and 4th year work and prepared lessons for Friday.

4.4.82 Before school, set up projector in Hall for Assembly. Took daily staff briefing and then assembly. Met with Head and Deputies periods 1 and 2. Discussed Curriculum, Schools Council document, prefects and other day to day admin. Before lunch read Maths Dept. paper, dealt with post, organised equipment for next week's Science lessons. After lunch — completed programming and demonstration of nominal roll programme. After school checked bus duties. Evening meeting of Curriculum Working Party.

This 'new recruit's' experience makes one thing clear. Perhaps one should not be looking at tasks performed as a means of classifying deputy heads, for these cannot tell you the way in which the job is tackled. Even a tightly defined job description does not restrict the individual in the way a job is done. There are many paths to achieving the same goal. This may be the key to successful classification or it may also be its undoing. Dare one suggest that it's not the duties, drills, invigilations and school calendar that makes an *oiler* what he is, but the personality of the individual in post. The focus moves to role expectation, definition and performance rather than to specific tasks. But does this etch the wrong agenda? Have we got it wrong? What of those variables left untouched? The influence of friends, family and finance in choosing your move? The quality of life? Totnes, Toxteth or Tottenham? If we return to the beginning, it may not matter which 'side of the fence' one is on for there will always be competing claims on time, skills and priorities. Who is the deputy head serving and what freedom does he have to negotiate and develop ... and what is he negotiating and developing? Is he task-oriented; is that the source of his feelings of esteem and worth, or is he the setting of the ethos through an infectious enthusiasm that others cannot but fail to respond to — a juggler who constantly keeps the plates spinning, who inspires and pushes colleagues through their current boundaries?

# New Directions in Departmental Leadership

*Nicholas Tyldesley*
*Thornbridge School, Sheffield*

## Duties of a Head of Department As Perceived Just Prior to a Period of Crisis

According to Machiavelli, 'the first impression that one gets of a ruler and of his brains is from seeing the men that he has about him. When they are competent and faithful one can always consider him wise, as he has been able to recognise their ability and keep them faithful. The prince in order to retain his fidelity ought to think of his minister, honouring and enriching him, doing him kindness and conferring on him honours and giving him responsible tasks . . .' (Machiavelli, 1514, pp. 85–6). In many respects the functions of a head of department are defined by the job description issued by the headteacher. This will reflect the managerial style and institutional climate of an individual school and its head. An analysis of these instructions provides an initial key for understanding the job of a head of department as it might appear in the staff handbook. From this statement of duties and responsibilities a managerial structure may be deduced and a critique of present practice made.

The following list is an amalgamation of a number of job descriptions drawn from schools and represents typical examples of the genre:

1   to keep an eye on the changing nature of the subject, and try to keep abreast of specialist content and method, be mindful of curriculum development and in-service training and advise the headteacher on matters relating to the subject and its place in the curriculum;
2   to teach his/her subject and to promote the professional development of the skills of all department staff, especially probationary teachers, by providing a structural syllabus for all age and ability groups;
3   to hold regular, full meetings of the department together with informal meetings and sub-meetings as occasion demands;

4 to assess the financial needs of the department, present his or her case at the beginning of each financial year to the headteacher and make known any current adjustment of need;

5 to decide the examination syllabuses and options within the syllabus to be taught by the department;

6 to monitor the progress of students on teaching practice;

7 to prepare requisitions within the terms of his or her allowance, check the arrival and inventory of new books and materials, keep the necessary stockbooks and perform the annual stock-taking and checking;

8 to supervise the preparation of all internal examination papers and to ensure that copies are available by the appropriate fixed date;

9 to liaise with other heads of departments to secure integrated courses if these are considered appropriate and take responsibility for liaison with feeder schools;

10 to discipline pupils who have disrupted lessons within the department;

11 to write draft references for departmental staff who have applied for posts outside the school;

12 to monitor the progress of pupils by systematic record-keeping.

Such a list of duties and responsibilities gives the raw material for looking more closely at the managerial role of departmental heads. As 'middle' managers they have a multi-purpose role: 'They are both members of a higher echelon management body and leaders of their own sub-system' (John, 1980, p. 52). At the same time, as classroom teachers, they are on a par with colleagues facing the same demands, although there may be an expectation that they will be coping more effectively. Perhaps the primary task is to weld a team of teachers together and ensure that a department works towards a set of agreed and clearly understood objectives. Because of the complex web of the school as a social organization in which one can distinguish several authority systems — subject teacher, head of department, headmaster; classroom teacher, school secretary, headmaster — and because all teachers have a managerial function, the successful head of department has to use a variety of skills, several at a time, to focus on this fundamental objective. No manual can hope to cover every contingency. This fact emphasizes the current debate on the value of management techniques applied in a scientific way to education.

Efficient administration seen in the planning of lessons, establishing and servicing the needs of different classes and teachers, as well as the completion of reports and marking assignments, is essential to underpin the day-to-day activities of a timetable in action. Important though this 'clerical' function may be in avoiding simple administrative chaos, the value lies in enhancing the reputation of the head of department as a 'super-professional' making it easier to exercise a charismatic style of leadership, borrowing from the notion described by Weber but shorn of some of his historical excesses and references to the rule of prophets, warrior heroes and demagogues.

Personal qualities required for such a leader seem daunting when listed; seemingly only paragons of virtue need apply for the job: 'The knack of relating well to people, and being able to serve their needs and their special qualities, immense energy, a highly developed sense of organisation. Perhaps among the most important is the ability to articulate points of view clearly and persuasively' (Marland, 1971, p. 98). Other qualities are contained in such words as judgement, self-confidence, decisiveness, and are revealed in participation and communication: 'Decisions and politics follow from talk, but words are the thing in school, there is no other product or outcome only transient, constantly changing relationships and permanently indelible language, refined to the highest degree of truth' (Barker, 1982). A wealth of skills, tactics and psychology is required by chairmen and participants in meetings: 'The room fills up; the sociologists and social psychologists, sophisticates of meetings, readers of Goffman who all know intimately the difference between a group and an encounter, who are expert in the dynamics of interaction come in and pick their places with care, examining existing relationships, angles of vision even the cast of the light' (Bradbury, 1977, pp. 153–4).

Michael Marland refers to the element of continuous tension in the task of a head of department: 'The tension comes from the problem of balance, balance between the overall school requirements and the narrower subject needs; between organisational possibilities and theoretical ideas; between flexibility and rigidity . . .' (Marland, 1971, p. 99). Reference was made at the beginning to the need for Machiavelli's prince to appoint the right sort of minister. Rulers and presumably headteachers prefer faithful courtiers motivated by honours. This role of representing the department and its needs to the headteacher and senior management team is an important one. It is necessary to argue effectively for extra resources, favourable timetable considerations and leave of absence for visits, courses and trips. Whereas a rational case has its own force, it would be naive to claim that this is sufficient to obtain a decision. Departments have to organize their own public relations within the school in order to curry favour from others. An element of dissimulation may be required and even courtiers may profit from some of Machiavelli's advice given to his prince: 'Nothing causes a prince to be so much esteemed as great enterprises and giving proof of prowess' (Machiavelli, 1514, p. 81) This may be translated into good exam results, adoption of a fashionable curriculum project or historical pageant, favourably reviewed in the local press. According to Marland, the sharpest problem of balance is 'between long-term planning and today's problems' (Marland, 1971, p. 99). Clearly, the departmental head has to be a change-agent and responsible for developing the curriculum. To achieve this chosen aim, all the skills and personal qualities mentioned above need to be exploited, the emphasis of one or other skill or quality depending on the circumstances.

It is necessary at this stage to pause in the explanation of the role of a head of department and to offer a critique of the analysis given so far.

## Effects of Contraction within Education

In some respects the description of duties and responsibilities has been two-dimensional. What has been lacking is an appreciation of the real everyday problems that occur in schools and modify the behaviour and reactions of all to be found in the institution. There are some significant items missing from the example of a job description which ignore the current climate of educational contraction which must modify the expectations of the role in important ways. Some duties originally outlined will, conversely, become increasingly redundant for the same reasons.

It is perhaps axiomatic that handbooks on school organization make two necessary assumptions: first, that the traditional hierarchical model of a school is acceptable and that this is a fixed structure, although interpersonal relationships may well be highly flexible, and participatory management appears to be in fashion; secondly, the situation in which well-read education managers find themselves seems more idealistic than reality would indicate, with sufficient opportunities for staff development and promotion when the management of large schools was the norm. Whereas the head of department is expected to show a concern for the career development of those within his department, which lies at the base of staff motivation, the advice has tended to ignore the head of department and the motivation of senior staff who are assumed to be creative and charismatic under generally depressing circumstances.

It is appropriate therefore to look particularly at the role of the head of department during a period of crisis involving financial and staffing cutbacks, a falling school population and increasing outside interest in what goes on in the classroom. In the process there will be some significant modification to the position and duties of our archetypal head of department and some assumptions about leadership will need to be re-examined.

For the moment it will be assumed that the present hierarchical structure will continue to exist; we shall consider how the leadership role of the head of department will alter to cope with changing conditions. Obviously many policies have to be imposed upon schools from outside as the curriculum contracts as a result of staffing reductions and the axing of uneconomic classes. This gives less scope for individual initiatives and the head of department will be faced by a number of difficult problems, if not for him to resolve, at least for him to mitigate the harsher effects.

Staffing cuts may have deeply disruptive consequences in forcing a radical rethink about the allocation of responsibilities and the deployment of staff. If departments are asked to nominate a colleague for voluntary redeployment, a period of inevitable tension must occur. The results of staff cutting may force unpopular policies to be adopted, e.g., mixed ability teaching, reductions in timetable allocation, integrated studies and the removal of options for examination classes. These are measures that in happier times the department for its own good reasons would be reluctant to entertain. It is not difficult to imagine the traumas involved in discussing which colleague should be sacrificed in the name of redeployment.

The head of department is faced by a dilemma in the exercise of leadership. Colleagues will naturally expect a vigorous defence by him of the department's position, in the manner of a feudal baron defending his fief: 'One must therefore be a fox to recognise traps and a lion to frighten wolves' (Machiavelli, 1514, p. 64). However the objections may be overruled after ritual opposition has been offered. A number of effects may be the consequence: the political standing of the head of department can be adversely affected in the hierarchical pecking order; but paradoxically, the debate and discussion prior to an unpopular decision can bring a department closer together, fostered by a fortress mentality and a more participative modus operandi. The impetus for curriculum change can occur as a result of the need to abandon streaming and to consider the arguments for subject integration.

## Political and Social Skills Required by a Head of Department

A head of department needs to be a super-professional, able to respond flexibly to changing circumstances in a spirit of genuine open-mindedness rather than political dissimulation. Creating a climate of optimism under such conditions and being able to motivate staff are the most important tasks facing the departmental head. Unfortunately, whilst accepting that men are indeed led by baubles, few of these are available to reward good service. More responsibilities can be allocated, resulting from a departing colleague's portfolio being redistributed which may help some staff to gain experience whilst waiting for promotion. Working in a team teaching situation may have similar effects to the mutual ego support gained from participation in a Californian encounter group.

Paradoxically, if the head of department is being forced to concentrate on departmental needs instead of being involved with students, probationers and too many in-service courses, this fact alone may help to bring a department closer together. But the dangers of a frustrated, immobile staff still remain and, although it may be patronizing to say so, necessity may prove to be the mother of invention; simply following different schemes of work and syllabus options may provide a degree of intellectual stimulation.

For those departments which may be understaffed and allowed to recruit, there may be difficulties when they are forced to accept a colleague redeployed from another school who may or may not be totally suited to departmental needs as perceived at that level. Smoothing a squarish peg into a roundish hole requires tact and diplomacy as well as some initial induction procedures.

At the same time as a head of department is being forced to play a more overt political role, defending a particular subject area, there are conflicting arguments for saying that a more subtle, conciliatory style of leadership can be more appropriate as a response to changes forced upon the subject allocation on the timetable. If related subjects are integrated, a high level of negotiating skills will be needed by the participants involved, both to establish new schemes of work and to enable teams of teachers to work together. In some respects a higher degree of compatibility is required from staff involved in these projects than might be required in a department where individuality may be seen as a positive virtue. Departments need to be aware of trends that emphasize a skills and attitudes approach to the curriculum (e.g., health education, careers and guidance) that cut across and draw from a variety of subject areas. A word of warning may be sounded here: 'It is vital that the question of how this is conveyed to youngsters is carefully considered. It would be easy to subscribe to these ideas and yet practise so badly that they would be ineffective' (PAL, Careers Dept Sheffield LEA, 1982). Constructing a curriculum matrix based on this philosophy involves time and energy, with a consequent proliferation in working parties and discussion documents.

The committee skills referred to earlier now come to the fore, plus the appropriate backup support from the advisory service and outside documentation. It is essential that the climate in which these discussions take place is 'sympathetic' and directed towards task achievement, without the feeling that a bandwagon is rolling merely for reasons of fashion or to enhance an individual's career prospects or personal reputation. The choice of chairman, the physical setting, membership and agenda (both official and unofficial) are crucial. Setting up an ever-increasing number of meetings, however laudable the intention in terms of professional obligation, does create problems of defining the nature of a teacher's job at a time when teachers find themselves working harder than ever before with diminished public recognition and lower morale. This sort of time and effort can be justified to staff on the grounds that the managerial function is enhanced through the means of school-based in-service training. Attention needs to be paid to this contentious issue by all interested parties within and outside schools.

The rise in long-term unemployment seems to be calling into question the value of the Protestant work ethic, which in turn influences in the classroom where the necessity of working towards achieving exam success is queried. The philosophical framework of such an examination-oriented curriculum is being attacked and debate is centred on the question of the ultimate aim of formal education — should we be training pupils for specific jobs, to cope with unemployment/enforced leisure, to undergo several stages of career reorientation. Teachers are also involved in a personal capacity so that the idea of a logical career development through the Burnham Scales is becoming increasingly unrealistic. These pressures put a department on the defensive if they want to justify the place of subjects in the curriculum if tradition or academic standing are used as the criteria. The principle of utilitarianism can be used by some subjects to more effect than others, leaving some departments vulnerable to the harsh realities of market forces.

Some nimble intellectual footwork will be required by department heads when representing their subject areas to timetable planners, academic boards, as well as parents and governors. Particular emphasis ought to be placed on the qualities of effective advocacy which can be used to defend an entrenched position or to argue for changes. Two levels of attack may be necessary: the marshalling of arguments to convince professional colleagues, couched in the language of familiar educational jargon; the same arguments may also need to be translated into a less technical mode in order to convince lay members of governing bodies and parents whose participation in educational decision-making is a factor to be considered seriously. Theatrical talents of a subdued nature are not out of place in the service of public relations.

As important members of a hierarchy within a complex social organization, heads of department may exhibit signs of role strain. Thus he tends to become more concerned with organizational values which emphasize order, co-ordination and other aspects of the needs of organization. He becomes more bureaucratic, while many of his teachers remain academically and professionally orientated. There may be a reluctance, therefore, to accept the implications of changes which criticize the status quo mentioned above. To behave with such an ostrich-like mentality may not be a viable option in the face of outside pressures from politicians and education departments. Heads of department can respond to the demands of a fundamental revision of the existing curriculum pattern by moving away from the snares of bureaucracy and allying themselves more with their colleagues as classroom practitioners. This is part of the process of changing from an authoritarian, directive style of leadership to a more open grouping, complementary to each other, sharing a common set of aims but each having an acknowledged expertise in a specific area: 'I like to think of these people as "advisers" to the rest of the team' (Marland, 1971, p. 18).

The managerial style that slots into this situation has been characterized by Andrew Pettigrew of the School of Industrial and Business Studies at Warwick University as 'the fixer' who acts as follows: 'Fixers display great skill in assembling resources such as people, power and finance in order to release social deadlocks and bring about change. They are often intuitive, rather than rational or programmatic thinkers and may have the necessary ability to bring together the bureaucratic skills of the systems administrator, and the visionary and social skills of the change-manager to effect change. Fixers are much in demand at the moment' (Pettigrew, 1982).

## Predicting the Future of Educational Change

Predicting the direction of educational change is an exercise fraught with problems eloquently argued by Karl Popper, but there can be value in some intelligent speculation about the future as a way of exciting debate and the posing of questions which then might influence policy-making. It is appropriate therefore to reconsider the leadership function of a head of department in the light of changes that are beginning to influence education policy.

It is clear that a neatly defined job description is too simplistic and ignores the complexities of the real world. Teachers are being forced to react to crises and to some extent to be on the defensive, with scope for positive creativity reduced. Leadership is more concerned with survival: 'The result is the appearance of the rhetoric of finance, economics and accounting linked to strongly articulated values about efficiency, and all these harnessed to the new preoccupation of resource management' (Pettigrew, 1982). There is the risk, according to Bernard Barker, 'that the rhetoric of the staff college and the mystique of administration may take us further away from children than we intend' (Barker, 1982). But this danger could be minimized if the notion of formalized bureaucracy as presently practised is re-examined.

This brings the argument back to the structure of advisers advocated by Marland, which could provide the basis for a new form of subject organization. As it seems to be generally agreed that all teachers are managers, so it follows that all teachers possess particular areas of expertise. So far as individual subjects are concerned, in the field of routine classroom management, a form of collective leadership could be developed. Depending on the agenda for a particular meeting, different teachers can act as chairman, produce documents and suggest new policies. This model derives from two sources: the board of directors of a commercial company with specialist directors concerned with finance, marketing, public relations; and the notion of an elected, rotating chairman common in faculties of higher education. As departments contract both in size and importance, subject sectors will be substituted, and a less hierarchical framework would seem to be appropriate. Although the school population will fall, the existence of a pool of unemployed adults, combined with fewer workers than in the past who acquire a single skill early in life which they continue to deploy until retirement, will create demands for continuing education with a structure from pre-nursery to post-retirement. Teachers should be able to exploit these opportunities for career enhancement, and this growth of additional areas of expertise may make a monolithic departmental structure obsolete.

The weakness in this scheme of expanding the role of subject adviser lies in the need for an individual with negotiating clout to represent a subject's needs to educational planners. Delegates with the skills of advocacy and a mandate to argue with headteachers may prove to be less effective, since the consultation procedures between academic boards may well be extended with the danger of losing flexibility. Where integrated schemes are in operation, the activities of a collective leadership need to be coordinated by someone with a wide breadth of vision going beyond the perspectives of a single subject area. For convenience, this function can be described as curriculum evaluation, showing the way in which the job of the head of department can adapt to new circumstances whilst trying to avoid the problems of too rigid hierarchies and bureaucracy. The system should be flexible enough to cope with the demands of a skills-based curriculum matrix. From the consideration of such a possible structure, some managerial skills can be extracted, and a new job description be established.

Whilst the organization of subject advisers can be retained, a separate team of curriculum evaluators within the school would operate on a roving peripatetic commission. Their task is to ensure that the broad aims of the school are interpreted at a classroom level and to ensure that the curriculum remains coordinated and balanced. They would be free from specific timetable commitments although it would be logical to use individuals with the appropriate subject background within a related group of subjects. A number of short- and long-term assignments will occupy the team ranging from the management of resources to team teaching, evaluating a specific scheme of work, advising on teaching methodology, monitoring the progress of pupils. The job is to support classroom teachers with materials and practical help, as well as to encourage ongoing innovation whilst relieving colleagues of some routine clerical administration. The curriculum evaluators could act as the channel of communication between subject teachers and academic boards. At a time of staffing changes resulting from deployment and school amalgamations, the advantages of this structure lie in its flexibility, since the members of the team need not be fixed for all time and can take account of changing staffing allocations.

For this type of role a combination of skills is required, contained in the term 'change-managers' who 'require good diagnostic skills to unravel the problems and priorities of the day, a clarity and simplicity of vision of where they would like to be . . .' (Pettigrew, 1982). To this we can add the need to have a specialist knowledge of the technical aspects of such matters as evaluation, and skills matrices, with an understanding of the process of getting innovation under way. Some general guidelines may help to summarize the duties and responsibilities of teachers with an enhanced managerial function; these modify and refine the list given at the beginning of this chapter.

A shift in emphasis may be noted. This is not intended to be a prescriptive recipe, to be regarded as a comprehensive manual for survival for the simple reason that schools are such idiosyncratic institutions. Further, educational management is a sub-branch of that social activity which may be designated 'politics': 'for the most part politics consists of a complicated game of move and counter move . . . and while all parties may claim a far-sighted vision of what they will achieve in the future, in practice they simply follow their noses as they smell out where their interests lie' (Cornforth, 1968, p. 172). Thus the job description is a series of signposts or warning cones, alerting the reader to the implications of a particular action.

## A Revised List of Duties for the Head of Department

1   To exercise a style of leadership that is direct and very open, carried out by someone who can stand, but not always remain, aloof;
2   to give clear, simple messages, maintaining these consistently and without dilution;
3   to give due consideration to establishing the most sympathetic climate before the launch of projected change;
4   to represent departmental needs to senior management; in a vigorous yet subtle manner;
5   to be constantly aware of the need to motivate colleagues to give of their best efforts, often under difficult circumstances;
6   to understand the institutional climate of a school and the political sub-structure as a guideline for exercising leadership;
7   to be able to articulate effectively in words and print departmental policy for both internal and external requirements;
8   to be able to relate schemes of work to general institutional aims;
9   to evaluate and monitor progress;
10   to be able to combine an action-oriented, short-term, task achievement style of management with the subtle approach of the 'fixer' in understanding the processes involved;
11   to be creative: rocking the boat yet not sinking it;
12   to be *simultaneously* a listener, judge, decision-maker, observer, orator and intermediary.

This list can be seen as building upon the more administrative duties already considered.

## New Directions for In-Service Training

'Whatever the form of education management, whatever the institutions in which education for management may be conducted, if we fail to clarify our aims and intentions we will achieve little or nothing' (Poster, 1976, p. 165). Before any management techniques are put into practice, a transitional period of in-service training must be instigated. The emphasis should be on developing the skills of negotiation and chairmanship within the broad context of the chequerboard of political relationships. Role play and case studies enable staff to practise without the tension involved in referring to named individuals in the school. Standing apart from a problem in this respect can lend more objectively to the attempt to solve difficulties. Time must be allocated for this valuable activity. Determining the most appropriate aims and objectives should involve the professional educator in wide reading and discussions, and it is vital that the necessary information from agencies concerned with policy-making be obtained. There is a place for deliberately provoking reactions about alternative organizations as a means of debating the status quo but not in any narrow, politically partisan manner. In this task, schools will have to work in a close relationship with the careers service and agencies concerned with information technology and youth training initiatives.

Achieving the new directions which have been suggested is a daunting task in terms of the time and energy required from individuals. 'But whereas some new people are born new people, natural intimates of change and history, the Kirks arrived at that condition the harder way, by effort, mobility and harsh experience' (Bradbury, 1977, p. 18). Middle management can be helped to reach these goals with the support of headteachers. This starts a new area for debate. As Martin Buber states: 'Genuine responsibility exists only when there is real responding' (Green, 1982, p. 363).

## References

BARKER, B. (1982) 'Root based leader or cloud based manager', *The Times Educational Supplement.*

BRADBURY, M. (1977) *The History Man*, London Arrow Books.

CORNFORTH, M. (1968) *The Open Philosophy and the Open Society* London, Lawrence & Wishart.

GREEN, J. (1982) *A Dictionary of Contemporary Quotations*, Oxford — Oxford Univ. Press, quote from M. BUBER.

HOUGHTON, V. *et al.* (1975) *Management in Education: The Management of Organisations and Individuals*, articles by L. WATSON and M. WEBER.

JOHN, D. (1980) *Leadership in Schools*, London, Heinemann.

MACHIAVELLI, N. (1514) *The Prince.*

MARLAND, M. (1971) *Head of Department*, London, Heinemann.

PETTIGREW, A. (1982) 'Problems of managerial response as organisations move from rich to poor environments', paper read to BEMAS Conference.

POSTER, C. (1976) *School Decision Making*, London, Heinemann.

*Preparation for Adult Life; Curriculum Framework*, discussion document from Careers Dept, Sheffield LEA.

# The Role of the Head of Department: Some Questions and Answers*

R.G. Bloomer
University of Southampton

## Introduction

It is possible to distinguish at least four reasons why departmental organization in schools and colleges is not always as efficient as it might be:

1   The organizational problems have become greater in recent years as, partly through schemes of comprehensive reorganization involving mergers, schools have increased in size, with the consequence of larger departments, sometimes under the umbrella of a faculty structure, and the added complication in some cases of a split site. The intake of pupils into schools is much less homogeneous in range of ability than it once was, and therefore there is a need for a greater diversity of courses. Moreover, major national schemes of curriculum development put pressure on schools to rethink their courses and styles of teaching, and many of the modern approaches — integration of subjects, mixed ability classes, team teaching and inquiry-based methods — offer a greater challenge to middle management. Heads of departments increasingly find that they may be asked to draw up their own timetables and programmes.

2   Modern 'democratic' management styles, predicated on belief in a 'climate of discussion' (Marland, 1971) and in 'coordination rather than dictation' (Skelton, 1977) while they may well lead to an enrichment of school work also call for greater skills and adaptability in heads of departments.

3   There is ambiguity as to the definition of the role of heads of department. Detailed contracts are rare, and most heads of department learn their role 'on the job' through their perceptions of what others heads of department do and of the expectations of head-

---

* This is an edited version of the article which appeared in *Educational Research*, 22, 2 February 1980, pp. 83–96.

265

teachers. The wide divergencies of view of the role have been made clear by Lambert (1975), and his research exposes the dangers, not only of friction through role conflict, but also of failure to take the work of management seriously.

4  Training for the work of management in schools and colleges is comparatively rare, and people are promoted on the strength of their expertise in one kind of work (teaching) to posts involving another kind of work (management).

Between May 1977 and October 1978 two series of evening workshops were held at the University of Southampton Department of Education, and a third series at Bournemouth Teachers' Centre, in order to investigate two major problems in middle management: (a) What sort of functions should a head of department have? (b) How should these functions be carried out? A total of ninety members from Hampshire, Dorset and Sussex attended the workshops, of whom forty-four were from comprehensive schools, sixteen from bilateral schools, eight from sixth-form colleges, six from grammar schools, five from primary schools, three from independent schools, two from technical colleges and one from a tutorial centre. The remainder of the workshop members were a local authority adviser, a head of a teachers' centre, a head of a field study centre, a lecturer from an institute of higher education and the author. Of the eighty-three members who were teachers in primary or secondary schools fifty-six (68 per cent) were heads of department, including year heads and heads of houses as well as subject heads, while the remainder held posts below this level. In more detail, the teachers were distributed among the scales as follows: Scale 1, seven (eight per cent); Scale 2, thirty-one (37 per cent); Scale 3, twenty-one (25 per cent); Scale 4, twenty-four (30 per cent). In the workshops members were free to contribute to discussions information, ideas and queries so that their collective wisdom could be brought to bear on a series of questions relating to three areas of the head of deparment's role: those concerned with the departmental meeting, with staff and pupils, and with the teaching prog- ramme and resources. The questions, which are reproduced below, were formulated after many discussions with teachers and after consulting the literature listed in the bibliography. Each workshop meeting concentrated on one of the three areas, and there was some division of labour in that different groups of members considered different sets of questions, though there was an opportunity for any member to comment on any question in the latter part of each meeting, when the groups reported back to the whole workshop.

The workshops differed from previous explorations of the role of the head of department in three ways: in the wide range of institutions from which members contributed; in the fact that the views of teachers who were not heads of departments were taken into account; and, above all, in the attempt to discover views of the role of the head of department *after discussion* rather than simply through the use of a questionnaire. As chairman of the workshops, I was impressed by the considerable degree of consensus which emerged, much of it in the form of prescriptive conclusions, and it is that consensus which I have attempted to outline in the following pages. In doing so I gratefully acknowledge the debt which I owe to all the workshop members and, in particular, to those who acted as recorders; the responsibility for interpretation must, of course, be mine.

## The Questions

### (A) *The Departmental Meeting*

A1   In what ways may departmental meetings help to achieve the following purposes:

    A1 (a) Communication
    A1 (b) Formulating departmental objectives and policy on courses, material resources, and assessment
    A1 (c) Delegation
    A1 (d) Evaluation of departmental policy and courses
    A1 (e) Further education and training of junior staff (and students?)
    A1 (f) Giving advice on new staff appointments
    A1 (g) The creation and maintenance of a happy, cooperative team

A2   What other purposes may departmental meetings serve?

A3   *A case study*
A teacher who has held his first post as head of department for two terms is keen on updating the syllabuses and methods used in the teaching of his subject. A senior teacher in the department, older but less well-qualified than the head of department, for whose post he was a candidate, shows no support whatever for any sort of change, and even avoids attending departmental meetings
What advice would you give to the head of department?

A4   Should departmental meetings

    A4 (a) be timetabled?
    A4 (b) have an agenda?
    A4 (c) include discussion papers circulated beforehand?
    A4 (d) have an 'outsider' present, e.g., the director of studies, a member of the pastoral staff or of the county advisory staff?
    A4 (e) keep a record of their decisions?
    A4 (f) report back their findings to an appropriate person or committee?

### (B)   *Pupils and Staff*

B1   *General.* 'It is the business of the head of department to help people to realize their full potentials; he should reduce tension, minimize constraints and aim to promote goodwill and a happy working atmosphere.'

B1 (a) What are the implications of this statement?
B1 (b) How far is the statement acceptable?

B2   *Pupils* To what extent and in what ways should a head of department be concerned with

B2 (a) diagnosing pupil's abilities
B2 (b) arranging pupils in groups for teaching
B2 (c) organizing the provision of appropriate courses
B2 (d) monitoring the progress of individual pupils
B2 (e) discipline problems in the department
B2 (f) pastoral guidance
B2 (g) careers advice
B2 (h) other activities connected with pupils?

B3   *Staff* To what extent and in what ways should a head of department be concerned with

B3 (a) helping each member of staff to feel part of a team
B3 (b) spreading the load of teaching
B3 (c) encouraging staff to extend their professional abilities
B3 (d) delegating the non-teaching work of the department
B3 (e) evaluating the work of members of staff
B3 (f) assisting in the process of appointing new staff
B3 (g) supervising probationers
B3 (h) supervising students in training
B3 (i) other activities connected with staff?

### (C)   *The Teaching Programme and Resources*

C1   What does the term 'curriculum' now imply?
C2   Curriculum development usually involves taking decisions about the following: aims and objectives; content; methods of working; assessment.
C2   (a) What kinds of things should a head of department consider under each of these headings?
C2   (b) What connections are there between the different headings?
C2   (c) On what principles and by what means may a head of department arrive at appropriate curriculum decisions?

C3 How may a head of department evaluate a scheme of work which has been in operation for several years?

C4 What are the essentials of team teaching?

C5 What dangers and difficulties might there be in introducing a team teaching programme?

C6 What benefits might a head of department expect from a team teaching approach?

C7 What different kinds of resources are available to heads of department in support of their teaching programmes?

C8 What factors should a head of department take into account in deciding what resources he needs?

C9 'It is just as important to think *when* things are needed as to think *what* is needed.' How far do you agree?

C10 How can a head of department most effectively make choices between alternative forms of any one resource?

C11 To what extent and in what ways should resources be produced within the department?

C12 'Many resources which have been requisitioned nevertheless do not exist, because nobody can ever be sure where they are.' (Bailey, 1973.) What can a head of department do to ensure the safety and accessibility of resources?

## The workshop's answers

### (A) *The Departmental Meeting*

#### A1 (a) *Communication*

Staff cannot work efficiently unless they are well-informed about the facts, problems and constraints of the situation in which they are working. Communication is not, however, a one-way traffic from the head of department: it often needs to be two-way or multi-way.

The need to use a departmental meeting for communication will vary somewhat with the size of the school and its physical layout. In a small school, and also in some larger ones where the staff of a department works in a suite of adjacent rooms, communications can sometimes be achieved informally. In many larger schools, however, especially where there is a split site or where a number of part-timers teach in the department, the departmental meeting can be a very necessary means of communication.

#### A1 (b) *Objectives and policy*

In spite of (or perhaps because of) the danger of deep disagreements, there is a need to maintain what Michael Marland calls 'a climate of discussion' in the department because the formulation of objectives and policy needs the combined wisdom of the whole team of staff, and needs to take into account the personalities and capabilities of individual teachers as well as the needs and abilities of the pupils. Clarity about policy is one mainstay of departmental efficiency, and teachers who have contributed to the forming of policy through discussion are likely both to see objectives more clearly and to show a greater commitment to achieving them.

### A1   (c) *Delegation*
A head of department should give some responsibility to each of his staff, partly in the interests of sharing work out fairly and promoting efficiency through the division of labour and specialization in particular departmental jobs, and partly also to give staff the chance to 'grow' as professionals and to realize that they have a distinctive contribution to make to the department's work. Delegation is not, however, something to be done 'blind'; the head of department needs to know both the strengths and weaknesses and the interests of his staff, and these often become apparent in discussions at the departmental meeting about jobs which need doing; there may even be volunteers! At all events the head of department needs to make sure that the member of staff undertaking a particular job has a clear idea of the work involved.

### A1   (d) *Evaluation*
Evaluation is necessary periodically both to assess the extent to which the department's current courses are achieving their objectives and to consider whether the department's objectives, and therefore courses, need to be modified in the light of changes in the needs of the pupils and in the personnel, interests and skills of the staff. Full-scale evaluations of school courses are rarely possible. One of the best practical means of evaluation is by discussion of courses, perhaps once a year, at the departmental meeting, when decisions are based partly on the results of examinations and tests and partly on the feelings of teachers about the department's programme of work and the outcomes of the programme.

### A1   (e) *Staff training*
Participation in discussions about the department's work is a valuable continuing form of education and training for all staff and it is important, not least because they have new perspectives, that probationers and other junior staff as well as newcomers should be drawn into the discussions of departmental meetings. At meetings, too, heads of department can publicize in-service activities relevant to the field of the department's work; discussion as to the appropriateness of the courses may take place, and members of staff may be encouraged to attend. The departmental meeting may also be used as an opportunity for those who have been on courses to report back to the rest of the staff, stressing key ideas which have a bearing on the department's work.

### A1 (f) *Staff appointments*

The staff of a department, particularly in a department which has clear aims and differentiation of functions between individual teachers, will often have valuable views regarding the appointment of new colleagues. A new appointment may be a straight replacement but, equally well, it may be either an opportunity for some area of work which the department feels has previously been neglected to be taken up, or an occasion when an existing member of staff may change the direction or emphasis of his work. Perhaps more frequently than at present, the advice of the department staff on new appointments could with profit be arrived at through discussion, and made available, through the head of department and head teacher, to the appointing body.

### A1 (g) *The department as a team*

'The creation and maintenance of a happy, cooperative team' through the holding of departmental meetings will be promoted by careful attention to each of the headings in this section. The key factor is the encouragement of a feeling of involvement in the life of the department, its work and its decisions.

### A2 *Other purposes of departmental meetings*

The departmental meeting is an occasion when the joint thinking of staff can be brought to bear on matters such as discipline problems, the learning difficulties of particular pupils, the organization of the department's contribution to schemes of integrated studies, or the planning of a programme of team teaching. The departmental meeting may also serve as an opportunity for ideas, feelings and questions about general school policy to emerge.

### A3 *A case study*

The situation outlined is a familiar one at a time of comprehensive reorganization and often rapid developments in curriculum. The ideal solution is to avoid such a situation arising by careful planning from the beginning. Real change takes years and requires the commitment of those who will implement it; a head of department who wishes to update syllabuses and methods of teaching, bearing in mind the high degree of freedom which teachers have in this country, needs to hold consultations with his staff, both individually and through department meetings, to generate enthusiasm and to get the backing of the department for a programme of change arrived at by consensus.

A head of department who is trying to carry through changes solely on his own initiative may well find himself in the situation of the case study; he will need to talk with the teacher concerned and, perhaps, to compromise, in order to create a niche for the teacher where the recognition of his responsibility and seniority would in time rebuild an injured ego.

## A4   (a) *Timetabled meetings?*

Attendance at departmental meetings is a normal part of the professional work of teachers. Some meetings will be of a non-timetabled, informal character but there is also a need for regular, more formal meetings either on the timetable or after school for routine decision-making as well as for longer meetings before term in order to formulate overall strategy. Meetings should not, however, be held just for the sake of holding them.

## A4   (b) *An agenda?*

For the more formal type of department meeting an agenda is desirable. The agenda represents a kind of plan of campaign for the meeting, and ensures that thought has been given beforehand, not only to what matters need discussions, but also to the order of priorities. The agenda should be open to the suggestions of all members, preferably made prior to the meeting.

## A4   (c) *Discussion papers?*

As long as there is time for members to study them beforehand short discussion papers are often valuable: they can save time at the meeting in communicating facts and ideas and, by taking everyone to a common starting point, can help to ensure that discussion is not held up or taken along blind alleys for lack of appropriate information. Friction, which is bound to exist between colleagues, and which may stultify discussion, may be relieved by having a subject introduced by a paper from a third party. Papers tend to promote a more tightly controlled discussion and may therefore help keep the thinking of the meeting to the point, though a head of department needs to be alert to the danger that issues which are relevant, but not raised in a paper, may be ignored by the meeting.

## A4   (d) *An 'outsider' present?*

On occasions the presence of an outsider may be valuable for specific purposes, for example: (i) offering a 'neutral' or more informed view of particular issues; (ii) providing feedback as to how the decisions of the department would affect others; (iii) giving speedy communication of the department's views to higher authorities (often very useful when the department is making requests).

## A4   (e) *A record of decisions?*

Decisions (preferably reached by consensus rather than by voting, which, in setting one person or group against another may help create factions) should be noted and kept openly on record for the guidance of staff in some kind of minute book. In the larger departments it may be desirable to circulate duplicated minutes, and in all cases it should be possible for staff to raise for further discussion items which seem to them to have been incorrectly or insufficiently fully minuted.

A4  (f)  *Reporting back?*
Schools are whole entities and in general it is desirable that departments should not try to exist in isolation but should make information about their thinking and activities readily available, especially to the head teacher and senior staff, who have an overall responsibility for the pupils and teachers.

### (B)  *Pupils and Staff*

### B1  *General*
The statement has the overriding implication that a head of department should take a close interest in the people in his department both staff and pupils, and should be prepared to develop his social skills, particularly in promoting healthy, pleasant and productive interpersonal relationships. 'Potential' may be viewed differently by different heads of department: subject heads may put most stress on teaching and learning whereas pastoral heads may be more interested in such things as ethical potentials, public spiritedness, capacity for leadership, and general contribution to the life of the school. The constraints which a head of department has to face may include uncooperative, factious or poorly qualified staff, shortage of money for resources, without which new courses or approaches to work cannot be introduced, and rigidities in timetabling, sometimes caused by the employment of part-time staff, which may make it difficult, for example, to take classes out of school for fieldwork or to 'block' several parallel forms for a 'lead lesson'. The statement also suggests that people are likely to work best in a happy atmosphere, an atmosphere which will not exist if, for example, staff are understretched, overloaded or required to teach in a way which runs contrary to their beliefs; a head of department who wishes to make changes will need to build up a climate of opinion in favour of change and to compromise, if necessary.

The statement gives, on the whole, an adequate, even an ideal, description of the role of the head of department, though it must be recognized that the personal traits, e.g., aggressiveness, very strong ambition or lack of social skills of some heads of departments might militate against the fulfilment of the aims listed. The latter part of the statement should not be taken as a recipe for complacency; heads of departments should certainly seek to reduce frustrating tension, but some tensions, for example a conflict of views in ordered discussion, can be productive and can lead to a richer synthesis of ideas. The head of department must aim to stimulate vitality. His overriding responsibility is to the pupils and, if it becomes evident that the education of pupils and the goodwill of the staff are in conflict, a head of department must, in the last resort, be prepared to be autocratic in safeguarding the interests of pupils.

B2   (a) *Diagnosing pupils' abilities*

From many points of view the diagnosis of pupils' abilities is an essential activity in schools. If pupils are to be helped to realize their full potentials, it is necessary to have some indication of what these potentials are in each individual case, so that, for example, persistent 'underachievers' may be recognized and given appropriate stimulus and support.

In the diagnosis of pupils' abilities, a head of department has the function of being a monitor of a monitoring system. He has, first, the duty of satisfying himself that proper diagnosis is made. He may feel that the needs of his department are already well served initially by the tests carried out by the feeder schools, by the LEA or by other departments in his own school. Alternatively, he may feel it necessary, or, in the case of the basic subjects, the school may feel it necessary, for his department to test pupils in its own area of work, perhaps using some form of standardized test. However, pupils' interests, and therefore abilities, change over time, and periodic tests or examinations are among the means of keeping a check on current abilities. Secondly, as regards the non-academic abilities, a head of department can encourage his staff to keep systematic records of their pupils' interests and achievements, and he will have the responsibility for seeing that information relating to the abilities of a pupil in his department is available to those who have a valid reason for wanting it.

B2   (b) *Arranging pupils in teaching groups*

In general the arrangement of pupils in groups for teaching depends upon the school policy with regard to streaming, banding or mixed ability classes and decisions about the composition of particular teaching groups are likely to be the province of the headteacher, sometimes with the assistance of the deputy head or head of upper or lower school. Heads of department are, however, often called on for advice, and may well have a say, for example, in the transfer of pupils between streams or classes on academic or other grounds. Direct departmental involvement in grouping pupils is increasing in some schools where heads of departments on some occasions may be allocated on the timetable a block of time and a large number of pupils (perhaps a whole year) whom they then have the responsibility for arranging in appropriate groups.

B2   (c) *Organizing courses*

Heads of departments responsible for subject areas, in consultation with their staffs, should have a large amount of autonomy in the planning of courses. There is a clear need for heads of departments to be outward-looking and able to take initiatives in modifying courses in the light of changes in their subjects, in their staffs and in the needs of the pupils. Providing appropriate courses may also imply some say in timetabling since certain kinds of work, e.g., fieldwork, require blocks of time.

**B2   (d)** *Monitoring the progress of pupils*
A head of department needs to be in a position to be able to know and report on the performance of all pupils in his department. Assessments of pupils' standards will normally be partly the responsibility of the individual class teacher and partly based on departmental examinations supervised by the head of department who can often gain a valuable insight into the needs and problems of staff and pupils by monitoring the progress of a sample of pupils forming a cross-section of the department's intake. Heads of subject departments will normally aim primarily at monitoring academic progress and maintaining systematic records but should be ready to exchange with pastoral staff knowledge which may have a bearing on the work and welfare of individual pupils.

**B2   (e)** *Discipline problems*
A head of department should aim to establish by his personal example and guidance a well-ordered overall atmosphere for the department's work, which will show itself in such matters as the care of books and other resources and the promotion of good standards of presentation of work. There is a need for the head of department to help inexperienced teachers to build up their disciplinary skills, for example by avoiding giving them over-difficult classes, by offering advice and by 'calling in' for short periods on classes in progress. In general individual cases of indiscipline are not the responsibility of the head of department.

**B2   (f)** *Pastoral guidance*
In order to be effective either in an academic or in a pastoral role teachers need to know pupils as whole individuals. All teachers have some responsibility for pastoral care of pupils, and the head of department, who is also often a class tutor, should stress the need for staff to be alert to pupils' interests and problems, including home difficulties.

The head of department should show concern for pupils who are evidently unhappy in their work. It may be necessary in some cases to consider transfer, either to another group in the same department if, for example, there are serious incompatibilities in personal relationships, or to a course in another department if, for example, it becomes clear that an unsuitable initial choice of option has been made.

Where a head of department deals with serious academic shortcomings, or becomes aware of serious pastoral problems of pupils, he should notify the specialist pastoral staff, since these staff cannot function efficiently unless they are well-informed.

**B2   (g)** *Careers advice*
A head of department should not try to rival specialist careers staff who have a wide knowledge of job opportunities, but nevertheless both pupils

and parents tend to expect a subject head to be able to give advice as to where his subject could 'lead'. The head of department is also in the best position to advise as to whether it is worthwhile for a pupil to continue with his subject, for example, to go on from O- to A-level, and this advice may be crucial to the choice of a career.

### B2 (h) *Other activities*

A head of department should encourage out-of-school activities associated with his subject, for example, clubs or societies, day visits or holidays abroad. Activities such as these can do a great deal to promote both enthusiasm for a subject area and better relationships between staff and pupils.

### B3 (a) *Helping staff feel part of a team*

This is often easier in a small department than in a large one, where there is often the danger of the development of factions, sometimes partly because of the geographical separation of staff. The head of department should actively promote communication within the team, aiming at the sharing of ideas and the involvement of all members in departmental decision-making. These purposes can be achieved partly through the holding of departmental meetings and partly by the readiness of the head of department to be available to staff for consultation and discussion of ideas and problems. A head of department can also encourage staff to cooperate in extra-curricular departmental or school activities; such shared experience helps to draw both staff and pupils together.

### B3 (b) *Spreading the load of teaching (see also B3 (d))*

Heads of departments should, where possible, encourage staff to teach a wide cross-section of the department's courses and classes, so that, for example, no one takes all the academically able or all the 'difficult' classes; where staff have teaching interests in common they can support each other in contributing to the discussion of common problems. The interests and abilities of individual staff should be taken into account and, in fairness, the total loads of staff, allowing for administrative and pastoral responsibilities and time teaching outside the department, should be approximately equal.

### B3 (c) *Encouraging staff to extend their professional abilities*

A head of department should take a general interest in the professional expertise of his staff: he needs to be available to discuss professional problems, and should tactfully encourage staff individually to develop some of their strengths and reduce some of their weaknesses. For this purpose, and on account of his other numerous responsibilities, a head of department needs a personal timetable with an allocation of 'free' periods distinctly greater than average. For probationers and junior staff it is often particularly helpful to see more experienced teachers at work, not for the sake of slavish copying, but in order to extend their repertoire of possible lines of approach. A head of department should be open-minded and courageous enough to encourage from time to time experimentation with new teaching techniques and materials, and may sometimes introduce change by asking members of staff to review new books and other teaching resources on behalf of the department. There is increasing recognition nowadays of the importance of in-service education and training in extending the professional abilities of teachers, and a head of department has a duty to see that details of relevant courses are available to staff and to encourage attendance, for example, by rearranging teaching commitments. Many heads of department themselves help to enrich in-service provision by their willingness to run or to contribute to courses on subjects in which they have special expertise. Much of the potential impact of in-service activities will, however, be lost unless the head of department facilitates feedback to the department of the knowledge and ideas which participating members have gained. A head of department must also recognize that his staff are not just members of his department but also members of the school and foster their wider interests in the school and contributions to its life. (B3 (b) and (d) are also relevant to this section: staff can 'grow' as professionals both by gaining wide experience of teaching and by the exercise of delegated responsibility.)

### B3 (d) *Delegating non-teaching work*

The non-teaching work of a department may include jobs such as the following: monitoring the department's funds, ordering, storing, issuing and maintaining books, stationery and apparatus, including audio-visual equipment, the preparation, storage and retrieval of 'home-made' teaching materials, e.g., worksheets, the supervision of technical or clerical staff, arranging internal examinations for the different courses and years, monitoring external examination entries, dealing with general correspondence and returns, the overseeing of safety apparatus and precautions, looking after a departmentally-based society, making arrangements for fieldwork and leading or helping to lead a school visit or holiday.

Duties should be spread out, both to avoid overloading any one person and to allow staff to grow in exercising responsibility and in a sense of involvement in the department's business.

### B3 (e) *Evaluation of staff*

The head of department may need to evaluate the work of members of staff for a variety of purposes, for example, the writing of references or the supply of information to the headteacher as material for references when a teacher is seeking another appointment, the production of reports on the progress of probationary teachers and, not least, for his own purposes in monitoring the functioning of the department. Some evaluation is inevitably unconscious and intuitive; it is in any case difficult to avoid forming some general impression of a teacher's work. But conscious evaluation is also necessary, though it should be unobtrusive and rarely involve formal 'sitting in' on lessons, The head of department can have informal, routine, one-to-one discussions with staff about their work with different classes, their methods of approach, the problems they are meeting and the progress of their pupils. Some heads of department study samples of written work from different classes in rotation. A teacher's capacity to generate ideas and to solve problems, to cooperate with others and to show powers of leadership and, above all, to show commitment to the work of the school will also often be apparent in work outside the classroom.

### B3    (f) *Assisting in the appointment of staff*
The head of department needs to be the spokesman for the department in this respect, as in many others, though he will normally consult his colleagues perhaps at a departmental meeting, as to the kind of appointment they feel is desirable. The influence of the head of department may be simply through consultation with the headteacher but a head of department should also be prepared to help in framing advertisements, making out short-lists and attending interviews.

### B3    (g) *Supervising probationers*
The supervision of probationers is an important commitment for a head of department. Probationers are vulnerable and usually need substantial support and guidance mainly through one-to-one discussions. They should not be given classes with which even experienced staff find it difficult to cope; nor, however, should they be sheltered to the extent that they never meet any discipline problems or that their authority is constantly undermined by the intervention of the head of department, so that they have no chance to grow in stature as teachers.

### B3    (h) *Supervising students*
It is a mark of any profession that its members take some responsibility for the education and training of their future colleagues and heads of departments supervising students in training in schools are acting as essential partners of the staff of colleges and university departments of education. The head of department will need to gain from the student's tutor knowledge of the precise purposes of any particular period of school experience and of any strengths or weaknesses which the student has previously shown so that these things can be taken into account in composing the student's programme. There is usually a need for some observation, especially during the early stages of a period of teaching practice, since, by seeing experienced staff at work, students can gain valuable insights into the norms of the school and can extend their ideas on lines of approach to classroom methods, the design of teaching materials and discipline. Students normally benefit from teaching a cross section of courses, and the head of department will take care to see that students are

not given unduly difficult classes and that they have adequate time for preparation and reasonable freedom to experiment with different methods of teaching.

The head of department will need to be able to provide a report on each student's work, but school practice periods are not primarily for assessment; they are learning situations and therefore the experience, the advice and the encouragement which the school is able to offer the students are the things which really count.

### B3 (i) *Other activities*

Heads of department should be approachable to members of staff and willing to discuss with them problems relating to their careers as well as to teaching and personal relationships in the department.

### (C) *The Teaching Programme and Resources*

### C1 *The term 'curriculum'*

Every school has both a formal curriculum, expressed in such things as the subjects taught, the syllabuses, methods used in the classroom, timetables and rules, and an informal curriculum which may be taken to include not only the activities of school clubs and societies but also what is sometimes called 'the hidden curriculum', important elements in which are the attitudes and values of the staff and the ethos and culture of the peer groups of pupils. The curriculum, then, may be said to be the sum total of all the experiences and influences which the school makes available to its pupils. There can be no ideal curriculum, for what a school offers must be open to influence both by the needs of its pupils and by the outlook and economic pressures of society, and these things vary not only from place to place but from time to time.

### C2 *Curriculum development* (a) *Meaning of terms*

An 'aim' in education is usually considered to be a broad intention achievable only over a substantial period of time, whereas an 'objective' is a limited step, often achievable in a single lesson, towards the general aim. Under the heading of 'Aims and objectives' a head of department will need to consider the kinds of knowledge and skills of which he feels pupils should gain mastery at different levels of the course. Increasingly nowadays, in spite of the dangers of indoctrination, the formation of attitudes and values by pupils in relation to the material studied is also considered a proper part of the framework of aims and objectives.

By 'content' is meant the actual subject matter which makes up each stage of a course.

'Methods of working' include a whole spectrum of possible approaches to teaching and learning, ranging from traditional expositional teaching to project methods, assignments, programmed learning, groupwork, team teaching, seminars, field studies and the use of audio-visual aids and of games and simulations.

'Assessment' may be taken to imply all methods of ascertaining the state of progress of pupils and their degree of success with their courses: different forms of external examinations as well as the school's internal examinations, short tests given in class, and the impressions gained by the teacher during oral teaching or the marking of course work may therefore all be included under this heading.

## C2   (b) *Relationships between aspects of curriculum development*

The key category here is undoubtedly 'Aims and objectives': clear decisions taken under this heading must have a strong influence on the nature of the material to be placed under each of the other headings. The subject matter under 'Content' may be selected for its own sake, because it is felt that pupils should know about it or it may well be selected wholly or partly because it provides suitable exemplar material for the building up of skills or the formation of key concepts. As regards 'Methods of working', an expositional style may serve perfectly well where the acquisition by the pupils of a body of fact is the prime aim, but where the aim is to foster the skills of problem-solving through the gathering, weighing, and interpretation of evidence, then methods involving a 'project' style of approach, perhaps including fieldwork or experimentation, may well be more productive. Pupils may be helped to decide on, or to become aware of, their own attitudes on controversial issues by the process of discussion in the light of the available evidence and perhaps also by role-playing games which may enable them to achieve a degree of empathy with the outlook of other people in situations very different from their own. 'Assessment', too, needs to be planned with close reference to the initial 'Aims and objectives', since it has the purpose of discovering how far these have been achieved.

## C2   (c) *Principles of curriculum decision-making*

In formulating departmental aims and objectives, a head of department must keep in mind the overall policy, the framework of aims and objectives of the whole school and the factors which have influenced its composition. Schools should design their curricula so as to have relevance to the interests, needs and problems of the pupils and of society, taking account of the basic skills and concepts which pupils will require both as citizens and as individuals at work and at leisure. The catchment area of the school, its culture and outlook, must be considered, while the right of parents to have a say in the education of their children is recognized in the 1944 Education Act and in the report of the Taylor Committee. It is a well-established teaching principle that we need to start from where pupils are, both intellectually and physically in their daily lives, but the school and its departments will also benefit by reference to other wider authorities, among whom may be cited the Schools Council, the local authority advisers, the inspectors of the DES, educationists, researchers and curriculum developers in universities, colleges and other institutions, the subject associations and the national climate of opinion about education as evidenced in the media. Curriculum, however, achieves practical existence where teachers meet pupils, and a head of department would do well, therefore, to harness the expertise and support of his staff in seeking solutions to curriculum problems.

## C3 *Evaluating a scheme of work*
Because of the need to keep up-to-date, to avoid staleness and to give pupils and staff the stimulus of new ideas, a lively department will keep its schemes of work under continual review, evaluating one or more of the major divisions of its courses each year. Evaluation of such regularity and frequency must necessarily be done mainly from within the department, and the head of department will be concerned to make his staff active partners in the process. The staff will need to meet to discuss the outcomes of courses in terms of the learning and the attitudes of pupils. The outcomes will need to be weighed in relation both to the aims and objectives formulated for the courses and to the constraints of, for example, timing, resources and assessment under which the courses have operated. Among the sources of guidance available to aid staff in the process of evaluation may be included the results of external and internal examinations and tests and any comments from senior staff of the school or from moderators, inspectors, advisers, teacher educators or colleagues in schools which are fellow members of a local examination consortium. Account should also be taken of the feelings of pupils about courses (some schools systematically sample pupil opinion) and, by no means least, the feelings of the staff themselves as professionals about the quality of the work and the kinds of response which were evoked. The views of staff who have joined the school fairly recently after experience of different teaching situations or who have been on in-service courses relevant to the particular problem under discussion may be especially valuable. Inevitably there must be a large subjective element in evaluation: not all the outcomes of courses are quantifiable, or even necessarily identifiable. Nor should the process of evaluation end with the consideration of outcomes; after deciding how far the aims and objectives have been achieved, it is at least equally important to evaluate the aims and objectives themselves: are they still appropriate or do changes in the school, in the subject or in society, call for a revision of course intentions which will have repercussions on content and methods of working and assessment?

## C4 *Essentials of team teaching*
By team teaching is meant a system in which a group of teachers, working cooperatively and each contributing from his own strengths, plan, teach, assess and evaluate a course of work for several classes. The process of team

the major requisitions, a medium- to long-term programme of resource planning which will ensure that his department has available the right resources in the right order.

### C10  *Choosing between alternative forms of a resource*

Resources are selected to satisfy the teaching and learning needs of staff and pupils, and the choice of a particular form of any kind of resource should be made from as wide a knowledge as possible of the alternatives available. Initial cheapness is not always the overriding criterion; account needs to be taken also of the toughness and probable longevity of resources, their maintenance costs, whether they are foolproof and easy to safeguard, and the extent to which they may be too intricate and troublesome or intimidating for staff to use. In selecting hardware such as projectors or tape recorders it is often wise to choose types which are similar to those already in the school because then spares are more likely to be available, money and time may be saved on maintenance and software may be more easily used in different places. The time and energy of staff can sometimes be conserved, and their impact heightened, by the acquisition of forms of equipment such as heat copiers which can be applied to a variety of reprographic purposes. Printed books, including textbooks, are still perhaps the commonest resources in schools, and the number and kinds of books which a department buys depend very much on its overall philosophy: some departments prefer to rely to a larger extent on books in libraries, many feel that there is a great value in each pupil having a textbook of his own, not just as a source for reference and revision but also because of the psychological security it offers, while others believe that small numbers of a variety of texts which complement each other should be available in each class. Selection between alternative books should be based partly on comparison of specimens, and partly on the knowledge and experience of colleagues.

### C11  *Production of resources within the department*

Purchaseable materials often need supplementation, and the expertise of the teaching staff will certainly be needed in the design of 'extras', which is often best done by a pooling of effort, since wider participation tends to bring richer results and fewer snags. The actual process of production may be carried out by office staff, by technicians, or sometimes by pupils, parts of whose courses may consist of making equipment for their own use, for example, musical instruments, tools for handicraft or clinometers for surveying.

### C12  *The safety and accessibility of resources*

One way in which the safety and accessibility of resources can be ensured is by the setting up of a central department store, under the supervision of a teacher or technician and preferably in a separate lockable room, accessible from the corridor, to which all staff of the department have keys. The store should have a card index of all the resources, with their locations, a means of booking resources in advance, and a book in which items removed can be recorded. Departmental technicians, where they exist, may be given charge of the issuing and return as well as of the maintenance of resources. Staff will not regard equipment as accessible to them if they do not have the necessary skill to use it, and the head of department may feel it necessary to see that periodic training courses are available which will enable staff to operate particular kinds of machinery efficiently. Increasingly nowadays, one of the most effective ways of ensuring the safety and accessibility of resources is by using an 'a.v.a. room' or 'resource centre' serving the whole school.

### Conclusion: A Check List for Heads of Department

The profile of the head of department which emerges from the foregoing pages is clearly that of a 'democratic' as opposed to an 'autocratic' or a laissez-faire type of leader, and the check list below is an attempt to sum up some of the characteristics of departmental leadership which have been identified as desirable. The list is a formidable one but arguably no more formidable than lists appropriate for other professionals at a similar level of managerial responsibility.

A head of department should:

1. recognize that his major function is to promote a situation in which staff and pupils approach as closely as possible their full potentials in teaching and learning;
2. aim at creating and maintaining a happy, cooperative team by involving staff fully in the life of the department, its work and its decisions;
3. ensure effective communication of information and ideas among the staff of the department by holding regular departmental meetings;
4. arrange that departmental meetings have a suitable agenda, that, on appropriate occasions, discussion papers are brought forward and people outside the department are invited to contribute to discussions, and that the decisions made are recorded and reported to higher authority;
5. seek to promote discussion and achieve consensus on the major features of departmental policy;
6. enable staff to cooperate as a team in planning courses and in solving problems such as teaching and learning difficulties;
7. keep the courses of the department under periodic review, recognizing the primacy of aims and objectives both in the initial planning and in the subsequent modification of courses;

8 secure the support of the departmental staff before introducing innovations in teaching programmes and methods;

9 recognize that ways of working may have just as much importance in curriculum as content, and therefore be willing to consider experimentation with alternative strategies, such as the use of simulation or team teaching;

10 ascertain and report to a higher level the department's views on the appointment of new staff and be ready to help in the preparation of short lists and in interviewing;

11 see that probationers and students are welcomed into the department and given ample opportunities to develop their professionalism;

12 encourage all staff to extend their professional abilities by delegating responsibility, spreading the load of teaching and of other work as evenly as possible and supporting attendance at relevant in-service activities;

13 take a continuing interest in the professional capacities and careers of the department's staff and be ready where necessary to provide material for references;

14 take a due share of the responsibility for ensuring that pupils' abilities are properly diagnosed, that pupils are placed in appropriate courses and groups for teaching, that their progress is systematically monitored and that reports on their work are available;

15 help by example and guidance to maintain good discipline and a well-ordered atmosphere for the department's work;

16 cooperate with the pastoral and careers staff in providing advice and guidance for pupils;

17 encourage extra-curricular activities associated with the department's specialism;

18 develop a wide appreciation of the range of resources relevant to the department's work and, in consultation with the staff, be able to select resources wisely, supplementing purchaseable with home-produced materials where necessary or advisable;

19 take care, with the help of any technical and clerical staff available, to see that material resources are kept securely, and that they are catalogued, maintained and readily available to a departmental staff with the ability and confidence to make full use of them.

## References

BAILEY, P. (1973) 'The functions of heads of departments in comprehensive schools', *Journal of Educational Administration and History*, January.

BISHOP, A.J. and WHITFIELD, R.C. (1972) *Situations in Teaching*, Maidenhead, McGraw-Hill.

FREEMAN, J. (1969) *Team Teaching in Britain*. London, Ward Lock.

LAMBERT, K. (1972) 'The role of the head of department in school', unpublished University of Southampton MA (Ed.) dissertation.

LAMBERT, K. and MARLAND, M. (1975). 'Research report: The role of the head of department in schools', *Educational Administration Bulletin*, 3, 2, Summer.

MADEN, M. (1974). 'The departmental meeting: Its role in curriculum reform', *Secondary Education*, 4, June.

MARLAND, M. (1971) *Head of Department*, London, Heinemann.

POLOS, N. (1965) *The Dynamics of Team Teaching*, Dubuque, Iowa, W.C. Brown.

SKELTON, I.A.N. (1977) 'A case study of curriculum integration in the lower years of the secondary school: A geographer's evaluation', unpublished University of Southampton MSc (Ed.) dissertation.

WARWICK, D. (1973) *Team Teaching*, London, ULP.

# Leadership and the Teacher

*Steve Murgatroyd*
*Open University in Wales*
*and*
*David Reynolds*
*University College, Cardiff*

The concept of 'leadership' has had a variety of usages, as is clear from the variety of definitions it has been given. For example, it has been defined as 'the initiation of new structure' (Lipham, 1964, p. 122), as a 'curious blending of leading, following, provoking and calming' (Cunningham, 1976, p. 324), as 'introducing something new or helping to improve present conditions' (Sergiovanni, 1977, p. 140) or more radically as the capacity of 'inducing new, more activist tendencies in their followers' (Burns, 1978, p. 48). Clearly, none of these definitions overlaps completely with another and few will stand the test of time according to some authorities (Spikes, 1979).

Because the nature of leadership as a process has been difficult to define and study objectively, a considerable effort has been expended on the study of the traits of leaders (see Marshall, 1970; Taylor, 1978; Stogdill, 1974; Jentz and Woford, 1979; Abrell, 1979 for examples). Whilst this has been revealing at one level — especially concerning the importance of motivation — at another it has helped hardly at all in the identification of potential leaders or in the understanding of the failure of leadership within educational organizations.

The inability to define leadership objectively and then measure it in a way that is methodologically acceptable, coupled with the general lack of utility of the 'leadership trait' school of thought, led many to study leadership in terms of situational and positional roles (Hersey and Blanchard, 1977; Reddin, 1970; Saville, 1971). Whilst there are obvious problems in equating potential for leadership with the position of a person within an organization, such work has enabled some reviews of effective versus ineffective leadership to be conducted (see Murgatroyd and Gray, 1982). What such studies tend to ignore, though, is the fact that leadership within an organization can occur at a variety of levels in response to a variety of situations and is not necessarily tied to possession of a formal organizational role.

In this chapter we explore ways in which teachers who do not hold senior management positions within a school (i.e., persons other than the head, deputy heads, senior teacher and in some schools the senior master or mistress) can produce leadership. We take the view that leadership is best defined in terms of the capacity to inspire followership. Whilst this conception of leadership has been criticized (see Paisey, this volume), it nonetheless remains a valid view of the reality of leadership within the school as an organization. This view of leadership makes possible the location of leadership at *any* point within the school as an organization, given a degree of followership for a person or group with purposive intentions. Often the outbreak of non-line management leadership relates to specific issues — the structure of the school day, the allocation of resources, staff promotion and development or specific changes in routines. Exceptionally, non-line management leadership ability will relate to the personality of a specific person (what Philip Rieff terms 'charismatic authority') who is seen as able to command followership across a variety of different issues. Here we shall concentrate on the specific leadership roles that emerge in relation to specific, rather than general, issues.

The 'outbreak' of non-line management leadership within an organization where it was previously absent can be of especial significance to that organization. First, these leadership occasions can change the role boundaries within that organization — executive leaders may feel a need to change or modify their roles so as to incorporate the new leaders in the decision-making process. Secondly the emergence of non-executive leaders can change the social relationships which exist within the school, thus changing the informal decision-making networks within the organization. Finally, a difference of view between formal and informal leaders over specific issues can lead to the polarizing of views within the organization. For these three reasons, non-line management leadership is a subject of considerable importance to those concerned with school change, with understanding the ethos of school organization and with those interested in teacher-teacher interaction.

The data on which this contribution is based are our observations of schools in Wales and outside over a ten-year period. Whilst much of this work has concerned questions like the sociology of pupil achievement (Reynolds, 1976a; Reynolds *et al.*, 1976b; 1980) and pastoral care and counselling within the school (Murgatroyd, 1974; 1976; 1977), we have increasingly become associated with the study of school change and development (Murgatroyd and Gray, 1982). In particular, we have been attending to the underlying assumptions made by a particular school's management team about the ways in which the process of change within the school as an organization can be achieved. Whilst these observations are part of our note-books over this ten-year period (especially since 1981, in the case of the above school), we do not claim that we are presenting here the results of a systematic study of non-line management leadership within secondary schools. Rather, this contribution should be regarded as our attempt to establish some pattern of data — a benchmarking exercise that indicates directions for future study and research.


## Classrooms and Leadership

One observation documented in Murgatroyd and Gray (1982) is of central importance to our observations here. It is that there is a strong relationship between the type of negotiation that exists within the classrooms of a school and the type of negotiations which take place in the context of the overall management of the school. Teachers who seek to control classrooms dogmatically and rigidly, who permit no room for pupil negotiation and who discourage the sharing of thoughts and feelings in a non-evaluative social climate also behave like this in the context of decision-making. Conversely, teachers who see their role in the classroom as facilitative rather than dominative, remedial or explicative (Murgatroyd, 1980), seek to adopt this style in the context of decision-making. A considerable amount of conflict within organizations can result from a conflict between these two styles.

As a case illustration consider the following:

> The Headmaster of a school decides that his senior staff will explore the quality of pupil experience by undertaking some pupil pursuit work in each teacher's class during a given term. This means that one of the senior staff will sit in and watch the teacher teach.
>
> This decision produces two reactions. First, the teacher union representative challenges the legitimacy of the Head's decision in respect of the senior staff as a group. He is adamant that, whilst the Head has a right to visit any classroom in the school at any time, he does not think that this right should be extended to the Deputy Heads or Senior Teacher. The Head of English, in contrast, is happy with the decision but unhappy with the detail she has been given as to the focus of the observations — what would the Senior staff actually be looking at? The Head of English wishes to explore possible evaluative criteria for such observations as a group exercise amongst the staff.
>
> The Head diffuses criticism by playing off the Union leader and the Head of English and the criteria go undiscussed.

In this incident, the potential for non-executive leadership on an issue of some controversy within the school is diffused (from the head's point of view) by the failure of potential leaders within the staff to produce an effective leadership style. What is more, the ease with which the 'divide and rule' tactic could be employed by the head ensured that the key question — what is the purpose of the exercise and what will be observed? — became lost in a dispute about how effectively to challenge the role envisaged by the head and his senior staff colleagues. This emphasizes the point (made earlier in this collection) that, in the followership view of leadership, sovereignty lies with the followers. Had one or other of these opponents of the head's position achieved a followership of substance then the head would not have been able to use the tactic of 'divide and rule' so effectively. (Note here that we are making no judgements about the position taken by the head, the head of English or the union leader — we are simply providing an account of an event in terms of leadership.)

A second point about the relationship between the classroom and leadership concerns competency. A person's ability to teach and control a class affects their standing within the school as an organization. In a school with which the authors have a long association, those staff who have least power within the organization both in terms of the line-management hierarchy and in terms of the potential for followership are those who have the poorest teaching reputation and the highest rate of discipline problems within the school. Though some of these staff sometimes seek to achieve followership over some issue, their status as teachers being unable to perform that 'basic job' seriously impairs their ability to command followership.

A final point about the classroom and leadership is the corollary of the previous point. It is often the case that the status of a person in an organization is greater outside than within that organization. For example, those strongly associated with curriculum innovation at county, regional or national level often have more status within their curriculum association (the Modern Language Association, National Association of Careers Guidance Teachers, etc.) than they do within the school in which they work. Whilst this would appear to be generally the case, there are specific occasions when it seems possible for the external recognition of a person to become a significant feature internally in generating leadership potential. In part this is because the external recognition is seen as a measure of the person's competence within their own field of work, and in part because they are seen as trustworthy and competent *organizationally* elsewhere. It seems as if there is some potential for the transferability of recognition *in relation to specific incidents and situations* from external to internal sources.

These are merely some preliminary observations. They help to set the scene for our more detailed review of some of the ways in which non-executive leadership can affect the way in which school organizations function.


## Non-Executive Leadership and School Change

In this section we wish to describe four ways in which we have observed non-executive leadership to contribute significantly to school change. These four are not an exhaustive list; they are simply a classification of our direct observations collected over ten years. We present them here, together with examples, to show the ways in which the non-executive leader can act to secure followership and change.

### 1   *Changing the Fantasies of Organizational Members*

Many school staff at all levels have fantasies about who should do what in an organization and about the kinds of things it is possible and impossible to do. These fantasies extend to such things as 'it is not possible to change the structure of the school day', or 'we have to teach X this way because that's how it has always been done' or 'it is the head's job to make decisions and our job to do our best to meet his demands'. These fantasies about school organization have also been well described by Putnam (1981) and Gray (1980).

These fantasies are in fact the beliefs which govern the response of staff to some activating event, and these beliefs determine the consequences for those staff of perceiving some event in a particular way. Ellis (1962) presents us with a simple schema for understanding the ways in which these fantasies about organizations affect organizational behaviour. He calls his approach the A-B-C approach (or, more technically, the rational-emotive approach). He suggests that the 'A' is some activating event (e.g., the allocation of resources); the 'B' is a belief held about that event (e.g., that the allocation of resources should always be fair and equitable, if it is not then this is awful); and the 'C' is the consequences of holding the belief about A (e.g., resources are allocated on a formula basis in terms of contact time and student numbers).

Many of the fantasies (or 'Bs') held by school personnel are irrational. For example, it is irrational to expect that resources be allocated equitably: it may be nice to hope that they will, but the reality of school life suggests that they won't. A second example may make this point more forcefully:

The A is: five members of staff are to be made redundant.

The B is: There ought to be some clear criteria (i.e., last in first out, or competency, or early retirement, or utility) by which this decision can be made.

The C is: no one is willing to make any decision in the end because there is no agreement on the criteria.

One of the ways in which we have observed non-executive leadership to emerge concerns the ability of such leaders to dispute the 'Bs' in such situations — to be rational in the face of irrationality. In the last example, the teacher concerned successfully used a Socratic method to show that there was no rational way in which a 'fair' decision could be made, since at least five people would always think it to be unfair. He also demonstrated, again by disputation, that there were benefits in asking the local authority to decide on the issue so that the close working relationships that existed within this (relatively small) comprehensive would not be unduly disturbed by the decision of the head, which would be arbitrary. Finally, he argued (having obtained a substantial followership by this time) that a decision made by the local authority as to who should be made redundant would be more open to challenge than a decision made by the head. In the end, the school challenged the education authority to name the staff it thought should go and the number 'lost' was reduced from five to two, both of whom volunteered to retire early. The role of this ordinary (and junior) teacher in the two staff meetings concerned with this issue was pivotal in the decision of the school to take a combative position.

There is not space here to provide a great many illustrations of this process at work. The point to note is that the systematic disputing of irrational beliefs is a task that can be performed by any member of a school staff and can affect the way in which that organization functions.

### 2   Contrasting the 'Clingons'

In the previous form of non-executive leadership we suggested that leadership role could be performed by disputing the irrational beliefs that were determining the consequences of particular actions. In this next form of leadership, the teacher needs to do more than dispute the irrational belief. He needs to illustrate by example or case study that there is an alternative way of dealing with some event than that currently being considered. Such use of innovative examples helps to disturb the belief pattern by showing that others have overcome their fantasies and irrational beliefs and have gone some way towards 'solving' the problem. The word 'clingons' is used here, not as a reference to the Star Ship Enterprise and the leadership qualities of Cpt Kirk (though much can be gained from a pursuit of this analogy!), but as a description of the way in which organizations seek to cling to irrational beliefs.

Three examples will suffice to make the point:

1   A teacher in a school is frustrated by the 35 minute period day and raises this at a staff meeting. He makes little progress, with many of the staff (including the senior management team) not being able to see advantages of moving to another scheme (e.g., the five period day). He identifies the 'clingons' as 'we've always done it this way' and 'there is no alternative (TINA)'. He decides to tackle TINA by demonstrating that there are alternatives and that these alternatives produce considerable advantages for the school. He circulates a

description of the five period day timetable, lists the advantages and disadvantages, contrasts this with the disadvantages of the 35 minute period day and seeks out each head of department to discuss the five period day personally. Six months later, the heads of department meeting recommends the adoption of the five period day — whilst the teacher concerned gets little recognition for this, at least the school has lost a tradition and changed in the direction he desired.

2    A group of four (mainly younger) teachers was concerned at the way in which the school was failing to respond in curriculum terms to youth unemployment. Whilst they did what they could to achieve curriculum relevance in their own classrooms, they wanted the school to develop an integrated curriculum response. When they first discussed this with others they heard the clingon, 'if we can get these kids through A levels they'll be OK and they'll get work' — not at all the reality of the situation in this area of Wales. They decided to explore the responses of schools elsewhere and contacted the National Institute for Careers Education Counselling (NICEC). NICEC provided them with a detailed description of several developments, including a curriculum programme in Saskatchewan devoted to Co-operation and Co-operatives. They then sent for this programme. In ten weeks they had rewritten this curriculum programme for use in their school. Now they are seeking to enlist support for a detailed programme of work rather than an idea. This programme will operate from September 1983 as a replacement for the social studies programme.

3    A member of staff of a department observed that the way in which the head of department ran departmental meetings always meant that none of the items submitted by staff other than the head was discussed, even though they were agenda items. She explored the reactions of others to this observation and received the clingon that 'heads of department always run their departments as they want to'. She soon found a journal article written by a head of department at a neighbouring school which argued the case for rotating chair-manship of departmental meetings. She circulated this to her colleagues (but not the head of department). They now operate a rotating chairmanship of departmental meetings.

These examples are of different kinds. Some have major impact on all staff of the school (especially the first which affects every teacher, pupil and worker in the school); others are of minor importance to the school as a whole, but do affect the conduct of a section of it. The point to note is that all of them involved the teacher in producing evidence which challenged the irrational belief which others wished to cling on to.

Lancashire 'Active Tutorial Work Programme' two years ago. The tutorial classes are now the single most obvious source of discipline problems within this school.

## Leadership Networks in the Staffroom

Many of the situations we have used to illustrate the four particular forms of non-executive leadership described here rely on one or more members of staff acting in concert on some specific issue. This is the most common form of non-executive leadership we have encountered. But there is a second pattern of non-executive leadership that relates to specific issues: leadership networks within a school's staff. (Readers will recall that it is not our intention here to document features of merely charismatic leadership within the school.)

There are some issues which affect the whole staff. The examples of the five staff to be made redundant and the change in the school day are illustrative of this. For many such issues, and most especially in relation to key appointments within the school for which there are internal candidates, leadership is not overt but covert and is not concerned with direct change but with indirect influence. Our observations suggest that the most effective form of non-executive leadership in these circumstances is achieved through the use of staff peer group influence in formal networks within the school.

Three common devices are used by those seeking to exert informal influence in this way: (1) the artificial creation of opposing schools of thought — their artificial creation soon leads them to be real; (2) the spreading of rumours — sometimes these rumours are believed to have their origin in fact; and (3) the encouragement of speculation so as to elicit views as to where people stand.

One example is that of a headmaster who, on retiring, wished to know the views of his staff about two internal candidates for his job. He confided in one of the authors that he need not seek their views but had simply to listen more attentively than usual to the 'vibrant ear lobes'. During a five-week observation of the school, the particular author noted these indicators: (a) one of the staff from woodwork/technical drawing was keeping a book on the appointment of one of the internal candidates who was showing better in the betting than another; (b) one of the candidates constantly checked the opinions of others within the school as to his chances, the other maintained a dignified position and simply repeated that it was a 'matter for the authority'; (c) the heads of department discussed the position and gave private advice to the head: (d) the matter was discussed thoroughly in the staffroom in the twelve-week period during which the 'race was on'. What this process did was to substantially reduce the chances of one of the two candidates commanding respect from the school staff, at least in the eyes of the head. At the beginning of the race, however, the head was not sure which way the staff would go.

This informal influencing process is a form of implied leadership in which non-executive members of the school as an organization can participate with some effect in taking important decisions affecting school life.

## Conclusion

In this chapter we have attempted to describe a variety of forms of leadership undertaken by ordinary teachers within the school. Whilst these descriptions are tentative, largely because they have the status of the first ordering of some observations collected incidentally over a ten-year period, they do provide a framework for thinking about the precise ways in which non-executive leadership operates within the school. In particular, we have highlighted the similarity between leadership tasks and rational-emotive tasks (Ellis, 1962).

There remain some observations about the importance that should be attached to such leadership. We began by suggesting that the outbreak of non-executive leadership within the school was likely to be of some significance to it. We end with the suggestion that, in our experience, such forms of leadership as we have noted are becoming more frequent features of the school situation. As Cooper (1981) observes, the current management style of effective organizations crucially involves participation and an emphasis on 'tolerance for multiple interpretations and the ability to explore and create alternatives' (Van Avery, 1980). The top-down model appears to be being supplanted by the bottom-up model of change and development within the school (Ferguson, 1980). Non-executive leadership significantly contributes to this process.

## References

ABRELL, R.L. (1979) 'Education leadership without carrot and club', *Clearing House*, 52, pp. 280–5.

BALDWIN, J. and WELLS, H. (1979) *Active Tutorial Work. Years 1–5*, Oxford, Blackwell.

BEST, R. *et al.* (Eds) (1980) *Perspectives on Pastoral Care*, London, Heinemann.

BURNS, J.M. (1978) 'True leadership', *Psychology Today*, 12, pp. 46–54.

COOPER, C.L. (Ed.) (1981) *Developing Managers for the 1980's*, London, Methuen.

CUNNINGHAM, L.L. (1976) 'Education leadership: The curious blend', *Educational Leadership*, 33, pp. 324–37.

DEBONO, E. (1982) *Lateral Thinking: The BBC Course*, London, BBC Publications.

DEDE, C. and ALLEN, D. (1981) 'Education in the 21st century', *Kappan*, 62, pp. 362–6.

ELLIS, A. (1962) *Reason and Emotion in Psychotherapy*, New York, Lyle Stuart.

ELLIS, A. (1972) *Executive Leadership: A Rational Approach*, New York, Citadel Press.

FERGUSON, M. (1980) *The Aquarian Conspiracy: Personal and Social Transformations in the 1980's*, New York, St. Martins Press.

GRAY, H.L. (1980) *Change and Management in Schools*, Driffield, Nafferton Books.

HAMBLIN, D. (1978) *The Teacher and Pastoral Care*, Oxford, Blackwell.

HERSEY, P. and BLANCHARD, K. (1977) *Management of Organisational Behaviour*, New York, Prentice-Hall.

HOPSON, B. and SCALLY, M. (1981) *Lifeskills Teaching*. London, McGraw Hill.

JENTZ, B.C. and WOFORD, J.W. (1979) *Leadership and Learning*, New York, McGraw Hill.

KIESLER, C.A. and KIESLER, S.B. (1969) *Conformity*, Mass., Addison-Wesley.

LIPHAM, J.M. (1964) 'Leadership and administration', in GRIFFITHS, D. (Ed.), *Behaviour Science and Educational Administration: 63rd Yearbook of the National Society for the Study of Education*, Chicago, Ill., The Society.

MARSHALL, S. (1970) 'Leadership and sensitivity training', *Journal of Education*, 153, pp. 6–37.

MURGATROYD, S. (1974) 'Ethical issues in secondary school counselling', *Journal of Moral Education*, 4, 1, pp. 27–37.

MURGATROYD, S. (1976) '"Care": The case of Paulette', *British Journal of Guidance and Counselling*, 4, 1, pp. 98–104.

MURGATROYD, S. (1977) 'Pupil perceptions of counselling: A case study', *British Journal of Guidance and Counselling*, 5, 1, pp. 73–8.

MURGATROYD, S. (1980) 'What actually happens in tutorials?', *Teaching at a Distance*, 18, pp. 44–53.

MURGATROYD, S. and GRAY, H.L. (1982) 'Leadership and the effective school', *School Organization*, 2, 3, pp. 285–95.

NEIBUHR, H. (1981) 'Teaching and learning in the 1980's', *Kappan*, 62, pp. 367–8.

PUTNAM, S. (1981) 'The reality of school organization', *School Organization*, 1, 3, pp. 255–66.

REDDIN, W.J. (1970) *Managerial Effectiveness*, New York: McGraw Hill.

REYNOLDS, D. (1976a) 'The delinquent school', in WOODS, P. (Ed.), *The Process of Schooling*, London, Routledge and Kegan Paul.

REYNOLDS, D. *et al.* (1976b) 'Schools do make a difference, *New Society*, 29 July, pp. 223–5.

REYNOLDS, D. *et al.* (1980) 'School factors and truancy'; in HERSOV, L.A. and BERG, I. (Eds) *Out of School*, London, John Wiley.

SAVILLE, A. (1971) 'Conflict: A new emphasis in leadership', *Clearing House*, 46, pp. 52–5.

SERGIOVANNI, T.J. (1977) *Handbook for Effective Departmental Leadership: Concepts and Practices in Todays Secondary Schools*, Boston, Mass., Allyn and Bacon.

SHANE, H.G. (1981) 'A curriculum for the new century', *Kappan*, 62, pp. 351–6.

SPIKES, F. (1979) 'Choosing a personal leadership style', *Lifelong Learning*, 3, pp. 8–9.

STOGDILL, R.M. (1974) *Handbook of Leadership*, New York, Free Press.

TAYLOR, I.A. (1978) 'Characteristics of creative leaders', *Journal of Creative Behaviour*, 12, pp. 221–2.

VAN AVERY, J. (1980) 'Futuristics and education', *Educational Leadership*, 37, pp. 441–2.

WAGSCHAL, T. (1980) *Learning Tomorrow*, New York, Praeger.

# Subordinates' Strategies of Interaction in the Management of Schools*

*Simon Pratt*
*University of Bristol*

Throughout the 1970s we have been interested at Bristol in thinking about the various strategies which might be available to a 'manager of change' in education. Writings of Miles (1965), Jones (1969) and of Benne and Chin (1970 and 1976) have been absorbed by our students and we have made much of Hoyle's observation that the sets of three principal strategies for bringing about change in human systems identified by those writers bear a peculiar resemblance to one another (Hoyle, 1970). We have invited our students to examine the potential of these strategies — power-coercive, empirical-rational and normative-re-educative — in the context of Havelock's 'RD and D', 'social interaction', 'problem solver' and 'linkage' models of innovation processes (Havelock, 1971), and we have stressed that these processes can be helpfully seen as interactions between three systems, those of the change agent, of the innovation itself and of the client or host system (Bolam, 1975); the change process over time we see as one of mutual adaptation among these three interacting systems, and we have explained 'failures', following the case study of Gross *et al.* (1977), in terms of lack of understanding not only of the nature of changes proposed but also of the settings in which they were to have been implemented and institutionalized and of the change agent systems responsible for their introduction. We have written about these things for other students as well as our own (Bolam and Pratt, 1976).

In a world eager for educational reform with the necessary resources relatively easy to find we might have left it at that, regarding 'innovation' and 'change' as synonyms, interchangeable in our writing in pursuit of literary style. But then came the holocaust — the oil crisis and strikes of 1973/74, rising underemployment of school and college graduates, local government reorganization, the Tyndale affair, the threat of falling rolls in

* This is an edited version of the article which appeared in *Educational Administration* 9, 2, 1980, pp. 71–8.

the secondary schools, college closures, cash limits, teaching career prospects sharply curtailed, Callaghan's 'Ruskin speech' and increasing militancy among the teachers ... the convenient assumption that 'planned change' was synonymous with 'desirable innovation' was no longer tenable. Senior management in schools now began to find collaboration, as distinct from compliance, less easy to come by from their junior colleagues who grew understandably less ready to risk their vital interests in the cause of change which took the form of contraction of their service. We had advised heads to lean as far as they could, while retaining the confidence of those (superordinates) to whom they are themselves accountable, towards the adoption of a participative managerial style, employing influence rather than control strategies and inviting collaboration rather than compliance from their subordinates (Bolam and Pratt, 1976). There are schools (and hopefully there always will be) where this advice we offered in the mid-seventies to heads still holds good. But there are other schools (far too many of them) where this advice must now be called into question. Today the interests of senior management (or of those to whom senior management is responsible) are often apparently directly opposed to those of assistant teachers. Change strategies which are intendedly influence-based rather than reliant upon sanctions are increasingly suspect. More subordinates respond to managerial initiatives not so much with offers of collaboration as with compliance, resistance or even by ignoring the superordinate move.

In three Avon secondary schools in 1980, faced with mid-year cuts in staffing which could not be implemented without significant revision of school timetables, members of the National Union of Teachers took industrial action in protest. Although this was at first sight unsurprising, there were features of particular interest about the strategies which the teachers employed. First, it was evident that they did not necessarily regard themselves as having withdrawn from participation in the work of their schools — they made themselves available in school to teach classes on the 'old' timetable and, in at least one case known to the writer, an active NUT member had agreed to prepare the revised timetable but without commitment to participation in teaching it; they regarded their action as being in support of the case, argued with the LEA by their heads among others, that damage inflicted by the proposed cuts upon their pupils' education would far outweigh any savings achieved. They therefore refused to participate in the LEA's planned change and, instead, set out to get it renegotiated. In pursuance of this objective the teachers in the three schools initially concerned adopted tactics which could be interpreted as 'regrouping' — or, in political science terms, the formation of new coalitions — once their early protests had brought no result. Action was organized on a rota system, involving many more schools with aims which included maintenance of a high level of protest while minimizing the impact upon individual children. Teachers from one school were shown on television organizing alternative educational activities outside the school premises. Appeals were being made to the public not only over the heads of the heads, but also over the heads of the LEA. The eventual outcome? This still looks different from different viewpoints. In negotiation the LEA gave little, if any, ground in terms of restoration of teaching posts during the academic year but no one can ever know to what extent the strength of the protest and its surrounding publicity will have conditioned the future handling of teaching staff deployment. Many will believe, and act on the belief, that employer-employee relations will never be quite the same again and that, should the issue ever come up again, what was once regarded as a purely managerial issue could now be seen as a proper subject for delicate 'political' negotiations. In this context it is interesting to observe the possible development of a managerial technique, in which the staffing ratio for each school would be derived from curriculum considerations rather than the curriculum from the pupil-teacher ratio. Whether this will be enough to establish new legitimated routines and so to take the issue back out of politics into the managerial sphere, or whether political negotiations over staffing ratios will be transformed into political negotiations over the organization of the curriculum — and whether such negotiations, if they come to pass, will be contained within the schools or extended to the LEA or beyond — only time will tell.

The key issues no longer surround the question as to whether teachers can be helped to respond, in their own self-interest, to the initiatives of enlightened benevolent heads. Today we need to understand the interactions between superordinates defending the interests of the providers of the education service, and subordinates defending their opposing interests. Common interests remain, or so it is claimed on all sides, although they seem to have slipped down the agenda of priority matters for attention. Such interactions are indeed 'negotiations' in the sense of the word adopted in *Negotiating the Curriculum* (Weston, 1979) which develops the idea in explaining pupil/teacher transactions in the classroom, thus 'Negotiation implies that there are different interests to be reconciled. But it also implies some element of common interest on which the parties can agree' (p. 41). One response to recent trends, and it is indeed the response of some teachers, is to turn to their union at the first sign of difficulty. Another is to eschew the use of strike action in particular, even in the last resort, and to seek 'professional' recognition through taking this stand. But most teachers, I suspect, fall somewhere between these positions in their feelings and in their behaviour. Can we identify a range of 'response' or 'interaction' strategies, complementary to the change strategies available to management, from which we would expect these teachers to choose? Can we even move towards associating a teacher's track record, in the perception of those to whom he is responsible, with a concept of 'managerial style' which we proposed five years ago?

... but in choosing his administrative strategy (i.e. his intended combination of control and influence strategies) for dealing with such a problem, the head is not a free agent; he is constrained not only by the nature of the particular task in hand and by his own personal inclinations, but also by the social and professional context in which the change is to take place *and by his staff's perception of his own past record as a manager.* ... In the short term he is a captive of his own managerial *style*; the head who suddenly adopts an uncharacteristic administrative strategy invites scepticism — indeed he courts disbelief and distrust. (Bolam and Pratt; 1976, p. 19)

Since the concept of managerial style was built up from subordinate perceptions of superordinate strategic choices, this may be the best point from which to develop these ideas.

We may perhaps assume that, in one kind of ideal world, superordinates only use 'pure influence' strategies, that these are perceived by subordinates as intended and that collaboration duly follows; whether a superordinate initiative is accepted or rejected appears to be of secondary importance to the spirit of the interaction which, if advice offered is seen as rejectable without penalty, is one in which trust is built up and in which the prospects for subsequent collaboration are enhanced. We can also envisage another ideal or polar type of situation in which all superordinate strategies are intended as, and are perceived as, acts of control, inviting compliance as the response — but being met sometimes by active countermoves or by what may be best called passive resistance.

Here are the first elements of a range of 'confront-comply' strategies which might be adopted in response to superordinate control strategies. But before analyzing these further we should perhaps turn our attention away from ideal types to the real world in which 'compounds' of confront-comply and collaborative strategies are to be found. These compounds (of which that adopted by the timetables in Avon cited above appears to be a good example) can then be regarded as subordinate negotiating strategies complementary to the earlier concept of administrative strategies as used by Hoyle (1970) and discussed by Bolam (1975) in suggesting that the use of incentives rather than sanctions can be seen as a significant variant on the power coercive strategy. We can for the sake of consistency now relabel both 'managerial' and 'administrative' strategies simply as superordinate (negotiating) strategies. Similarly, following Weston (*op. cit.*, p. 42) who sees negotiation 'lying on a continuum somewhere between confrontation at one end, and at the other committed co-operation', we can envisage subordinate negotiating strategies which are compounds of cooperating with confront/comply. So it is the propensity of a subordinate to attach weight to considerations of common purpose (i.e., to collaborate rather than merely to comply) which is seen by superordinates as determining that subordinate's negotiating style.

## Influence Strategies and Collaborative Response

Two main types of influence strategy have already been identified, by Benne and Chin among others, i.e., those which rely primarily on mutually recognizable expertise, irrespective of its source, to resolve essentially technical problems and those which rely on the acceptance by both change agent and client that effective innovation requires a change of attitudes, relationships, values and skills on the part of any or all concerned. The response, in either case, may be made by an individual or a group and may or may not rely on resources which are contained within the span of control of the superordinate in question. Thus, from a superordinate perspective, we can recognize four main possibilities:

*collaborative/individual/contained* — e.g., the response of a trusted confidential adviser

*collaborative/group/contained* — e.g., when the response to the head comes from a group of staff within the school

*collaborative/individual/extended* — e.g., the trusted adviser with out-of-school resources

*collaborative/group/extended* — e.g., the characteristic response of the 'problem-solving group' with external linkage which 'progressive teachers' of educational administration have advocated, indeed eulogized, in the 1970s (see, for example, Baker, 1980).

## Control Strategies: The Range of Responses

Although the variety of control strategies appears to be less than that of influence strategies, most of the argument centring on the question of whether the recognition of some classes of sanctions is to be regarded as 'rational' or as 'compliant' behaviour, the range of responses appears to be wider. As in the case of influence strategies it seems important to recognize that the response may come from individuals or from groups and that respondent(s) may or may not call upon resources outside the span of control of the superordinate. The added complexity comes from the recognition of three modes of response to a perceived control strategy, rather than one. These appear to be made by *complying*, by *passively resisting* the superordinate move, or by actively *confronting it*. The twelve-fold typology generated is exemplified below

| *Response strategy* | *Example* |
|---|---|
| *Mode scope level* | (as perceived by superordinate) |
| *comply/individual/contained* | The response of a 'yes man'. |
| *comply/group/extended* | A group, such as a subject department in |

| | a school might use significant external resources (e.g., contact with an adviser) in choosing to comply. |
|---|---|
| *passively resist/individual/ extended* | The response of an individual who has sought advice from his union, but has been advised that his case is 'unwinnable'. |
| *confront/individual/extended* | Adviser or union invoked by individual teacher (who may be bluffing) resisting what he claims is an instruction to behave 'unprofessionally' (the invoking of the head or a deputy in a dispute between an individual teacher and his head of dept, would also fall within this category). |
| *confront/group/extended* | 'Official' action in which outsiders are involved, leaving the superordinate unable to settle the issue by negotiation without prior reference to others to whom he is accountable (e.g., CEO, LEA, Chairman of Governors, or if superordinate is, say, the CEO, the possibilities multiply again — DES, ACC, Chief of Executive of LEA, etc.). |

So what? For the present there is little to add, except to note the possibility of further variants such as apparent collusion between superordinate and subordinate who may 'forget' and 'ignore' an instruction respectively in the shared but unstated recognition that 'hassle' is hardly conducive to creative teaching. Nor do effective managers look for Pyrrhic victories, as many canny teachers know — but few wise teachers risk calling the bluff of a superordinate who doesn't seem to know what it would cost him to win. It is, of course, the last two strategies which are of particular interest. Why do particular teachers in particular circumstances respond in these ways? Do we know? Is it researchable? Could the results of such research be used to clarify, and therefore improve, relationships within school hierarchies even where interests are conflicted? These are for the moment open questions, well worthy of our attention.

A final point concerns the vexed conceptual relationships between 'management' and 'politics' and between 'participation' and 'negotiation'. Is it the case that in 'managerial' thought not only the face of hierarchy is treated as a given, but also many facets of its form? Is 'participation' then granted as a concession by those with access to legitimated control strategies to those without such access? Is it the case, by contrast, that in 'political' thought the form of hierarchies, if not the fact of hierarchy, is regarded as problematic, as potentially renegotiable at any time or place? Can 'counter' strategies be understood as a rejection not only of compliance, but also of the managerial notion of participation, in favour of negotiation between parties neither of which is capable of completely controlling the actions of the other?

Seen in this light the behaviour of subordinates who seek to form coalitions (a political activity if ever there was one) to negotiate with their members' (managerial) superordinates cannot be regarded as perverse; it is only to be expected. But so, too, should superordinates who are threatened with outflanking be expected by subordinates to seek to join strong coalitions. Whether such escalation improves the quality of decisions negotiated, or whether it merely serves to make less satisfactory compromises stick a little longer, is a moot point which can probably only be answered instance by instance. But perhaps all parties to disputes could usefully think through issues prior to their escalation?

If they do so, it seems that questions of 'autonomy' will come quickly to the fore — autonomy of teachers in schools, of schools in LEA education systems, of education committees in local government, of local government in the national context and, increasingly I suspect, of pupils and their parents in relation to the whole gamut. Those institutions which survive with their autonomy more or less intact seem likely to be those which can develop internal political systems, using locally available knowledge, expertise and political clout to resolve problems which are incapable of 'managerial' resolution without escalation. Is it schools not school systems, and teacher-learner relationships not organized classes, which ought to be the focus for development? Would the adoption of such an approach necessarily entail an unacceptable (i.e., non-legitimate) forfeiture of control by the higher echelons of government? If, as the growing insistence on accountability seems to indicate, this does seem to be the case in practice, what can be done?

Surely the problem will not go away? The crystal ball is but dimly lit, but perhaps real progress might be made by developing frameworks within which everyone, even the child, counts as a potential negotiator. It is in this sense that I believe politics, with a small 'p', should be a central activity in education — but perhaps it already is, although many of us in our managerial roles find this hard to recognize or to accept. It is more comfortable to think of oneself selectively granting rights of participation to others than it is to come to terms with our partial dependence upon them, especially where these 'others' are people we regard as less expert than ourselves. But if we are to be truly accountable for the things we do in their interest, then I believe we have to be willing to negotiate with them, thus simultaneously recognizing their legitimate interests and expressing our accountability. The problem of accountability will not go away, but it can be worked through.

*Simon Pratt*

## References

BAKER, K. (1980) *The Schools and Inservice Teacher Education (S.I.T.E.) Project; Report on the First Year, 1978–9*, University of Bristol School of Education (Research Unit), mimeo.

BOLAM, R. (1975) *The Management of Educational Change* in HARRIS et al. (1975)

BOLAM, R. and PRATT, S. (1976) *The Management of Innovation in Schools*, Million Keynes, Open University Press.

CHIN, R. and BENNE, K.D. (1976) 'General strategies for effecting changes in human systems', in BENNIS, W.G. et al. *The Planning of Change* 3rd ed., New York, Holt, Rinehart and Winston.

GROSS, N. et al. *Implementing Organisational Innovations*, New York, Harper and Row.

HARRIS, A. et al. (Eds) (1975) *Curriculum Innovation*, London, Croom-Helm.

HAVELOCK, R.G. (1971) 'The utilisation of education research', in *British Journal of Educational Technology*, 2, 2, pp. 84–97; also in HARRIS, et al. (1975).

HOYLE, E. (1970) 'Planned organisation change in education', in *Research in Education*, 3, pp. 1–22; also in Harris et al. (1975).

JONES, G. (1969) *Planned Organisation Change*, London, Routledge and Kegan Paul.

MILES, M.B. (1965) 'Planned change and organisational health: Figure and ground' in HARRIS et al. (1975).

TAYLOR, W. (1978) 'Power and the curriculum'; in RICHARDS, C. (Ed.) *Power and the Curriculum: Issues in Curriculum Studies*, Driffield, Nafferton.

WESTON, P.B. (1979) *Negotiating the Curriculum; a Study in Secondary Schooling*, Windsor. NFER Publishing Co.

# 5
## Higher Education

# Introduction

An examination of leadership within the educational system would be incomplete without an examination of the leadership role in, and of, higher education. This section includes two original papers which consider separate, but equally important, influences.

In the first paper Brian Fidler outlines the decision-making and leadership processes in higher education. He suggests that the style of leadership which is found in institutions of higher education is very sound, reflecting the professional nature of the staff of such institutions while being organizationally suitable for the current structure of the system. It is with obvious regret that he notes that the collegial type of leadership is not found in sectors which deal with 'students' of earlier age-groups, although it has proven benefits.

The second paper by Ivor Goodson is, in contrast, an examination of the ways in which the system of higher education, and its personnel, exert a 'pull' on the schools sector by effectively deciding upon the respectability and credibility of the 'subjects' of the school curriculum, thereby forcing various degrees of status upon certain teachers and school departments. It will provide stimulating and provocative reading for any school subject specialist who believes that he, or the school, has decided whether to include a particular subject in the school curriculum and has therefore become an innovator and leading light. It is also a reminder that there are less overt influences at work within the educational system which are able to exert considerable unofficial pressure to change, or maintain, the current situation. Others will be considered in section 6 of this book.

# Leadership in Post-Compulsory Education

*Brian Fidler*
*Bulmershe College of Higher Education*

Compared to other sectors of the educational system, leadership in the post-compulsory sector is much more concerned with the ways in which organizations conduct their affairs than it is about key roles and the characteristics of those who occupy such positions. This is not to deny that there are some positions within such institutions which are particularly influential, nor to deny that the characteristics of the individuals who hold these positions make a great deal of difference to what happens in a particular institution. But the thesis is that these effects have declined over the last twenty years whilst there has been a corresponding rise of collegial authority. This in turn has required a change of leadership style to prevent the working of the institution becoming dysfunctional.

The second thesis to be elaborated here is the spread of collegial authority both throughout higher and further education and also to lower levels within each institution. It will be noted that this process has stopped, at least as a formal requirement, when it reached the school sector.

The post-compulsory sector of education covers an enormous range in terms of age of students and in terms of the academic level of the work being carried out. As will be shown, in the spread of participative decision-making and academic self-government, it is the level of work being carried out in the institutions which has been the major determinant rather than the degree of maturity of their student populations.

## Post-Compulsory Sector

The 1944 Education Act defined virtually all education beyond school level but outside the universities as further education. However, subsequently a distinction has arisen between advanced further education (AFE) and non-advanced further education (NAFE). Whilst this distinction arose as a result of different financial and other control mechanisms, it has proved important in charting the spread of collegial authority. Advanced further education is defined as work beyond the level of GCE A-level.

The work of universities and the advanced part of further education is usually called higher education. Thus AFE is often called public sector higher education whilst when reference is made to further education without any qualifier it is usually NAFE which is intended. Except where greater precision is necessary, these terms will be used in what follows.

Today higher education covers all the work of universities, almost all the work of polytechnics, and the majority of work of most colleges and institutes of higher education. Meanwhile, further education is carried out in about 500 colleges variously called technical colleges, colleges of technology or further education colleges. In addition, 'further education' is the term which embraces the work of evening institutes and adult education but its use here will not be taken to encompass this additional area of diversity.

## The Robbins Report

The Robbins Report of 1963 was a landmark in higher education. It proposed that the number of student places be increased from 216,000 in 1962/63 to 560,000 in 1980/81, but it proposed few structural changes other than the incorporation of teacher training colleges into university schools of education. The major institutions of higher education would remain the universities, whilst a limited number of the more experienced further education establishments would provide high level courses and so gradually transfer to the university sector as they acquired the necessary credentials.

Both proposals to transfer institutions to the university sector were not accepted by government. Instead, in 1965 Anthony Crosland announced the binary policy for higher education which has endured ever since. In place of a single sector to which all aspired there were to be two sectors — the university sector and the public sector of higher education. At that time the public sector was expected to consist of thirty newly created polytechnics and a much larger number of colleges of education (the renamed teacher training colleges).

As will be seen, it was the university model of self-government which was seen as appropriate for higher education. The Robbins Committee had not proposed any radical changes to the government of the universities but it did recommend that as regards academic self-government the process should become more participative as far as ordinary members of staff were concerned.

## The University Model

It would be quite wrong to suggest that the organizational structures of all universities in England and Wales are similar. Exceptions must be made for the collegiate universities of Oxford and Cambridge, and for the federal universities of London and Wales, but the remaining universities have much in common and it will be a model taken from this remaining group which will be used.

The autonomy of the universities flows from their Royal Charters. These allow them to award qualifications, receive income, own property and carry out other activities to further their objectives — usually teaching and research. Despite their increasing reliance on state finance, the universities are still largely self-governing. Self-government does not, however, imply a lack of lay or outside representation.

The supreme governing body of a university is the court or court of governors. This was originally representative of those who financed the university (local authorities and other benefactors). It is a very large body and does not supervise the day-to-day management of the university. It appoints the titular head of the university, the chancellor. Much more important, however, is the smaller executive body dealing with finance and external relations — the council. Some members of the council are appointed by the court and some by the senate. It is the council which appoints the vice-chancellor or executive head of the university.

It is in the realm of academic and internal matters that the notion of a university as a self-governing institution is most appropriate for it is the senate which deals with such matters. In the past this consisted mainly of professors when they formed the bulk of academic staff, but this began to change and was hastened by the Robbins proposals. Representation was widened to include ordinary members of the academic staff and a small number of students. The senate not only deals with course proposals, awards and other academic matters but also with the promotion and appointment of academic staff (in some cases technically these are only recommendations to council). Below the level of senate are faculty boards which deal with the academic affairs of groups of related departments, and finally at departmental level there are departmental boards on which all academic staff sit.

Whilst the reform of senates to include a less hierarchical representation of academic staff and some students took place in the 1960s, any more radical changes in the government of universities were expected to come from the group of nine new universities founded in the early 1960s (East Anglia, Essex, Kent, Lancaster, Stirling, Sussex, Ulster, Warwick and York). The charters of these universities retained a very large court (of up to 400) as the most senior body in the university, but only in the usual titular sense. Its function was generally reduced to receiving annual reports and as a forum for discussion, whilst power went to a much smaller council. This was a more manageable size of between twenty-five and forty people. It still consisted of a majority of lay members with only a minority of academic staff including the chancellor and vice-chancellor. This was the executive body which was to be responsible for all except purely academic matters, although it would receive advice from senate on important non-academic matters.

Some of the new universities have chosen to have a more executive-style senate. The senate of the larger civic universities can number over 100, which is too large to create academic policy rather than merely to approve it after its formulation elsewhere. Some of the newer universities, however, have adopted a senate of the more manageable size of their councils. Numbers have been reduced by having only a small number of ex-officio seats and having only a small number of members elected from academic staff and students. As an alternative to this approach, in the larger universities with unwieldy senates, smaller standing or steering committees have been set up to provide an effective executive body for academic policy.

It is acknowledged that the question of appointments, and particularly promotions, is a problem for widely representative bodies. At a number of the new universities these questions are dealt with by a professorial board. The reasoning behind this is that they are disinterested since they are not in a position to profit from further promotion. A further innovation at a number of the new universities was the creation of a general assembly of all staff periodically to hear a report from the vice-chancellor and to discuss policy.

However, it is at the level of organization below that of the whole university that the more innovative ideas have been tried. Traditionally, the basic building block of the university has been the academic department headed by an appointed professor. Related departments were grouped into a faculty which was presided over by an elected dean. Clearly strong departmental boundaries, which are a consequence of this mode of organization, make interdisciplinary courses much more difficult to mount and operate, and, indeed, cooperation of any kind is inhibited. Several of the newer universities have tried to tackle this problem. Some have tried to create super-departments (often called schools) which cover the work of several subject areas, whilst others have created boards of studies to group teachers for each degree course. Despite such attempts to break the departmental mould, it still in various guises seems remarkably resilient.

From this description of the university model it is clear that important leadership roles are taken by departmental heads. Their position is so particularly important because in the university system, as in the remainder of higher education, the major flow of policy proposals and suggestions for innovation is upward from departments rather than downwards from the vice-chancellor. It is perhaps this which provides the greatest contrast to the situation in schools where the headteacher has such a dominant role. What then of the vice-chancellor? He is the chairman of senate but other than that, according to the statutes, the post is one with very little formal power, and yet the position of the vice-chancellor is generally agreed to be a very influential one. He has been described as a chairman of a body of equals, but that is to understate the case, for, as a former president of the NUS said, 'he is usually very much of an executive chairman proposing decisions rather than someone to arbitrate between debators'.

### The Weaver Proposals

In evidence to the Robbins Committee the former teacher training colleges' representatives complained bitterly about their relationship with their maintaining authorities. They claimed that they were treated according to regulations designed for the schools. The Robbins Committee's solution to this problem was to transfer the colleges to university schools of education. The government did not accept this proposal but, under pressure, did undertake to review the government of the colleges of education. A study group under the chairmanship of Mr. (later Sir) Toby Weaver of the DES was set up in 1965. This group was to negotiate how much freedom and responsibility could be given to the colleges and how much power and control the local authorities would be prepared to give up. Representatives of the universities were present for most of the group's meetings and were able to present the university model for consideration.

In the Weaver Report, which was to be seminal to the government of public sector higher education institutions, the view of the Robbins Committee was endorsed, 'that academic freedom is a necessary condition of the highest efficiency and of the proper progress of academic institutions.' Further it was stated, 'The academic affairs of a college are primarily for academic people to deal with.' The way in which this was to be done was thought sufficiently self-evident that there was very little supporting justification in the report for the proposals which emerged.

The basic proposals were:

1  the governing body should be responsible for the general running of the college;
2  the academic board should, subject to the general approval of the governing body, be responsible for the academic work of the college;
3  the principal should be responsible to the governing body for the internal organization and management of the college.

The composition of the governing body was to reflect the various interests concerned with the work of the institution. Thus there were to be representatives of LEAs, universities and school teachers, and in addition to the principal as an ex-officio member, the academic board was to nominate representatives.

The academic board was to consist of the principal and vice-principal and 'those members of the teaching staff who carry the main weight of responsibility in the college together with reasonable representation of other teaching staff'. The lack of precision in the composition reflected the lack of management structure prescribed by the Pelham salary structure of the time (there were no appointed heads of department, for example).

There was at this time, before the student disturbances of 1968, no suggestion of students being offered representation on either academic board or governing body.

These proposals, it should be remembered, were for the colleges of education. It was with some chagrin, therefore, that the colleges watched the newly created polytechnics being offered this structure of government before them. Since the polytechnics were to be designated by the DES, it was made a condition for this privilege that the maintaining authority had to be willing to accede to this measure of academic self-determination. Such was the competition among authorities to have a polytechnic in their area that, given time, they were willing to accept this reform.

However, the remaining public sector institutions had to wait for the Education (No. 2) Act, 1968, to lay down the pattern of academic self-government for the colleges of education and also for all further education colleges. The implementation of this change in the case of further education colleges was detailed in Circular 7/70 to come into force on 1 September 1972.

## The Government of Further Education Colleges

The governing body of a further education college was to consist of LEA representatives (in a minority), industrial representatives and the principal and not less than two members of the college's academic staff. Student representation was suggested where there were substantial numbers of students over the age of 18. The composition and powers of any academic board were similarly to vary with the age of students in the college and also with the level of work undertaken. For those colleges with a substantial amount of advanced work there was to be an academic board with substantial powers. It was to be the Weaver blend of ex-officio and elected members. For colleges with no advanced work an academic board was to be optional but the governors were to make arrangements for teaching staff to be regularly consulted about the 'organisation and regulation of the academic work of the college'.

Thus most colleges were given an academic board but this could be either policy-making or advisory (to the principal). Many of the larger colleges had previously had a board of studies or similar forum for academic discussion but this had not usually been policy-making. So since 1972 there has grown up a working relationship between the principal of a college and its academic board.

Empirical evidence for the changes in the distribution of power and leadership in the colleges as a result of the appearance of academic boards has been rather sparse. The situation previously was that as the colleges were highly departmentalized, the heads of department and the principal were the power centres within a college. There is some evidence that the consultative and participative structures which have appeared at college level have tended to reduce the influence of heads of department at college level, but the lack of departmental boards or formal consultative and participative procedures at departmental level has led to staff frustration when departments have continued to operate in an authoritarian manner.

Whilst the influence of heads of department may have been reduced, this is not the case as far as the principal is concerned. However, to preserve his pre-eminent position the principal has had to adapt his style of leadership. He now has to argue his case and persuade the academic board to his point of view. Although as the chairman of the academic board his formal position is of primus inter pares with respect to academic policy-making, he is also the chief executive officer of the college. He is thus concerned with the day-to-day management of college affairs including appointments, promotions and the distribution of college resources. In addition to the internal sources of power, the principal is also the college's representative to the outside world, and, of course, he has close contact with the college governors and LEA officers and is able to judge and pronounce upon the college in relation to external forces.

Another source of power in the FE college is the branch of the lecturers' association, NATFHE (National Association of Teachers in Further and Higher Education). This union has been influential in pressing for participatory government of the colleges. In 1981 the union conducted a questionnaire survey into the operation of academic boards in colleges. About a third of college union branches replied and in about half of these colleges the academic board was only consultative. The replies indicated that in many colleges there was a clear distinction between the theory and practice of the part academic boards played in determining policies concerning the academic work of the college. Many comments indicated that principals apparently tried to obstruct the proper operation of the academic board and only just over a third of academic boards could be considered as 'a genuine and effective instrument for staff participation'. That principals also have differing views on the usefulness of academic boards is illustrated by two principals writing about the changing face of further education. One principal broadly welcomed the appearance of academic boards as very helpful to college principals whilst the other thought academic boards were ineffective in times of stress.

Although there have been these changes to the policy-making process and organization of colleges at the level of the whole institution, there have been few corresponding changes at lower levels in the institution. There have, however, been some attempts to devise alternative structures to the conventional department.

### Internal Organization of Colleges

There are three quite widespread patterns of internal organization of colleges — departments, faculties and the matrix.

*Brian Fidler*

## 1   The Departmental Model

This is the most common pattern, particularly in NAFE. The college is divided into a small number of relatively independent departments. This is a strictly hierarchical form of organization. There will be a head of department, a deputy and section leaders responsible for the main areas of work. Each course taught by the department will have a course tutor to organize it. There will be a fair amount of line management, with perhaps a departmental committee or board to take account of the more participative trends within college organization. Clearly, without such a committee the hierarchical character of departmental organization is increasingly in opposition to the more participative style of leadership indicated by the presence of an academic board.

Many departments in FE are very large (up to fifty or so staff). This follows from the attempt to divide the college into a relatively small number of sub-units combined with the very rapid increase in the size of some units in the recent past. Some departments, therefore, represent very diffuse areas of work which are quite unrelated to each other and are brought together for administrative reasons. These are usually concerned with finance and representation on college committees. Where these large departments are rigidly sub-divided into sections these may be very isolated (sometimes geographically) and to a large extent self-regulating. There may be problems of communication between the sections of such a large department.

## 2   The Faculty Model

In AFE, particularly the polytechnics, departments are generally smaller than is the case in the remainder of FE. These smaller departments are then grouped into faculties rather like the university model. Because of the greater diversity of work compared to universities, some problems have occurred in trying to group departments by any wholly academic criteria. Part of the reason for faculty groupings is to reduce the number of sub-units of the institution to a small number for at least some purposes. This is a compromise between individual departmental autonomy on the one hand and the needs of efficient organization of the whole institution on the other. It is simpler to plan for, administer and negotiate with four or five faculties rather than twenty or more departments. From the point of view of departmental staff the faculty structure facilitates communication across departments of the faculty and the faculty board extends the participative structure down below the level of the academic board. Thus common problems have a forum and the interdisciplinary work within a faculty is facilitated.

320

### 3 The Matrix Model

A much more radical development which has been attempted in a number of institutions from tertiary colleges to polytechnics is the matrix organizational structure. This aims to create the maximum flexibility in utilizing staff expertise, particularly in the design and teaching of interdisciplinary courses.

The basis of the matrix approach is the realization that staff do not always need to be grouped in the same way for all purposes. They will sometimes need to group together in one way for a certain purpose and at other times in a different way for a different purpose. For example, for teaching, especially on an interdisciplinary course, the appropriate grouping is by the course and teachers may teach on a number of them. However, by academic discipline the grouping will be different. The matrix structure is an attempt to offer a flexible grouping system to deal with these varying requirements. The matrix approach originated in industries where there was a need for rapid innovation using interdisciplinary teams which would come together for a short period and then disperse when their work was completed.

In colleges the permanent grouping is by academic subject discipline with a section leader as head, whilst the temporary groupings are by courses taught. These temporary groupings are headed by course leaders. The title of matrix model follows from the diagrammatic representation of this structure as a matrix, as shown in Diagram 1. Clearly, in such a structure power and leadership are diffuse since they are divided primarily between section heads and course leaders. At its best such a system is flexible, facilitates innovation and establishes clear priorities between teaching and other college duties since for each activity there is a clearly identified leader without any conflicting loyalty. However, it is also quite clear that there are many potential areas for conflict and it has been suggested that conflict can only be resolved by mutual agreement or by appeal to the most senior management in the college and much time may be spent in attempting to resolve such conflict which often has no simple solution.

### Participatory School Government?

Academic self-determination has been shown to be a trend which has spread from the universities to public sector higher education and then to the remainder of further education. Paralleling this diffusion of academic self-determination has been the spread of participatory academic policy-making. The spread of these two forces has, however, not reached school level in any formal sense. Control of the curriculum in schools formally rests with predominantly lay governors, whilst participatory academic boards for

Diagram 1.   Matrix Organization

| | | Teaching Sections | | | | | | |
|---|---|---|---|---|---|---|---|---|
| | | Academic Disciplines | | | | | | |
| | | A | B | C | D | E | F | G |
| | Course 1 | × | | × | | × | | |
| | Course 2 | × | × | × | × | | | |
| Course Teams | Course 3 | × | | | × | × | × | × |
| | Course 4 | × | | × | × | × | × | |
| | Course 5 | × | × | | | × | × | × |

A cross indicates that staff from an academic teaching section make a ccontribution to a particular course.

schools have rarely been seriously considered. The Taylor Committee in looking at the government of schools left it to governors to ensure that there was adequate staff consultation in schools, yet in other respects their proposals for school governors reflected similar developments in further education.

Thus there is the anomaly that tertiary colleges for 16-19-year-olds operating under further education regulations generally have an academic board responsible for academic policy-making whilst sixth-form colleges catering for full-time courses for 16-19-year-olds and operating under school regulations have no such participative machinery.

Whilst there are many in further education who are critical of the time consumed by the more participatory style of academic self-government, there are few who would wish to return to the old, more autocratic style of leadership. Much still remains to be worked out in terms of the relationship of the principal and senior staff to the academic board since this calls for a new style of leadership.

### References

ATCDE (1968) *The Government of Colleges of Education*, London, ATCDE.

BRANNEN, R. *et al*. (1981) 'Departmental organisational structures in further education', *Journal of Further and Higher Education*, 5, 3, Autumn, pp. 22–32.

EBBUTT, K. and BROWN, R. (1978) 'The structure of power in the FE college', *Journal of Further and Higher Education*, 2, 3, Autumn, pp. 3–17.

MOODIE, G.C. and EUSTACE, R. (1974) *Power and Authority in British Universities*, London, Allen and Unwin.

OPEN UNIVERSITY (1977) *Management and the Academic Board in FE Colleges*, Unit 12, Course E321.

PARKES, D. (Ed.) (1982) *The Changing Face of FE*, London, FEU.

PERKIN, H.J. (1969) *New Universities in the United Kingdom*, Paris, OECD.

PURSAIL, A.J. (1976) 'Staff development in FE at a time of crisis', *Coombe Lodge Reports*, 9, pp. 277–85.

ROBBINS REPORT (1963) *Higher Education*, Cmnd 2154, London, HMSO.

THOMAS, K. (1981) 'College democracy: Which way forward?', *NATFHE Journal*, October, pp. 22–4, 34.

WEAVER REPORT (1966) *Report of the Study Group on the Government of Colleges of Education*, London, DES.

# Beyond the Subject Monolith: Subject Traditions and Sub-Cultures

*Ivor Goodson*
*University of Sussex*

A number of studies have confirmed the central role which subject sub-cultures and subject specialisms play in the preparation of teachers. In 1970 McLeish's research on college students and lecturers found that: 'The most remarkable differences in attitude of any in the total sample appear to be between subject specialists.'[1] Developing a more differentiated model of 'subject sub-cultures', Lacey noted in 1977 that 'the subject sub-culture appears to be a pervasive phenomenon affecting a student-teacher's behaviour in school and university, as well as their choice of friends and their attitudes towards education.' This leads on to arguing the case for 'considering the process of becoming a teacher as a multi-stranded process in which subject sub-cultures insulate the various strands from another.'[2]

Whilst studies of teacher preparation have thereby pointed up the part played by subject specialisms and sub-cultures, these have often been presented as 'undifferentiated epistemological communities sharing knowledge and methodology'.[3] This paper will contend that a variety of 'traditions' exists within subject sub-cultures. These traditions initiate the teacher into widely differing visions of knowledge hierarchies and content, teacher role and overall pedagogic orientation.

To understand subject sub-cultures as a 'pervasive phenomenon' in teacher preparation the major 'traditions' within these sub-cultures need to be identified and studied. We shall see that just as 'there are important differences within subject boundaries of the same order as the differences between subjects',[4] so also are there certain major 'traditions', which exist with varying degrees of articulation and allegiance, *within* most school subjects. It is these subject 'traditions' which act as the main agency of teacher initiation into subject communities, so that they are at the sharp end of the 'pervasive phenomenon' of the subject sub-culture.

The study of school subject 'traditions' should focus on the intentions and forces which underpin such traditions. Hopefully it will be possible to discern certain patterns underlying subject traditions, and this paper argues that by studying school subjects and subject cultures in evolution certain historical imperatives can be identified. The forces which lead school subjects to follow broadly similar patterns of evolution are inevitably related to the forces which intrude on each individual teacher's judgement of how his career and material interests are pursued during his working life. However, the focus of this paper is on academic subject cultures and as a result teachers involved in mainly pastoral careers are not considered. Above all, the paper follows the aspiration voiced in an earlier paper from Mardle and Walker which viewed the location of classroom processes 'as part of a patterned historical framework' as a way of developing links between current micro and macro levels of analysis.[5]

## Subject Tradition and Sub-Cultures

School subjects are made up of groups and individuals with varying identities, values and interests. One is often reminded of Bucher and Strauss's characterization of professions as: 'loose amalgamations of segments pursuing different objectives in different manners and more or less delicately held together under a common name at particular periods in history.'[6] The study of school subjects in evolution discerns a close relationship between the promotion of certain 'traditions' and sub-cultures and the pursuit of status and resources. Layton's study, *Science for the People*, traces a number of traditions in nineteenth century science which sought to relate science to people's lives.[7] The book generates a number of hypotheses as to why this version of science was ultimately replaced by a more thoroughly academic version pursued in laboratories and defined in new textbooks and syllabuses. The focal role played by subject associations in this pursuit of more academic status is documented by Hanson with reference to the Society of Art Masters.[8] The Society showed great concern for the academic dress and titles which bestow, or appeared to bestow, high status on other knowledge categories.

Dodd has recently reviewed the history of design and technology in the school curriculum, following earlier work on design education by Eggleston. A major theme in the work is the desire among teachers of the subject for higher status:

> Heavy craft activities have been referred to by a number of different titles as their nature and contribution has changed. Concealed in this ongoing discussion is the matter of 'status' and 'respectability', and although the most recent change from Handicraft to Design and Technology reflects a change of emphasis, there is something of the former argument. 'Practical' describes quite adequately an essential part of the subject, but it is an adjective which is little used because in the terms of the Crowther Report, it is an 'emotionally charged word'. As the subject has developed there have been efforts made to

encourage its acceptability by participation in certain kinds of external examinations (which have not always been the best instruments of assessment), the use of syllabuses (often malformed to make them acceptable by other institutions), and by euphemisms like the 'alternative road', but these have failed to hide the underlying low status which practical subjects have by tradition.[9]

Among more general studies of the history of curriculum, Raymond Williams' brief work relating educational philosophies to the social groups holding them is deeply suggestive. He writes: 'an educational curriculum, as we have seen again and again in the past periods, expresses a compromise between an inherited selection of interests and the emphasis of new interests. At varying points in history, even this compromise may be long delayed, and it will often be muddled.'[10] This view of the history of curriculum has been recently extended by Eggleston who contends that: 'The fundamental conflicts are over the identity and legitimacy of the rival contenders for membership of the groups who define, evaluate and distribute knowledge and the power these confer.'[11]

Banks' study of *Parity and Prestige in English Secondary Education*, written in 1955, though even more out of date than Williams' work, is a valuable complement. The same theme relating curriculum to social class emerges. Williams had noted that the academic curriculum was related to the vocations of the upper and professional classes. The curriculum related to the vocations of the majority was slowly introduced, and Banks notes that 'as the proportion of children from artisan and lower middle class homes increased, it was necessary to pay more attention to the vocational needs of the pupils, and even to amend the hitherto academic curriculum to admit subjects of vocational nature.'[12] But the subjects related to majority vocations were persistently viewed as of low status. Banks quotes a TUC pamphlet which in 1937 maintained: 'School time used for vocational training not only gives a bias to study but takes up valuable time and effort better employed in a wider and more useful field. Moreover, it stamps at an early and impressionable age the idea of class and inferior status on the scholar, which it is the aim of a noble education to avoid.'[13]

Viewed in this way, vocational training is seen not to refer to the pervasive underlying objective of all education as preparation for vocations but to the low-status concern of preparing the majority for their work. The academic curriculum is, and has historically been, in purpose vocational, but the preparation is for the high-status professions. Indeed, Banks' study concludes that 'the persistence of the academic tradition is seen as something more fundamental than the influence, sinister or otherwise, of teachers and administrators. It is the vocational qualification of the academic curriculum which enables it to exert such a pressure on all forms of secondary education.'[14]

Layton has analyzed the evolution of science in England from the nineteenth century, and suggests a tentative model for the evolution of a school subject in the secondary school curriculum. Layton has defined three stages in this evolution. In the first stage:

> the callow intruder stakes a place in the timetable, justifying its presence on grounds such as pertinence and utility. During this stage learners are attracted to the subject because of its bearing on matters of concern to them. The teachers are rarely trained specialists, but bring the missionary enthusiasms of pioneers to their task. The dominant criterion is relevance to the needs and interests of the learners.

In the interim second stage:

> a tradition of scholarly work in the subject is emerging along with a corps of trained specialists from which teachers may be recruited. Students are still attracted to the Study, but as much by its reputation and growing academic status as by its relevance to their own problems and concerns. The internal logic and discipline of the subject is becoming increasingly influential in the selection and organisation of subject matter.

In the final stage:

> the teachers now constitute a professional body with established rules and values. The selection of subject matter is determined in large measure by the judgements and practices of the specialist scholars who lead inquiries in the field. Students are initiated into a tradition, their attitudes approaching passivity and resignation, a prelude to disenchantment.[15]

Whilst the conflict between vocational and academic traditions is studied in Williams, Banks, Dodd and Eggleston, Layton's work points towards a more complex and differentiated model of subject traditions. Layton's first stage clearly shows the 'pedagogic' as well as vocational origins of school subjects: not just 'utility' but also 'relevance to the needs and interests of the learners'. The concern with pupil relevance constitutes another tradition, and a continuing one, in the definition of the subject's content. In short, Layton's model warns against any monolithic explanations of school subjects and leads us towards identifying the motivations behind certain traditions and to studying the fate of these traditions as school subjects evolve over time.

### Defining Subject Traditions: Academic, Utilitarian and Pedagogic

The historical study of school subjects defines certain 'traditions' which can often be related to the social class origins and occupational destinations of their pupil clienteles. Hence the curricula of public and grammar schools aimed mainly at the middle and upper classes preparing for professional life were primarily academic; whilst the elementary schools educating the majority stressed vocational training.

Writing of the 'traditions' in English primary education, Blyth discerned three different trends: the preparatory, the elementary and the developmental. The preparatory tradition was 'almost exclusively related to what we now call grammar school education, which developed in its turn mainly as an upper middle class phenomenon', the elementary tradition 'with its characteristic emphasis on the basic skills' was aimed at the lower classes. 'For those who were unfortunate, indolent or culpable enough to be poor, the minimum of education was proper and sufficient.' The third tradition, the developmental, bases its principles on concern with each child along the lines recommended by Rousseau or Pestalozzi. Broadly speaking, Blyth's three primary traditions can be equated with the three traditions discerned within secondary education: the academic, utilitarian and pedagogic traditions.[16]

The definition of public and grammar school subjects in the nineteenth century, established in the 1904 Regulations and confirmed in the School Certificate Examinations, clearly followed the aims of education as a preparation for professional and academic life. Eggleston, commenting on the early nineteenth century, states:

> A new and important feature of the time that was to prevail, was the redefinition of high-status knowledge as that which was not immediately useful in a vocation or occupation. The study of the classics now came to be seen as essentially a training of the mind and the fact that a boy could be spared from work long enough to experience this in full measure was in itself seen as a demonstration not only of the high status of the knowledge itself but also of the recipient — the mark of a 'gentleman' rather than a worker.[17]

Eggleston's last sentence points up the contradiction: it was not so much that classical liberal education was non-vocational but that the vocations were only those fit for upper-class gentlemen. 'As educational history shows', Williams reminds us, 'the classical linguistic disciplines were primarily vocational but these particular vocations had acquired a separate traditional dignity, which was refused to vocations now of equal human relevance.[18]

For this reason we have avoided the use of the terms 'vocational education' or 'vocational knowledge'. Instead, we refer to the subject-based curriculum confirmed by the examination system as the *academic* tradition, and to low-status practical knowledge as the *utilitarian* tradition. Utilitarian knowledge thus becomes that which is related to those non-professional vocations in which most people work for most of their adult life. In addition to the basic skills of numeracy and literacy, this includes commercial and technical education.

Neither commercial nor technical education was ever seriously considered as a new dimension which could be added to the existing classical curriculum. It was specialized training for a particular class of man, and its confinement to low-status areas of the curriculum has remained a constant feature of English curriculum conflict. For example, Layton's research on the development of science education in the nineteenth century has shown how the emphasis was increasingly placed on abstract knowledge with a consequent separation from the practical world of work. Nevertheless, the alternative view of a narrowly utilitarian curriculum is still powerful, as is shown by the constant pressure for utilitarian subjects in spite of their recurrent failure to earn high status. The manpower needs of a changing industrial economy demand that utilitarian training will be consistently advocated by many industrialists. When widespread industrial failure is endemic the continuing ambivalence of educational status systems causes serious concern and pressure for change. The Great Debate was one symptom of this concern, and as was recently argued in *The Times*:

> Strategies for furthering the inter-relationship between industry and the educational system need to address the complex question of status systems. The established patterns of status represent an enormously powerful historical legacy, a kind of indirect pressure group. Only if high status areas in the educational system such as the public schools and Oxbridge are willing to remodel their value systems do current strategies stand any chance of success.[19]

The low status of utilitarian knowledge is shared by the personal, social and common sense knowledge stressed by those pursuing a child-centred approach to education. This approach with its emphasis on the learning process can be characterized as the *pedagogic* tradition within the English curriculum. Child-centred or progressive education does not view the task of education as preparation for the 'ladder' to the professions and academia or as an apprenticeship to vocational work but as a way of aiding the child's own 'inquiries' or 'discoveries', and considers that this is best facilitated by 'activity' methods.

The pedagogic tradition normally challenges the existing professional identity of teachers at two levels: (1) as a 'specialist' in a school subject, for which the teacher had normally been specifically trained; and (2) as an all-pervading authority figure within the classroom. The Interdisciplinary Enquiry (IDE) workshops run by Goldsmiths College in the sixties clarify and exemplify the dual nature of the challenge. The workshops were specifically instituted as pilot courses for experienced teachers involved with those school leavers staying on as a result of ROSLA.

The IDE booklets contained a series of stark messages for teachers of traditional subjects:

> We suggest that the subject based curriculum has fundamental educational disadvantages. The school day is fragmented into

subject periods and time allocated to each subject is always regarded as insufficient by the subject specialist, as indeed it is.

Apart from the disadvantages in terms of time:

> The arbitrary division of knowledge into subject-syllabuses encourages a didactic form of teaching with the pupil's role reduced to passive assimilation. Any enquiry resulting from a keen interest shown by children in a section of work they are doing in a subject inevitably takes them over the boundaries of the subject into another, perhaps several others. Good teachers would like to encourage this evidence of interest, but they simply cannot afford the time, especially if their syllabus is geared to external examinations.[20]

As a solution to the problems engendered by the didactic teaching of traditional subjects Goldsmiths' team advocated organizing schemes of work around interdisciplinary enquiries.

Another curriculum project aimed at young school leavers underlined both the need to reappraise 'subjects' and to clearly define new pedagogic relationships. The Humanities Curriculum Project (HCP) began in 1967 with Lawrence Stenhouse as its director. HCP pursued the pedagogic implications of curriculum reform through the notion of 'neutral chairmanship'. This meant 'that the teacher accepts the need to submit his teaching in controversial areas to the criterion of neutrality ... i.e. that he regards it as part of his responsibility not to promote his own view', and further that 'the mode of enquiry in controversial areas should have discussion, rather than instruction as its core.'[21]

The pedagogic tradition has been closely allied to the so-called 'progressive' movement in education. As Shipman noted in 1969, the more progressive curricula have come to be concentrated on those sections of the pupil clientele not considered suitable for O and A-level examinations. In this way the pedagogic tradition has often suffered from the comparatively low status also accorded to the utilitarian tradition.

## Examinations and Academic Subjects

The connection between certain subjects taught in school and external examinations was established on the present footing with the birth of the School Certificate in 1917. From this point on the conflict over the curriculum began to resemble the contemporary situation in focussing on the definition and evaluation of examinable knowledge. The School Certificate rapidly became the major concern of grammar schools and because of the subjects thereby examined confirmed that academic subjects would dominate the school timetable.

By 1943 the Norwood Report assessed the importance of examinations in the following manner:

> A certain sameness in the curricula of schools seems to have resulted from the double necessity of finding a place for the many subjects competing for time in the curriculum and the need to teach these subjects in such a way and to such a standard as will ensure success in the School Certificate examination. Under these necessities the curriculum has settled down into an uneasy equilibrium, the demands of specialists and subjects and examinations being nicely adjusted and compensated.[22]

Despite the warnings, the academic subject-centred curriculum was strengthened in the period following the 1944 Education Act. The introduction of the GCE in 1951 allowed subjects to be taken separately at O-level (whereas the School Certificate was a 'block' exam in which the main subjects all had to be passed), and the introduction of A-level increased subject specialization in a manner guaranteed to preserve if not enhance the largely 'academic' nature of the O-level examination. There was little chance that a lower-status examination, such as the CSE, which was introduced in 1965, would endanger the academic subject-centredness of the higher-status O and A-levels.

Indeed, it has proved remarkably adaptive to maintaining the status differentiation noted by Shipman and has even extended it. A recent study by Ball shows four bands within a comprehensive school allocating pupils as follows: Band 1 to subject-based O-levels; Band 2 to subject-based CSE Mode 2; Band 3 to integrated or watered-down subjects (e.g., Maths for Living) for CSE Mode 3; and Band 4 to non-examined 'remedial' classes.

The hegemony of the academic subject-based curriculum for O-level candidates was confirmed by the organizational structure of the Schools Council. An early role for the Council in the examinations field was advising the Beloe Committee set up to consider the proliferation of examinations in secondary modern schools. Beloe employed the subject-based framework of the Secondary Schools Examination Council, set up in the inter-war years to ensure uniformity of examinations, mainly at O and A levels. As Robert Morris, one of the two founding Joint Secretaries, explained:

> You can now see why the Schools Council developed a committee structure based on subjects. It was simply logical ... we just inherited the structure of the Secondary Schools Examination Council who had already developed a pattern for examinations in academic subjects. (personal interview)

The attempts of interest groups to promote new subjects have focussed since 1917 on the pursuit of high-status examinations and qualifications. Subjects like art, woodwork and metalwork, technical studies, book-keeping, typewriting and needlework, domestic science and physical education have consistently pursued status improvement by arguing for enhanced examinations and qualifications. But as we have seen, few subjects have been able to challenge the hegemony of the academic subjects incorporated in the 1904 Regulations and 1917 School Certificate. This academic tradition has successfully withstood waves of comprehensive reorganization and associated curriculum reform. The upheaval of the Great Debate is a reminder that this survival appears to have been at the expense of certain 'dominant interests' in the economy.

## Academic Subjects, Status and Resources

The historical connection between academic subjects and external examinations is only partly explained because of 'the need to teach these subjects in such a way and to such a standard as will ensure success in the School Certificate examination'.

The years after 1917 saw a range of significant developments in the professionalization of teachers. Increasingly with the establishment of specialized subject training courses teachers came to see themselves as part of a 'subject community'. The associated growth of subject associations both derived from and confirmed this trend. This increasing identification of secondary teachers with subject communities tended to separate them from each other, and as schools became larger, departmental forms of organization arose which reinforced the separation. Thus the subject-centred curriculum developed to the point where the Norwood Report in 1943 expressed considerable concern:

> Subjects have tended to become preserves belonging to specialist teachers; barriers have been erected between them, and teachers have felt unqualified or not free to trespass upon the dominions of other teachers. The specific values of each subject have been pressed to the neglect of the values common to several or all. The school course has come to resemble the 'hundred yards' course, each subject following a track marked off from the others by a tape. In the meantime, we feel, the child is apt to be forgotten.[23]

Norwood summarizes the position by saying that 'subjects seem to have built themselves vested interests and rights of their own.' In explaining the continuing connection between external examinations and academic subjects the part played by the vested interests of the subject groups needs to be analyzed. The dominance of academic subjects with high-status examination credentials would need to be in close harmony with the vested interests of subject groups to explain the strength of this alliance over so long a period.

The 'subject' label is important at a number of levels: obviously as a school 'examination' category, but also as title for a 'degree' or 'training course'. Perhaps most important of all the subject defines the territory of a 'department' within each school. The subject is the major reference point in the work of the contemporary secondary school: the information and knowledge transmitted in schools is formally selected and organized through subjects. The teacher is identified by the pupils and related to them mainly through his subject specialism. Given the size of most comprehensive schools a number of teachers are required for each subject and these are normally grouped into subject 'departments'. The departments have a range of 'graded posts' for special responsibilities and for the 'head of department'. In this way the teacher's subject provides the means whereby his salary is decided and his career structure defined.

Within school subjects there is a clear hierarchy of status. This is based upon assumptions that certain subjects, the so-called 'academic' subjects, are suitable for the 'able' students, whilst other subjects are not. In her study of resource allocation in schools, Eileen Byrne has shown how more resources are given to these able students and hence to the academic subjects:

> Two assumptions which might be questioned have been seen consistently to underlie educational planning and the consequent resource allocation for the more able children. First, that these necessarily need longer in school than non-grammar pupils, and secondly, that they necessarily need more staff, more highly paid staff and more money for equipment and books.[24]

Byrne's research ended in 1965 before widespread comprehensivization, and therefore refers to the tripartite system. However, referring to the now comprehensive system, she wrote in 1974:

> There is ... little indication that a majority of councils or chief officers accept in principle the need for review and reassessment of the entire process of the allocation of resources in relation to the planned application, over a period of years, of an approved and progressive policy, or coherent educational development.[25]

Hence it is likely, if Byrne's judgement is correct, that the discrimination in favour of academic subjects for the able pupils continues within the comprehensive school.

That comprehensive schools do place overwhelming emphasis on academic examinations, in spite of the growth of 'pastoral systems', has been recently confirmed by Ball's study of Beachside Comprehensive. He notes that 'once reorganised as a comprehensive, academic excellence was quickly established as a central tenet of the value system of the school.'[26] He provides a range of qualitative and statistical indicators to confirm this contention and concludes that 'while the division is less clear-cut and stark than in the grammar school' nonetheless it is evident that 'the teacher-resources within the comprehensive school are allocated differently according to the pupil's ability.' Thus the most experienced teachers spend most of their time teaching the most able pupils. This is a reflection of the fact that the social and psychological rewards offered by the school to its pupils accrue to those who are academically successful and that academic achievement tended to be the single criterion of 'success in the school'.[27]

Through the study of Beachside Comprehensive considerable evidence is assembled to prove Marsden's prediction that 'if we give the new comprehensive the task of competing with selective schools for academic qualifications, the result will be remarkably little change in the selective nature of education. Selection will take place within the school and the working class child's education will still suffer.'[28]

The importance of different curriculum traditions for each ability band of pupils is central in confirming these selective patterns. After the first term we learn 'the increasing differences of syllabus and curriculum which develop between the bands mean that band 2 or band 3 pupils would have to perform exceptionally well if not brilliantly to overcome the limitations placed upon them by the organisation of the syllabus.'[29] Ball notes that the pattern of curriculum differentiation is 'not unlike that made in the Norwood Report for fourth and fifth year pupils.'[30] At the top of the hierarchy of subjects are the traditional O-level subjects like maths, English, the languages, sciences, history and geography. These high-status subjects have 'an academic orientation in common; they are concerned with theoretical knowledge. They are subjects for the brighter, the academic, the band 1 pupil. Below these in status come O-levels in practical subjects like technical studies and metalwork. For band 2 and 3 pupils there are traditional CSEs and lowest of all in status new Mode III CSEs.'[31]

In a detailed and illuminating study of how the option system works it is possible to discern how curriculum categories and pupil clienteles (and futures) are 'matched' by the teachers. Ball shows how this works for two classes — the band 1 class 3CU and the band 2 class 3TA. After the option system has worked the '3TA pupils have been directed away from the "academic" to the practical, while the reverse has happened for the 3CU pupil'.[32] The study shows clearly that working-class pupils concentrate in bands 2 and 3 and further that the 'differentiation of access to high status knowledge with high negotiable value is crucially related to socio-economic status.' He concludes:

> Option-allocation is a point at which school careers become firmly differentiated and at which the informal differences between pupils in terms of social reputation and their experiences of the curriculum lower down the school are formalised into separate curricular routes and examination destinations. It is here that the stratified nature of the occupation structure is directly reflected in the ability stratification within the school.

Both the differential status of the knowledge areas in the curriculum and the access to the sixth form that certain courses provide are aspects of the selection of pupils for further and higher education and the occupation market. The selection process and negotiation of meanings that go to make up the option-allocation procedure are part of the structural relationships within the school which label pupils with different statures and educational identities.[33]

But the study of internal process in an individual school can only take us so far. Reflecting the reality of the teacher's views inside the school, such a study takes the differentiated curriculum traditions which play such a central part in pupil differentiation as given. Truly 'men make their own history but not in circumstances of their own choosing.' The comprehensive school has had to accept the 'circumstances' of curriculum traditions derived from the tripartite system and earlier.

A number of studies confirm the status hierarchy of subjects. Warwick reports that a 1968 survey showed that over 7 per cent of male teachers who had studied within the languages and literature group (forming just over 19 per cent of the total sample) had become headteachers, compared with less than 1 per cent of those who had studied in the field of technology and handicraft (who formed just over 11 per cent of the total sample). Similarly, among male teachers 'former students of languages and literature had apparently four times as many chances as former students of music and drama, and one and a half times the chances of former students of science and mathematics of becoming headmasters.'[34]

The hierarchy of subjects is clearly derived from traditional grammar school preferences. Stevens reports that here 'English, Science, Languages and Mathematics are in general the subjects in which success or lack of it is significant for the children. The fact that practical subjects come low on the scale does not in itself support an assumption that more intelligent children are weak, even comparatively, at practical subjects.... The figures are rather as indicating the degree of importance with which several people, but chiefly the staff, invest subjects for the children.'[35]

## School Subjects and Teachers' Interests

Three major subject traditions have been identified: the academic, utilitarian and pedagogic. The link between external subject examinations for the able student and the flow of status and resources has been clearly demonstrated. Conflicts between separate subject traditions have to be viewed within this context of status and resource allocation.

The aspirational imperative to become an academic subject is fundamental and very powerful and can be summarized as follows: school subjects comprise groups of people with differing interests and intentions.

Certain common factors unite these sub-groups, most notably that the material self-interest of each subject teacher is closely connected with the status of the subject in terms of its examinable knowledge. Academic subjects provide the teacher with a career structure characterized by better promotion prospects and pay than less academic subjects. Most resources are given to academic subjects which are taught to 'able' students. The conflict over the status of examinable knowledge is above all a battle over the material resources and career prospects available to each subject community or subject teacher.

The definition of a subject as an O and even more as an A-level examination postulates acceptance of the academic tradition. Even subjects with clear pedagogic or utilitarian origins and intentions such as art, craft (in aspiration design and technology) and rural studies (in aspiration environmental studies/science) have had to present themselves as theoretical academic subjects if A-level status is to be seriously pursued. Of course, once granted, A-level status, alongside acceptance as a university discipline, ensures 'establishment'. Layton's profile brings out the often contradictory directions in which pupil relevance and teacher and pupil motivation move as against the pursuit of academic status and the consequent definition of subject content by scholarly academics. The fate of subject traditions is clearly exhibited in close linkage with knowledge patterns and classroom pedagogy: the historical imperative in the case of science is clear but so also are the implications in terms of teacher preparation.

A more recent historical study (Layton's model was devised in 1972) has allowed some of the tentative assertions he made from the case of science to be tested for geography, biology, and rural studies.[36] In the case of geography, the subject was initially dominated by utilitarian and pedagogic arguments: 'we seek to train future citizens' and the citizen 'must have a topographical background if he is to keep order in the mass of information which accumulates in the course of his life.'[37] At this point the subject was largely taught by teachers untrained in geography. In 1903 Mackinder has outlined a strategy for the improvement of geography: the first demand was that 'University Schools of Geography' be established 'where geographers can be made.'[38] By this time the Geographical Association, which had been formed in 1893, was actively promoting the subject's academic potential, so much so that when the Hadow Report came out in 1927 it contended that: 'The main objective in good geographical teaching is to develop ... an attitude of mind and mode of thought characteristic of the subject.'[39]

By that time the university schools of geography demanded by Mackinder were being established for, as Wooldridge noted: 'It has been conceded that if Geography is to be taught in schools it must be learned in the universities.'[40] However, not until after 1945, Garnett tells us, were most school departments of geography directed by specialist-trained geographers. As a result of this training, she noted, 'most of the initial marked differences and contrasts in subject personality had been blurred or obliterated.'[41]

In fact, for several decades university geographers were plagued both by the image of the subject as essentially for school children and by the idiosyncratic interpretations of the various university departments, especially in respect to fieldwork which encapsulated many pedagogic and utilitarian objectives. Thus, while establishment in universities solved the status problems of the subject within schools, within the universities themselves the subject's status still remained low. The launching, in the 1960s, of 'new geography' with aspirations to full scientific or social scientific rigour is therefore to be largely understood as a strategy for finally establishing geography's status at the highest academic level. New geography stressed the 'scientific' and theoretical side of the subject at the expense of 'fieldwork' and 'regional studies'.

The history of biology, from low-status origins in elementary and secondary schools to establishment in universities, is similar to that of geography. The utilitarian and pedagogic elements in biology which so retarded its progress were mainly confirmed by the fieldwork aspects of the subject. Hence, the development of field biology ran counter to the pressures for status escalation. Status through a vision of biology as 'hard science' was increasingly pursued in the 1960s through an emphasis on laboratory investigations and mathematical techniques. In 1962 Dowdeswell had conceded the crucial importance of laboratories as status symbols and had directed much of the Nuffield Foundation's money and resources towards their development.[42] The rise of molecular biology with the work of Crick and Watson finally confirmed biology as a laboratory-based hard science. As a result, the subject was rapidly expanded in the universities (themselves expanded apace). With the training of a new generation of biology graduates the subject's incorporation as a high-status O and A-level school subject was finally assured.

The case of rural studies provides a different pattern of evolution. The origins of the subject were clearly and avowedly utilitarian, and pedagogic arguments for the subject were continuous, but academic arguments were never seriously entertained or deployed. After 1944 the subject was almost exclusively confined to the secondary moderns and with the growth of comprehensives in the 1960s it was faced with extinction as schools were reluctant to teach an ex-secondary modern subject with no examination status. As a result the newly-formed rural studies subject association began to promote the subject as an 'academic discipline'. The name was changed to 'environmental studies' and a protracted battle ensued to have the subject accepted at A-level. Unfortunately, although one board did accept the subject at A-level, there was never any possibility of a university base and hence no specialist scholars to define the discipline for broad-based A-level acceptance. Lacking this university base, status passage to academic acceptance has been denied to environmental studies.

Whilst aspiration to academic status has been discerned by Layton for science and confirmed in the case of biology and geography and (unsuccessfully) in the case of rural studies, utilitarian and pedagogic traditions and sub-groups owe their existence to radically different visions about the assumptions and intentions which underpin school subjects. Despite the continuing support for these traditions, the flow of resources and attributions of status plainly operate against them and in favour of the academic tradition. The implications of this imperative for the individual teacher's specialization and career pattern are fundamental and wide-ranging, affecting his view of his role and associated pedagogic predictions. In the study of the history of geography the author concluded:

> To further their own material self-interests school subject teachers must hand over control of their subject to those who are given the power to define 'disciplines'. Inevitably the subject is now defined by university scholars for their peers and students in line with the pervasive theoretical and scientific vision which characterises our academic institutions . . . whatever the original intentions or content areas of that subject may have been.[43]

In the evolution of the subject and through the promotion of different traditions over time the teacher's role therefore moves (following Layton) from an initial stage as 'an untrained specialist' to a final stage where as 'a professional' he is trained to teach pupils an examination subject defined by university scholars and examination boards. The stark differences in the teacher's role and associated pedagogy reflect the different visions embodied in the various subject 'traditions'.

### Conclusion

Sub-cultures, as well as initiating teachers into particular subject traditions, also offer arenas wherein those teachers can redefine and redirect educational patterns. But the direction in which school subjects move towards the culminating academic tradition is a reflection of the patterns of material interest and career aggrandisement which receive support inside the educational system and which crucially influence an individual teacher's assessment of the sub-cultural tradition which gains his allegiance.

The material interest of subject teachers is closely connected with the status of the subject in terms of examinable knowledge. 'Academic' subjects provide the teacher with a career structure characterized by better promotion prospects than less academic subjects. More resources are given to those academic subjects which are taught to 'able' children.

Hence the historical imperative is towards socialization into and acceptance of the academic tradition within subject sub-cultures. This tradition predicates fundamental assumptions about teacher role, pedagogic orientation, hierarchies of knowledge and the fabric of relationships which underpin these. We have noted that Layton sees the academic tradition as the prelude to disenchantment for pupils; likewise Witkin has shown how working-class pupils actively prefer and choose lessons they can relate to the everyday world; and Halsey's recent research shows the radical difference between working-class recruitment to technical schools (utilitarian tradition) and the far lower take-up of grammar schools (academic tradition). Plainly, the historical imperatives which lead teachers into acceptance of the academic tradition will be at the expense of other aspirations encapsulated within pedagogic and utilitarian traditions.

We have noted the recurrence of challenges to the dominance of the academic tradition and to the emergence of 'pastoral' careers within schools. At the present time, under the threat of falling rolls, some education authorities are reviewing their fundamental assumptions about curriculum planning. In some areas this has led to a concern for 'whole curriculum needs' which leads to planning according to the range of subjects required by all pupils. Were this questioning of assumptions to become more general, it would clearly question the mechanisms which currently maintain the academic/able pupil alliance.

Detailed consideration of subject traditions, together with an appraisal of the benefits and costs of each for the individual teacher, might seem a useful perspective from which to begin teacher preparation. By focussing on these themes teacher trainers could ensure a discussion about teacher roles, pedagogies and relationships which were closely related to actual choices with which the teacher will be confronted in his or her working life.

## Notes

1 McLeish, J. (1970) *Students' Attitudes and College Environments*, Cambridge, quoted in Lacey (1977), p. 64.
2 Lacey, C. (1977) *The Socialisation of Teachers*, London, Methuen, pp. 63–4.
3 Ball, S.J. and Lacey, C. (1978) 'Subject disciplines as the opportunity for group action: A measured critique of subject sub-cultures', paper presented at the SSRC Conference, Teacher and Pupil Strategies, St Hilda's College, University of Oxford, September.
4 *Ibid.*
5 Mardle, G. and Walker, M. (1980) Introduction to book on Teacher Preparation, mimeo.
6 Bucher, R. and Strauss, A. (1976) 'Professions in process', in Hammersley, M. and Woods, P. (Eds) *The Process of Schooling: A Sociological Reader*, London, Routledge and Kegan Paul, p. 19.
7 Layton, D. (1973) *Science for the People*, London, George Allen and Unwin.
8 Hanson, D. (1971) 'The development of a professional association of art teachers', *Studies in Design Education*, 3 February.
9 Dodd, T. (1978) *Design and Technology in the School Curriculum*, London, Hodder and Stoughton.
10 Williams, R. (1961) *The Long Revolution*, London, Penguin, p. 172.
11 Eggleston, J. (1977) *The Sociology of the School Curriculum*, London, Routledge and Kegan Paul.

12 BANKS, O. (1955) *Parity and Prestige in English Secondary Education*, London, Routledge and Kegan Paul, p. 5.
13 TUC (1937) *Education and Democracy*, London, TUC.
14 BANKS (1955) *op. cit.*, p. 248.
15 LAYTON, D. (1972) 'Science as general education', *Trends in Education*, January.
16 BLYTH, W.A.L. (1965) *English Primary Education: A Sociological Description*, Vol. 2, London, Routledge and Kegan Paul, pp. 21, 30, 124–5.
17 EGGLESTON (1977), *op. cit.*, p. 25.
18 WILLIAMS (1961), *op. cit.*, p. 163.
19 GOODSON, I.F. (1978) 'Why Britain needs to change its image of the educated man', *The Times*, 14 February.
20 UNIVERSITY OF LONDON, GOLDSMITHS COLLEGE (1965) The Raising of the School Leaving Age: Second Pilot Course for Experienced Teachers, Autumn Term.
21 THE HUMANITIES PROJECT: AN INTRODUCTION (1972) London, Heinemann, p. 1.
22 THE NORWOOD REPORT (1943) London, HMSO, p. 61.
23 *Ibid.*
24 BYRNE, E.M. (1974) *Planning and Educational Inequality*, Slough, NFER, pp. 29, 311.
25 *Ibid.*
26 BALL, S.J. (1981) *Beachside Comprehensive*, Cambridge University Press, p. 18.
27 *Ibid.*
28 *Ibid.*, p. 21.
29 *Ibid.*, pp. 35–6.
30 *Ibid.*, p. 138.
31 *Ibid.*, p. 140.
32 *Ibid.*, p. 143.
33 *Ibid.*, pp. 152–3.
34 WARWICK, D. (1976) 'Ideologies, integration and conflicts of meaning', in FLUDE, M. and AHIER, J. (Eds) *Educability, Schools and Ideology*, London, Croom Helm, p. 101.
35 STEVENS, F. (1972) *The Living Tradition: The Social and Educational Assumptions of the Grammar School*, 3rd ed., London, Hutchinson, pp. 117–18.
36 GOODSON, I.F. (1982) *School Subjects and Curriculum Change: Case Studies in Curriculum History*, London, Croom Helm.
37 COUNCIL OF THE GEOGRAPHICAL ASSOCIATION (1919) 'The position of geography', *The Geographical Teacher*, 10.
38 MACKINDER, H.J. (1903) 'Report of the British Association meeting, September 1903', *The Geographical Teacher*, 2. pp. 95–101.
39 BOARD OF EDUCATION (1927) *Report of the Hadow Committee*, London, HMSO.
40 Quoted in DAVID, T. (1973) 'Against geography', in BALE, J. *et al.*, *Perspectives in Geographical Education*, Edinburgh, pp. 12–13.
41 GARNETT, A. (1969) 'Teaching geography: Some reflections', *Geography*, 54, November, p. 368.
42 W.H. DOWDESWELL as Director of the Nuffield Biology Project.
43 GOODSON, I.F. (1981) 'Defining and defending the subject', paper presented at St Hilda's Conference, September.

# 6
## Quangos and Other Influences

# Introduction

It is possible to name almost all of the officially designated parts of the leadership process in our educational system and, to some degree, to describe and assign a level of authority and power to each. The previous sections of this book have fulfilled that task. The papers in this final section have been chosen and/or commissioned to highlight some of the less 'official' sources of leadership and pressure.

The first contribution is an original paper by John Brand who examines the contribution of the now defunct Schools Council and the professional centres/teachers' centres to the encouragement of change in the educational system of England and Wales. He looks carefully at the development of these bodies as concepts and as real organizations and poses a number of ideas about formal and informal networks of curriculum and organizational initiatives which have had significant bearing on the detailed actions resulting from official leadership of our schools.

The second contribution, by Paul Lodge and Tessa Blackstone, examines the important, and ever changing, influence of the teachers' unions and associations, exemplified by the National Union of Teachers and one of the newer interest groups who work on the fringes of the system to encourage development along particular lines. The important point about these influences is that to a large extent they are motivated by self-interest and the wish to have particular aspects of the system changed to suit their particularly idiosyncratic needs. Therefore while they are indeed 'a power to be reckoned with' their role is, and should be, merely advisory if elected and appointed leaders of the 'official' system are to avoid losing control of the direction of general issues in education.

A particularly apposite example is illustrated and discussed in the paper by Brian Holmes. 'Parental choice' is a cliche, bandied around by politicians and others as though it is a solution to the whole problem of maintaining democracy in our society. Unfortunately the superficial appeal of the concept hides important ramifications for the conduct of effective leadership in the educational system, and Brian Holmes has examined them with clarity and skill, finally advocating a closer relationship between the rhetoric and reality of education.

The final paper is an original, and tentative, examination by Dan Wicksteed of the role of the media in decision making about the primary school curriculum. He concludes with a question: have you, as a member of the profession, something to contribute to the media as well as something to gain from them? Perhaps this is the crucial question to ask after reading this book: is it time for the various sectors and interests in our educational system to bury differences, forget historical accidents, professional obstinacy and political expediency, and begin to learn from each other? If we could do that, we would probably experience the most important new direction of all.

# The Schools Council, the 'Professional Centre' Concept and the 'Teachers' Centre' Movement

*John Brand*
*Hipper Teachers' Centre, Chesterfield*

Accelerated change would now appear to be a key characteristic of contemporary society and its disturbing and frequently disorienting impact has already been well documented by Alvin Toffler.[1] It is perhaps symptomatic of this all too swiftly changing set of circumstances, as reflected in the current schizophrenic atmosphere which pervades the education community, that positive responses to the situation, such as the Schools Council, are now subject to complete closure, or doomed largely to unimplemented concept status, as in the case of 'Professional Centres' as envisaged by the James Committee, or simply left at the discretion of the politically pressurized and financially crippled LEAs, as is the situation with the 'Teachers' Centre' movement.

The 'teacher as researcher' movement, has largely developed during the last two decades, and it is certainly no coincidence that the Schools Council, the 'Professional Centre' concept and the 'Teachers' Centre' movement have emerged during the same period, as has the equally significant notion of 'process as content', in which Stenhouse suggests that 'the teacher be committed to inquiry in the process of his teaching, on the grounds that nothing he is offered by teachers of teachers should be accepted on faith.'[2] In essence, the emergence of the 'teacher as researcher' and the 'process as content' developments are clear evidence of a new thrust in educational leadership, which takes full account of the importance of the 'grassroots' teacher's contribution to curriculum enquiry and in-service strategies, both as a participant and as a leader. Furthermore, it strengthens recognition of the fact that situations are increasingly being allowed to determine and generate the varying types of leadership they require. Thus it is my purpose here to identify for the reader the ways in which the Schools Council, the Professional Centre concept and the 'Teachers' Centre' movement have contributed to the growth and significance of all these comparatively recent ideas and developments in the context of the shifting emphasis and pattern of educational leadership and policy within our state system.

*John Brand*

## The Schools Council

### *The Schools Council As a Leader*

The open flexible style of the Schools Council leadership was partly reflected in its established identity as a democratic non-government organization with an independent view of education and also by those who ran it, including democratically elected representatives of parents, teachers, heads, employers, unions, together with representatives from polytechnics, universities, further education, examination boards, churches, local education authorities and the Secretary of State. In essence, it was the nearest thing we ever had in this country to a national education forum.

Equally significantly, the Schools Council's express purpose, which was to help improve what was taught, how it was taught and to encourage a better and fairer system of examinations, when coupled with those who ran it, clearly influenced the evolution of this particularly flexible style of leadership. Therefore, it tended to employ or fund a few experts and mobilized the voluntary help of literally thousands of practising teachers. Inevitably this mode of functioning swiftly filtered through to all those involved and in particular to the teachers concerned, which encouraged the almost parallel growth of the concepts of 'the teacher as researcher' and 'process as content'. It is now clear that the style of leadership of the Schools Council as a body became increasingly consistent with its process, particularly in the latter years of its functioning. This dynamic state of affairs undoubtedly contributed momentum to another emerging concept, that of the 'professionally developed teacher'.

### *The Schools Council As an Influence on Leadership Styles*

Paradoxically enough, the committee structure of the Council was at the same time a weakness and a strength: weak in the sense that the committees were thought by the Trenamen enquiry to be overpopulated, and strong in that they did seek to be representative and democratic in their functioning. In any case the process of involving classroom teachers and headteachers in national level deliberations and decisions on matters of educational policy, strategy and provision, alongside their peers, partners and normally hierarchical superiors in the system, inevitably contributed to the development of a fresh, broad and in-depth understanding of our educational structure. Perhaps more significantly, it also enabled them to assimilate the appropriate types of experience to develop their confidence, ability and enthusiasm in the application of a whole new range of process-oriented, democratic leadership skills. As a direct consequence, 'grassroots' classroom practitioners were soon provided with multiplying opportunities to participate in the curriculum review and development process, nationally, regionally and locally on a much larger and more co-ordinated scale than ever before.

### *The Schools' Council Process*

Whenever the average teacher's topic of conversation focusses on the relative scarcity of educational resources for doing the job properly, the teacher's available time inevitably figures prominently. A further analysis of the ways in which this time could be allocated has to take into account such diverse factors as the ridiculously high and counter-productive pupil/teacher ratio which exists in many LEAs, contracting resources, rapidly disappearing classroom assistance of any kind, an expanding role, a dynamic curriculum and mounting accountability. Inevitably this produces a situation in which the average teacher can no longer find the time to keep abreast of the appropriate literature emerging from various sources, relating to developments at his/her own level of functioning or subject area, nor the wider developments in education and the social and political events which eventually have a profound influence on the functioning of the state education system and society in general. Evidently forms of support, guidance and leadership were clearly needed in order to assist the already overburdened public sector teaching force, in their endeavour to remain aware, positively motivated and responsive in an increasingly change-prone society. Here it was that the Schools Council set a particularly good leadership example, by fostering the development of a 'grassroots' style of involvement through its committee structure and project process.[3]

I suspect that the process and outcome aspect of the Schools Council projects will eventually be recognized as the most important contribution to the furthering of education in this country, for it was in this way that increasing numbers of practising teachers became involved in in-depth curriculum review group coordination and membership situations with their colleagues and partners in the field. This process also nurtured the expansion and enrichment of democratic and cooperative leadership tendencies. Such field leadership opportunities as participation in Schools Council committees, project monitoring and steering groups required that those concerned should undertake an extensive amount of reading, including appropriate HMI documents, draft project materials and relevant background books and articles. This in turn meant that those involved had to acquire new skills in the realm of 'speed reading' and as a direct consequence expanded their fund of knowledge, objectivity, confidence and professional grasp. Eventually they were in a position to view curriculum developments in prospect more objectively from the 'chalkface'. This in turn enabled the heads and teachers concerned to be in a position, alongside LEA advisory services, to alert their staffroom colleagues as well as those in other schools within their locality as to key issues and appropriate strategies. (The mediums they might have used for this purpose could have included school-focussed INSET and local teachers' centres among others.) More significantly, they constituted a practical manifestation of a fresh form of leadership by example. Thus these participants in the Schools Council committee structures, working parties and programmes of work, had demonstrated the vital 'leadership through group process role' that can and should be played and shared by teachers with their professional peers, alongside all their appropriate colleagues in the field, in the evolution of a curriculum which can meet the needs of a society beset by continual change.

### Schools Council — The Network Dimension

The term 'network' is probably one of the more practical, positive, and useful words to be added to the vocabulary of educational terminology in recent years. It is practical in the sense that it implies that partnership and communication between schools and other educational institutions should be the norm in this era of declining resources and increased social and political pressures; positive in that cooperation and shared responsibility are eminently desirable educational objectives; and useful in that the process of an effective network can spread positive and desirable trends and strategies thoroughly and economically.

The Schools Council by its very nature and composition was un-doubtedly the first effective, national educational 'network' to be established and in view of the democratic leadership influences which are an integral part of 'network' functioning, it will suit our purpose to take a brief look at the Schools Council 'network' and its legacy to the nation. Here it becomes apparent that a natural 'network' was immediately created by means of the Schools Council's interrelated committee and project functioning referred to earlier. However, the Council was perceptive enough to recognize the need for 'communication and coordination' agents at an early stage, and it was the Schools Council field officer team which was developed to carry out this ambitious function. Unfortunately, the complexity of the role and the sheer amount of work involved were never matched by the size of the field officer team. Even so the field officer concept was a sound one, in that those involved in the work forged new links in the chain of communication from the national level through to the regions and thence to the localities, fostering the idea of democratic involvement in curriculum review and shared responsibility leadership in the education process as they did so. This they partly achieved through their involvement with the Schools Council committee structure and, more significantly, through their increasingly active participation in and promotion of programmes of project work. Their widespread liaison at all levels in the field (LEAs, schools, teachers' centres, colleges of higher education) in connection with the identification of curriculum and teacher needs was fundamentally beneficial to all concerned.

The creation of the Schools Council largely corresponded with the evolution of the Teachers' Centre movement and certainly in the initial stages the Council was apt to regard teachers' centres as its local 'agents'. However, while this could be near the truth in some sense and cases, teachers' centres were never able to be solely committed to the promotion and support of Schools Council initiatives in quite the manner of the field officer team. This was simply because teachers' centres by their very nature have to be unbiased, being expected to respond equally enthusiastically to curriculum initiatives from a variety of sources. Even so, as the Schools Council network developed, it became noticeable that in some cases the working relationship between field officers and teachers' centre leaders had become increasingly productive. This was self-evident in the sense that the exchange of information and contacts concerning in-service leadership, proven and potential, and individual and group curriculum initiatives in the school situation had blossomed, albeit on a limited scale. HM Inspectorate has frequently gone on record recently as stressing the need for initial and in-service training to equip teachers to become agents of change. Clegg, for example, observes: 'As H.M.I. with a particular interest in the professional development of teachers, I believe we shall only see the implementation of a better school curriculum if we can attract and select good staff and encourage them to engage in in-service activities.'[4] However, there has been scant recognition at this level of the degree to which the network influence of the Schools Council, with its 'democratic leadership through process' outcome, has shifted the emphasis of both curriculum review and the initial and in-service training strategies in real terms.

In effect, 'democratic leadership through involvement in the education process' emphasizes that professional development is not something that can be done to anyone, but that essentially it requires the conscious participation of the individual concerned — in other words, it is not simply a 'top-down' exercise or a prescriptive event. Certainly Brown was shrewd enough to acknowledge this, through his recognition of the crucial relationship that exists between curriculum development and teacher development: 'Schools themselves either individually or in consortia must afford the conditions and the inducements for the continuous in-service development of their teachers, as the crucial component in the whole apparatus of maintaining a modern, professional service, and that curriculum development is inseparable from teacher-development. Furthermore, if favourable conditions are not built in to the workaday functions of the profession, then waste, frustration and inefficiency will proliferate.'[5]

Regardless of its shortcomings, the Schools Council always conducted its affairs in an open, friendly and non-hierarchical manner. It was always most accessible and responsive to criticism, whatever its source. Similarly, it was always prepared to bend a sympathetic ear towards ideas and suggestions relating to possible improvements to the education process and its climate. All of this not only constituted an admirable form of open democratic leadership in itself, but also created the climate and conditions to foster the emergence of grassroots forms of process-oriented leadership on a hitherto unprecedented scale.

### The Schools Council and Its Successor

The Schools Council was established to help to improve what is taught and how it is taught, and to encourage a better and fairer system of examinations. The evidence indicates that the Council's full impact as a leader and as an influence on the leadership process throughout the field of education will not be fully understood and appreciated until well after its most untimely demise in real terms. The sudden and unexpected decision by the government in 1982 to remove the Schools Council, although clearly consistent with current pressure for a move towards a centrally controlled curriculum, obviously runs counter to major trends in leadership involvement and the decision-taking process which have evolved during the last twenty years within the state education system, under the close scrutiny of successive administrations of contrasted political hues and the watchful eyes of HMIs and the DES.

The successor to the Schools Council should concern us here in view of its undoubted present and potential impact on existing educational networks, on the curriculum process and, by implication, on leadership trends. However, the situation is complex in that while the Schools Council was accountable to all its constituent member interests and, therefore, democratic in its purpose, with an independent view of education, its successor is essentially a nominated body, with the Secretary of State for Education and Science retaining the power of veto over membership and deciding what it will and will not do. It was not encouraging to learn that initially it was intended that there should be two separate bodies, with a clear indication that the examination element would be both bigger and better funded, while the curriculum body would follow a largely 'gap-filling' role, which seems more consistent with the notion that the closure of the Schools Council may have been originally intended as a cost-cutting exercise. None of this matches up with a sympathetic yet sensible understanding of the current needs of either the children or the teachers, or an appreciation of the intrinsic value and importance of the move towards an increasingly dynamic and democratic mode of functioning within the state education system, which has occurred during the past two decades. More significantly, it demonstrates quite graphically the comparative lack of awareness by the government of the day of the impact and influence which the Schools Council has had throughout the field of education as a leader, an influence and a source of initiative in the drive to stimulate 'chalkface' involvement in the leadership processes which are now associated with some in-service education and curriculum development endeavours.

How can a national curriculum body which is by definition politically controlled, prescriptive and constituted on a nomination basis hope to fill the not inconsiderable 'gaps' created by the removal of the Schools Council and what are the implications for the potential health and vitality of our public education system?

## The Professional Centre Concept

### The Theoretical Ideal

The James Committee report of 1972 attached more importance to third cycle in-service activity provision proposals than to anything else because, it was argued, 'they determine a great deal of the thinking which underlies the report as a whole.'[6] In the Committee's view, 'The third cycle comprehends the whole range of activities by which teachers can extend their personal education, develop their professional competence and improve their understanding of educational principles and techniques.' Here it can be argued were some key notions which subsequently contributed to theoretical discussion, relating to the evolution and expansion of such concepts as 'the teacher as researcher', 'process as content', and which in turn increased the momentum of 'chalkface' involvement in in-service and curriculum development leadership strategies.

The sheer scale of the James Committee's proposals, encompassing as they did the ambitious third cycle, together with an element of the largely school-based induction year of the second cycle proposals, was intended to depend on the creation of a 'country-wide network of centres'[7] in which case it was envisaged that existing professional institutions, including colleges and departments of education, further education colleges, teachers' centres and schools could assume the function of professional centres. As the report has it, 'They would become centres for expertise in learning and teaching and for curriculum development, would act as channels for interpreting the results of educational research and, in some cases, would conduct research themselves.'[8] Furthermore, 'it would be essential for all schools and further education colleges to have easy access to at least one professional centre.'

The third cycle professional centre proposals generated widespread and healthy debate. However, on reflection, reality has fallen far short of the theoretical model, because although university education departments, colleges of higher education and teachers' centres were in one sense or another already 'a forum for the exchange of ideas, information and experience between new and experienced teachers, teacher-trainers and

L.E.A. advisers',[9] money was never made available to cover the formidable costs involved in funding nationwide resourcing, staffing and secondment of teachers which full implementation would have necessitated.

As is too often the case, individual LEAs were left to contemplate the financial burden involved without any central funding assistance, and a swiftly deteriorating economic situation and increased political intervention in the education process did not help matters.

### The Practical Reality

Although the 'Professional Centre' as defined and envisaged in the James Report[10] has never really materialized, the ideas contained within the theoretical model clearly assisted the move towards more democratic and task-oriented forms of leadership and increased professional autonomy within the teaching profession, as was clearly reflected in the work of the Schools Council and teachers' centres.

The James Committee requested that 'the proposals should reflect and help to enhance the status and independence of the teaching profession.'[11] Consequently they argued that 'for too long the teaching profession has been denied a proper degree of responsibility for its own professional affairs'. They further expressed the hope 'that the implementation of this report would do much to encourage the profession to move forward to a new degree of independence and self-determination.'[12] Evidently no one at the time questioned the credibility of the James Committee's deliberations and certainly the pedigree of its membership was never questioned, although ironically enough it was Margaret Thatcher who as Secretary of State initiated the James Committee enquiry originally. Why then did 'Professional Centres' as defined by the James Committee Report never leave the drawing board stage?[13] There is no doubt that the implementation of the third cycle proposals in general and the 'Professional Centre' concept in particular, would have been expensive, particularly in a generally deteriorating economic climate. However, given the undoubted importance of education as a 'natural' resource and the likely high potential of yield in terms of improved motivation, involvement and general accountability of the teaching profession, it seems at least strange that such an opportunity to improve the quality of our public education system was passed up at the time and has been ignored ever since. Unless, of course, the distinct move towards democratic teacher involvement in their own professional development, as well as curriculum review leadership strategies at all levels, is now in the process of being reversed. Even more disturbing is the notion that such a strategy might be connected with the current lobby for a centrally determined curriculum operating in a much diminished public education system, as too often has been the case in the USA in recent years.[14]

## The Teachers' Centre Movement

*The Chameleon Tendency*

Teachers' centres are apt to respond to situations, needs and circumstances in much the same way that the chameleon invariably blends with a change of background. However, this particular 'chameleon' is indeed subtle in its colouring, in the sense that not all the 250 plus institutions[15] which are currently termed 'teachers' centres' can fully, or even in some cases marginally, justify the description. Therefore, it is my first concern here to attempt to lead the reader through some of the subtleties of organization and functioning which characterize teachers' centres, to enable a fuller appreciation of situations where the fresh and more progressive forms of educational leadership which are now in evidence are most likely to be encountered.

Arguably, by the very nature of its name, a 'teachers' centre' ought ideally to be largely an institution with a preponderance of democratic teacher participation in policy-making, decision-taking and general functioning. In reality the most practical and effective interpretations have to date constituted a balanced, non-authoritarian working partnership between LEA representatives and teachers in the locality. The situations where this combination works most effectively are those where the LEA concerned is shrewd, sensitive and imaginative enough to recognize the need to appoint a teachers' centre leader who could also operate as an area INSET coordinator, who not only possesses the appropriate flexible yet strong leadership qualities, but is also provided with scope to function effectively. The evidence would seem to suggest that only in such circumstances can policies of delegated leadership be pursued with confidence. Clearly it is extremely desirable to promote the delegation of leadership in a teachers' centre context, in relation to the needs satisfaction of its working groups, projects and courses. Nevertheless, it would seem unwise to apply such an approach, unless the centre concerned has the benefit of strong yet flexible leadership. Evidently there are implications for the LEA concerned, in terms of the quality, experience, relative autonomy and status it is prepared to invest in its teachers' centre leadership.

Certainly anyone would need to possess well-established feelings of personal security and self-confidence before they were able to manifest the assertive behaviour which in one form or another characterizes all types of leadership. Therefore, it is worth bearing in mind that the trend towards the encouragement of democratic and process-oriented forms of leadership in the evolution of INSET and curriculum review strategies has only developed comparatively recently. Even so there are still an encouraging number of areas where teachers have been able to experience in-depth exposure to shared leadership situations through involvement with forward-looking teachers' centres. Unfortunately, in many areas previous long-term exposure to conditioning from 'top-down' authoritarian leadership remains unaltered. This in itself has severely hindered the progress of our education system on a broad front, since the first era of 'payment by results' in the mid-nineteenth century. Furthermore, evidence of the approach of a second such era is now accumulating, alongside the trend towards a centrally controlled curriculum and a diminishing public sector school system. All of this constitutes a formidable and growing threat to the survival of the fledgling, democratic, shared leadership processes, which are intrinsic elements of the centre leader's professional role and vital features of any dynamic teachers' centre.

While variations in the role and status of the teachers' centre leader do have a fundamental effect on the nature and efficiency of delegated leadership in a centre, there are other relevant factors such as physical building provision, its location and staff allocation. Decisions on such crucial matters are currently left at the discretion of individual LEAs, as is the local status of the teachers' centre and the incidence of teachers' centres within a particular LEA. As a consequence, the spectrum of such INSET provision is wide and full of contrasts, ranging from very thorough and well-organized, to extremely inadequate to the point of non-existence. Such a state of affairs has serious national implications for the even distribution of positive developments in democratic leadership in its education context.

Our analysis would be incomplete without some consideration of the size, balance and geographical location of the teacher population within a centre's catchment area, and their combined effect on the 'ways of working' which the centre leader will be able to employ. Thus urban and rural teachers' centres are inclined to adapt to their very different local circumstances in a predictably individual fashion, in order to meet teacher and pupil needs. In this way they are apt to remind us again of that 'chameleon tendency' which is a key characteristic of any active teachers' centre.

### The Teachers' Centre Activity Process: A Key to New Leadership Trends

The atmosphere of a teachers' centre is frequently viewed as a key enabling aspect of its appeal and functioning. However, although the friendly welcome and the informal discussion over 'a cup of tea' are both notable elements in the 'mix', they are only 'outriders' to the quietly dynamic underlying flexible framework and process of the actual activity and resource service patterns. The cumulative impact of all these 'ingredients' on teacher group behaviour in general and its leadership in particular is only now being accorded the attention it merits. Nevertheless, the outcome constitutes a formidable foundation on which our attempts to interpret ongoing shifts in the identification, emergence and development of educational leadership in a growing range of contexts can be built.

The key to this spread of involvement in the leadership process in its teachers' centre context appears to depend on the existence of certain conditions. Among those which figure prominently are the teachers' belief in their own professional ability, standing and security; the absence of all forms of unnecessary authoritarian control; the availability of a reasonably well-resourced developmental pattern of democratically determined in-service and curriculum review within a locality.

Therefore, in talking about the growth and characteristics of this leadership tendency, we are touching upon a crucial dimension of teachers' professional development, which is reflected in Stenhouse's notion of 'process as content'[16] and the 'teacher as researcher' concept. Thus it seems likely that:

1  teachers need not consciously be pursuing an aim of personal professional development when their involvement with a teachers' centre commences;
2  their personal awareness as professionals appears to grow in direct relation to the extent of availability and nature of opportunities to participate in their own INSET and curriculum review processes;
3  teachers' ability not only to participate in their own in-service needs identification process, but also the degree to which they can articulate those needs, both tend to evolve as their professional development proceeds;
4  a sharpening perception of their own INSET outcomes can ensure that the flow and quality of constructive feedback improves as their professional development progresses;
5  the balance of involvement between school-initiated INSET and curriculum review endeavours and activities organized by their local teachers' centre becomes more subtle, interrelated and mutually beneficial;
6  teachers are more likely to contribute to the leadership in group situations where:
    a  they can feel in control of their own involvement and contribution;
    b  they can feel the support of their colleagues;
    c  the group is organized on democratic lines, where the climate is right for 'shared leadership' to emerge;
    d  teachers' centre activity patterns allow for developmental participation (gentle induction process, leading to increased motivation, voluntary participation, involvement and commitment);
7  teachers' ability to participate in the initiation of fresh self-help support group endeavours and other innovatory inter-school collaborative strategies develops as their own professional development reaches an advanced stage;
8  teachers' ability to view the education process with growing objec-

tivity increases with the depth and breadth of vision which personal professional development brings;

9 increased understanding and appreciation of the subtle benefits to be gained by 'tapping' local, regional and national networks, in support of their own as well as their group professional needs, reflect the alertness and mobility of thinking which are fundamental elements of the professional development process.

Thus different aspects of the professional development process combine to create the climate, conditions and events which enable more teachers than ever before to assume multiplying task and process-oriented leadership roles with confidence.

### Informal Networking: A Teachers' Centre Way of Life

The term 'networking' has been aptly interpreted as describing 'ways in which individuals link and develop'. My intention here will be to demonstrate some of the positive links which can be made between 'networking' and the current democratic trends in educational leadership, as they are reflected in the work of teachers' centres.

The term 'network' is capable of describing 'collaboration along a continuum from local informal individual links to a national strategy.'[17] This indicates the potential scope for individual teachers and, by implication, teachers' centres' involvement in and influence over the educational decision process at all levels.

'Networks' in a real sense have their own leadership function and therefore the members of a 'network' tend to share the decision-taking procedures; certainly 'networking is an active process with no place in it for a passive person or institution.'[18]

Another notion which is intrinsic to 'networking' is that of cooperative endeavour, to share problems and their solutions; it can be seen that this is the teachers' centre's fundamental way of working.

Looking at a network involving a teachers' centre and other in-service agencies from another perspective, the fact that representatives from other institutions are participating in a group alongside teachers who could well possess higher status than those teachers with a decision-taking role to match, demonstrates that they are setting aside their hierarchical status and, by implication, sharing the decision-taking process. Put in another way, 'Relationships within a network tend to reflect the quality of the contribution made by an individual rather than their formal status within the group.'[19] A sense of partnership is implicit in 'networks'; this underlines the fact that the concept of 'the professionally developed' teacher is not only gaining acceptance and respect, but also that its evolution can have profound implications for future trends in educational leadership, if the economic, social and educational climates are right.

## Notes

1 TOFFLER, A. (1970) *Future Shock*, Pan; (1980) *The Third Wave*, Pan.

2 STENHOUSE, L. (1979) 'Research as a basis for teaching', inaugural lecture, University of East Anglia.

3 Some good project examples include: 'Communication Skills in Early Childhood', 'Science 5–13', 'Geography for the Young School Leaver' and 'Breakthrough to Literacy'.

4 CLEGG, A. (1981) 'The Role of H.M. Inspectorate in In-Service Training', in *The Teacher and the School*, Open University set book published by Kogan Page.

5 BROWN, P. (1973) 'Developing the teacher with the curriculum', *Secondary Education*, Autumn.

6 JAMES COMMITTEE REPORT (1972) *Teacher Education and Training*, London, HMSO.

7 *Ibid.*

8 *Ibid.*

9 *Ibid.*

10 *Ibid.*

11 *Ibid.*

12 *Ibid.*

13 *Ibid.*

14 HOLT, M. (1981) *Evaluating the Evaluators*, London, Hodder and Stoughton.

15 WEINDLING, D. *et al.* (1983) *Teachers' Centres: A Focus for In-Service Education?* Schools Council Working Paper 74, Methuen, April.

16 STENHOUSE (1979), *op. cit.*

17 BERESFORD, C. and GODDARD, D. (1981) 'Networking: Some contexts and characteristics', in *Making INSET Work: Myth Or Reality?'* Faculty of Contemporary Studies, Bradford College.

18 *Ibid.*

19 *Ibid.*

# Pushing For Equality: The Influence of the Teachers' Unions and Other Pressure Groups*

*Paul Lodge*
*University College, Cardiff*
*Tessa Blackstone*
*Institute of Education, University of London*

This paper examines certain sources of external pressure on the politicians, civil servants and local authority administrators. We have divided these sources of pressure into two main categories, namely the teachers' organizations and the ad hoc pressure groups. To cover all of these in one paper would be an impossible task. For this reason we shall be highly selective in what we choose to examine. We shall look first at the NUT and its attitudes towards educational inequality. Our justification for this is that it is by far the largest and most influential of the teachers' unions, and it has immersed itself in policy questions beyond those of pay and working conditions far more than have the other unions, including its closest rival the National Association of Schoolmasters and Union of Women Teachers (NAS/UWT). We shall look then at the Campaign for the Advancement of State Education (CASE). Because it is the most general and most universal in its coverage, it is the most interesting of the pressure groups from our point of view, though admittedly it is in some respects atypical just because of this.

The main difficulty we have faced in examining the role of the NUT and CASE in promoting equality in education is deciding what constitutes valid evidence. In the case of the NUT we have concentrated on an analysis of the content of its publications during the 1960s and 1970s and on conference resolutions and any other public statements of its position. We have not tried to piece together the less public activities in which the Union may have been involved, such as planted parliamentary questions or private meetings with Ministers or DES officials. One of the problems in relying on content analysis of the kind we have undertaken is that it focuses on printed comment. Absence of comment may itself constitute evidence too; so may

* This is an edited extract from Paul Lodge and Tessa Blackstone (1982) *Educational Policy and Educational Inequality*, Oxford, Martin Robertson.

all kinds of behind-the-scenes activities. Sometimes evidence may conflict. For example, in the written evidence that the NUT sent to the Tenth Expenditure Committee[1] it suggested that it had a great deal of influence on policy-making. Yet in the oral evidence it gave to the same Committee it listed a number of examples of its lack of influence! As far as CASE was concerned, we were not able to rely as extensively on publications or even unpublished documents. While we were able to undertake a content analysis of its one regular publication, it was necessary to fill out the information thus provided with informal, unstructured interviews with members of the executive. Earlier documents had not been systematically filed and therefore provided a somewhat incomplete basis for reaching any conclusions.

In spite of the methodological difficulties just described, our view is that although there may be some disagreement about our interpretation in places, we have nevertheless sifted and presented enough evidence to be confident that our arguments are supported by the facts.

## The NUT

About half Britain's teachers belong to the NUT. The proportion of *unionized* teachers who belong to this particular teachers' union is, of course, higher. It draws its strength in particular from primary school teachers, most of whom are women, although the executive has tended to be dominated by male headteachers. At the secondary stage over the last twenty years it has lost some ground, in membership terms, to the NAS/UWT, which has substantially increased its members. However, in spite of the growing strength of the NAS/UWT and the growth in importance of the specialized associations such as the Secondary Heads' Association, few would deny the continuing predominance of the NUT. Yet there are a number of other teachers' associations, several of which have considerable strength. This lack of unity sometimes reduces the power of the NUT to influence policy. Indeed, the NUT, particularly under Sir Ronald Gould, a previous General Secretary, has favoured the creation of a single teachers' organization. Gould himself wrote in the early 1960s: 'If the administrative power in education which was once diffused is now being concentrated in the Minister, then the power of the teachers, which is at present diffused, should be concentrated too'.[2] But unity has not taken place, and the NUT's view that the teachers' potential influence is consequently dissipated still stands. However, the major disagreements between the teachers' organizations tend to focus on the handling and content of pay negotiations and conditions of service, not on questions of general educational policy. On such policy questions the NUT, largely because of its size, tends to have a near-monopoly when it comes to public statements. It is also rather more widely represented on various bodies directly or indirectly concerned with the making of educational policy than are the other associations. However, the DES consults them all on many questions of policy and consults, too, individual associations whose sectional interests may be at stake. Thus it certainly does not have an exclusive relationship with the NUT. In this sense the NUT might be accurately described as *primus inter pares* among the teachers' organizations.

It is difficult to trace the NUT's influence on educational policy. Ronald Manzer has described[3] the existence of an 'educational sub-government' in which the various parties, the DES, local authority associations and teachers' unions consult, bargain and negotiate until an educational consensus emerges. Much of this discussion takes place privately between officials. In certain circumstances, however, Manzer suggests:

> bargaining inside the education sub-government may break down and the participants have to appeal to the political system at large for a settlement. For educational pressure groups in England and Wales such an appeal is usually made with a 'public campaign'. The public campaign is an exceptional event in the politics of the education sub-government, however; and, in general, access to political as opposed to administrative arenas is definitely of secondary importance for all the groups in the sub-government.[4]

The methods that the NUT employs to influence policy are various. They include direct dealing with departmental officials, deputations to Ministers, planted parliamentary questions and membership of official working parties. At any one time it is likely to be represented on nearly a hundred bodies, including various unofficial groups as well as the more formal official ones. By this means it may exercise considerable influence on policy questions, sometimes obtrusively but, more often than not, in an unobtrusive way. It works through an extensive network of contacts, bringing pressure to bear on those with power or influence to get its views on a wide range of matters accepted. For example, there are a number of ex-teachers in the House of Commons, especially in the Labour Party. Moreover, the NUT actually sponsors several MPs. One instance of rare direct and visible NUT influence on educational developments is cited by Manzer. The publication in the early 1960s of a pamphlet entitled *Fair Play for Our Primary Schools* sparked off a parliamentary debate on the neglect of primary schools and probably contributed to the setting up of the Plowden Committee. For the most part, the process is less visible and, as a consequence, open to a variety of possible interpretations.

The degree to which the political arena is used may have grown somewhat in recent years, however. In the climate of rapid growth in educational expenditure which existed throughout the 1960s and the early 1970s there was less pressure on the teachers' unions to move out of the charmed circle of negotiations between the DES, the local authorities and themselves. Like Manzer, Coates argues:

> Their [the teachers' unions'] additional reliance on parliamentary pressure and the mobilization of public opinion are secondary forms of behaviour (in which not all participate to the same degree), whose purpose ultimately is to affect the terms of reference within which that consultation with the Department takes place.[5]

Since the mid-1970s, however, the almost automatic assumption of high growth that existed before has been challenged by the circumstances. The harsh combination of public expenditure constraints, a declining birth rate and some disenchantment with the importance of educational expansion to achieve economic growth or redistribution has meant that cosy discussions about how best to spend a growing budget are over. There are already signs that to defend what they have already, all the teachers' unions are resorting to a more public and political role. Moreover, a concentration on fighting to retain the *status quo* may well detract from attempts to redistribute. It may also be the case that the DES has somewhat changed its style. The Department now consults more widely through the publication of Green Papers and consultative documents of one kind or another. This widens the debate beyond the 'education industry', makes it more public and may also serve to push the unions into a more overtly political arena.

Another aspect of the NUT's political position is its relationships with the major political parties. Manzer argues:

> on the whole the relationship between the Union and the parties is deeply inhibited, reflecting the low temperature of educational politics, the disinclination of the Union to become involved in party politics and the irrelevance of party educational policy to the overwhelming amount of national educational policy[6]

In taking this point of view, he ignores the much closer connection the Union has with the Labour Party than with the Conservative Party and overstates the 'irrelevance' of party policy to national educational policy. Although it is true that there is some caution about identifying too closely with one or other political party (many of the union's ordinary members are Conservative voters), there is little doubt that most of the union's senior officials have an affinity with the Labour Party. Their contacts with Labour Members of Parliament, with members of the Labour Party's National Executive Committee's sub-committee on education and with Labour Ministers are likely to be closer and more extensive than those with their Tory equivalents. The Union's executive clearly draws its members from a range of political opinion. Two of its more prominent members over the last two decades have been members of the Communist Party, and there have been Conservative as well as Labour presidents. However, in general it is fair to say that the Union's political position has been to the left of centre rather than to the right, in terms of both its leadership and the policies it espouses.

This has implications for the stance that it is likely to take upon most questions of educational equality. The union is likely to attach some importance to achieving greater equality in general and, more specifically, greater equality through education. The Labour Party is committed to change in order to bring this about, while the Conservative Party on the whole is not, and Labour policies on education have been more in line with NUT policies than have Conservative educational policies. The Union has tried to influence the policies of both parties in government in order to create more equality. Its advocacy of certain policies may, however, have less to do with its commitment to such an ideal and more to do with self-interest. Cynics might argue that any espousal of greater equality has as much to do with trying to expand the system to create more jobs and more opportunities for promotion for teachers as with trying to improve the opportunities of certain groups of children. The real test comes, perhaps, when self-interest and moves designed to create greater equality conflict with each other. There are special tensions which are peculiar to 'professional' unions. On the one hand, they wish to represent the interests of their members with respect to pay, job opportunities and working conditions; on the other, they wish to be a responsible and influential force in the pursuit of wider aims concerning professional standards which they perceive to be in the national interest.

The rest of this section will examine the view that the NUT has taken of some of the relevant policy areas, namely, nursery education, positive discrimination, the abolition of selective schools and the raising of the school-leaving age. In so doing, it will from time to time touch on the professional/union conflict.

The union has long espoused the case for education for children under 5. Since the early 1960s it has produced several documents on the need to expand nursery schools and classes. The first of these involved a survey of maintained nursery education, carried out in 1962. It found that all the nursery schools in the sample, and most of the nursery classes, had long waiting lists. More than half of the schools had more names on their waiting lists than pupils in their schools. In the period leading up to the creation of the Plowden Committee, the Union was the first organization to emphasize the large gap between demand for, and supply of, nursery places and to stress the need to close the gap. In its own evidence to Plowden it recommended that nursery education should be available at the age of 3 and that 'there should be a statutory obligation on the local authority to provide facilities on the scale necessary to meet the full demand for such education in its area'. It explained the need for nursery education partly in terms of 'waste of ability' and 'differences of opportunity between one area and another', commenting particularly on the importance of the child's linguistic environment: 'Of all the cultural inequalities that widen the differences between child and child, it is the richness or poverty of its early linguistic development which demands most attention.' It went on to say that 'an adequate nursery-school system and the provision of infant school education from the age of 5 are both indicated if there is to be equal educational opportunity for all our children.'[7]

The emphasis was thus clearly on nursery education as an equalizer. There was no direct reference to its developmental role in early childhood outside the context of the elimination of inequality or deprivation. Although the references to cultural and linguistic disadvantage now seem crude and simplistic, they reflected the conventional wisdom of the time. Reference was made to work done in other countries, notably the USA, 'with its negro problem', and Israel, 'with its problem of the oriental Jewish immigrant'. There was also reference to high levels of provision in France, in spite of a later start to compulsory schooling there. The union's evidence rightly pointed to a third of 3-year-olds and two-thirds of 4-year-olds at school in France in the early 1960s. In an attempt, presumably, to draw the Plowden Committee's attention to the importance of employing fully trained teachers with this age group, it wrongly stated that French teachers in nursery schools had the same training as those in elementary schools, preference being given to those who had taken a special section concerned with very young children. In fact, although this was true of some French nursery teachers, many did not have the same training as primary teachers. Instead they took a more practical course with lower entry requirements and, probably, lower status.

The evidence also referred to the need to help parents of deprived children because of the strong link between early nurture and later ability to benefit from schooling. Interestingly, however, the document did not advocate bringing parents into the nursery schools but suggests instead the expansion of services available to mothers through child welfare clinics and education for parenthood in the secondary school curriculum. This may simply have reflected the view that intervention should take place only before the child starts school, or indeed before the child is even thought about. It may also have reflected the union's wariness of proposing that parents should be brought into the schools on a large scale. It did, however, suggest that informal contacts between parents and teachers were important elsewhere in the report. It backed Parent-Teacher Associations but sounded a note of caution about their development replacing these informal contacts.

The document concluded by stating: 'we have emphasized but not, we think, over-emphasized the social role of the primary school as the great provider of equal opportunity for all our children.' To achieve this, it argued that it was essential that children should enjoy 'the benefits that highly skilled and therefore highly trained teachers can confer'. It went on to warn against any possible departure from this desideration for purely economic considerations.

To some extent, the Plowden Committee made just such a departure. It recommended a major expansion of nursery education along the lines proposed in the NUT's evidence, so that eventually it would be available for all children whose parents wanted it. However, the expansion was to be staffed in part by nursery assistants rather than entirely by fully qualified teachers. There would be a minimum of one teacher per two nursery classes, and the nursery assistants would work under her supervision and guidance. In its public response to Plowden, in a document in which it commented on the major issues of the report, the union said nothing about this recommendation. Indeed, its comments on the nursery education proposals were confined to three sentences. However, in its private negotiations with the Labour Government at the time the latter was considering the Plowden Report's recommendations, it strongly opposed the proposal to staff the expansion partly with nursery assistants. In a relatively recent series of lectures on aspects of government, Shirley Williams castigated the NUT for doing so.[8] She had been a Minister of State at the DES at the time and argued that the union's opposition prevented the Government from expanding nursery education at a time when there were still serious problems with teacher supply in primary schools, as well as constraints on public expenditure, making the cheaper nursery assistants doubly attractive. She put this forward as an example of the undesirability of excessive secrecy in British government. Had the union's opposition been made public, there would, she implied, have been a public outcry, which would have greatly strengthened the Government's hand in innovating in a way which the union opposed. Alternatively, the union might have been more constrained to avoid the embarrassment of public criticism. How far this was true is, of course, a matter for speculation. It is, however, hard to escape the conclusion that in this case the union's legitimate concern with the interest of the teaching profession was in some conflict with its desire to expand nursery education in order to equalize opportunity for all children. The case that no expansion was better than some expansion partly staffed by nursery assistants was and is hard to sustain. However, it can perhaps be understood in terms of a dilution of the quality of the professionals working with young children at the time when emphasis was being placed on imposing higher standards through, for example, longer and more demanding training.

The union persisted in its opposition to the employment of nursery assistants in the 1970s. In a comment on a DES Draft Administrative Memorandum on their employment, it stated that its attitude was governed 'by its long-standing policy that all teachers in primary and secondary schools, including nursery schools, should be qualified teachers.'[9] It went on to say:

> in welcoming the expansion of nursery education, [the union] was concerned that such expansion should not result in an increase in the number of unqualified persons employed as teachers in nursery schools and classes. Indeed this is one of the reasons why the union object so strongly to the proposal of the Secretary of State to cut down the number of places in colleges of education.[10]

It also continued to advocate nursery education expansion in order to alleviate inequality throughout the decade. It issued four different pamphlets. The first was a survey of nursery education in Wales.[11] The Welsh report stressed the importance of giving priority to areas of social need. Consistent with the Welsh tradition of an early start to primary education, it recommended provision from the age of 2. This was followed by another pamphlet on pre-school provision in England and Wales.[12] The pamphlet was marked by its attack on playgroups. By this time the playgroup movement had become an established form of provision rather than just a stop-gap, which was how it had been perceived in the 1960s. Moreover, it had a number of powerful advocates. Bridget Plowden had retracted from the commitment of her Report to nursery classes on the grounds that the participation of parents was crucial and that this could be more easily achieved in playgroups. A.H. Halsey, whose action research studies in educational priority areas had examined the work of playgroups,[13] was also giving them his support partly because of teacher opposition to parental help in schools. The NUT appears to have been willing to accept them as long as they were seen as a temporary expedient. As soon as they become more than this, it took a different view.

In a 1977 publication, *The Needs of the Under Fives*, the union again criticized playgroups, although perhaps a little less forcibly than before. It argued:

> Playgroups are not educational establishments, and as voluntary organizations rely predominantly on fees charged and occasional grants from local authorities, nor can they always draw on the advisory help of local education departments. Playgroups are not established on the basis of nationally agreed criteria, nor do they all belong to the Pre-School Playgroups Association. This results in an haphazard distribution and great differences in the quality of the service and accommodation provided. The Union is concerned that little attempt has been made by either central or local government to monitor the standards and quality of playgroup provision.[14]

It went on to say:

> The Union recognizes that the expansion of nursery education in the context of priorities for deprived areas means that there will continue to be a role for playgroups, particularly in more favoured areas, as an interim measure, while nursery education is being expanded. Nevertheless, we consider that there is a very real risk that any allocation of resources to playgroups would be prejudicial to the interests of nursery education and so to the children themselves.[15]

As far as the NUT was concerned, playgroups were second-best, stop-gap measures. This was partly because of a genuine belief that standards are higher where professionally trained staff are employed and partly, no doubt, to protect the role and status of nursery teachers.

Not only did the NUT oppose the expansion of nursery education using nursery assistants rather than teachers, but it also criticized the 1971 White Paper's proposals to expand provision by attaching nursery classes to primary schools.[16] It also criticizes the White Paper for failing to allocate sufficient financial resources to nursery education, claiming that it would cost more than anticipated. Whether the union was correct about this or not, in general such criticism may well be counter-productive when governments are under severe public expenditure constraints, since it may serve to discourage them from expanding at all rather than encourage them to provide further funds. The union then argued: 'we strongly disagree with the almost total exclusion of nursery schools from the proposed provision.' It admitted the advantage of nursery classes, particularly that of greater continuity, then went on to claim that nursery schools had many advantages too. However, the only one it cited was that nursery classes were likely to be accommodated in mobile classrooms or in inadequately converted infant classes. Any objective observer would regard this as a somewhat weak claim for nursery schools. In fact, the real reason for the NUT preference for nursery schools was its belief that they provided better promotion prospects for nursery teachers. Although it did not reveal this in the 1974 document, it made the point quite clearly in *The Needs of the Under-Fives*:

> The Union believes that authorities should seek to ensure that nursery teachers have an opportunity to obtain promotion without necessarily having to apply outside of the nursery sector. This requires a restoration in the balance in the programme so that the number of places in nursery schools and nursery classes is nearly equal.[17]

Since nursery schools are considerably more expensive than nursery classes, their development might well have slowed up the expansion of the number of available places. This is another example of a conflict in the union between its goal to promote opportunities for its members and its genuine desire to obtain more nursery provision, especially for the disadvantaged child.

One further example of this concerns its views on parental participation, which have already been touched on. In the 1974 document it argued:

> Teachers welcome parental support and are prepared to put their training and experience at the disposal of parents. Nevertheless, we see dangers in that it may be assumed that such community of interest confers an unqualified right upon parents to intervene in the educational function of the school as and when they see fit ... teachers are responsible for the welfare of all children and have to hold a balance between the needs of the individual and the

community, in a way parents do not normally have to bear in mind. The Union therefore believes that the Department of Education and Science and the local education authorities should give proper emphasis to this responsibility, and that they should institute further consultation on this matter with the teachers through their professional associations.[18]

Its attitude to parental participation was thus somewhat grudging. By 1977, however, its attitude seemed to have softened, although it is not clear why. In a section on home-school relations it endorsed parent education, suggesting guidance 'in techniques directed at the development of cognitive and perceptional skills'. The union also claimed: 'it is vitally important that all parents are conversant with techniques in child development and can make assessments of the child's progress.' It also reported, with apparent approval, the Red House project in the West Riding action research study[19] where parents worked with small groups of children in the nursery school and accompanied them on neighbourhood visits. However, the union also warned that 'a lack of professional expertise among these adults can cause more problems than are solved', although it did not elaborate on how this happens.

The union has backed nursery education for many years, however. While in its 1977 statement it advocated expansion to meet the developmental needs of all children, it has consistently advocated priority for the disadvantaged child in the interests of equality and has castigated the DES for failing to provide the resources for this. In its response to the DES 1977 Green Paper it disputed the DES claim that there had been a big expansion in nursery education, rightly stating that it had been limited and uneven and advocating 'further substantial investment in this sector of education'.[20]

One of the more radical policies put forward over the last twenty years has been that of positive discrimination in education. The concept was first propounded by the Plowden Committee. The Committee had been influenced by the Poverty Program in the USA, which was trying to channel resources in the direction of the deprived or disadvantaged by a variety of different means. Under this influence, Plowden coined the term 'positive discrimination' and recommended that an attempt should be made to reverse the disadvantages suffered by various groups by discriminating in their favour in certain ways rather than against them, as normally happened. The development of positive discrimination is described in greater detail elsewhere. It suffices to say here that it involved providing extra resources for certain schools (in the first instance, mainly primary but, later, secondary as well), mainly in the poorer areas of large cities. The policy was thus based to a large extent on a geographical theory of poverty, which emphasized the concentration of low incomes, low skills, poor housing, poor amenities and low educational standards in the inner city. The educational remedy centred on the idea of educational priority areas. Such areas would benefit from extra money for school building, and certain schools within these areas would be designated as schools with special needs operating in circumstances that became known in some LEAs as conditions of 'exceptional difficulty'. These schools would be given extra resources, including staff, and their teachers paid a special allowance. The main aim of the social priority allowance was to encourage teachers to remain in such schools and thus reduce the high teacher turnover which characterized these schools at the time. Lastly, the nursery education expansion programme was to give priority to areas with special needs.

In its published response to the Plowden proposals the NUT welcomed the principle of positive discrimination, stating 'this has always been a feature of our educational system as applied to children with physical and mental handicaps, and we fully support its extension to those children whose deprivation is of a social, emotional and linguistic nature.'[21] The union also accepted that priority areas should have primary school classes reduced to thirty or below before other areas, though it emphasized the need to make the reduction universal. The union made surprisingly few other comments in this document on positive discrimination and priority areas. However, on the related subject of the integration of the school with the local community, to which Plowden attached particular importance in priority areas it took a more protective union stance as far as the teaching profession was concerned. Although accepting the need for close school-community links, the union stated: 'we believe that it could be unreasonable to base proposals of this kind, which might make inroads into the teacher's private life in excess of that required from other members of the community, on the assumption that they would be universally adopted.'[22] At the time it was also both complacent and half-hearted about the community use of school buildings. It argued that this was already 'not uncommon', and went on: 'many teachers have accepted the inconveniences arising from the dual use of buildings. We suggest, however, that the analogy of maximum utilization of industrial plant cannot be applied to a living community like a school. . . .'[23]

The Plowden proposal for teachers' aides to help out teachers in the classroom was regarded with unequivocal hostility by the NUT. Again this was a reflection of the union's belief that teachers are the only adults suitable to work in the classroom with children and its wish to avoid a possible loss of status for teachers which might result from an inadequate definition of the boundaries between the roles of teachers and aides. However, opposition of this kind seems likely to have reduced the chance of increasing the manpower resources available to work in disadvantaged schools at that period, so it could be argued that the NUT's line did a disservice to those children it claimed it wished to see helped. In its anxiety to preserve the teacher as the only trained person working with children in the classroom, the union also opposed Plowden's proposals for the extension of training opportunities for aides. Instead it preferred on-the-job training in areas such as first aid and the maintenance of equipment for ancillaries. Since adults working in primary schools are bound to have a fair amount of direct contact with pupils, even if they never play formal pedagogic or instructional roles, the case for their understanding of children and their needs is a strong one. The NUT can therefore again be accused of failing to act in the best interests of pupils.

The recommendation to pay teachers in priority areas an extra allowance posed problems for the NUT. In its published response to Plowden it made no reference to this proposal, possibly because of divisions which existed within the union. One view held by some officials of the union was that it would have been better to allocate the extra funds to the schools rather than to teachers' salaries. Banting suggests:

> even before negotiations began, the representatives of both the teachers and the local authorities indicated coolness towards it. The NUT, however, was the major stumbling block. During the 1960s the union's primary goal was a much higher basic salary scale and it was not happy about the endless variety of special supplements that were regularly proposed. They felt that such differentials created troublesome distinctions between teachers and drained away resources from a higher basic scale.[24]

On the one hand, the proposal meant higher pay for teachers and, if the policy worked, more and better teachers in areas of need and lower teacher turnover there. On the other hand, it meant more pay for only a minority of teachers. Hence the measure was seen as potentially divisive within the profession and, possibly, as unpopular with the majority of the union's members who would not benefit from it. Moreover, difficulties about defining and identifying schools in priority areas would probably have meant rough justice for some teachers doing demanding jobs in poor areas in schools which just missed qualifying for extra help. In the event, the union's initial resistance to this recommendation declined, and it accepted a modified version of the Plowden proposal. However, when the 1974 Labour Government wished to replace it with the Social Priority Allowance for teachers, the union was again opposed on principle. It argued that it was educationally unsound to channel extra resources to deprived areas by this method.

Racial minorities in Britain are not only at a disadvantage because their members are concentrated in the lower socio-economic groups; they are also at a disadvantage because they suffer from discrimination. Another form of positive discrimination has been the use of legislation to provide extra resources for schools with high proportions of immigrant children. Under Section 11 of the 1966 Local Government Act, local authorities are able to claim 75 per cent of the cost of the staff who are employed to make special provision for 'immigrants from the Commonwealth whose language or customs differ from those of the indigenous community'. Any local authority is eligible to make this claim if 2 per cent or more of its school population are the children of Commonwealth immigrants. In July 1978 the NUT issued a report which was critical of the operation of this legislation.[25] Its criticisms were based on a survey of local authorities, which revealed that the amount of grant claimed varied enormously between authorities and that it bore little relationship to the number of immigrants within their boundaries. It also showed that staff employed under Section 11 were frequently not being used to carry out specific tasks to help minority group children. Indeed, some headteachers did not even know that they had Section 11 staff.

The union put forward a number of positive proposals to improve both the Act and its implementation. These included abolishing certain limitations (such as those that restricted the application of the Act to people from the Commonwealth and those resident in the country for less than ten years) to take in all minority groups and some constructive suggestions on how much extra staff might be used. Among them were recommendations to use liaison officers between the community and the schools, to create education visitors to visit homes and to provide more resources for the teaching of English. It could be argued that in backing amendments to Section 11 and more effective use of the legislation, the union was in the enviable position of being able to support change which would benefit disadvantaged children and would also provide staff in schools 'extra to establishment' and thus benefit the teaching profession. In this case there was no conflict of interests. However, some of the NUT's proposals for use of Section 11 staff were unlikely to have a direct impact on reducing the burdens of the classroom teacher. It would therefore be unduly cynical, and rather unfair, to argue that this was the union's main goal with respect to Section 11.

A further report was produced the following year[26] in response to a Home Office Consultative Document on replacing Section 11 of the 1966 Local Government Act. This welcomed some of the Home Office's new proposals and reasserted the NUT's view that ethnic minorities must be given high priority in educational programmes within a wider strategy to deal with racial disadvantage. The second report confirms the view that the NUT has played a positive role in trying to improve educational opportunities for ethnic minorities.

There is further confirmation of its consistently concerned record in this area in two other publications. *All our Children*, published in 1978, summarized the way in which the union believes schools can contribute to a tolerant multi-racial society. In its conclusion it recommended that all teachers should 'champion the cause of social justice for all students in their classes, schools and communities'. It also suggested that the schools could and should be seen as agents of racial harmony. In this context it backed a curriculum that recognized cultural diversity in schools. One practical outcome of this was a Schools Council project on need and innovation in multi-racial education, which the NUT proposed along with the National Foundation for Educational Research and the National Association for Multi-Racial Education. There was, however, a touch of complacency about the document's definition of the role of the school when the NUT quoted from its own evidence to the 1973 Select Committee on Race Relations: 'our educational system [is] non-discriminatory in intention and in fact.' The union went on to explain the fact that children separate into different minority groups as they get older and become more ethnically aware, or indeed intolerant, in reaction to pressures in the wider society. Such pressures are undeniable but do not mean that the educational system has nothing to answer for with respect to discrimination against minority groups. There was, in fact, no reference in this document to the need for positive discrimination towards minority group children. The DES argued at the time that general policies towards the disadvantaged would benefit black and brown children. The Department tended to down-play the extra dimension to the social and economic disadvantages from which these groups often suffer. Possibly to avoid stigmatization, it argued that policies should be geared not specifically towards minorities but towards the disadvantaged generally.[27] While the NUT did not actually say this, its omission of any reference to positive discrimination for ethnic minorities could mean that it accepted the DES line. However, it is perhaps dangerous to interpret lack of explicit comment as acquiescence. All the indications, including its strong stance on Section 11, are that the NUT has favoured positive discrimination for ethnic minorities.

One way in which the DES decided to tackle disadvantage was to found the Centre for Information and Advice on Educational Disadvantage. This was set up in 1975 as an independent body to promote good practice. The union gave the new centre strong backing in *All our Children*. However, it did not say anything in this pamphlet about its potential role with the disadvantaged among ethnic minorities. When the new Conservative Government took office in 1979 it embarked on an attempt to reduce greatly the number of QUANGOs. Although it was not especially successful and the great majority of QUANGOs remained intact, the Centre for Educational Disadvantage was one of the victims. The NUT roundly condemned the Government for its decision to close the Centre. Max Morris, an ex-president of the union and vice-chairman of the Centre claimed that its valuable work on ethnic minorities and the 20 per cent of the school population who get no qualifications would be wiped out.[28]

The second document which demonstrates the NUT's commitment to minority groups is *Race Education and Intelligence: A Teacher's Guide to the Facts and the Issues,* also published in 1978. This pamphlet was commissioned by the NUT from biologists and psychologists at the Open University, including Steven Rose, a well-known critic of Jensen's and Eysenck's theories about racial differences and levels of intelligence. The pamphlet set out clearly for practising teachers the arguments against assuming any biological basis for differences that may occur. How much influence a document of this kind has is, of course, impossible to assess.

The third area of policy in which we wish to examine the NUT's position over the last fifteen years or so is the abolition of selective schools. It is a policy that the NUT has forcefully advocated since the mid-1960s. Prior to this there is not much evidence of extensive NUT initiative to promote this cause. The reason for this is unclear. It perhaps reflects a tendency by the union to support certain changes when they become part of the political agenda rather than to fight for their inclusion on the agenda in the first place.

It was not until the election of a Labour Government in 1964 that the union apparently considered it worth devoting much time to the advocacy of comprehensive schools. In that year it published *The Reorganisation of Secondary Education*. This seems to have been designed as much to demand that certain conditions, such as adequate accommodation, should be fulfilled in the reorganization schemes as to make the case for reorganization. It was no doubt issued in an attempt to influence a new Labour Government not to proceed too fast *if* that meant that schemes would not be backed by extra resources and teachers would not be extensively consulted about the planned changes. The same year the NUT submitted its evidence to Plowden. In a long section on the transition from primary to secondary education it made its case for comprehensive schools. This case was not based on the socially divisive effects of failing to provide a common schooling for all at the secondary stage; it was based instead on the harsh effects of selection and failure on individual children and on the distorting effects of the 11 plus examination on the primary school curriculum. The emphasis was on psychological and educational matters rather than on the broader social and political implications of different forms of schooling, and the document listed

> the unreliability of the final results, the strain on the child, the tendency for the success of the school and its teachers to be judged by the number of children who gained places in selective schools, the inequalities resulting from coaching and homework and the effect on those children who failed the examination, and who suffered a loss of confidence and acquired a feeling of resentment as a result.[29]

The document argued that even where the methods of selection had been chosen with great care in the interests of maximizing fairness and reliability, many of the undesirable effects of selection remained. It recommended a system in which the primary school assessed the child and made a recommendation but considered that even this would not 'abolish completely the strain on children and parents'. Reference was also made, however, to the fact that secondary schools vary in the provision of amenities, standards of staffing and equipment, as well as in function: 'Such a position can be defended only on the assumptions either that some children do not need or deserve as good an educational opportunity as others, or that the nation cannot afford to find the money or the manpower to equalize opportunity.'[30] Both of these assumptions, it was implied, should be rejected.

A careful reading of the NUT's evidence to Plowden leaves little doubt that the union was in favour of the abolition of selection at the time. However, its view was often expressed in an oddly muted way. Whether this reduced the impact of what it said is hard to say. One example of its reticence and caution is as follows. The Plowden Committee had asked in its list of questions for those giving evidence whether selective education was desirable. In its reply the NUT said, 'In some ways we regret that we are called upon to answer the question at this particular time.' Because some authorities had already begun reorganizing 'in a very hasty and ill-considered way', decisions about this question were in some ways too late, it argued. At the same time, in some ways they were too early, it claimed. It was hoped that effects of Plowden's recommendations, including demonstration of the potential of all children, would help in the battle to persuade parents and teachers of the effect of environment upon the educational development of children (a surprising admission). This needed more time. In the light of all the evidence on this subject already available at that time, this is a strange statement. However, perhaps the findings of research had not yet percolated through to many teachers.

Although there is no doubt about where the union stood on this issue — it was in favour of comprehensive schools — its advocacy of the abolition of selection was certainly cautious and pragmatic rather than uncompromising and idealistic, perhaps because it was anxious to ensure that the reform would work. Its advocacy of change was hedged about with preconditions, notably those concerning buildings. Much emphasis was placed on the need for purpose-built accommodation. Constraints on new building were accepted as a reason why the tripartite system should continue in some areas. There are two possible interpretations of why the NUT placed so much emphasis on school buildings. The first is that it was anxious that comprehensive schools should succeed and therefore insisted that, for example, schemes which put together two schools on different sites should be avoided. There was not, however, much evidence to support the importance that it attached to buildings. The second interpretation was that it was primarily concerned with the job opportunities and working conditions of teachers and was anxious to protect these even at the risk of slowing down the development of comprehensive schooling. There were certainly fears that the senior posts in comprehensive schools would all go to ex-grammar school teachers and that ex-secondary modern teachers would suffer accordingly. After the publication of Circular 10/65, which invited local authorities to submit plans for the reorganization of secondary education, the NUT's house journal, the *Teacher*, came out in support of the Circular.[31] However, the editorial also criticized the Government for failing to provide extra money, which it claimed could delay the exercise by up to thirty years. It also indicated concern that reorganization would be at the expense of primary education, stating, 'the inequalities that the present tripartite system tends to encourage find their first beginnings in the primary school.' As many of the union's members were primary school teachers it was presumably politic to say this. However, if the Government had acted upon the criticism, there would have been even fewer resources for comprehensive schools and therefore, on the NUT's own argument, an even greater delay in establishing the new system.

By the end of the 1960s the NUT had adopted a tone of greater urgency about the implementation of secondary reorganization. Possibly fearing the return of a Conservative Government, which might have stopped further progress towards comprehensive schools, it began to demand legislation to enforce reorganization on local authorities. At the 1969 Conference it passed a resolution calling on the Government to provide the necessary money and to legislate in order to bring about comprehensive education. From then on practically every annual conference of the NUT has passed a resolution on comprehensive schools. During the 1970s there were only three years when such a resolution was not passed, and the topic was the subject of resolutions more often than any other. This perhaps indicates better than anything else the degree to which, by then, the NUT attached importance to the issue in spite of a somewhat cautious position earlier. Moreover, many of the Conference resolutions were phrased in terms of a belief that the comprehensive principle is the only basis for providing equal opportunity for all children. And by 1977 the demand was for 'an immediate end to all forms of selection'. Two years later Conference instructed the executive to encourage the membership to refuse cooperation in selection procedures. By the end of the 1970s, then, the union was taking a fairly militant position about selection.

Several possible reasons can be postulated to explain this change. First, the political climate was marked by a sharpening of the debate. With each change of Government there was an immediate attempt to change the policies of the previous Government. The NUT was drawn into this debate and could not easily sit on the fence. Second, there was probably a change in the general attitudes of the NUT's membership: teachers trained in the 1960s were exposed to educational research which demonstrated that social as well as academic selection was taking place. Third, dissatisfaction over the fairness and reliability of selection methods had probably grown.

Beside Conference resolutions, there are three documents, published between 1969 and 1979, which reveal a certain amount about the NUT's position on reorganization. One of the ambitions of Edward Short, who was Secretary of State for Education during the latter part of the 1966–70 Labour Government, was to produce a new Education Act to replace the 1944 Act. His hopes were not fulfilled. However, he did prompt others to think about what a new Act should contain. Among them was the NUT, which produced a document entitled *Into the Seventies*, in which it put forward its ideas. In the introduction it made clear its views about the essentially regressive nature of educational expenditure. The more privileged the pupil, the more money is spent on him. Second, it identified wastage.

> The outstanding characteristic of the system is its profligate waste of ability. There is waste of ability before the child enters school, waste at 11+, waste at school leaving age ... The present distribution of educational resources still very often means that the 'haves' receive positive discrimination in their favour, while the 'have nots' lose even the little that might be theirs.[32]

It went on to propose that the new Act should legislate for comprehensive education over the whole of the compulsory age range. It defined comprehensive education not just as a non-selective system but also as a system in which each school has a representative cross-section of the full ability range, and it admitted that legislation might not be enough to secure this. It recognized that it might also be necessary to limit parents' choice of school. Since most parents have never been able to exercise such a choice, it did not consider this restriction unacceptable. It also argued that the advantages of comprehensive schools far outweighed the disadvantage of some limitation of choice.

The second of the documents mentioned above addressed itself specifically to attacking the Conservative Government's slowing down of the process of going comprehensive in the early 1970s. In a pamphlet provocatively entitled *What is Mrs Thatcher up to?* it launched a personalized attack on the Secretary of State for Education. It was more 'political' than any previous statement on this subject published by the union. One of the devices it used was to quote from Conservatives who had either made speeches or written articles in support of comprehensive schooling. Lord Boyle, a former Conservative Minister of Education was frequently quoted. There were also quotations from Edward Heath and Rhodes Boyson, at that time a comprehensive school head and since a Junior Minister at the DES. The introduction noted that in successive deputations to Mrs Thatcher when she was at the Department of Education the Union had failed to persuade her to change her policy. She was damned with faint praise for having proceeded with the raising of the school leaving age and the allocation of extra money for building primary schools but scornfully reproved for 'the outdated nature of her attitude and the harmful effect of certain of her decisions' on secondary education. She was tellingly contrasted with Lord Boyle, who was described as having shown 'a deep awareness of the way in which the organization of secondary education had to be reformed'.

The fact that many Conservative as well as Labour councils had rejected selection in favour of comprehensive schools was emphasized, and reference was made to the fact that in Margaret Thatcher's own constituency of Finchley a referendum of parents produced a four-to-one majority in favour of ending selection. The fact that 1,000 comprehensive schools had been approved by the DES during Thatcher's term was attributed to the fact that she was unable to find any good reason for turning down LEA plans to establish them. The accusation was made that she used delaying tactics, that in some cases she gave only partial approval, thus leaving some authorities with a messy mixture of grammar and comprehensive schools and that she had no clear criteria or guiding principles for her decisions. The fact that grammar schools could not exist alongside comprehensive schools without the latter being no more than 'misnamed secondary schools' was stressed, with a quote from Rhodes Boyson saying just that.

*What is Mrs Thatcher up to?* is an example of political pamphleteering at its best. It is cleverly conceived, punchy and persuasive. If Mrs Thatcher were the kind of politician who could be embarrassed by attacks of this kind, it might have succeeded in making her feel uncomfortable. The third of the 1970s NUT pamphlets, entitled *Education in Schools*, which touched on secondary reorganization is in a quite different style, perhaps because it was published in a different political context. It listed and briefly commented on the main recommendations in the Government's Green Paper, *Education in Schools* (1977). This Green Paper followed the 'Great Debate' which was stimulated by the speech of the Prime Minister, James Callaghan, at Ruskin College, and it covered a wide range of issues. One of its many recommendations concerned secondary reorganization. It stated that comprehensive reorganization must be completed, though it was self congratulatory about the substantial progress so far and went on to argue that what was needed in the wake of reorganization was a period of stability during which standards might be improved. The pamphlet questioned the Government's claims about the extent of the achievement so far. It suggested that although 75 per cent of pupils were nominally in comprehensive schools, this figure exaggerated the true proportion. It included pupils in schools where only those in the lower forms were in 'comprehensive' classes because of the recent nature of reorganization. It also included pupils in comprehensive schools which were coexisting with selective schools. The NUT went on to urge the implementation of the 1976 Education Act requiring all authorities to submit plans for reorganization. Only then, when recalcitrant authorities had been brought into line, would the period of stability be justified.

Thus by the end of the period we are considering the union was strongly committed to the abolition of selective schools, in strong contrast to its slightly tentative position a decade or so earlier. Its position on the raising of the school-leaving age to 16 seems to have been strong and consistent advocacy of it from the early 1960s. Some might argue that adding an extra compulsory year to secondary education greatly increased pupil numbers and therefore the demand for teachers, so that the union could hardly have advocated anything else. However, some teachers' organizations, notably the NAS, strongly opposed raising the leaving age significantly, to the detriment of existing pupils and their teachers. The NUT did not accept the arguments of the other associations. In a short paper stating its view of the issue the union explicitly attacked the argument that resources should be directed towards those who went to learn rather than those who are unwilling. It pointed out:

> views not so very dissimilar were being expressed a hundred years ago, when the principle of compulsion was being applied for the first time at a much earlier age. But more important, the fact that teachers were aware of the hostility of some of the present leavers, against the school and its ethos, should be taken as a criticism of our present attitudes and methods, rather than as a reason to welcome the departure from school of such youngsters at the earliest possible opportunity.[33]

It is difficult to detect exactly what position the NUT took on the question after the Crowther Report was published in 1959 recommending that the school-leaving age should be raised. However, once the Government had announced in 1964 that it would implement the recommendation, the union was active in encouraging preparation for it and in demanding extra resources for buildings, staff, in-service courses and curriculum development. However, its commitment to raising the school-leaving age was not sufficiently influential to prevent the Government from deciding in 1968 to postpone the measure by two years, from 1970–1 to 1972–3, as part of a package of public spending cuts. The NUT's Annual Conference in 1968 adopted a resolution deploring the decision to delay implementation. Among the reasons cited were that it would 'deny opportunities to underprivileged children' and would 'delay the satisfactory reorganization of secondary education', as well as restricting 'the output of better trained and skilled manpower'. Thus it emphasized both redistribution and manpower requirements. Voluntary staying on, which had increased, was thought to be insufficient; moreover, those who left early were most likely to be those who had already suffered other social disadvantages.

After this the union concentrated on the problem of how to implement the change, dismissing as irrelevant any further discussion of whether it should be introduced. It carried out a survey of all LEAs to find out what was being done to prepare for the raising of the leaving age and published its findings in a pamphlet entitled *16: Raising the School-Leaving Age*. The pamphlet claimed that many authorities complained of being hampered by inadequate resources, and as a consequence the union pleaded for greater generosity on the part of central government. However, it went on to say that there were substantial differences between LEAs in the quality of preparation, which had little to do with resources. One of the less obvious issues it touched on was the influence of examinations on the secondary school curriculum. The retention of all pupils until they were 16 would require that more thought be given to the examination system, though few authorities had apparently considered this. Finally, the pamphlet foresaw that the raising of the school-leaving age would strengthen the case for abolishing two separate systems of school-leaving examination. This is a policy which the union advocated as early as 1970 and has strongly espoused since then.[34] One of the reasons it put forward in favour of a common system was that it would remove 'the divisive element implicit in the present dual system'.[35] In backing five years of compulsory secondary education for all children, the union did not explicitly anticipate the need for completely different forms of assessment, such as pupil profiles, which would be required if a substantial minority of pupils were not to be left without any form of paper qualifications whatsoever on leaving school.

The union's position on the raising of the school-leaving age can be summed up as the conventional liberal progressive one, which backed the measure strongly as a means of extending opportunities to less privileged children. Disparities in staying-on rates between different social groups and different parts of the country could be wiped out by this means. It did not question whether the extension of compulsion was desirable in principle. It did not consider whether the most obvious alternative method of extending opportunities in this age group — the expansion of part-time education for 15–18-year-olds, possibly on a compulsory basis — might be a more desirable use of the resources. It was, however, hardly in the NUT's interests to do so. The union represented schoolteachers, and the alternative policy would have meant expanding the further education sector rather than the secondary schools.

In this paper so far we have examined the position that the NUT adopted on the key issues of policy designed to create greater equality. What conclusions can we draw about the NUT's influence? As we said in the introduction to this chapter, it is not possible to prove influence. We can only speculate on the basis of the fairly limited evidence we have available.

What we have said has been based largely on an analysis of NUT publications and Conference resolutions. What is difficult to ascertain is the impact of such publications. Who reads NUT pamphlets? How many people read them? How seriously are they taken by policy-makers in central and local government? How far do they influence ordinary NUT members? Are the members' attitudes and practices modified as a result of reading these pamphlets? If so, presumably this will have some indirect effect on policy formulation at the local level, and possibly at national levels, insofar as the teaching profession as a whole, rather than just its representatives, is seen to be strongly opposed or strongly in favour of particular changes.

Another important question is how closely the public position taken by the union in the pamphlets it produces accords with the position it takes up in the private negotiations it enters into with central government in particular. When attempting to put pressure on the Government through deputations to Education Ministers or through private discussions with senior officials, it may adopt a stance slightly different to the one it adopts publicly. It may feel able to take a more self-interested position than it would if its views were exposed to public scrutiny. In some circumstances the reverse may be true. It may feel more able to advocate policies in the interests of children, parents or the nation, rather than simply in the interest of teachers, when it is not exposed to its own members' scrutiny. Whichever is correct, it must be emphasized that the extent to which the union can privately depart from the public position it takes must be constrained. If it did so frequently and extensively, it would rapidly lose credibility with the 'insiders' in the decision-making process and would probably eventually lose some of its influence.

Where the union does adopt a somewhat different position in different contexts, this may not necessarily be the result of a cynical disregard for the principles of consistency and integrity. It may be because there are genuine differences of opinion between different sections of the union. So far we have assumed homogeneity. In fact, as in all large organizations concerned with political and policy issues, there are differences of opinion which are sometimes of a serious kind. Most of the work that goes into NUT publications is done by full-time officials, mainly in the Education Department. This work is scrutinized by members of the executive and its committees before being published. Hence it often represents a consensus and may mask differences of opinion that emerge elsewhere. However, in spite of all these provisos, it seems reasonable to assume that the publications are a fairly accurate reflection of the union's general position and that they are read by those responsible for making policy, who have to take into account the likely response of the teaching profession as a whole and of the NUT in particular.

Apart from the example of the pamphlet on primary schools mentioned at the beginning of the chapter and the 1970 proposals for a common examination at 16, there is no other evidence of the NUT's actually initiating new policies in the areas we are considering. Its mode is, in general, responsive rather than initiatory. Its opposition to particular proposals, such as the partial staffing of nursery classes with nursery assistants, may serve as an informal veto. Its opposition to extensive parental involvement is another example. Its views on this are in part a function of strongly-held professional values about freedom and autonomy in the classroom. Professionalism of this kind has undoubtedly produced tensions when certain kinds of change have been advocated. As the *Schoolmaster* stated with respect to the Beloe Report, 'it has always been a source of pride to the profession, and a very proper one, that in this country the teacher has the unalienable right to decide what to teach and how to teach it, and insofar as he is the best judge of the child's readiness to learn, when to teach.'[36] On the other hand, its continual backing of certain policies may help to speed up their implementation. Its espousal, if a little belated, of the abolition of selection at the age of 11 over a number of years may have helped somewhat to reinforce the introduction of comprehensive schools.

We suggested earlier that the union's position has been on the radical side of the political spectrum rather than the conservative. (One result of this is that its public stance may vary a little according to which party is in power.) However, Manzer has argued that 'in promoting the education of working-class children the NUT was part of a general movement in British society to improve the condition of the working class.'[37] He suggests there was a social idealism that was shared by administrators and teachers alike during the post-war years. He does not give the union any special credit for espousing the cause of equality. On the contrary, he claims that the NUT

> must now be regarded as a powerful conservative influence in the politics of English education. This conservatism is explained by the Union's traditional professional concern for the education of the individual, its refusal to sacrifice long-standing educational ideals, the distractions created by divisions inside the teaching profession, and the threat to the collective role of teachers in the policy-making process posed by a more national orientation and centralization of educational policy.[38]

Does this judgement stand up in the light of our analysis of the NUT's position on our four policy issues? What has emerged shows the NUT as both idealistic and self-interested, both conservative and radical. In certain respects it has dragged its feet, as a consequence possibly reducing the educational opportunities of working-class children. In other respects it has fought hard to expand educational opportunities for the less privileged members of the community. Its record is by no means unblemished, as we have indicated. Nevertheless, Manzer's assessment seems a little too sweeping and harsh.

### The Campaign for the Advancement of State Education

We turn now to a different kind of pressure group: the Campaign for the Advancement of State Education (CASE). It differs from the NUT in every conceivable respect, except that it shares with the union a commitment to improving the quality of state education and to extending to more children the opportunities that offers. Its influence and importance are small compared to those of the NUT. It has few resources, a much smaller membership and no teeth.

Its origins may be traced back to Cambridge in 1960. Like many pressure groups, it began when a small group of people formed to try to resolve a particular problem. Parents of children at an individual primary school were united by the poor provision offered, and they attempted to persuade the local authority to do something about it. They were surprised to be told that their children were fortunate. The conditions at many other primary schools were much worse. As a result, the parents set up a pressure group to try to improve matters. It became known as the Cambridge

Association for the Advancement of State Education. One of its members wrote to the *Guardian* expressing concern. Soon after this a similar group was set up in Oxford, sparked off, as in Cambridge, by poor facilities in a particular primary school. The first secretary in Oxford was Peter Newsam, who has since become the Chief Education Officer in London. By coincidence, both primary schools were called St Andrews. What is probably less coincidental is that the first groups were formed in the university towns of Oxford and Cambridge. Both these cities have an uncommonly high proportion of upper-middle-class parents, who attach great importance to education and many of whom send their children to local primary schools, even though they may opt out of the state system at the secondary stage. They belong to a highly articulate group, underterred by the barriers put up by local bureaucracy, well-informed and therefore well able to complain to some effect. Soon after the Oxford group was formed, new groups began to spring up elsewhere, predominantly but not exclusively in the middle-class areas of big cities (Hampstead and Richmond) or in middle-class towns (Chester and Stockport). By the middle of 1962 there were twenty-six groups in existence, and in the same year a national joint committee for the advancement of state education was formed.[39] This became known as the Confederation for the Advancement of State Education. Each local association was to have autonomy but to be affiliated to the national association; affiliation fees were to be related to size. The policy of the central association was to be made by the Annual Conference, with a small executive to implement it. CASE has retained all these features since its origins.

Its membership is predominantly middle-class. Many of its most active members have had some professional interest in education. This is reflected in the present national executive of twenty people, whose members include three college of education lecturers, two university lecturers, a primary headteacher and two ex-teachers. As one member of the executive put it, CASE has attracted those members of the teaching profession who are critical of existing organizations and the level of resources provided to support them and who presumably believe reform can and should be promoted from outside the system.

CASE operates largely at the local level. In this respect it is unlike most of the other educational pressure groups, such as the Advisory Centre for Education (ACE), the Campaign for Nursery Education (CNE) and the Campaign for Comprehensive Schools (CCE), which operate mainly at the national level, or the National Confederation of Parent-Teacher Associations (NCPTA), which operates mainly at school level.

In CASE the role of the national executive is confined largely to supporting the local groups by providing them with information about what is happening, notably with respect to central government policy. Its main independent role has been to secure an annual meeting initially with the Secretary of State, now with the minister, to pass on National Conference resolutions. However, it has decided recently to maintain a higher profile and to try to sharpen its impact by examining a series of central policy questions on which it will produce a national CASE line by focusing on a number of issues. In this way the executive hopes to increase its influence nationally, which up until now has probably not been very extensive. It is exceedingly difficult to measure such influence. The hope is that the policy papers which emerge from examining the issue will in future serve as guidelines for local associations. Whether the local associations accept them will be entirely up to them. The local associations are totally autonomous — a state which they jealously guard. Thus greater control by the national executive would probably be resisted and might provoke some local associations to opt out. Basildon did so, not so much on the issue of autonomy as on political grounds; it considered the national executive's position on the reorganization of secondary schools and on subsidies to private schools too left-wing.

This example highlights the problems of a pressure group of this kind. As long as it keeps a low profile nationally, without stating too clearly the policies it advocates, it is able to hold together in a loose-knit confederation a fairly broad range of local activists anxious to improve state education. As soon as it becomes more precise and specific about the policies it advocates, it may lose some of its support. CASE altered its name from Confederation to Campaign in 1979, partly to give itself a clearer, more forceful and more militant image. The organization as a whole had in any case suffered some decline during the 1970s. Its officers believed that the attempts of a new Tory Government to cut expenditure on education increased the need for a national voice lobbying for state education across the whole social spectrum. One of the activities that the national body initiated at this time was a lobby of Members of Parliament against the cuts. It also arranged a meeting on the 1980 Education Bill with the Child Poverty Action Group (CPAG) and various trade unions, including the National Union of Public Employees (NUPE), the NUT and the National Association of Teachers in Further and Higher Education (NATFHE), to which it invited all Members of Parliament. Its aim was to point out to MPs the undesirable aspects of the Bill and to provide them with ammunition with which to attack it.

In spite of such activities, it remains true that CASE's activities are concentrated at the local level. During the 1960s the number of local groups grew substantially, so that by the end of the decade there were about 120. By 1974 this had fallen to 105 and by the beginning of the 1980s to sixty. There are two possible explanations for this decline. The first is that a number of local associations were set up to fight for the reorganization of secondary education in their areas. When this was achieved, they collapsed. The second is that the arrival of a Labour Government in 1974 seemed to herald a commitment to various advances in state education, so that in some places complacency led to the collapse of associations.

The size of local associations has varied considerably. Some have 150 members, others as few as twenty. The largest has well over 200. They are concentrated in the south of England. Their style appears to vary considerably from the militant and radical to the more timid and conventional. Some groups have tried to widen their membership to achieve a broader representation of the community; many have remained strongly middle-class. Particular battles sometimes bring in a wider range of members. The campaign to retain the Inner London Education Authority (ILEA) was one example in the London area. Many parents did not want to see ILEA broken up and some of them were persuaded to join CASE, which was campaigning against the dismemberment of the authority.

Lack of funds has frequently been a constraint on activities at both local and national levels, as is the case with most pressure groups of this kind. Voluntary effort keeps the organization going. However, a small, non-renewable grant of £3500 per annum for three years was obtained from the DES in April 1979, which helps to pay for a part-time executive officer. The executive does not appear to believe that this will reduce its independence in any way. Another source of funds is the Home and Schools Council. This body was formed by CASE, ACE and NCPTA to publish pamphlets. Because of the political nature of its work, CASE cannot be classified as a charity, which reduces its access to funds. One way round this problem is to set up a separate charitable arm, whose brief is to seek additional funds mainly in order to carry out research. This happened in 1980. The presence of a number of different educational lobbies, all seeking funds, parallels in certain respects the existence of a number of different teacher unions. One proposed solution to the dissipation of effort that may take place is for a number of the pressure groups to get together and to share a simple set of premises, thereby reducing overheads and increasing contact between them. So far lack of capital has prevented this. A single building would not mean a single educational pressure group pursuing the expansion of educational opportunities. Many of those involved would advocate a more pluralistic system rather than the unification of CASE, ACE, CCE and CNE into a single body. However, a reform of this kind would probably reduce some duplication of effort, although it would leave out organizations such as the National Association of Governors and Managers (NAGM) and NCPTA, because their private-sector members would make them unacceptable to the other pressure groups.

CASE has attempted to co-operate rather than compete with these other pressure groups, although it is difficult to assess how successful it has been in this respect. Mutual suspicions do exist. For example, CASE has been suspicious of the consumer-orientated ideology of ACE and believes that ACE has been over-concerned with what it believes to be fringe issues, such as corporal punishment or the unavailability of school records to parents, as compared with the more important issues of the under-resourcing of education, the divisive nature of much of the educational structure and the lack of positive discrimination. ACE, for its part, has been suspicious of CASE, particularly on the grounds that it has not been critical enough of the teaching profession or of its authoritarian and secretive approach adopted in relation to parents. However, these suspicions have not prevented a certain amount of collaboration, nor have they prevented CASE from continuing to work with the teachers' organizations where possible. It does so because it believes that reform and advance are difficult without teacher commitment. There has been considerable antagonism between CASE and the NUT at certain times, however, notably on the issue of parent participation in the reform of school government. On the other hand, on such matters as the state's buying places in the private sector and cuts in educational expenditure there is strong agreement, so the Assisted Places Scheme is a target which brings the NUT and CASE together. Collaboration between rather different types of pressure groups, such as CASE and the NUT, is based in part on exchange and reciprocity.

In this particular exchange CASE is much the less significant partner. There is a sense in which it needs the NUT, but the NUT does not need CASE: that is, the NUT is one of the bodies CASE wishes to influence, whereas the reverse is not true to anything like the same extent.

The methods employed by CASE to get its views known and accepted are similar to those used by other pressure groups. From the centre it publishes three times a year a newspaper, *Parents and Schools*, which is circulated to about 3,000 subscribers. Rather surprisingly, it does not send this to those whom it is trying to influence. Its role, therefore, appears to be primarily to provide information and guidance for local members. Recent editors have started to devote themselves to particular themes, such as exemplary comprehensive schools, which demonstrate good practice across a number of different areas. The national officers of CASE try to make themselves generally available to the media and to respond to journalists positively. They write letters to the national newspapers. As already indicated, they meet the Minister for Education once a year. They lobby Parliament and have given evidence to the Select Committee on Education. CASE also submits evidence to government inquiries into education, and in the case of Plowden and Taylor two of its active members were appointed to the Committees.

At the local level the tactics are similar: letters to the local press, the use of local radio, public meetings, petitions, pressure on education committee members, discussions with chief education officers and their colleagues. Some local associations have also carried out surveys of various aspects of education. Three recent examples serve to illustrate this. In 1979 Oxford CASE carried out a survey of mixed-ability teaching in the middle age range.[40] It provided the facts about the extent of streaming, setting and mixed-ability teaching for 9- to 12-year-olds in Oxfordshire schools, which responded and listed the reasons given for different forms of organization. It made no judgements about the findings. The introduction to the report said: 'this report will provide a factual basis for informal discussion on the methods of organizing teaching at the middle age range in schools. We also hope that it will encourage parents to inquire about the system in use at schools their children are attending or are likely to attend.' In 1980 south-west Surrey CASE produced a pamphlet providing basic information about all the secondary schools in Guildford, in the hope that it would be 'useful to families moving into the area, to parents with children at middle schools, and all those interested in education generally'.[41] It is the kind of document that a local education authority might be expected to distribute to parents at the time of their children's transfer to secondary education. The third document is rather different. It is an attempt by the St Albans association to document the effects of cuts in the education budget during 1979–80. All the heads in the St Albans area were interviewed and their responses collated for each sector. The pamphlet concludes that 'basic educational standards, supposedly preserved despite budgetary cuts, have *already* fallen, particularly for children in need of remedial help.' It goes on to say:

> there will be increasing discrimination against children in poorer families because they may not be able to pay for services which have historically been provided as an integral part of their education. Since they will probably attend schools in poorer neighbourhoods, they will be at a great material disadvantage — soon.[42]

It is a much more political document than the other two. It implicitly criticizes the Government and the local authority, and it makes judgements about the quality of the education being provided.

The documents reveal the dual role of CASE at the local level. On the one hand, it is an information-providing service for parents, increasing knowledge and 'raising consciousness' about education. On the other hand, it is a campaigning body setting out to explore undesirable aspects of education and to fight for improvements. Some local associations appear to emphasize one role rather than the other; others seem to try to fulfil both roles, sometimes a little uneasily. The more traditional concentrate on uncontroversial activities, particularly in the sphere of home-school relations. These include holiday play schemes, 'meet the head' meetings, parent help on school outings and governor training. Some of the newer CASE groups born as a result of the cuts are more inclined to campaign directly in association with local branches of the NUT, NUPE or CPAG. The stance the national executive takes is to try to emphasize the organization's campaigning role. This is embodied in a policy statement produced in 1979, in which it listed its main aims. These included pressing for greater involvement of parents in education; campaigning for the abolition of the remaining forms of selection for secondary education and for the establishment of a 'genuinely comprehensive system'; campaigning for the extension of co-education; and pressing for the furtherance of community schools. It advocated the development of programmes to prepare young people for adult life and opposed corporal punishment, compulsory religious education and all subsidies to independent schools from public money. In its overall goal of increasing the quality and size of state education, CASE aimed to press for increased public expenditure in this area. It stated that it would campaign for higher expenditure on deprived areas, better provision for handicapped children, more opportunities for the education of children under 5 and for young people in higher and further education.

Thus its aims cover a wide range of educational issues. Undoubtedly, throughout the history of CASE two issues have been of dominant concern. These are the reorganization of secondary education and parental participation in education. It has sometimes been seen as a parents' group,[43] partly because of the emphasis it places on the second of these issues. However, as already indicated, professional educationalists are fairly prominent on its national executive committee, and it counts a substantial number of teachers among its members, although it is not possible to be precise about the numbers and how many of them are also parents. It asserts that it is not a parents' organization but welcomes as a member anyone who is dedicated to improving state education. Nevertheless, parent participation in decision-making has been one of its most important causes, which unites its members, unlike some of the other issues it has espoused, which have caused some dissension. One of its most prominent members over the years became a member of the Taylor Committee on School Government, where she fought for strong representation on school governing and managing bodies.

In spite of its general backing for the expansion of nursery education and its inclusion of this in its list of policy aims, CASE does not appear to have given nursery education very high priority in its campaign activities. The existence of another pressure group exclusively devoted to this question may be the explanation. One of the difficulties CASE has faced in this area has been uncertainty about where it stands on the question of pre-school playgroups. The hard line or purist position has been to back state-financed and state-run nursery schools and classes and playgroups. But CASE draws many of its members from just the kind of social group which has been most prominent in the playgroups movement — middle class mothers. Also its commitment to parent participation places it in a dilemma when it is argued that playgroups are model organizations in this respect. It is an area which demonstrates quite well the loose relationship between CASE at the centre and its local associations. The national executive has strongly backed state nursery education; many of the local associations have flirted a great deal with playgroups. In its guidelines the national executive gets round this as best it can. Guideline No. 6, on the early years of schooling, says:

> We recognize the valuable part played by pre-school playgroups, but do not consider them to be a substitute for adequate and properly equipped state provision. Some play groups have developed a high degree of parental involvement, and our ideal would

be to see all under-5 provision fully involving parents on the lines of the best practice in both playgroups and nursery schools at present.

There is little evidence that CASE has advocated nursery education as an equalizer. In a leaflet entitled *The Kind of Nursery Education CASE Wants*, it lists 'many more nursery classes' but only points out that the first five years of a child's life 'are vital for his or her future development'. In a series of information sheets produced as guides for parents, one on nursery education is included.[44] Again, it concentrates on the developmental advantages of nursery education for all children rather than its social role for the less privileged sectors of society, although it makes passing reference to the needs of children in depressed neighbourhoods.

There is also relatively little reference to the Plowden policies of positive discrimination in CASE documents. Leading members of the national executive admitted when interviewed that this was partly a reflection of the organization's middle-class membership and the concentration of local associations in middle-class areas. 'Even nice people do not like giving up privilege' was the way one of them put it. The complexity of many of the issues involved in making positive discrimination work renders it a difficult area on which to campaign for a group such as CASE. Some of its own members have criticized the organization for mouthing the right sentiments but doing very little. One aspect of positive discrimination, to which it devoted an article in *Parents and Schools* in spring 1979, is multi-cultural education. It comments that both Section 11 of the 1966 Local Government Act and the Urban Programme 'were devised rather hurriedly'. Its criticisms of Section 11 are similar to those of the NUT: no monitoring of the use of additional staff appointed under it, no money for capital expenditure, too narrow criteria in the allocative procedure. It goes on to urge that the highest priority should be given to resources for multi-cultural education and lists various policies to improve it.

In the early years of its existence CASE backed the raising of the school-leaving age. However, it was not a policy for which CASE fought very hard. As one executive member put it, 'It swam with the tide.' Once the decision had been made, it did advocate thorough preparations, including an overhaul of courses to ensure that they would be an appropriate preparation for adult life. In a Parents and Schools Information Sheet[45] it reported on an essay competition on the extra year that the Richmond local association had organized for the first group of children affected. It wrote up their responses, which strongly emphasized a demand for vocational education, for more practical information about various aspects of adult life such as family finance and work experience. Its findings thus confirmed those of the earlier survey by the Schools Council.[46] It ought to be asked what purpose their publication would serve in a series of guides to parents, most of whose children would stay on at school anyway. We can only speculate that their inclusion in the series was to help persuade such parents that a purely academic curriculum for all 15-year-olds was not what was required.

It seems unlikely that CASE has had much influence in three out of four of our case studies. They are not issues on which it has joined battle very often. The last of them, secondary reorganization, is quite a different story, however. The reason why CASE has attached so much importance to this is not altogether clear. One suggested reason is 'agonized liberal consciences' among the liberal-radical membership. (If this is correct, it is hard to explain why these consciences have not been active with respect to positive discrimination.) It is possible that at least a minority of CASE members have had children or friends and relatives with children who failed the 11-plus and whose dissatisfaction with what secondary modern schools were offering has been vociferous. Among the more radical members there has been criticism of the 'old-fashioned' curricula of the grammar schools and a belief that comprehensive schools would offer a better education for all children including their own, who were at or would go to grammar schools. The simple explanation is that the reorganization of secondary education on comprehensive lines has arguably been the most important issue facing state education during most of the period of CASE's existence. It is hardly surprising that an organization dedicated to improving the quality of state education for *all* children should have devoted a good deal of attention to it.

National CASE committed itself to supporting and fighting for a policy for a fully comprehensive system in 1966, about the same time as the NUT started to push hard for it. Since then it has campaigned consistently to achieve this. In 1971, perhaps rather surprisingly late in the day, it produced a Parents and Schools Information Sheet, *Going Comprehensive*.[47] This answered a series of questions which might have been put by doubting parents, such as 'What is wrong with the old system?' 'Why destroy the grammar schools?' 'Won't comprehensive schooling mean levelling down?' It also listed a series of points which parents might use as a check list when looking for a good comprehensive school. Its newspaper, *Parents and Schools*, has given the issue coverage. For example, it compiled a two-page item in 1976, at the time the Labour Government's legislation forcing LEAs to comply with the Government's policy in this area was going through, which included a progress report on the number of schools and authorities going comprehensive, implicit support for the legislation, as well as some criticism of various local anomalies in comprehensive schemes. More recently, CASE has produced a series of short discussion papers on various policy issues. One of these was on selection. It argued that selection is wrong because no tests can accurately measure a child's intelligence, because 'it is a competition for an arbitrary number of places available locally' and because it damages children's self-esteem and wastes talent.

In some areas 'comprehensive' or 'all-ability' schools exist in name alongside selective practices. This is an abuse of language, since any schools which co-exist with a selective system are secondary moderns, whatever they are called. In some areas, like Kingston, the 11+ has become 'optional' which as well as adding social to academic selection, puts cruel burdens on the consciences of parents who are opposed to selection and therefore also opposed to second-rate alternatives.[48]

However, it is the local associations that have probably campaigned most successfully for comprehensive schooling. Indeed, as suggested earlier, the decline in the number of local associations is partly a reflection of success in the area. Once an authority had decided to reorganize, for some members the main purpose of the association had vanished, and they drifted away, leaving behind a core which was not large enough to sustain the association's continuation. Nevertheless, a number of the most successful of the local associations have continued to exist. Perhaps the best example is Richmond. In what is a relatively right-wing Tory authority with a large middle-class population, the local CASE battled for a comprehensive system over a period of several years. It can justifiably claim that, along with Richmond Parents' Association, it got the authority to move from non-action to action, and the submission of plans, using a variety of tactics. These included persistent lobbying of councillors and officials and extensive exposure in the local press. Its success was based partly on its committed and determined leadership and partly on the breadth of its support. Its membership has been larger than that of most other CASE local associations. Success on one issue often spills over to others. Not only has Richmond CASE fought successfully for comprehensive schools, but it has also campaigned with success for the reform of school governing bodies (organizing a successful day training course for governors) and for the much more extensive consultation of parents.

In conclusion, there is little doubt that CASE has espoused the cause of greater equality in education. CASE believes that every child has a right to the facilities he needs to achieve his best. Those who start with disadvantages need more from schools. There are strong pressures in our society to concentrate on a 'quality education for a few', but 'we have paid dearly in the past for our failure to educate the majority', stated a CASE handout prepared for the 1979 election. It went on to say that CASE should urge 'extra help on a scale never before contemplated for schools in areas with special difficulties, so that children who most require it, for whatever reason, get more individual attention and learning aids'. These quotations reflect the national organization's general commitment to the cause of greater equality. They do not, of course, indicate how much campaigning effort has been put into pursuing them. We have suggested that of the four areas of policy we identified, CASE has not pushed very hard to initiate policies of positive discrimination, but it has fought hard to establish comprehensive education. This is also the area of policy in which it has had the greatest success.

Its very success in this area in a number of local campaigns has perhaps posed problems for it. For example, in certain local authorities, especially where Labour is in power, there have been invitations to CASE to put forward someone to take a place as a co-opted member of the education committee. Recognition of this kind is, in certain respects, a demonstration of success. Yet where such invitations are taken up CASE may become part of the local 'establishment', thereby losing its independence and capacity to criticize, thus jeopardizing its future success as a campaigning pressure group. Rick Rogers points to a rather different kind of problem that success may bring. He suggests that CASE has failed to capitalize on past success, notably in comprehensive reorganization, through a failure to identify other important issues so that local associations faded away.[49] He also suggests that middle-class loss of confidence in certain aspects of comprehensive schools, and thus in state education, may have contributed to the relative quiescence of CASE in the second half of the 1970s.

A Conservative Government bent on major cuts in educational expenditure may well change all this. It is possible that cuts will provide the rallying force needed for CASE to expand its network of local associations and their membership. It is possible that it may again become the source of considerable pressure in certain local areas, this time on the matter of cuts. There are signs that in this context it will collaborate with the NUT more than it has in the past to try to make any pressure that it exerts more effective. The more the local associations do this, the more likely it will be that any existing gaps between them and the central organization will close.

Both CASE and the NUT seem likely to go on being part of what Kogan has called 'the progressive consensus'. On past evidence neither seems likely to be innovative, in the sense of producing new ideas about educational policies which may enhance equality. The NUT has, however, probably had some impact in advancing existing policy proposals which have not yet been implemented. It may also act as a constraint on the introduction of other policies which it perceives to be in conflict with its general commitment to equal opportunities. Similarly, on a much smaller scale CASE has had some impact in certain areas in forcing local authorities to advance more quickly or to change the substance of their policies. But the influence of those pressure groups remains fairly small compared with the power wielded by central and local government on the policy areas with which we are concerned. However, as Maurice Kogan has eloquently put it, 'the sources of policy generation are so difficult to locate, let alone place in any logical pattern, that detecting the changes in values, or the pressures by which change is effected, is more a matter of art than of analysis.'[50]

### Notes

1 *Policy-Making in the Department of Education and Science,* Tenth Report from the Expenditure Committee London, HMSO, 1976.
2 SIR RONALD GOULD (1963) *The Teacher,* 19 April, p. 5
3 RONALD A. MANZER, (1970) *Teachers & Politics,* Manchester University Press.
4 *Ibid.,* p. 3.

5 R.D. COATES, (1972) *Teachers Union & Interest Group Politics* Cambridge: Cambridge University Press, p. 12.
6 MANZER, (1970) *Teachers & Politics*, p. 19.
7 *First Things First*, memorandum submitted to CACE, under the chairmanship of Lady Plowden London, NUT, 1964.
8 SHIRLEY WILLIAMS, (1980) 'The Decision Makers', in *Policy and Practice: The Experience of Government* London, Royal Institute of Public Administration.
9 *Nursery Assistants*, comments on DES Draft Administrative Memorandum, (NUT, mimeographed, 1972), p. 1.
10 *Ibid.*, p. 2.
11 *Nursery Education in Wales* London Welsh Committee of the NUT, 1972.
12 *The Provision of Pre-School Education in England and Wales* London, NUT, 1974.
13 A.H. HALSEY (1972) *Educational Priority: EPA Problems and Policies* London: HMSO.
14 *The Needs of the Under Fives* London: NUT, 1977, p. 17
15 *Ibid.*, p. 17.
16 *The Provision of Pre-School Education in England and Wales*, p. 15.
17 *The Needs of the Under Fives*, p. 29.
18 *The Provision of Pre-School Education in England and Wales*, p. 12.
19 HALSEY, (1972) *Educational Priority: EPA Problems and Policies*, Volume IV.
20 *Education in Schools* London, NUT, December 1977.
21 *Plowden: The Union's comments on some of the major issues of the Plowden Report* London, NUT, 1969, p. 2.
22 *Ibid.*, p. 5.
23 *Ibid.*, p. 6.
24 KEITH BANTING, (1980) 'The case for revival', *Times Educational Supplement*, 13 June.
25 *Section 11* London, NUT, 1978.
26 *Replacing Section 11* London, NUT, 1979.
27 *Educational Disadvantage and the Needs of Immigrants:* Observations on the Report of the Select Committee on Race Relations and Immigration, DES London, HMSO, 1974.
28 MAX MORRIS, (1979) quoted by MARY CASTLE, 'Second thoughts urged on 'arbitrary' closure of disadvantage centre', *Teacher*, 23 November.
29 *First Things First*, p. 17.
30 *Ibid.*, p. 17.
31 See issue of 12 July 1965.
32 *Into the Seventies* London NUT, 1969, p. 4.
33 *The Union View of ROSLA* London, NUT, 1971.
34 See A Certificate of General Secondary Education, London, NUT, March 1970.
35 *Examining at 16-Plus: The Case for a Common System* London, NUT. 1978, p. 5.
36 See issue of 30 September 1960.
37 MANZER, (1970) *Teachers and Politics*, p. 38.
38 *Ibid.*, p. 158.
39 ROGERS, 'The case for revival'.
40 *Mixed-Ability Teaching in the Middle Age Range* Oxford, CASE, 1979.
41 *Secondary Schools in Guildford* Guildford, CASE, 1980.
42 *The Effects of Budgetary Cuts on Education in the St. Albans Division*, 1979–80 St. Albans; Association for the Advancement of Learning, 1980.
43 MAURICE KOGAN (1975) *Educational Policy-Making* London: Allen & Unwin.
44 *Nursery Education* Billericay; Home and School Council, 1973.
45 *Raising the School Leaving Age* Billericay, Home and School Council, 1972.
46 *Young School Leavers* London, HMSO, 1968.

47 Published by the Home and School Council in 1971.
48 *CASE Guidelines No. 5: Selection. Favoured Few or Selection for All?* London, CASE, 1981, p. 3.
49 ROGERS, (1975) 'The case for revival.'
50 KOGAN, (1975) *Educational Policy-Making*, p. 23.

# Parental Choice in Education*

*Brian Holmes*
*University of London Institute of Education*

Every parent wants an educational system which satisfies the needs, interests and expectations of his or her own child. Some parents are willing and able to pay the market cost of providing the kind of education they want for their own child. What they want varies. Some parents expect a school to be run in accordance with their own religious beliefs. Others are determined that the school shall prepare their child for competitive examinations. Less overt in their demands are parents who hope that a particular school will improve the social, economic and political life chances of their child. The schoolteacher who claims to be providing an all-round education in the child's own interests is likely, cynically, to be accepted by parents as just rhetoric.

In most countries a majority of parents are either unable or unwilling to pay the high costs of providing for their children an education of their choice. If within the publicly maintained system some schools meet their wishes, parents will do all in their power to ensure their children 'get in' to a favoured school, even to the extent of moving house. Other parents attempt to change the system by engaging in political action in the hope that their children will benefit. One consequence of such moves has been the increasing politicization of education. Once its provision has been taken out of the realm of private finance, it becomes a matter of patronage by church or state. For many years this patronage has been mediated by university academics and school teachers. In many countries their authority is now being questioned and whereas previously, even in systems of compulsory education, the question who shall be educated was answered by priests and teachers, politicians are no longer willing to accept this arrangement. And parents are the allies of politicians whether at national or local level.

There is no doubt that, in this sense, the whole worldwide educational scene has been transformed since the Second World War. International declarations made education a universal human right. Left-wing politicians in Britain, France and Sweden immediately pressed to introduce secondary

---

\* This is an edited version of the article which appeared in *Education Today*, 32, 3, 1982.

education for all. Communist governments in Eastern Europe proposed to follow Soviet practice by introducing common or comprehensive schools. The Americans in Japan urged the post-war government there to expand education at all levels. In the USA, Japan and India enrolments in higher education rose rapidly in the fifties. Elsewhere similar levels of expansion occurred in the sixties. Baby booms everywhere meant that primary school enrolments escalated from the beginning of the fifties, and pressure on the secondary schools became intense in the sixties.

At the same time politicians and educationists were aware that, for social and economic reasons, some children were 'disadvantaged' in traditional systems of education. For the most part the blacks in the USA were forced to attend less good schools than those for the whites, in spite of the Supreme Court ruling that 'separate' facilities for whites and blacks were only constitutional if they were 'equal'. Working-class children in Western Europe were held to be at a disadvantage because of the class position of their parents. Clearly in India the caste system operated in favour of children from higher castes and against 'outcastes'.

In most industrial-urbanized countries, city schools were regarded as better than rural schools on most criteria. In newly independent countries foreign Christian mission schools were regarded as centres of privilege. Private schools, whether catering for members of a particular religion, which historically many did, were thought to convey privileges on children whose parents could afford to pay for their schooling. In those countries, such as France and Japan, in which publicly maintained schools enjoyed the highest prestige, it was claimed that through their positions of wealth and power well-educated parents were able to use the system to their advantage.

Given this very complex state of affairs, should parental choice be supported and, if so, how can it be realized?

### The UK 1944 Education Act

Hotly debated, the 1944 Education Act was approved by a coalition government in a wartime Parliament. English legislation is, of course, notoriously vague (compared with that enacted in most other countries), leaving deliberately or by chance enormous room for interpretation and political manoeuvre. Thus while the Act, in Section 76, very explicitly gave parents the right to have their children educated in accordance with the wishes of parents, the omission before 'parents' of 'their' might have been deliberate — leaving open the question of how parents could be identified and through which agencies their wishes should be expressed. Common sense suggests that parents are interested in the education of their own children. Political rhetoric implies that parents should be interested in the education of other people's children. The cynicism with which some politicians and educationists advocate comprehensive secondary schools for the children of other parents, while sending their own children to private schools, is encouraged by the vagueness of English laws.

Of course this Section of the Act allowed even greater room for manoeuvre. Section 76 stated that education in accordance with parental choice should be compatible 'with the provision of efficient instruction and training' and the 'avoidance of unreasonable public expenditure'. For many years the first clause left the admission of children to publicly maintained schools in accordance with the wishes of parents to the patronage of teachers who were in a position to decide which of the many children competing for admission to grammar schools should be allowed to enter them. The second clause — 'unreasonable public expenditure' — legitimizes attempts by national government or local authorities to restrict parental choice by saying that to meet the wishes of all parents would be too expensive.

At the macro level only a small number of parents can influence public provision. In England and Wales they may act through local or national political parties, less effectively through parent teacher associations, and hardly at all through financial arrangements. Public funding of schools is too remote from individual parents for them to increase, in accordance with their wishes, public expenditure or to reduce it if the schools do not meet the their expectations. This is in sharp contrast to the situation in the USA, where property owners living in a school board district have to agree to a specific education tax to meet recurrent costs, and bond issues have to be approved and taken up to provide capital costs. Industrialists finding the education tax on their property too high, may well pull out of a community and move to a less highly taxed location. Local school boards are consequently much more aware of collective economic pressures than in England, and parents in the USA can actively participate in the political processes which lead either to an increase or to a decrease in funds for local schools. One consequence is that as between local school systems in one state and between school systems in different states, the range of per capita expenditures in education is enormous.

Nevertheless this method of financing publicly maintained schools does allow parents a measure of choice. American traditions confirm that these who pay the piper should determine the tune, even though their influence is mediated through agencies of representative government. It may account for the fact that the private schools of America, with few exceptions represented by Gorton, Andover and Phillips, are less highly regarded than local neighbourhood publicly financed schools. Trouble has arisen in the USA because, in ensuring that their children received the kind of education they want, middle-class, white, Protestant parents paid little attention to the kind of schooling the children of black parents should receive, and have consistently supported decisions which allow Roman Catholics to run their own schools, provided they do not expect to receive substantial financial support.

The Supreme Court decision of 1954, that segregated schools were inherently unconstitutional, gave rise to prolonged debates about the right of white parents to retain and support schools for their own children, if it meant excluding black children from them. Historically in most towns residential areas were segregated and big cities had, and have, their ghettoes. The principle that schools should serve a neighbourhood resulted, even after 1954, in de facto segregation. Attempts to integrate schools, by 'bussing' blacks from one area into predominantly white schools and whites into predominantly black schools, have met fierce opposition and increased support from among white parents for private schools.

Parental pressure in England and Wales is less direct, but in a curious way affected the outcome of debates about the comprehensive schools in the sixties. It is ironic that a policy advocated by members of the Labour Party and resisted by members of the Conservative Party was first realised in practice by the Leicestershire County Council. With the help of individual headteachers and the support of members of local communities Stewart Mason, with the agreement of the chairman and members of his education committee, persuaded a Conservative county to go comprehensive in a piecemeal fashion. Major resistance came from the headteachers, governors and former students of some well-established grammar schools. They were by-passed until throughout most of the county the policy was a fait accompli.

It should be noted, however, that successful conversions to a comprehensive system took place in what were evidently prosperous, middle-class, professional, residential areas, suggesting that with rising pupil numbers and greater competition for grammar school places these parents, rather than face the prospect that their children would fail to get into a grammar school, were prepared to support the establishment of comprehensive schools. Such articulate parents were less and less willing to accept that teachers could judge the potential of individual children and place them accurately on a scale of aptitude and ability. In other words, they were no longer prepared to allow the life chances of their children to be subject to patronage of teachers.

This is the issue facing advocates of a selective secondary school system in which, for historical reasons as well as present-day considerations, one kind of school is more highly prized than the others. After the 1944 Act abolished tuition fees, the only criteria of selection and admission to grammar schools were academic. No parent could excuse his failure to send his child to a 'grammar' school because he could not afford the fees — a reason, or excuse, which could be made in the 1930s. The establishment of comprehensive schools only partially resolved the issue.

Where parents were fairly certain that their local 'comprehensive' would be a 'good' school, admitting only children from their immediate neighourhood, support for such a school was forthcoming. In large city conurbations, however, very large comprehensive schools drew their entry from a very large area, including a range of residential districts. Consequently there was no guarantee at all that in such schools the wishes of all parents could be met. Undoubtedly some parents expected comprehensive schools to prepare pupils as successfully as grammar schools for public examinations and university entrance. Other parents were less clear and perhaps less articulate. In any case it seems unlikely that they had clear alternatives to secondary education to propose. It was left for teachers to propose what pupils ought to receive in the way of education. Their desire to accommodate pupils who were unlikely to pass O-level General Certificate of Education examinations led to the creation of a 'second class' Certificate of Secondary Education.

It soon became apparent that not all comprehensive schools, even in a fairly circumscribed area were regarded by parents as equally 'good' or desirable. There is evidence to show, for example, that some parents preferred their children to attend an old-fashioned school, where they would be among friends, rather than go to a newly built, less crowded school somewhat farther away from their homes. Evidently Roman Catholic parents preferred Roman Catholic comprehensive schools. Some non-Catholics also preferred these schools because of the academic results achieved and the discipline they imposed. Some parents preferred single sex to co-educational schools. Some no doubt wanted schools where the ethnic composition was more homogenous. Since these desires cut across religious, cultural and ethnic differences it is apparent that, even if on certain criteria of quality every comprehensive school could be made the same, all schools are unlikely to be regarded by parents as equally acceptable because they apply a different set of criteria. Hence, to satisfy parental preferences in a multicultural society or local community, simply to make one school similar to all the others will not meet the case. It is evident that schools (overtly comprehensive) establish their own reputation among interested parents and that, at the point of transfer, some schools will receive more applicants for admission than can be accommodated, others will receive fewer applicants than they can take.

While it may be theoretically possible to equalize provision, given the socio-economic circumstances in which schools are located, it is unlikely that provision can be equalized in practice. In the USSR every effort is made to make schools as similar as possible, so that no child has an unfair advantage over another. Superficially schools in the large cities are very much alike in terms of buildings, routine and curriculum. There are however obvious differences. Some schools offer a modern foreign language in the second grade (age 8) rather than as in most schools in the fifth grade. Such schools are popular among parents who want their children to go on to a famous university, polytechnic or pedagogical institute. More subtly, each school has its own ethos, frequently associated with the personality of the principal. It is evident that some schools are more favoured than others. How then can parents choose? Soviet schools are neighbourhood schools. But the allocation of accommodation is regulated by local committees. It is possible therefore that a neighbourhood school serves a fairly homogenous group of either factory workers or professional people and it is not surprising to find a high proportion of children in a school for professional parents who want to become like their parents, doctors, lawyers and engineers. Since movement in terms of residence is not determined by market forces, it is not easily possible for parents to move into a neighbourhood in which there is a favoured school.

In Japan curricula are established centrally, teacher qualifications are carefully monitored and, since 1945, the system of education has expanded enormously. Progress through the system is open virtually to all children and young people, so that practically all children attend school until the age of 18, and a very high proportion of young adults are enrolled in junior colleges, liberal arts colleges and universities. Yet educational institutions can be ranked in order of prestige. The former Imperial university of Tokyo is at the apex of the vast triangle of national and private institutions. Other national universities such as Kyoto and Kyushu rate very highly as do some well known private universities such as Keo and Waseda. In Tokyo are found some of the most prestigious upper secondary schools and clearly even down to the level of kindergarten some schools are regarded as better than others. Japanese parents are extremely anxious to ensure that their children attend the *best* schools and university. They are prepared to make many sacrifices to guarantee this. They either send their children to private schools or have them coached intensively to gain admission to a favoured school. Indeed, coaching may be necessary if a child is to get into a good private kindergarten or school. The competitiveness of the system and its consequences have been described as the 'examination hell', which places financial and academic constraints on the exercise of parental choice of school or college.

Academic achievement on the part of individual children and young adults has traditionally been the criterion on which access to prestige institutions in France has been based. The concept of an aristocracy of talent has informed French education, certainly from the time when, in the late eighteenth century, Revolutionary leaders and their successors proposed to establish a universal system of local primary schools and selective state secondary schools. Care was taken to make the national *lycées* as similar as possible. Boarding schools were set up to allow rural children to enjoy the same standard of education as that provided in the cities. Yet the *lycées* in the Sorbonne areas, for example, Henri Quatre and Louis Grand, enjoy a national reputation far higher than even those other *lycées* which prepare students not only for the universities but for the *grandes écoles*, admission to which is on the results of competitive entrance examinations. Catholic parents can choose to send their children to Catholic schools but, until de Gaulle's legislation in 1959, such schools received no financial help from public sources. Many of them prefer to enter their children for state secondary schools and consequently exert pressure on the Catholic authorities to make their schools as 'academic' as the *lycées*.

Choice of school is the most obvious way in which parental preferences can be expressed. In most countries success depends on one or all of several criteria of admission or exclusion. Ability to pay full or partial fees is one. It is decisive in those countries such as England, USA, Japan, Egypt, India and France, where private schools are allowed to operate, can charge high fees and are extensive in number. Choice is allowed to Catholic parents, many of whom are very anxious to ensure that the school's ethos is Catholic. In some countries such schools are heavily subsidized, for example, in Italy and in the United Kingdom. In other countries they receive modest support — France, and in some countries they receive virtually no help at all — USA. In the USSR religious schools are proscribed.

The growth of multiculturalism has and will further complicate the picture. Many parents wish to send their children to schools where the medium of instruction is the mother tongue. Such a choice is open to the many linguistic groups in the USSR and India. In many African countries mother tongue instruction is prescribed for the first years of schooling. Private schools in Egypt, however, offer parents the possibility of having their children educated through the medium of a foreign language. Claims by the French-speaking inhabitants of Quebec that instruction should be in French have been accepted in Canada. Similar claims by linguistic groups in nineteenth century USA were resisted. Recently Hispanic parents have succeeded in their campaign to have Spanish medium schools. In England the proliferation of religious (Moslem, Hindu and Sikh) and linguistic (Turkish, Greek and Urdu) groups raises major questions of parental choice against a background of special provision for Christian denominations and Jews, but in the same national language — English.

The complexity of providing schools acceptable to all these groups is enormous, since so many of them live in multicultural communities in the urban areas and cities. Financial constraints will probably make it impossible to establish separate schools for all the groups regardless of size or place of residence. Moreover, it should be noted that any attempt to segregate children on the basis of race, language or religion would probably be resisted — at least by some parents if not others. The categorization of parents into these groups presents a relatively new problem in the UK. The solution to it is by no means clear and alternatives are bound to be advanced and rejected according to the groups of parents involved.

### Parents per se

If the difficulties of meeting the preferences of groups of parents are considerable and solved in a variety of ways to the satisfaction or otherwise of the groups, then problems individual parents face are immense, unless they can afford to pay the full cost of educating their own children and have the chance to do so. The abolition of private fee-paying schools seriously restricts the choice of some parents even though these may be in a minority.

Such parents have rarely been organized into pressure groups, and in England are regarded by some politicians and educationists as somehow disloyal to the public system because they seek to opt out of it. Threats to deny them freedom of choice will mobilize them. Who can blame them, moreover, if the public system offers them neither choice of school, nor choice of curriculum, or if the kind of choices now available in the English school system were threatened?

Apart from arguments that Section 76 of the 1944 Act does not really mean what it states, either in terms of choice of school or choice of content, the choices open to individual parents are minimal and hedged round with all kind of constraints and reservations. The situation is chaotic. It is time this Section of the Act was either repealed, as many egalitarians might desire, or clarified to include individual parents as well as parents representing organized groups. The intentions of Mrs. Thatcher's Conservative administration to extend parental choice were written into the 1980 Education Act. One clause made it possible for parents to take advantage of the 'assisted places' scheme so that, if selected, their children could attend private-independent secondary schools at public expense. Another regulation gave parents the right to apply to maintained secondary schools of their choice and appeal against a local education authority's refusal to accede to their request. It should be noted that, for the most part, choice of secondary school is restricted to one of several comprehensive schools under the local authority's jurisdiction. Gossip, appearances, proximity to home, adverse or favourable publicity, public examination successes and a brief visit to competing schools help to place them in a hierarchy of prestige. Those with the highest rating on these very subjective tests have no doubt, as in the ILEA, more applicants than they can accept.

The 'banding' system of allocating children to secondary schools is an example of the cynicism of social engineers. It is based on the assumption that children can be graded — the good, the average and the indifferent. To ensure that a full range of abilities is in every comprehensive, proportions from each group are allowed to enter. But on what criteria are children assessed and placed into an appropriate 'band'? Modern educationists, having heard about intelligence, partially understood debates about the validity and reliability of IQ tests and rejected the use to which they were put in the nineteen fifties to 'cool' children out of the academic grammar schools have, it seems to me, thrown the baby out with the bathwater. To retain the notion that children can be banded and at the same time to reject tests as many teachers do, which while by no means perfect, have been standardized, is foolish. What can replace them as measures of ability on the basis of which a child can be placed in Band 1, Band 2 or Band 3 — the results of achievement tests? And on what subjects? General knowledge, mathematics, English, Bengali, Urdu, modern Greek, history, religious knowledge? It is the practice in the USSR to award a mark 1 to 5 to a pupil for every answer, oral or written, given. The result is recorded in a mark book so that, for each primary school child, teachers have a comprehensive record of achievement. It is unlikely that this alternative would be accepted as a satisfactory form of continuous assessment by many of our primary school teachers.

The favoured procedure, as far as I can judge, is teacher assessment — frequently a very subjective affair, but placing in the hands of teachers enormous powers of patronage. Can we be sure that the exercise of such patronage is just? Certainly a consideration associated with preferred choice of secondary school is the band into which an individual child is placed. Conscientious teachers, anxious to please parent and child, may be tempted to weigh up carefully which band is appropriate for the child in relation to his or her possibilities of being admitted to a popular secondary school. Pressure on Band 1 places is bound to be high if the school has an 'academic' reputation. Would a clever child stand a better chance of admission if he was placed in Band 2 or 3? The alternative is to rely exclusively on verbal reasoning tests and attainment in prescribed subjects. Neither teachers, parents, nor children should be faced with the possibilities of this kind of chicanery.

The semi-chaos which has followed the high number of objections from parents to the refusal of local authorities to accept their preference, reveals the extent to which the scheme will not work, unless parents can be absolutely satisfied that the system cannot be manipulated by teachers and have absolute trust in their professional integrity. A solution is to create among comprehensive schools 'parity of esteem' in the eyes of parents: a forlorn hope, as those who held in 1945–46 that parity of esteem could by fiat be accorded to secondary, grammar, technical and modern schools. Parents know what they want for their own children, and no amount of high sounding theory will persuade them willingly to accept unacceptable alternatives. Of course not all parents have the same expectations: what is deplorable is that some parents wish one thing for their own children while laying down what is good for 'other people's children'. I find this nauseating. There is abundant evidence to suggest that many individual parents are anxious that their children gain qualifications which will admit them to 'academic' secondary schools and a university. The present climate suggests that opportunities to gain admission to universities will decline rather than expand, making parents more anxious. Why should parents not have such ambitions?

It is no use trying to persuade a sizeable majority of them that secondary schools should emphasize aesthetic, moral and physical development at the expense of 'academic' qualifications. To do so is cant, unless we can create a society in which academic achievement is not rewarded in economic, status and political terms. Of course the 1944 Act provides for individual parents who want an 'academic' education for their children provided it is efficient and does not involve undue expenditure. Teachers have traditionally been granted the privilege of deciding for which children an 'academic' education could be provided efficiently. Many of them have rejected both publicly defensible criteria on which selection used to be made — IQ and achievement tests. Others maintain that parents should not want an 'academic' education for their children on the ground that it will give them an unfair advantage over other children. Others imply that children can be interested in all kinds of activity, but are bound to be put off by mathematics and other subjects, which depend upon cognitive ability and intellectual activities. Cynically, I believe that many of them rationalize their party political ideology and commitment by espousing educational theories which, while certainly worth discussing, are by no means absolutely true.

## Parental Choice and Primary Schools

This assertion applies particularly to many primary school teachers, whose rhetoric based on pragmatism has been elevated to an ideology. It commits headteachers and teachers to theories which are either very debatable or which cannot be realised in practice. I studied many excellent progressive primary schools in Leicestershire County Council when I undertook research for OECD. On the other hand, I have been in primary schools where the gap between rhetoric and practice is enormous.

At the same time, as Japanese parents realize, a good start has an important bearing on the chance a child will have of entering a prestige university. In Britain the relatively small size of the university population and the extraordinary prestige of Oxford and Cambridge means that a good start is thought to be very important by many parents. There is little point in teachers telling such parents that an 'academic' education in primary schools is not what they should want and that it denîes children of their childhood. So Rousseau might have claimed, but by what right do primary school teachers tell parents what they should want for their children? Certainly the 1944 Act does not give them that right.

Given the anxiety among individual parents that their children have a good start, what choices are open to parents?

Neighbourhood primary schools are usual. Admission is based on parental interviews and has not created enormous difficulties so far. Once a child has been admitted, there is little an individual parent can do to influence its education. In terms of school type, given a choice, parents may well wish to choose between a school with a 'progressive' ethos and one with a 'traditional' ethos. To the expert observer there are many differences between the two types both in terms of the theories held by teachers, methods of teaching, discipline, curriculum, the organization of teaching groups and classrooms, and methods of monitoring progress and achievement. Laymen and women are not in the same position to differentiate on these criteria. All of them have been educated, and most of them remember their school days. Parents' opinion may be based on the extent to which they liked or hated school. Judgements are more likely to be made on the basis of publicly known achievements. The grounds on which the reputation of an English primary school today are based are difficult to describe. Until it was abolished, the 11+ selection test was the benchmark against which the quality of a school was measured. High success rates made it a 'good' school, modest or low rates of success made it a 'bad' school. This single criterion has been rejected by a large number of teachers who regarded the influence of the 11+ selection examinations as wholly uneducational. Parents now have to trust teachers. I doubt whether in some cases they should.

The rhetoric of these teachers is that primary schools should cater for individual children. Individualized teaching and learning is a well-rehearsed slogan. Activity methods of teaching, family groupings, flexible timetables, the abolition of rote learning, an emphasis on creativity and aesthetic activities are held to be the ways of making sure that each individual child receives an education in accordance with its interests, aptitudes and abilities. Such progessive practices can, to be sure, be organized satisfactorily. They can however, as the William Tyndale affair demonstrated, result in chaos. In either case teachers are responsible for what goes on and individual parents can do little, or nothing, to influence the kind of individualized teaching their child receives. It is highly unlikely that, against a headteacher's wishes, a parent can insist that his or her child should receive an education which will prepare it for a preferred secondary school. At best, parents must take or leave what is offered and how it is offered. The illogicality of this kind of rejection is beyond belief.

If there is any logic in a refusal to accept as an individualized programme one in accordance with a parents' wishes, it is that teachers 'know best'. The rhetoric of community participation denies this. Can it be that teachers are interested in parental participation only when and if parents agree with them? In other words constraints are placed on the types of individualized programme by teachers. On this issue — namely, choice of curriculum — the gap between rhetoric and practice is enormous in some schools.

It is made more serious by the 1980 Act Section 17, which gives parents the right to take advantage of the assisted places scheme. The fees of children, whose parents are unable to pay secondary school fees, may be remitted if they can successfully pass an entrance examination at a high level. There is no reason why an education designed to prepare primary school children to take advantage of this scheme should not be given in schools where individualized teaching is proclaimed as the aim of the school. Whether or not such a programme is 'educational' is a matter of opinion. Neither teachers who think it is, nor those who think it is not, can claim they are incontrovertibly right. In publicly maintained schools their power makes them 'right', not their esoteric knowledge. Certainly there is growing disquiet about the content of primary school education and the standards of achievement expected of children and achieved by them. Unfortunately individual parents, having committed their child to a local primary school, have no way of influencing its education.

What is worse, many primary school teachers are not able to convince parents that to give their child an education in accordance with their wishes would be inconsistent with 'efficient instruction'. This clause in the Act implies that some children can be given one kind of education efficiently, others cannot. A teacher can justify his or her refusal to provide a desired education only if it can be shown that the child is one of those who cannot benefit. Teachers can 'cool' primary school pupils out of the academic system just as easily, and less publicly, now as when they operated the 11+ system. The difference is that parents have no public evidence to which they can appeal. The judgement of teachers, who have a vested interest in justifying themselves, can be virtually decisive. Their refusal to take, or make public, a child's IQ, protects them against parental protests. Laudable attempts by LEAs to 'band' children anonymously cannot prevent teachers from knowing each individual child on which they pass judgement.

Unless teachers can publicly demonstrate that a child they claim is unable to undertake a certain kind of instruction efficiently cannot do so, they abuse a position which for the most part in the past has been one of trust. Their refusal to supply parents with the evidence on which their judgement is based seems to me a denial of natural justice. Not to monitor carefully the progress of a child is a dereliction of duty. In spite of the move to progressive practices in the USA, every primary school child there is regularly tested, and teachers can tell parents in some detail how well their children are performing against standards of attainment related to chronological age. As stated, Soviet teachers mark and record every answer given by their pupils. By these methods teachers can at least justify their judgements. Too frequently English parents have to take teacher assessment on trust. It is not always valid or reliable.

Unless teachers reduce the gap between their rhetoric of individualized programmes and their practice, the confidence of parents is bound to decline. Until individual parents are convinced that their preferences will be taken seriously by teachers in publicly maintained schools, those who can will opt out of the system by sending their children to private schools. While teachers protect themselves by interpreting Section 76 as they think fit, the rights conferred on parents by the Section will remain a myth.

# Leadership in the Primary School: The Role of the Media

*Dan Wicksteed*
*Worcester College of Higher Education*

How can the media help those who wish to be leaders in the primary schools? The media include national newspapers, television and radio for the general public, professional literature and schools programmes on TV and radio, Open University courses, not to mention teachers' manuals, Schools Council project materials and all textbooks. Indeed microcomputer software programmes must be included now.

The particular feature of the media to be considered here is the virtues arising from lack of personal contact. The question is: what do the non-personal contact services provide as support and guidance in leadership in the primary school?

To answer this certain features of leadership must be contrasted. Personal contact skills, those dealing with negotiation in one form or another, are crucial, but there is a risk of undervaluing other skills which affect the way leaders form their own opinions as opposed to negotiating their adoption. How do they acquire their opinions, at best their vision? It is this which negotiations are designed to approach. Without the vision, leaders simply respond to the strongest outside pressure. It is a key danger of primary school leadership that this describes it too closely in too many cases. Responding to what the inner vision sees as a proper demand should not be confused with an inability to resist changes.

Whilst this is not to be an essay on how opinions are formed, it seems reasonable to summarize the features displayed by opinion leaders as being likable, powerful and knowledgeable (e.g., Gagné, 1977).[1] A leader must be powerful or not lead. To be likable without being powerful or knowledgeable is not to lead. Being powerful without being likable or knowledgeable is mere stubbornness. Being likable and powerful without being knowledgeable is the big fish in the little pool. Part of the concern of this article is whether primary education contains too many little pools. The media can link these pools.

Leaders, it is assumed, are those with wide contacts. Any head (or deputy) will have contact with the teachers in his own school. He will value contacts with other local heads, advisors and those he meets in normal duties. What the media provide is a wider range of contacts, albeit not personal ones.

In order to explore some of the things which can be expected of the media and some which cannot, I would like to draw attention to similarities in distinguishing between spoken and written communication and distinguishing between personal and non-personal or media contacts (see Diagram 1).

Diagram 1. *Differences between Spoken and Written Communications*

| Spoken | Written |
| --- | --- |
| Two-way flow of information | One-way flow of information |
| Audience known | Audience guessed |
| Modification during communication through continuous feedback | No modification during communication |
| Generally informal, impermanent | Generally formal, permanent record |
| Instantly public, to generally small audience | Delayed public access. Potentially to large audience |

It can be seen that the spoken mode is intrinsically a negotiation mode. The written mode by contrast encourages longer, more polished but also more lonely, even more private, products. It provides the author with opportunity to stand back and talk with him or herself, prior to going public. Once public it provides a private, usually self-paced, reflective opportunity for the reader.

The very nature of the media then provides access for all primary teachers, but particularly the leaders amongst them, to a wider range of contacts and a private, self-reflective opportunity. Awareness of the media may not increase a leader's likableness, but it should increase his knowledge and credibility and hence indirectly his power or potency.

What data do we have on teachers' use of the media? This is not the place for an exhaustive survey of audience ratings, readership numbers and market penetration, but a few selective findings can be quoted to show that teachers generally value the media for ideas and support, and that heads in particular value this source.

In March 1983 the Department of Education and Science estimated there to be some 189,000 full-time nursery and primary teachers.[2] These included 23,000 heads and 20,000 deputy heads.[3] Thus 12 per cent of primary teachers are heads and 11 per cent deputy heads. Approximately a quarter of the primary teaching force might be viewed as its leaders.

The Schools Broadcasting Council estimated in Autumn 1982 that 95 per cent of schools used *some* TV or radio series from BBC or ITA; 94 per cent of schools used some BBC series; and 81 per cent some ITA series.[4] The average school used 7.6 series, not just one. If ideas about what to teach are part of leadership, schools broadcasts are playing an extremely extensive and possibly underacknowledged role.

The idea that this use of the media is predominantly to provide supporting content for teaching approaches already settled upon is given some credence by the difference between this level of take-up and the take-up by teachers of previews put on by BBC or ITA. One estimate of the take-up of the available audience for such previews was as low as 0.2 per cent. What teachers say they want and what they watch do not match very closely it seems. However, we should not make too much of such a statistic taken out of context.

This high valuation of schools broadcasts is confirmed by data from the Schools Council Impact and Take Up project.[5] Some ninety-eight heads and 740 teachers were asked how frequently twenty-nine different 'sources of information' were found to be useful to 'obtain information and ideas for their teaching'. 'Television for Schools', 'Radio for Schools' and 'Associated BBC and ITA literature' obtained an average rating of between 'often useful' and 'sometimes useful'. The teachers, though not their heads, rated 'Television for Schools' as the second most useful source, below only 'Teachers in your own school'.

This project also provided data which distinguished between heads and others. The differences were interesting. Heads rated fifteen of the twenty-nine sources as frequently/sometimes useful compared to their colleagues who only rated nine sources this highly. Heads seem more hungry for information. Of their fifteen sources some eight were impersonal or media sources. The teachers only rated four media sources this highly, the three broadcasting ones already mentioned and 'book exhibitions.' Heads, in addition, rated 'Publishers Catalogues', 'Research Journals and General Books on Education', 'Educational Press', 'Schools Council Curriculum Development Projects' at this high level.

What emerges is a picture of heads seeking media sources to support their leadership role more energetically than their colleagues. A head who wishes to bring credibility to his work seems to appreciate the need for wider reference sources than his colleagues. Whilst heads seek wider sources of both personal and non-personal type they value twice as many impersonal media sources this highly.

Unfortunately, this research did not separate deputy heads from other teachers. It is a matter for speculation what would have been revealed had it done so, but some clues may be provided by considering printed sources more carefully. One of the most popular primary journals is *Child Education*. Its monthly UK circulation is some 50,000.[6] If we assume no dual readership, which is probably pessimistic since many are purchased by schools, then at least one in four primary teachers have access to this source. One follow-up survey by the publishers suggested 18 per cent of the readership were heads. This is a larger percentage than their previously mentioned 12 per cent within all primary teachers. In contrast, deputy heads took only 4 per cent, with class teachers taking 51 per cent. The rest was shared among advisors, lecturers, nursery nurses, play leaders and miscellaneous categories. The slightly less popular *Junior Education* had a circulation of 33,000. Here heads represented 16 per cent of the readers, deputy heads 10 per cent and class teachers 72 per cent. The 'miscellaneous' group was much less evident. Nevertheless, it seems reasonable to imagine one in six primary teachers having access to this source and a higher fraction of junior teachers.

Again heads seek this source more energetically than their colleagues. The data also prompt the speculation, though it can be no more, that junior deputy heads seek media support more energetically than infant and first school deputies.

If the 22,000 circulation of *Art and Craft in Education* is also considered it seems that about one in nine primary teachers seeks media support from this source. It may be that many of these readers are the same people taking *Child Education*, *Junior Education* and *Art and Craft in Education*.

A number of primary journals with smaller circulations exist, for example, the NUT's *Primary Education Review* (5000) and *Education 3–13* (2–3000).[7] Their existence even in small numbers confirms the value teachers place on media sources.

Research in which the author has recently been involved confirms the general picture revealed so far. A combined Schools Council and Primary Schools Research and Development Group (PSRDG) research project on 'Curriculum Responsibility and the Use of Teacher Expertise in the Primary School', asked some 465 teachers questions that included one on their 'Perceived sources of professional development'.[8] The personal contact sources were again rated more highly than the non-personal or media sources, but 43 per cent rated the 'professional literature' either 'extremely' or 'very' important as a source of ideas. Information and suggestions from national reports were rated this highly by 36 per cent. When the question was about 'support' rather than 'ideas', the percentage rating 'professional literature' this highly dropped to 31. One is tempted to speculate that much literature is used for ideas, not their detailed development. It may be that for the average class teacher this is the particular appeal of broadcast sources. A possible corollary is that heads value the ideas more highly and mind less about their detailed working out.

A variation between high levels of familiarity with some sources and a lower level with others has been a common characteristic of primary teachers for some years. In 1970 Cane and Schroeder in *The Teacher and Research* found 89 per cent having 'sometimes read' the *Teacher* and 87 per cent having 'sometimes read' *The Times Educational Supplement*, yet only 9.5 per cent having 'sometimes read' *Forum* or 13 per cent the *British Journal of Educational Psychology*. In the same year the DES published figures showing that 36 per cent of primary teachers had read all of *Mathematics in the Primary School* and a further 41 per cent had read part.[9] Comparative figures for *French in the Primary School* were 10 per cent and 20 per cent.

In summary, primary teachers, particularly heads, utilize the media.

Whilst some overall figures and some crude divisions between heads and others are available, it is a matter of speculation what use they make of these sources and what attracts teachers to them. The speculation presented in this brief article is that those who wish to lead are those who particularly value the media for the wider range of 'contacts' they make available, thus increasing leaders' knowledge and credibility.

A further more tentative speculation is that the media provide a relatively private arena in which teachers, particularly heads, can try out their ideas and relate them to those of others. In contrast, once a head says something in front of his staff it is likely to be viewed as part of a negotiation. Yet when heads are still forming their views they may particularly welcome this more private, reflective, non-intrusive format. With authors they can speculate, decide they are wrong perhaps and change their minds without any loss of face. In the process they become part of a larger pool of minds.

Primary education needs good leadership. Published articles and polished programmes are a crucial part of making the whole of primary education less parochial and more universal. They also provide an opportunity for private reflection and the emergence of a wider vision for these leaders. Authors and producers should be leaders of leaders. Perhaps the right way to end is to ask whether you have something to contribute to the media as well as something to gain from it?

### Notes

1 GAGNÉ, (1977) *The Conditions of Learning*, Holt Rinehart and Winston, p. 250.
2 DES (1983) *Teaching Quality*, London, HMSO, pp. 3–4.
3 If private schools are included, as was done in estimating the number of primary schools potentially seeking microcomputers, the figure rises from 23,000 to 27,000 primary schools.
4 Figures provided in telephone conversation with IBA Audience Research Department.
5 SCHOOLS COUNCIL (1978) *First Interim Report of Impact and Take Up Project*, London.
6 Provided by John Clark, Marketing Coordinator of Scholastic Publishing Ltd, to whom I am very grateful (April 1983).
7 Advertisers' promotional literature; and details from Studies in Education Ltd.
8 In press. Details available from the author.
9 DES (1970) *Survey of In-Service Training For Teachers*, 1967 Statistics of Education SS2, London, HMSO.

# Author Index

# Subject Index

accountability, 16–17, 70–1, 74, 151, 153–5, 177, 206, 211, 217, 296, 302, 307, 349
advanced further education (AFE), 313–14, 320
adult education, 64
Advisory Centre for Education (ACE), 181, 384, 386–7
Advisory Committee on Handicapped Children, 82
Advisory Committee on the Supply and Training of Teachers (ACSET), 154
Africa, 403
Allen, G., 91
Assessment of Performance Unit (APU), 91, 151–2
Assisted Places Scheme, 387, 404
Australia, 217, 232

Bains Committee, 113, 129
banding system, 404–5, 408
Beachside Comprehensive, 334–5
Beloe Committee, 332
Bevin, E., 231
binary policy, 314
biology teaching, 337–8
Blackie, J., 91
block grant system, 74
Board of Education, 81
Bournemouth Teachers' Centre, 266–86
British Association, 140
British Broadcasting Commission (BBC), 410–11
Browne, S., 91–2, 103, 104
Bryce Commission, 81
bureaucracy
and primary schools, 221–9

bureaucratic model
of organizations, 8–9, 11, 116
bureaucratization, 15, 16
Burnham Report, 92, 93, 259

Callaghan, J., 91, 92, 119, 151, 177, 178, 302, 279
Cambridge Association for the Advancement of State Education, 383–4
*see also* Campaign for the Advancement of State Education (CASE)
Campaign for the Advancement of State Education (CASE), 176, 361–2, 383–93
Campaign for Comprehensive Schools (CCE), 384, 386
Campaign for Nursery Education (CNE), 384, 386
Canada, 403
Carlisle, M., 68
cash limits, 63
central advisory councils, 81–2
central government
and the educational system, 53, 57–78, 79–87, 105–6, 116–21, 142, 144, 173, 175–86, 211–12, 217–18, 224–8, 352, 384–5, 393
Centre for Information and Advice on Educational Disadvantage, 374
change in schools, 292–8, 301–8
Chief Education Officers, 54, 73, 105–21, 123–36, 163, 206, 211, 213, 306
Child Poverty Action Group (CPAG), 385, 388
Churchill, W.S., 231
classrooms
and organizational leadership, 42–4, 49,